D0213910

NATIVES AND STRANGERS

A History of Ethnic Americans

Fifth Edition

LEONARD DINNERSTEIN

Professor Emeritus, University of Arizona

ROGER L. NICHOLS

University of Arizona

DAVID M. REIMERS

Professor Emeritus, New York University

New York   Oxford

Oxford University Press

2010

To Myra Dinnerstein, Marilyn Nichols,
and Cordelia Reimers

Oxford University Press, Inc., publishes works that further Oxford University's
objective of excellence in research, scholarship, and education.

Oxford   New York
Auckland   Cape Town   Dar es Salaam   Hong Kong   Karachi
Kuala Lumpur   Madrid   Melbourne   Mexico City   Nairobi
New Delhi   Shanghai   Taipei   Toronto

With offices in
Argentina   Austria   Brazil   Chile   Czech Republic   France   Greece
Guatemala   Hungary   Italy   Japan   Poland   Portugal   Singapore
South Korea   Switzerland   Thailand   Turkey   Ukraine   Vietnam

Copyright © 1997, 2003, 2010 by Oxford University Press, Inc.

Published by Oxford University Press, Inc.
198 Madison Avenue, New York, New York 10016
http://www.oup.com

Oxford is a registered trademark of Oxford University Press

All rights reserved. No part of this publication may be reproduced,
stored in a retrieval system, or transmitted, in any form or by any means,
electronic, mechanical, photocopying, recording, or otherwise,
without the prior permission of Oxford University Press.

Library of Congress Cataloging-in-Publication Data

Dinnerstein, Leonard.
  Natives and strangers : a history of ethnic americans / Leonard Dinnerstein, Roger L. Nichols,
  David M. Reimers.—5th ed.
    p.   cm.
  Includes bibliographical references and index.
  ISBN 978-0-19-536622-8
  1. Minorities—United States—History.   2. United States—Ethnic relations—History.
  3. United States—Race relations—History.   I. Nichols, Roger L.   II. Reimers, David M.
  III. Title.
  E184.A1D49 2009
  305.800973—dc22   2008047725

Printing number: 9 8 7 6 5 4 3 2 1

Printed in the United States of America
on acid-free paper

CONTENTS

PREFACE

American society began as a string of tiny, isolated settlements that spread inland from east, south, and west. The invading Europeans sought blacks from Africa to aid them, and together people of these two groups overran the Native American population inhabiting the present United States. From the start, immigration and the contests among and between distinct racial and ethnic groups played central roles in the development of the new colonies. Immigrants from the British Isles dominated the new settlements quickly, as did their customs throughout most of what became early American society. Once established, the English colonists raised concerns about which peoples to welcome and under what conditions newcomers were needed or desirable. These concerns have prompted national debates and political disputes down to the present. More often the communities receiving most of the immigrants became the local arenas in which such issues played out. Frequently, the newcomers increased tensions as they brought long-time ethnic, racial, or religious disputes along when they arrived. Those existing quarrels and the animosities between immigrants and groups already well established in America proved central to the nation's history.

Our purpose in writing this book has been to emphasize the role of immigrants, African Americans, and American Indians in the development of a national society. It concentrates on culture, politics, economics, the development of social attitudes, and how ethnic and racial groups affected and were affected by all of those. In this edition we have tried to integrate the experiences of racial, ethnic, religious, and national groups to explain how their histories have intertwined and how they bring clarity to understanding American society.

The book's title, *Natives and Strangers,* points to some interrelated questions that should help guide readers' attention. The first has to do with just who is an American. Related to that question, one needs to ask, how does a person who is not an American become one? Is it a matter of place of birth, self-identification, learning to speak English, acceptance by others, or some combination of these and other measures? Was there a recognizable process through which people who arrived as "strangers" changed or lost their differences enough to be accepted as "natives" by the rest of society? To what extent did all of the new-comers encounter similar or differing receptions? How may we explain the vari-ous levels of animosity or acceptance some groups received after their arrival? The answers to these questions illustrate major themes in the growth of the United States and demonstrate the complexities of minority peoples' experi-ences on their way to acceptance within the broader national society.

During much of American history, newcomers provided an abundant supply of labor. Although that fact, combined with natural resources and an inventive and entrepreneurial spirit, laid the foundations for success, mainstream histories of the United States until after World War II emphasized geographical advan-tages and technological and commercial innovations in explaining American progress. Before the 1960s average people, and particularly deprived groups and the poor, received little attention from most scholars. More recently, how-ever, social and cultural historians have focused much of their effort on exactly those people and, in doing so, have brought about a major shift in how scholars understand the past. This new emphasis showed clearly how millions of name-less people, often considered "strangers" by their neighbors, contributed to the economy and strove to make lives for themselves in the United States. This study is intended to explore their stories and to deepen and enrich our under-standing of the varieties and significance of minority group history. When read-ing it, be aware that the dates used with the chapter titles only suggest broad eras and are not meant as rigid demarcation points. Many of the central themes being examined overlap chronological periods, and in places ideas and movements from other eras seemed to fit better in a given narrative context.

The text uses the expression *ethnic group* to mean a people with a shared culture or sense of identity based on religion, nationality, or a common experi-ence. Although modern science informs us that there is no such thing as distinct biological races, ideas and conflicts about race and racism are so much a part of American history and public discussion that these terms appear in the text where appropriate. The reader should keep in mind that the social construction of race—its definitions—has varied widely over time. For example, at one time the Bureau of the Census considered "Hindus" to be a separate race rather than a term defining a religious or nationality grouping. Even in recent enumerations the Census has used terms such as *Chinese, Vietnamese,* and *Filipino* to repre-sent distinct races. Clearly there is no Chinese race. Rather, they represent an ethnic, language, and nationality group. In the Census Hispanics identify them-selves as white or other when noting their racial identification. Because of the growing number of multiethnic marriages in 2000, the Census offered a cate-gory for people to identify themselves as being of mixed race. Professional golfer Tiger Woods is a clear example of the current blurring and complexity of racial identities. His family background is one-fourth African American, one-fourth Chinese, one-fourth Thai, one-eighth Native American, and one-eighth Dutch. He describes the result as "Cablinasian," a combination of *Caucasian*, *bl*ack, American *In*dian, and *Asian*. Some social scientists now use the term "people of color," a recent social construction of a shorthand term to describe non-Europeans. Yet these people represent a great variety of different peoples. In the pages that follow, we hope to clarify what impacts ideas about race, ethnicity, nationality, and religion had on those people whom Americans saw as "natives" or "strangers" throughout the nation's history.

Although immigration and minority group experiences have dominated many periods of the American past, Native Americans remained on the scene, too. People long thought to have been destroyed generations ago—such as the Narragansett of Rhode Island or the Grand Traverse Ottawa and Chippewa of Michigan—have recently received acknowledgement as recognized tribes by the federal government. At present more than 560 tribes are scattered throughout most of the fifty states. Newspapers carry accounts of how particular reservations have discovered new riches through casino gambling on or near their homelands. Although not immigrants, by choice many of them remained "strangers" and on the outside of American society. At the same time their experiences gave them integral roles in the creation of an American national identity.

At the end of the first decade of the twenty-first century, immigration—composed mainly of peoples from Latin America, the Caribbean, Africa, and Asia—continues at record levels. For the first time in American history, one decade—the 1990s—witnessed the arrival of more than nine million people. After a dip following the September 11, 2001, destruction of the World Trade Center in New York City, the flood of newcomers increased again and has averaged about one million people annually. These figures do not include the post-1990 unauthorized immigrants, who also entered in record numbers.

That immigrants and native-born minorities will always be with us is perfectly clear. Peoples of European background now constitute about two-thirds of the population, but in many counties and cities, as well as at least two states, no single ethnic group can claim to be the majority. Perhaps sharing the experiences of people who came earlier in our history, as well as those of current entrants, will help both "natives" and "strangers" alike to learn how to deal with the complex issues tied to race, ethnicity, and acceptance that continue to bedevil modern American life.

Tucson, Arizona   Leonard Dinnerstein and Roger L. Nichols
Teaneck, New Jersey   David M. Reimers
February 4, 2009

1

Colonial Foundations

(1600–1780s)

They trudged eastward through arctic summers in small family groups. Nomadic hunters, they followed the herds of large mammals across Beringia, the one-thousand-mile-wide land bridge that connected eastern Siberia with western Alaska. Others, often hugging the coast, came east in small boats. For thousands of years the people came. Their descendants walked east and south across North America and beyond. Gradually, as they hunted, explored, and migrated, the Wisconsin glacial period ended. Temperatures increased, the glaciers retreated, and the worldwide warming that followed about ten thousand years ago raised sea levels by several hundred feet. The waters of the Bering Strait now flow between Siberia and Alaska and cover the routes of these first immigrants to America.

Ever resourceful, the people whom the early Europeans mistakenly called Indians populated the New World completely. Sometime after crossing into the Western Hemisphere they developed new spear points that helped them kill even the largest of the early land mammals. About eleven thousand years ago these people faced ecological disaster. They had become so skillful at killing the bison, mammoths, and other large creatures that the herds disappeared. Gradually they shifted to smaller targets, such as deer, and to gathering roots, seeds, nuts, and fruit. Over many generations their skills at hunting, gathering, fishing, and eventually agriculture allowed them to survive and even to prosper. About three thousand years ago agriculture spread throughout the fertile and well-watered parts of the country, bringing with it the development of stable villages and even larger groups.

Because most of the story of human occupation occurred prior to European contact with North America, its history is too dim to trace here. Yet it is important to realize that the continent has been inhabited for much more than ten thousand years, whereas Europeans and their descendants have been here less than five hundred years. By the time Columbus "discovered" America in 1492, native civilizations had come and gone. Vast complexes, such as Cahokia in Illinois, had witnessed perhaps as many as thirty thousand inhabitants, while the Mississippian and related cultures had populated much of the Midwest and East. During several centuries prior to the European intrusions into North

1

America, the native peoples became thoroughly familiar with their local environments. They had reasonable lives and developed complex societies, trading patterns, religious cosmologies, and diplomatic alliances. By 1492 somewhere between three million and five million people who lived as part of at least five hundred distinct tribes, bands, and other groups awaited the European strangers. Often without even realizing it, when they encountered the Europeans, the American Indians began a series of meetings between and among peoples living in what became the United States and the waves of others who came to this country later. That process continues to the present and provides the title for this book.

The story of relations between the groups that fused into modern American society began in the late fifteenth century. When the Europeans began to explore parts of North America, their actions launched powerful economic and social currents that first created and then shaped the United States. Within a few generations of the early explorations, knowledgeable Europeans realized the potential of North and South America. Moreover, the continents of the Western Hemisphere fit nicely into the evolving mercantilist economic theory of that day. According to this view, each government tried to organize and regulate its national economic activities to strengthen itself. Thus during the sixteenth and seventeenth centuries Spain, Portugal, France, Sweden, Russia, the Netherlands, and Great Britain established trading posts and colonies around the world. Those that flourished provided riches such as gold, silver, and precious gems, which the rapidly growing national governments needed to pay their debts. If no precious metals could be extracted from a colony, the mother country gained profits from selling manufactured goods there in exchange for inexpensive raw materials. In some cases colonists received bonuses for producing items needed by the mother country so that it did not have to spend its wealth buying such things from foreign competitors.

Coming of the English

Among the major powers, Britain proved most successful in North America and eventually gained control over most of the continent. Unlike the Spanish colonies in South and Central America, which quickly yielded immense treasure in gold and silver, as well as raw materials needed in Europe, the British North American colonies failed to bring instant wealth. Instead, they developed agricultural and commercial enterprises that often rivaled, instead of supplementing, economic activities in the mother country. Lacking resources that could be exploited rapidly for large profit, the British colonies needed increasing numbers of people to serve as a market for English goods, as well as to provide laborers for their own agricultural, chiefly rural societies. Their attempts to enslave large numbers of Indians, as the Spanish had done elsewhere, failed, and they had to look elsewhere for workers. Within only twelve years of the first successful Virginia settlement in 1607, the colonists began importing blacks to increase their labor force, but this effort also proved inadequate, and they called for continuing numbers of immigrants—at first from Great Britain, and later from the rest of Europe as well.

When the first Virginia colonists stepped ashore from the decks of the *Susan Constant,* the *Godspeed,* and the *Discovery* in 1607, they not only began the task of building a colony that was supposed to strengthen England in its international competition with its European neighbors, but they and the settlers who followed also brought ideas and customs that laid the foundations for continuing ethnic practices in American society.

First, they brought along a sense of English racial and cultural superiority. Many would have agreed with the cleric who in 1558 told his flock, "God is English." They considered Protestantism the true expression of Christian faith and, at least in the Massachusetts Bay Colony, believed that only the Puritans practiced it appropriately. Whether in New England or farther to the south, the colonists felt that in the new country they could make money—get ahead—and thereby improve their personal, economic, and social status. From the beginnings of settlement, this drive for economic gains motivated most Englishmen in the New World. The attitudes associated with commercial capitalism and economic expansion, therefore, became one of the dominant forces in early American development.

The English regarded those who differed from them as inferior. Toward the native American Indians they held two contradictory views. On the one hand, Englishmen hoped to meet friendly tribesmen who would help, guide, and trade with them. On the other hand, they feared these "savage and backward" people. Black Africans, because of their color and customs, were both feared and scorned. Toward Europeans from the continent, whose ways varied only slightly from their own, Englishmen felt a certain kinship, but they regarded their own practices as superior. In the New World these attitudes would prevail and leave their own mark on the development of American society.

The modernization process, which gradually transformed a few isolated settlements along the Atlantic coast into the United States, included several developments initiated during the seventeenth and eighteenth centuries. Transplanting English culture to North America occurred first. It took several generations, and its speed varied widely depending on time, place, and source of immigration. In colonies such as New York and Pennsylvania, large numbers of non-English people originally established a society that for a time was more European than English, but even the most cosmopolitan towns and regions bore distinctive English markings in language, laws, social customs, and economic patterns.

Indians and Anglo-Americans

When the English landed in North America, they found much of the coastal region heavily populated. Estimates of Indian population in the United States vary, but many scholars now accept the figure of three to five million people prior to colonization. Sharing elements of Eastern Woodland and Southeast cultures, the tribes had begun to emerge from their New Stone Age development, as evidenced by their tools, weapons, and household utensils made from wood, reed, clay, stone, or bone. They had no domesticated animals except dogs, no wheeled vehicles, and no written languages, but they lived in well-laid-out villages of comfortable lodges, longhouses, and wigwams. Skilled in farming, gathering, hunting, and fishing, they had mastered their environment, their technology permitting them to live in modest comfort.

The degree of social organization within individual tribes varied widely, from the tightly structured Natchez and Iroquois to much smaller and less firmly connected groups. Nevertheless, all were organized by family relationships into clans or kinship bands. Several related clans formed what the English often mistakenly called a tribe or a nation. Groups of several tribes might be part of still larger confederacies. In New York the five nations of the Iroquois Confederacy faced the Dutch, French, and English with a well-organized political and military force. To the south, in Virginia, Powhatan directed a group of thirty tribes. When the English arrived in 1607, the Virginia Indians had already been encountering Europeans for decades. Thus Powhatan considered the newcomers as just one more element in his already complex relationships with the nearby Indian groups. By manipulating the English, he hoped to strengthen his power over the groups in the confederacy and to use that strength against his nearby competitors. After a few months of observation, the Virginia tribal leader clearly felt little awe of the Europeans or most of their technology, so his people made few basic changes in their lives because of the whites. However, the early experiences had a more profound impact on the colonists. Once the English realized that their tribal neighbors had neither gold and silver nor interest in an extensive trade, their early dreams of wealth faded. This forced Virginia authorities to change their goals. What was to have been a trading post now became an agricultural settlement, based on the cultivation of tobacco; however, for that they needed large amounts of land, which could be obtained only from the Indians. At first the tribal people held the upper hand, but it was dangerous to have what the whites wanted. As would-be trading partners the Indians were essential to the English, but once farming provided the economic base for the colony, the Indians became an obstacle, and repeated clashes occurred. After five years of sporadic fighting, in 1614 the Indians accepted a peace settlement. The resulting calm lasted only a few years; as the Virginia Company sent hundreds of new colonists to America, pressures for more land increased. At Powhatan's death in 1619 his successor and brother, Opechancanough, assumed leadership. Three years later he directed an all-out war against the colonists. His 1622 attack caught the Virginians almost totally unprepared, and nearly a third of the whites died in the fighting. The English retaliated with crushing force, and for ten years they burned villages, killed people, and seized good cropland. Having failed to annihilate the English in 1622, the Indians lost what little chance they had to destroy the colony or even to halt its further growth. Although the warriors of the Powhatan Confederacy fought a second war in 1644, this too failed, and the Virginians forced the survivors west, away from the settlements.

Events in New England differed for a time. A series of European diseases carried by early settlers swept through the coastal tribes in 1616–17, killing thousands and causing the survivors to flee. As a result, in 1620, when the Pilgrims landed in eastern Massachusetts, cleared fields stood unused, villages lay in ruins, and few people remained nearby to contest English settlement. In fact, individual Indians such as Squanto and Samoset helped the struggling Europeans for a time. Despite this favorable start, within a decade the situation changed drastically, as growing competition with Dutch traders and rapidly increasing numbers of pioneer farmers strained relations between the tribes and the English. The whites' efforts to dominate the fertile Connecticut Valley farther west led to intrigue and war. Efforts by the resident Pequots to block Puritan expansion failed, and a bitter war in 1637 nearly destroyed the tribe. One group of Pequots, led by Chief Uncas, joined the whites against their relatives, and with additional help from the Narragansetts the New Englanders won. They sold some of the survivors into slavery, scattered the rest among other nearby tribes, and then began moving into Pequot territory.

Even those Indians who chose accommodation and negotiation rather than retreat or war fared badly. The Puritans segregated individuals who became Christians into the so-called Praying Towns and remained suspicious of Native Americans living there. During Metacom's War (also called King Philip's War) in the mid-1670s, these peaceful Christian converts barely survived efforts to destroy them as a subversive and dangerous element within the colonies. The war signaled the Indian realization that conciliation and negotiation with the whites had failed; for the Puritans this desperate struggle proved the need to remove or destroy the tribesmen whenever they thwarted English economic development or territorial expansion.

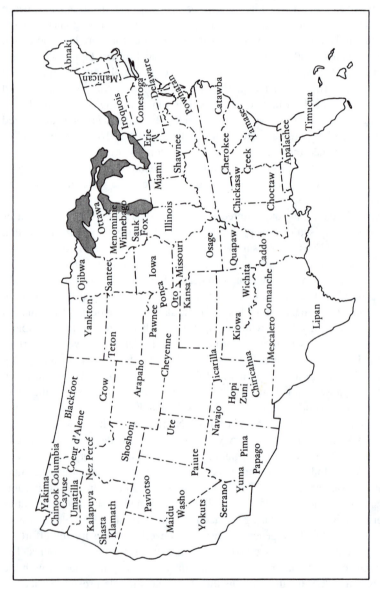

Major Indian Tribes

6

The patterns of events in Virginia and New England occurred elsewhere, but other models emerged, as well. For example, in South Carolina, within a single generation, the Indians provided a source of both wealth and power through furs and slaves. When the English arrived in the 1670s they found the coastal tribes caught up in bitter warfare. The whites capitalized on these conflicts, and within a few years both the colonists and the Indians had been drawn into an ever-widening circle of trade and warfare, which brought destruction to the nearby tribes. Thousands of deerskins provided the major staple for trade between Indians and whites for years. In addition, however, Carolina leaders aggressively sought Indian slaves by encouraging the coastal tribes to make war on their enemies. By rewarding their allies with guns and other goods in exchange for Indian prisoners, the Charleston traders stimulated intertribal warfare and hurried the depopulation process in the coastal region. Wars of virtual extermination against the Westo (1680–83), Savannah (1707–8), Tuscarora (1712–13), and Yamasee (1715–16) provided thousands of slaves. Not only did these wars open vast regions for settlement and trade, but they also strengthened the English while weakening the nearby tribes. These conflicts resulted in large part from the almost total adaptation of the Carolina tribes to the European trading system. The Indians' eagerness to acquire trade goods sometimes blinded them to the results of their competition with the whites. At the same time, some tribes gloried in their newly acquired firearms and the destruction of their enemies.

The bitter warfare in Carolina produced an active slave trade, as hundreds of captives arrived in Charleston annually as potential slaves. By 1708 the colony included 1,400 Indian and 2,900 black slaves. The authorities shipped thousands more Indian captives to the West Indies and to the port cities in other North American colonies. For example, as late as 1730, Kingston, Rhode Island, included 223 Indian slaves in its modest population. Despite the continued enslavement of tribal people, they proved dangerous prizes, as many sought to escape or otherwise cause trouble for their owners. Within a couple of decades after the slave trade began, major objections arose to this labor supply. Citing the Indians' "conspiracys [*sic*], insurrections, rapes, thefts, and other execrable crimes," in 1715 several New England colonies prohibited the importation of any more such slaves. These events and the continuing destruction of the tribes by European epidemic disease ended most efforts to enslave Indians in eastern North America.

Throughout the first century of English-Indian contact, the tribal situation shifted drastically. In 1607 the Indians were politically independent, economically self-sufficient, and superior to the whites in terms of using the natural environment. However, continuing relations with the English brought a downward spiral of major population loss, the erosion of tribal autonomy, and economic collapse, which left the tribes heavily dependent on the invading whites. At the same time, the English and the Indians developed ideas about each other that led to continuing trouble. The whites considered the tribal people to be hostile, untrustworthy, and dangerous. Meanwhile, the tribesmen came to view the Europeans as dangerous, unpredictable, and insatiable invaders who killed their people and stole their land. True, the whites' trade goods made villagers' lives easier, but the expanding English settlements brought frequent land surrenders and increasing cultural breakdown among the Indians. In addition, sporadic raids by pioneers and warriors and the four colonial wars between Britain and France all created suspicion and hatred between the races. The toast "Civilization or death to all American savages," given during a campaign against the Iroquois, illustrates these feelings.

Attracting Settlers

Because attempts to enslave the tribesmen were only partially successful, English colonial promoters soon realized that they needed to find other sources of labor. To meet growing demands for workers, colonial officials wanted to get whites over to the colonies. Both the Virginia Company and, later, the British government promised free land to colonists who brought other settlers to the New World. The Virginia Company also offered to pay the cost of passage for those unable to pay their own way across the Atlantic. Thus, in exchange for laboring for four to seven years, poor whites secured passage to America. At the end of their service these indentured servants, as they were called, sometimes received land. Such promises lured many lower-class Englishmen to the New World. During the seventeenth and eighteenth centuries the opportunities in English colonies encouraged other Europeans as well to leave their homes and settle in America. There was always a need for both skilled and unskilled labor. At the fringes of settlement, newcomers would help counter the potential Indian menace, for as the population increased in newly settled communities, attacks from Indian warriors diminished. As the colonial economy evolved, immigrants helped expand the market for farmers and businessmen. At the same time, the British government viewed prosperous colonies as national assets and therefore encouraged colonial economic development. The Crown also believed that England was overpopulated and that emigration would benefit the mother country.

Indentured servitude became the prime way of bringing poor people from the Old World to the New. It offered the underemployed indigent opportunities in America and provided additional workers to the labor-short colonies. The policy proved beneficial to the immigrants in the long run, but during the first few years the laborers' lot was little better than that of slaves. Planters drove them hard, and indentured servants were supervised by overseers who, as one historian wrote, "were not apt to be men notable for Christian charity." An observer recalled, "I have seen an Overseer beat a Servant with a cane about the head, till the blood has flowed, for a fault that is not worth the speaking of; and yet he must have patience, or worse will follow." There are also tales of a Virginia master who had his servant's ears nailed to a pillory and left him standing there for four days and of a Massachusetts master who punished a servant by "hanging him by the heels as butchers do beasts for the slaughter." American colonists, one scholar tells us, succeeded

> in treating their indentured servants as private property. They bought and sold them, sued each other for possession of them, and set up engines of law for the protection of their rights in them. Though on occasion the state took a servant away from a cruel master without providing due compensation, this was certainly avoided as often as possible, and many cruel masters, though losing their servants, received the sum procured by selling them elsewhere. To be sure, the servant had rights, but while he was in servitude these rarely conflicted with the conception of him as property.

If working and living conditions were harsh, so too were the general health conditions of early America, and many servants did not survive their terms. In spite of these hardships, indentured servants willingly provided the main source of labor for the southern colonies in the seventeenth century. Few economic opportunities and possibilities for social advancement existed for these people in England, whereas in the colonies, once the period of servitude had ended, one's origin presented no insurmountable stigma. Clearly, there was a real chance for betterment in the New World. As a result of such opportunities, it has been estimated that in the seventeenth century a majority of whites coming to America were indentured servants and that for the entire colonial era about one-quarter of all Europeans were indentured servants. But, combined with the number of slaves and convicts, more than one-half of all immigrants settling during the period from 1607 until the 1770s were bound laborers of one kind or other.

In addition to the volunteer white labor force, the English occasionally kidnapped people and sent them to America. They also used the colonies as a dumping ground for convicts, and between 1718 and 1775 the courts banished at least fifty thousand individuals to the colonies. Although England believed that this practice was a good way to get rid of undesirable prisoners, some of the colonists thought otherwise. In 1751 the *Virginia Gazette* complained that these people were "Serpents" and declared, "In what can Britain show a more Sovereign contempt for us than by emptying their jails into our settlements?"

Several colonies passed laws attempting to halt the shipment of convicts to America, but England disallowed them. Not all colonists opposed the incoming convicts; some planters welcomed persons of "evil fame" as cheap labor.

Development of Slavery and Racism

The desire for economic gain dominated American society for centuries. Almost every major movement or recruitment of peoples from outside the colonies or the United States would be rationalized on the grounds of adding needed laborers, who would work at wages so low that extraordinary profits could be achieved. During the colonial era changes in British government policies dictated the need for even cheaper labor, and this in turn resulted in the importation of African slaves on a grand scale.

Before the 1650s Virginia tobacco growers had been selling their produce to the mother country, as well as to other nations. But in 1650 and 1651 Parliament passed the first of the Navigation Acts, which regulated trade within the empire. Seeking to strengthen the English economy and to weaken competing Dutch shippers, the laws limited colonial exports to English ships. These acts also restricted the sale of colonial tobacco to Britain, Holland, and other parts of Europe and ultimately led to lower tobacco prices. The Dutch had often purchased inferior grades of colonial tobacco, but after the Navigation Acts, not only were they eliminated from the trade, but the British demanded only the first-quality leaves. During the 1650s and early 1660s overproduction also contributed to lower prices and reduced profits. Moreover, the fixed terms of English indentured servants resulted in a continual turnover in workers and a need to train new ones. This in itself would not have been a major burden, but on the restoration of the monarchy in England in 1660, Charles II and his ministers concluded that the country was no longer overpopulated. Having decided that it would be unwise to continue to allow members of the work force to leave, they inaugurated a policy to discourage emigration.

These factors—the Navigation Acts, lower tobacco prices, and difficulties in obtaining additional indentured servants from England—combined to make the colonists, especially the owners of large southern plantations, favor importation of African workers. In 1662 the British government granted a monopoly in the slave trade to the Royal African Slave Company, thus initiating a major new policy of bringing in blacks to help lower the costs of producing tobacco, rice, indigo, and other colonial staple crops. Slaves would not terminate their servitude, as did indentured servants; they would increase and multiply, thereby guaranteeing a permanent work force, and their purchase price and maintenance costs would detract only minutely from the ultimate wealth they would contribute to their masters. With such obvious economic advantages, moral concerns, if any, disappeared quickly. Entrepreneurs, in the seventeenth century or later, have rarely allowed moral scruples to affect the way they utilized people for economic profit. More often than not some heretofore unfamiliar minority group has appeared on the scene to provide the needed brawn. As a nation, the United States has always been fortunate that in times of its greatest needs conditions in other countries, or other sections of the nation, have been conducive to migration.

According to a number of scholars, some of the first Africans who arrived in Virginia in 1619 were treated not as slaves but as indentured servants. The colony had not grown sufficiently to envision the need for many blacks, and even though white Englishmen still came, large numbers of Africans seemed unnecessary. Although well entrenched in South America and the West Indies, the practice of slavery was not common in the British colonies of North America in the 1620s and 1630s but evolved as the decades passed. Before the 1660s, neither Virginia nor Maryland, the original southern colonies, formally recognized slavery. The status of blacks in these states had not been carefully spelled out. Sometimes courts treated blacks and whites in equal fashion, other times not. However, with the enactment of the slave codes in the 1660s, new laws clearly indicated the difference between African American slaves and white indentured servants.

The southern governments tightened their slave codes throughout the remainder of the colonial period. The colonists decided that conversion to Christianity did not bring freedom, and they made the status of the child follow that of the mother—a decision prompted by the fact that most interracial sexual unions were of white males and black females. Eighteenth-century laws made manumission more difficult. Slaves also lost their right to hold property and to testify in court and increasingly came to be considered property, not persons.

As white men enslaved blacks, they also regarded them with suspicion, fear, and contempt. We know little of how Africans viewed whites during the colonial period, but we have much evidence of the growing racism among whites. Even before the explorations of Africa, Europeans, especially the English, believed that black connoted evil and white, purity. The *Oxford English Dictionary* indicated that before the sixteenth century black meant "soil, dirty, foul...atrocious, horrible, wicked." To the first Europeans who explored Africa and encountered blacks, the difference in pigmentation made a profound impression, and, in the long run, skin color, more than any other factor, defined the relationships between blacks and whites.

Europeans also noted other differences. Africans were not Christians, and whites gradually began to consider blacks, as they considered Indians, savage and uncivilized. They started describing Africans as beasts and said they resembled the chimpanzees discovered in the African explorations. White men also viewed blacks as lustful, sexual beings. These ideas eventually led to the ethnocentric conclusion that their darker pigmentation symbolized the innate inferiority of blacks.

At first slavery grew slowly. In 1650 blacks made up less than 5 percent of England's North American colonies, and by 1671 Virginia counted only two thousand slaves in a population of forty thousand. During the eighteenth century the number of slaves increased rapidly, and on the eve of the American Revolution they constituted 22 percent of the colonial population. Most of these slaves lived in the southern colonies, particularly Maryland, Virginia, and South Carolina, where in 1770 they accounted for 40 percent of the total population. Virginia alone had 188,000 slaves, or about half of the slave population of the United States. South Carolina also had large numbers of slaves, especially

The cargo of a slave ship. The slave deck of the *Wildfire*, brought into Key West in 1860. From *Harper's Weekly*, 1860. (Library of Congress)

in the counties surrounding Charleston. In Charleston, as well as other areas of South Carolina in the eighteenth century, blacks outnumbered whites. This was also true of other areas in the tidewater regions of the Chesapeake Bay colonies.

Colonial slaves labored in nearly all occupations. Blacks had been imported for the cultivation of rice, indigo, sugar, and tobacco, but the slaves engaged in other tasks as well. They worked as carpenters, coopers, tailors, cooks, blacksmiths, and personal servants—indeed they labored in most of the South's occupations. For those few who lived in towns such as Williamsburg, Charleston, or Baltimore, a variety of skilled trades might be learned. In Charleston, for example, urban craftsmen sometimes trained slave apprentices, who then could be sold to the plantations for higher prices than common laborers. In the same city some blacks worked as fishermen, a skill they may have brought with them from Africa.

But skills acquired by slaves did not mitigate the harshness of colonial slavery. Life was cruel for black as well as white servants or offenders. Branding and public whipping provided common punishments for lawbreakers, and the slave might receive even more severe punishments. One observer noted of an especially brutal planter in the 1730s, "Colonel Lynch cut off the legs of a poor negro, and he kills several of them every year by his barbarities." Colonial documents record cases of maiming of slaves through castration, nose-slitting, and the chopping off of hands and ears. Such brutalities became less common in the eighteenth century, but rebellious slaves could always expect the worst. Slaves also worked long and hard, and they always had to fear that their families could be destroyed by sales of one or more of their members. During periods of great tension, particularly when fears of slave insurrections were high, the laws and their execution could be especially fierce.

In addition to harsh physical labor extracted from slaves and their inferior status, the owners attempted to impose English culture on the Africans. Historians know little about how much African culture slaves retained in colonial America, but judging from the more abundant sources of the nineteenth century and scattered earlier records, blacks managed to hang on to many of their ways and to blend their heritage with that of the English to form an African American culture. For example, part of the "seasoning" process involved teaching English to the slaves; most learned the language, but many flavored the new tongue with African words. In the Sea Islands along the South Carolina coast, the blend produced Gullah speech, which still survives. The slaves also withstood many of the early efforts to Christianize them, for they brought with them complex religious ideas that resisted destruction. Eventually, especially after the Great Awakening of the 1740s, Christianity made inroads on African religions and customs concerning life, death, and belief, but by the time of the

Civil War black religion was a blend of African beliefs and white Christianity, not a carbon copy of the latter.

White men feared the newly arrived Africans who seemed to resist slavery more than those who had been born in the United States. One South Carolina planter remarked, "The Negroes that most commonly rebel, are those brought from Guinea, and who have been inured to War and hardship all their lives; few born here, or in the other Provinces, have been guilty of these vile Practices." Planters, although eager to exploit African labor, feared having too many blacks in their area, possibly out of their direct control. They saw runaway and rebellious slaves as not only a labor loss but also a threat to white supremacy.

The most menacing form of resistance was open rebellion, and although insurrections were not common in the American South, a number occurred during the colonial era. Among the most famous was the Stono Rebellion in South Carolina. This 1739 uprising took the lives of approximately twenty-five whites and twenty-five blacks, damaged property, and frightened the colony. Whites took up arms to crush the revolt; afterward they attempted to bring the slaves under a tighter rein. Yet even more controls and a greater imposition of English culture on blacks brought no guarantee of security. Some of the most assimilated slaves, the artisans, led one of the most famous rebellions in Virginia in 1800.

Other slaves disrupted the system by refusing to work hard, breaking tools, destroying crops, stealing, feigning illness, or running away. But the chance of a successful escape was slight, and most blacks had to cope with bondage as best they could. If their master was well off or kinder than most, there might be leisure time, better food, clothing, housing, and concern for individual welfare. Regardless of their treatment, however, slaves found comfort in their religion, their music, and, above all, their families. Slave families had no legal standing but nonetheless provided the close human relationships necessary for survival.

The northern colonies also developed slave societies, but slavery never became central to their economies. Forty percent of the southern population consisted of black slaves compared with only 5 percent in the North. About 10 percent of Rhode Island's mid-eighteenth-century residents and a slightly higher proportion of New York's inhabitants were slaves. Northern regulations, and slavery generally, proved less harsh than in the South. In New England slaves were considered property, but they had more protection as persons than bondsmen and bondswomen in the South. As property, New England slaves resembled southern slaves—they could be bought, sold, and inherited, and they faced restrictions, such as curfews. Still, as persons they were entitled to jury trial, could testify against whites in some cases, and were able to acquire property. In the North, New York and New Jersey were the most oppressive. The slave codes there resembled those in the South. New Yorkers also shared the fear of rebellion, especially after an uprising in 1712, and, like southern whites, they retaliated with severe repression. Whether in the North or South, however, slavery provided cheap labor and often significant profits for the growing colonial society.

A few blacks obtained their freedom during the colonial era. Some had entered as indentured servants, such as those arriving in 1619, and became independent when they served out their indentures. Others were freed by their masters or managed to purchase their liberty. Their numbers remained small, and in 1770 only about 5 percent of the African Americans were free. Mostly they became modest farmers, but in some colonial towns they earned their livings by pursuing a trade or working as day laborers. Everywhere free African Americans were regarded as second-class citizens with limited legal rights.

Except in South Carolina, where the whites remained a small minority among large numbers of Indians and blacks, colonial Americans seem to have paid little attention to contacts between the two non-European peoples. In South Carolina, however, the colonists feared that Indians and slaves might combine forces and destroy them or that the tribesmen would offer a haven for runaways. To prevent these occurrences, whites spread tales of Indian torture and atrocities among blacks and at the same time paid the nearby Indian tribes to return escaped slaves. At other times colonial officials, lacking sufficient white manpower, reluctantly armed some blacks for campaigns against the Indians. This policy also made future cooperation between the two groups even more difficult. Whether or not the possibility of Indians and blacks launching a race war against whites actually existed, South Carolinians thought it did. Their policies offer yet another example of how the Anglo-Europeans dominated and used the other two races for their own benefit.

European Minorities

Blacks and Indians were not the only minorities to be exploited in colonial America. Europeans, although welcomed for their wealth or potential labor, also suffered from English domination. Nevertheless, both the Scots-Irish and the Germans played significant roles in the development of colonial society, especially during the eighteenth century, when as many as 400,000 of them arrived in America. In 1683 Francis D. Pastorius led the first German families to Philadelphia, responding to William Penn's advertising campaign and the promises of religious toleration and personal freedom. For the next century Germans poured into the English colonies, the largest number settling in Pennsylvania. By the 1760s they made up one-third of that colony's population.

From there some migrated slowly to the south and west, settling in Virginia, the Carolinas, and Georgia. To the north, Germans moved into New York, particularly along the Hudson Valley.

Getting to America from the German states and elsewhere in Europe could be a trial during the colonial era. Merchants and ship owners involved in the transatlantic trade in immigrants were eager to recruit passengers for their sailing vessels. If the prospective immigrant lacked funds for the journey, ship owners advanced the money in exchange for the immigrants' labor. Profits were good during the eighteenth century, but much depended on how many migrants could be packed into the ships. As one historian noted, "All ship owners and freighters wanted to fill their ships, so passengers were usually crowded together, along with their baggage, victuals, and other goods." Often such conditions brought disease. Although only a small percentage of passengers failed to reach their destinations, there were several deadly voyages. On one boatload of 312 Germans, for example, 250 died at sea, whereas on another that carried 160 people, only 10 arrived alive. Not until the end of the colonial era were laws passed requiring decent treatment for passengers.

The flood of non-English immigrants eventually caused friction and difficulties. Some of this resulted from long-held bitterness toward people from competing European nations, but many of the problems grew from local issues in the American colonies. Although it is not possible to consider all the nationalities and scattered settlements, the situation in Pennsylvania shows how negative feelings toward non-English peoples developed. There the Germans—incorrectly called Pennsylvania Dutch—were divided into several groups. Those who attracted the most attention were the so-called sect Germans: Amish, Mennonites, Moravians, and Dunkers. These people were pacifists and sided with the Quakers in matters of military service and defense.

Most Germans, aside from wanting to maintain their own language and customs, agreed with other pioneers about the need for strong action against the Indians, but they mainly wanted to be left alone. When the Quaker-dominated legislature refused to pass laws committing the colony to fighting in King George's War during the 1740s, Benjamin Franklin and other non-Quaker leaders tried to organize an unofficial militia for defense against the French and the Indians. They appealed unsuccessfully to the Germans for cooperation. This aloofness to the war between Britain and France convinced some Pennsylvanians that the Germans were unpatriotic and a potential danger to the colony.

The pacifist Germans in particular encountered hostility from other settlers, as well as from colonial officials. The Moravians, or Brethren as they called themselves, had been forced out of Georgia during the1730s for refusing to bear arms. A few years later New York authorities suspected their missionaries of persuading the Indians to join the French against the English and forced the Moravian mission in Duchess County to close. Then in 1747 Governor William Gooch of Virginia denounced the Brethren for their pacifism. As a result of these difficulties the Moravians received a promise from Parliament that they would not have to bear arms or take oaths in legal matters. After that they fared slightly better. By the 1770s the pacifist groups included no more than 10 percent of the German population in Pennsylvania, and they aroused less antagonism from the rest of the colonists.

Pennsylvania leaders suspected and feared the Germans not only because some refused to fight but also because they rejected Anglo-American customs and the English language. German immigrants separated themselves from the English-speaking population whenever possible during the middle decades of the eighteenth century, causing suspicion and some bitterness. Benjamin Franklin denounced them as "Palatine Boors" and in a fit of exasperation asked, "Why should *Pennsylvania,* founded by the *English,* become a Colony of *Aliens,* who will shortly be so numerous as to Germanize us instead of our Anglifying them?"

To break down the language and cultural barriers in the colony, English-speaking leaders organized a Society for the Propagating of Christian Knowledge among the Germans. This association proposed a system of twenty-five English "charity" or free schools for the German communities. These institutions could then "Americanize" the students. Leaders among the German community recognized why the schools had been offered and objected immediately. One wrote that the school supporters "care little about religion; nor do they care for the cultivation of the minds of the Germans, except that they should form the militia and defend their English-American properties." As a result, only about half of the schools got started, and by 1763 the last one had been closed.

The Scots-Irish constituted the largest number of non-English Europeans coming to the colonies during the eighteenth century. By the time of independence, these people numbered between 7 and 10 percent of the white population. Beginning in 1717 descendants of the Scots, who had gone to Ulster in northern Ireland a century earlier, started migrating by the tens of thousands. By 1776 nearly a quarter of a million Scots-Irish had entered the colonies. Although not English, these people spoke the same language as the English colonists and usually had little trouble adjusting to American society. They might well not have been considered as a distinct ethnic group except for their large numbers; their habit of settling together, which resulted in their domination of many frontier regions; and their open dislike for the English.

The flood of Scots-Irish pioneers landed in Philadelphia and moved west into central Pennsylvania and then either north or south following the mountain valleys into western New York, Pennsylvania, Virginia, and the Carolinas. Often within a few months or a year or two, they established communities in the West. There they quarreled with both their non-Scots-Irish neighbors and with government officials, but not because of ethnic differences. As Presbyterians, they encountered some religious persecution in those colonies in which the Anglicans received official recognition and tax support. The Scots-Irish objected not only to Anglican doctrines and practices but also to the prohibitions against having their own clergymen perform marriages. Nevertheless, such difficulties proved minor.

The major problems that the Scots-Irish immigrants faced resulted from their position as pioneers. They often asked for defensive measures against the Indians or expensive road-building programs. Such demands brought them into conflict with eastern-dominated legislatures that either would not or could not support these requests. In Pennsylvania, for example, riots during the winter of 1763–64 and the frontiersmen's march on the colonial capital at Philadelphia show the depth of Scots-Irish anger with the government. Inadequate defensive measures during the just-ended French and Indian War, the ensuing horrors of Indian raids during Pontiac's Rebellion in the summer of 1763, and the refusal of the Philadelphia-controlled government to offer protection produced the riots.

During the eighteenth century the Germans and Scots-Irish were the two largest European groups to enter the colonies. They both pushed to the newly opened frontier regions and peopled extensive areas. They provided substantial markets for American and English manufactured goods and brought immediate economic development just as a result of their numbers. They were, however, by no means the only European immigrants to British North America.

The Dutch had preceded the English to New Netherland—later New York—where they remained for generations. In the Hudson Valley land grants to patroons, or large landowners, led to the creation of semifeudal manors. At what became Albany, Dutch fur traders opened a successful trade, which the English later inherited, with the tribes of the Iroquois Confederacy. In New Amsterdam, the principal Dutch settlement, farmers and shopkeepers mixed freely with the people from other nations. When the British seized their colony in 1664, perhaps ten thousand people lived in New Netherland, and half of those were English. Dutch influence in New York thereafter declined rapidly except for the language, family and place names, and local architecture.

Refugees from religious persecution, such as the Jews and Huguenots (French Protestants), contributed to colonial economic development despite their small numbers. Jews settled first in New Netherland and in Rhode Island. Other colonies prohibited atheists, and even non-Christians, from becoming permanent residents—rules that slowed Jewish entry. By the middle of the eighteenth century Jewish merchants and shippers engaged in considerable trade between Rhode Island and the British West Indian colonies. In that same century Jews moved to Philadelphia, Charleston, Baltimore, and Richmond, but their population and influence remained small.

The Huguenots also populated a few colonial areas. Fleeing their homeland because of religious persecution during the late 1680s, they began arriving in the colonies in small numbers. These first French immigrants reached New England on the eve of an eighty-year series of wars between the British and French in Canada and received less than an enthusiastic welcome. French immigrants to South Carolina made more positive contributions—if only because they avoided the suspicion so prevalent in New England. They entered Carolina hoping to raise silkworms, olives, and grapes, but these ventures failed. The French then moved into Charleston, learned English, and became well-established merchants and businessmen. Others, Roman Catholics who had originally settled in Nova Scotia, were expelled, ventured further south, and located in and around present-day New Orleans.

Immigrants from Scotland, especially the Lowland Scots, who arrived in fairly large numbers between 1763 and 1776, also prospered as merchants. Whereas the Highland Scots were clannish and remained aloof from other colonists, much like the Germans, a minority of Lowland Scots played a vital role in colonial ports, acting as factors, or agents, for British merchants. Because of their economic ties to England, these Scots frequently became Tories during the Revolution, and some returned to England or migrated to Canada during the Revolutionary era.

Colonial Social Structure

By the time of the American Revolution the colonies had grown to a population of about two and one-half million, with much of the growth coming after 1720. Most of the people settled along the Atlantic seaboard, east of the Appalachian Mountains. Manufacturing remained chiefly a home industry, and most colonists made their living from the soil. Less than 10 percent of the population lived in towns. America needed profits from shipping or the exports of its farms and plantations for survival and growth. This need placed the colonists in competition with English shippers, farmers, and merchants, straining relations between the colonists and the mother country severely. During the eighteenth century British efforts to strengthen their mercantile controls over the colonies caused much resentment there, and, if adequately enforced, they would have caused much hardship.

By the end of the colonial era the patterns of future social and economic growth had emerged. In the Southern colonies the elite planters invested their capital in land and slaves in order to grow and export tobacco, rice, and indigo. They depended on merchants in the colonial cities and in England for their shipping and trade. The commitment to land and slaves and a plantation society would dominate the American South through the Civil War; the major difference was that by the middle of the nineteenth century cotton would replace tobacco as the chief export.

If the economic pattern was set, so too was the racial structure. The South did not attract large numbers of diverse European groups in colonial America and would not do so through most of the nineteenth century. White southerners looked to blacks for their labor supply, which they obtained either through the slave trade or the natural growth of the black population. Black slaves and white masters were the unique way of the South and remained so until the Civil War. Black servitude promoted the belief in white supremacy, a view that continues to haunt contemporary America.

Whereas staple crops and slavery characterized the southern states, the North had few slaves. Most of the blacks found in the North, however, were slaves. All blacks were treated as inferiors and did not figure prominently in the regional economy. Northern and especially middle colonies depended on the Germans and Scots-Irish for their new settlers and farmers. Northern colonies also had a more diverse economy and depended on their farms and shipping for prosperity. Cities were more important in the North, and four of the nation's urban centers, Philadelphia, New York, Boston, and Newport, Rhode Island, were located there (see Table 1.1). Charleston was the only southern colonial city whose population exceeded five thousand in 1776.

Although small by modern standards, the urban centers held the key elements for modernization. The business skills of the commercial class, risk capital obtained from business and local industry, and opportunities for larger economic profits than those from agriculture pointed toward the future. The modest colonial towns and cities attracted both the people and the capital needed to stimulate the burst of industrial and urban development that took place during the early decades of the nineteenth century.

The inordinate number of poor people as an aspect of colonial urban life received notice from contemporaries and increased as cities grew larger. Although outside of New York City and Pennsylvania most of the residents were of English descent, commonly and unfairly many people assumed that "foreigners" received disproportionate assistance. Some of the newly arrived immigrants received poor relief from local governments, but most of the poor were in bad health, elderly and incapacitated, or widows and orphans unable to provide for themselves. Many ethnic groups established societies to help keep

TABLE 1.1. Population of Colonial Cities, 1760–1775

	1760	*1775*
1. Philadelphia	23,750	40,000
2. New York	18,000	25,000
3. Boston	15,631	16,000
4. Charleston	8,000	12,000
5. Newport	7,500	11,000
Total	72,881	104,000

new immigrants from joining the ranks of the dependent. The first such immigrant aid society in colonial America, the Scots' Charity Box, was founded in Boston in 1657. Most of the others began between the 1760s and 1790s and included *Die Deutsche Gesellschaft,* the Friendly Sons of St. Patrick, and *La Société Française de Bienfaisance de Philadelphie.* The immigrant aid or benevolent groups would expand considerably in later centuries. Begun to improve conditions on emigrant ships and to provide food, clothing, shelter, and employment for newcomers of their nationality, they gave fellow countrymen opportunities for meeting one another. Eventually these organizations filled a central role in immigrant lives and appeared wherever large numbers of foreigners settled in the nineteenth and twentieth centuries.

The ethnic mixture of the Northern colonies led to conflicts as English Protestants distrusted other nationalities, Jews, and Catholics. Yet the non-English brought labor and skills and were generally loyal to the Patriot cause during the Revolution. As long as their numbers remained low and they seemed to accept American values, society accepted them, but tensions remained and would cause further clashes with the beginning of large-scale immigration in the nineteenth century.

Socially the South differed from the North. The planters dominated southern society. They held the best land and large numbers of slaves, and they controlled the political assemblies. The middle-class farmers usually showed both social and political deference to them. Southerners, even more than northerners, were of English descent; hence the planters' model was the English country gentleman.

In the North, society's orientation became more urban, educated, and middle class. The Puritan influence, in the form of Congregationalism, endured in New England and helped to mold the institutions and attitudes there. Northerners, and some travelers to the New World, thought the North was more fluid than Europe and the southern colonies with their large numbers of slaves. One observer declared that there was "scarcely any part of the world" in which the "lower classes" of people were better off than in New England. There the "ease of gaining a farm renders the lower class of people very industrious; which, with the high price of labour, banishes everything that has the least appearance of begging, or that wandering, destitute state of poverty, which we see so common in England."

Yet the North had its elites, too, especially the wealthy merchants in the major ports who dominated urban society. In places such as Long Island, the Hudson Valley, and the Connecticut Valley, powerful landowners controlled local communities. One traveler remarked of New England on the eve of the American Revolution that "gentlemen's houses appear everywhere" and that on the landed estates the "owners live much in the style of country gentlemen in England." In the eighteenth century these elites had grown rich. As a result the gulf between rich and poor had widened, as it had in the South, creating a propertyless lower class in northern cities. In 1687 the wealthiest tenth of Boston's population owned slightly less than half of the taxable property, and in the 1770s, about 63 percent, whereas the bottom third had practically nothing. In rural Chester County, near Philadelphia, the richest tenth of the farmers also increased its share of the wealth in the eighteenth century. But lacking large concentrations of slaves, the North was less stratified than the South and offered modest opportunities for social and economic advancement.

Racial Minorities and the Revolution

Throughout the Revolutionary era minority rights remained a major issue for policy and debate in the colonies. During the War for Independence Loyalists, who opposed the Revolution and supported England, proved a major threat to the Patriot cause. Strongest in the middle colonies of New York, New Jersey, and Pennsylvania, as well as in Georgia, these people soon became known as Tories. According to one popular definition, a Tory was "a thing whose head is in England, and its body in America, and its neck ought to be stretched." England drew support from perhaps one-third of the colonists, although the exact number of Loyalists remains uncertain. The Patriots had good cause to fear Loyalists in their midst. Some Tories served as spies or guides for the British, and about fifty thousand of them actually fought alongside the Redcoats. At least two of the colonies, New York and Georgia, provided more men for the armies of the king than they did for General George Washington.

Among colonial immigrants, at least three ethnic groups gave heavy support to the British. Although most of the Scots-Irish seem to have favored the Patriot cause, those near Philadelphia joined a Loyalist regiment known as the Volunteers of Ireland. In North Carolina bitterness caused by the earlier quarrels within the colony kept many Scots-Irish from joining the move for independence. Some Germans also became Loyalists. In the South they feared losing British protection from the Indians, but in Pennsylvania religious factors remained important. Britain had given them freedom from persecution less than thirty years earlier, and Revolutionary authorities still frequently fined them for refusing to swear support for the government despite their plea that taking oaths violated their religious beliefs. The Highland Scots were almost the only people who wholeheartedly became Loyalists, and the British organized units of these men to fight in both New York and North Carolina. Because the fighting lasted eight years, much bitterness toward British supporters resulted. Often the persecution of Loyalists had little direct impact on immigrant or ethnic minorities as groups in the colonies, but the use of violence and coercion to achieve conformity remained a threat to them.

For both Indians and blacks the War for Independence brought changes, but for the tribal people these proved mostly negative. During the years just preceding the war, British authorities had tried to satisfy colonial land hunger by concluding treaties with the Iroquois Confederacy of New York for land cessions just beyond Pittsburgh and in Kentucky. This brought outraged denunciations from Shawnee and Delaware bands that lived in the ceded areas, and violence spread along the frontier. When intruding whites killed the family of a tribal leader named Logan, who had worked for peace, retaliation was swift, and in 1774 Lord Dunmore's War occurred. Although isolated diplomatically by the British, the Shawnee launched a series of devastating raids on pioneer settlements, hoping to drive the whites east of the mountains, but these failed. Instead, the colonial troops forced Chief Cornstalk and his warriors to accept peace and American penetration of at least part of their homeland. In the South, too, similar incursions into Cherokee country kept the frontier tense.

With this background of white-Indian violence and suspicion, it is not surprising that the Second Continental Congress quickly turned its attention to Indian affairs. In July 1775 that body declared that "securing and preserving the friendship of Indian nations" is "of the utmost importance to these colonys *[sic]*." The desire to satisfy Indian demands resulted in Congress sending negotiators to the frontier. Unfortunately, they had little but talk to offer. As a result, when the American Revolution began, violence and ill will existed all along the frontier.

Certain that the British would enlist Indians to raid the frontiers, the authors of the Declaration of Independence denounced King George III for using "the merciless Indian Savages, whose known rule of warfare is an undistinguished destruction of all ages, sexes, and conditions," as allies. Bitter fighting between Indians and whites flared across New York, Pennsylvania, and the Carolinas as Mohawk leader Joseph Brant and Cherokee Chief Dragging Canoe led their followers down the warpath on the side of Britain. Most of the tribes remained neutral, and a few small groups even sided with the colonists. Despite that, a generation of bitter warfare just prior to independence had demonized Indians. When peace came in 1783 many white Americans considered Native Americans to be savages who had no place in the new country. George Washington stated this idea clearly when he wrote that "the gradual extension of our Settlements will as certainly cause the Savage and the Wolf to retire; both being beasts of prey tho' they differ in shape." Because of such attitudes, when control of eastern North America shifted from Britain to the United States, tribal people found themselves being treated like defeated enemies.

During the war, military demands for manpower enabled thousands of black slaves to obtain their freedom, while some free blacks also improved their social status through wartime service. Except in the Deep South, militia authorities welcomed both slaves and free blacks into army and naval units. A recent study estimates that some five thousand blacks served in American military units and perhaps another one thousand fought for the British. Tens of thousands more fled to the British, hoping to gain their freedom. In either case, whether serving in the military or running away, blacks used the War for Independence for their own benefit.

By the 1780s white northerners and southerners both agreed on one thing. They had obtained their independence from England and had won a large land mass reaching to the Mississippi River as part of the peace settlement. They meant to expand to the west and exploit the land. Farmers, planters, and land speculators sought new economic opportunities as worn-out soil or overpopulation of the eastern lands forced them to look west. An eager, restless people, Americans at the end of the Revolution were already pushing over the mountains and seeking new worlds to conquer.

2

Forging a New Nation
The South (1776–1840s)

A New Situation

In July 1776 the Declaration of Independence affirmed as self-evident "that all men are created equal, that they are endowed by their Creator with certain unalienable Rights, that among these are Life, Liberty, and the pursuit of Happiness." Theoretically this document put the new nation on record as supporting freedom for all people. Noble as these pronouncements were, they could not obscure the attitudes that individual Americans held or the actions their society took in relation to the ethnic minorities within it. As a result, the question of how Indians, slaves, and immigrants would deal with a society that wanted their labor or, in the case of the Indians, their land, plagued them and the new nation for many decades.

The American Revolution uprooted thousands of people, disrupted trade and commerce, discouraged immigration, and damaged farms, homes, and cities. Yet the former colonists soon resumed their economic activities, united behind a new government, and bound themselves into a nation. The process of nation building proved difficult at first, but important compromises by all groups enabled the thirteen states to discard the Articles of Confederation and ratify the federal Constitution. Even this new frame of government, however, could not overcome the sectional differences or solve existing problems to the satisfaction of all. As a result, during the pre-Civil War decades, two conflicting threads run through the pattern of American history. On the one hand, a deepening sense of nationalism and a growing optimism in the future of America are clearly evident. Most pronounced in the 1776–1820 era, and again during the 1840s, these feelings remained significant factors in national life. At the same time, however, differences in social patterns and economic development continued to exist. Increasingly the North developed towns and cities with expanded commercial enterprise and growing industries. Although some commerce and industry emerged in the South after 1820, it lagged far behind development in the North. Instead, many southerners invested their capital in land and slaves, concentrating most of their economic effort in staple-crop agriculture. People in the newly settled areas of the Mississippi Valley and beyond developed yet another society. Based largely on family farms and small towns, this region needed access to Indian lands and effective transportation. These diverging economic patterns both reflected and shaped the differing needs in the North, South, and West. By the 1830s there was an unmistakable trend toward sectionalism as the North and South drifted gradually away from their earlier feelings of nationalism. Now they looked on each other as competitors with dissimilar goals.

In the 1780s few Americans realized that the differences between the North and South were of long-range significance. Cotton had not yet become the mainstay of Southern agriculture, and slavery seemed to be dying out everywhere. Few could have predicted that the North would develop major urban centers and the industrial economy that emerged prior to the Civil War. Nevertheless, the gap between the two regions over slavery and economic development would grow and divide America into two nations, one slave and the other free.

Territorial Growth

The small but growing strains between North and South had little immediate relevance, and many Americans continued moving west. They looked in that direction for national expansion and coveted the foreign-owned and Indian territory that lay in their path. Beginning with the 1803 Louisiana Purchase, American leaders and citizens confidently predicted that settlement would eventually reach to the Pacific Ocean. Planning for the famous Lewis and Clark expedition that crossed the northern plains, Rocky Mountains, and Pacific Northwest in 1804–6 began before the United States had acquired any of the regions traversed by the explorers. New technological developments such as steamboats made settling the frontier easier than it had been during the early decades after independence. National pride, fear of European powers taking parts of North America, and the pressures of a growing population and economy impelled the federal government to gain new territory. In 1818 negotiators for Great Britain and the United States agreed on a boundary settlement between Canada and America for the lands west of the Great Lakes. The next year Secretary of State John Quincy Adams concluded the Adams–Onís Treaty with Spain, which gave Florida, as well as the Spanish-claimed portion of Oregon, to the Americans while defining the boundary between the United States and the Spanish territory in the Southwest.

For the next two decades pioneers moved west, and in the last half of the 1840s the nation experienced renewed territorial growth. In 1822 Mexico opened its northeast province of Texas to foreign settlers, offering some free and some cheap land. As a result of this inducement, Americans by the mid-1830s outnumbered Mexicans in Texas by a ratio of nearly nine to one. This frightened the Mexican government. As Protestants, the Americans had no desire to assimilate into Mexican society, yet Mexican law required that all immigrants be Catholic; as slaveholders, the Americans were aghast when Mexico outlawed slavery. After 1830 Mexico tried to prohibit further immigration of Americans into Texas. Obviously a clash between the Texans and the Mexicans lay ahead. In 1835 a series of minor disturbances culminated in revolution, and within a year the Texans had declared their independence and sought annexation to the United States. Domestic political wrangling prevented the federal government from immediate action; not until 1845 did Texas join the Union. The next year the United States and Great Britain settled their differences over the Pacific Northwest, and the Americans acquired the region between the 42nd and 49th parallels, from the Rockies west to the Pacific coast. Then in 1848, as a result of the war with Mexico, the United States annexed practically all of what are now California, Nevada, Arizona, New Mexico, and parts of Wyoming and Colorado. Six years later, through the Gadsden Purchase, American negotiators rounded out the southwestern border between the United States and Mexico.

Indian Relations

Before, during, and immediately after the American Revolution, Indians in the South faced heavy pressures to surrender their lands to the advancing pioneers. Although most of the tribes had remained neutral during the war, Indian–white violence occurred along all the frontiers. Responding to continuing demands for land during the 1780s, Cherokee, Choctaw, and Chickasaw leaders signed several treaties bringing peace, recognition of American control over the region, and specific tribal boundaries. The chiefs hoped that the agreements would stabilize relations with whites and limit state encroachments into their country, but in this they failed. Southern frontiersmen continued to seize Indian lands, so tribal leaders next turned to the Spanish in Florida and along the Gulf Coast for help. The mixed-race Creek leader Alexander McGillivray, who had been on the British army payroll a few years earlier, now became a paid Spanish agent among the tribes of the Southeast. With other chiefs he met Spanish officials repeatedly in an effort to forge an Indian confederacy, but they failed to reach any agreement to oppose the United States. Instead, American negotiators persuaded the Indian leaders to travel to New York for negotiations. There, McGillivray accepted the salary of a United States Army general and so lost at least some of his earlier enthusiasm for anti-American plotting. Yet other reasons proved more important in the collapse of the Indian confederacy. Certainly the defection of both the Cherokee and Chickasaw tribes during the 1790s hurt. In addition, when Spain and the United States signed the 1795 Treaty of San Lorenzo, the Spanish diplomats left their Indian allies to face the Americans on their own.

Although isolated bands of warriors and whites clashed repeatedly, the major Southern tribes remained at peace. Nevertheless, they faced continuing pressure to sell their land and experienced repeated incursions by the frontiersmen. Such provocations convinced many tribal leaders that war against the United States was futile, and when the War of 1812 broke out, most Indians in the South remained at peace, a stark contrast with their fellow tribesmen in the North. The only major exception grew out of the Red Stick War, a bitter Creek conflict in Alabama. Led by William Weatherford (Red Eagle), in 1813 Red Stick warriors attacked frontier settlements and destroyed Fort Mims in Alabama. Countering the Red Sticks, however, a majority of Creek warriors under William McIntosh, as well as companies of Cherokee and Choctaw troops, joined General Andrew Jackson's forces. Unfortunately for the Southern tribes, their cooperation with Jackson's army brought no relief from the repeated demands that they sell their land to the United States. Even before the war with Britain had ended, the Treaty of Fort Jackson had stripped them of most of their territory in Alabama and Georgia. Thus at the end of the War of 1812, the Indians once again found either that they had been on the wrong and losing side or that when they helped the Americans, it did them little if any good.

With peace in 1815 the federal government shifted its emphasis from forced land cessions to several related but different programs. Working with Protestant church groups, it encouraged missionary and educational activities among the villagers, hoping to interest the Indians in European-style agriculture so that the tribes would need less land to support them. At the same time the government began encouraging groups of Eastern Indians to sell or trade their lands for territory beyond the Mississippi River, which would also open more land for pioneer settlement. Clearly the programs worked at direct cross-purposes with each other, but then consistency was never a hallmark of federal Indian policy. Even if it had been, the tribes presented the government with a stark dilemma. Responsible officials wanted to maintain peace, but they had to satisfy the pioneers, too. Usually what satisfied the clamor of frontier whites angered the tribes. The problem became acute after the War of 1812 when settlers demanded that the government get the Indians out of their way. Technically the tribes had two alternatives: they could remain on a reduced portion of their land and farm as the whites did, or they could move west. But few Indians had a real choice, as greedy farmers, lumbermen, and miners swept onto tribal territory with little hindrance from the federal government.

In the face of increasing white pressure, Cherokee leaders sought to preserve both their culture and their land in several ways. They encouraged the acceptance of missionary-sponsored schools, thus benefiting from the education. They employed a newly developed Cherokee syllabary that enabled many villagers to read their own language for the first time, thus fostering a deep sense of unity and nationalism that swept through the villages. Whereas the Indians tried to deflect change, as early as 1790 Congress had authorized spending up to $20,000 a year to buy seed, livestock, and tools for tribal farmers. Some villagers accepted this help and modified their farming methods, but in the long run what they wanted most was to be left alone.

This wish was denied. Rather, in 1819 Congress increased its pressure on the tribes when it established an Indian Civilization Fund of $10,000. Through the new program the government paid churches and other benevolent groups that agreed to build and run schools for the tribes, whereas earlier it had only encouraged their efforts at acculturation of the Indians. The new program had widespread public support despite inadequate funding. By the 1840s the federal government still provided the same $10,000 each year, but private mission groups and even some of the tribes themselves spent a total of $150,000 annually to "civilize the savages and Christianize the heathen." In addition to building schools and churches, missionaries established model farms to teach the Indians updated agricultural techniques. Between 1783 and 1815 some of the tribesmen responded to these efforts by learning English, weaving, or use of the white man's farm implements. Others acquired skills as mechanics and blacksmiths. Many, however, clung to their tribal cultures, taking only those things in American society that made their lives easier or more comfortable and rejecting other aspects of white "civilization." In particular the tribesmen spurned or ignored efforts to make them individuals. They retained their allegiance to family and clan, which characterized Indian society, and thus retained an outlook different from most other Americans in the nineteenth century. By repudiating the popular goals of private property and economic advancement, Indians only proved their innate "inferiority" and "savagery" in the view of most other Americans.

This was not an accurate view of all Southern tribes. In particular among the Cherokee, located mainly in North Carolina, Tennessee, and north Georgia, tribal leaders had been fully bicultural for several generations. Literate, articulate, bilingual men directed tribal affairs in ways that served to increase Indian strength and wealth. By the mid-1820s the Cherokee owned at least 22,000 cattle, some 1,300 slaves, 31 gristmills, 10 sawmills, and 8 cotton gins. In addition, the tribe operated eighteen schools and published the *Cherokee Phoenix,* a bilingual Cherokee–English newspaper. With imposing brick plantation homes and successful slave-operated staple-crop agriculture, these leaders presented a serious challenge to southern whites. Such men could hardly be classed as shiftless savages or inferior vagabonds. Despite this obvious evidence of Cherokee achievement, some whites concluded that assimilation would take far longer than they had originally assumed, whereas others decided that assimilation might never work or that it might not even be a worthy goal.

As a result, in the years immediately following the War of 1812, pressure grew to find other answers to the Indian question. This led the federal government, while pursuing a policy of assimilation, to embark on another program, known as Indian removal. Through this program whites sought to persuade Indians to exchange their homes east of the Mississippi River for lands beyond that river. Officially announced by President James Monroe just before he left office in 1825, this program merely made formal what had been happening piecemeal for several decades. Working in direct conflict with the civilization approach, it appeared to offer a better way to end the continuing difficulties with the tribes. Also, once the Indians had left, new areas for settlement by immigrants and pioneers would open more quickly.

This removal policy had many supporters. Those who favored gradual assimilation of the tribesmen hoped to speed the process by isolating the Indians from the frontiersmen. Then they might learn from just and concerned whites. Monroe's secretary of war, John C. Calhoun, estimated that within thirty years after moving west the tribes might be "civilized" enough to join the white majority. A few federal officers actually envisioned Indian territories and states in the West, but that idea never had much support. Apparently no one in the 1820s anticipated the incredible speed with which white Americans would spread beyond the Mississippi, and it was the rapidly advancing frontier that destroyed any chance of achieving the goals of the removal program.

Not all whites favored pushing the Indians aside, and, particularly in the Northeast, public leaders spoke out against forced removal. John Quincy Adams, who followed Monroe as president, was among those who questioned American tactics toward the Indians. Expressing the unpopular view that the nation should deal fairly with the tribes, he hesitated to force them west.

His successor, Andrew Jackson, had no such qualms. A popular frontier leader and famous Indian fighter, "Old Hickory" announced in his first inaugural address his intention to push the Indians beyond the Mississippi. In May 1830, less than a year later, Congress passed the Indian Removal Act, which provided funds to buy tribal holdings and to pay the costs of relocation. The new law gave the president no authority to use force, but he did anyway. The pattern had been set; the Indians had to move or be destroyed.

The removal efforts applied to tribes in the North and Midwest, as well as to those in the South, and during the 1830s about 73,800 Indians moved west under this policy. Usually the federal government appointed a special agent to gather, organize, supply, and lead the migrants. Civilians supervised the moving of cooperative Indians, and army officers superintended the recalcitrants. Local businessmen provided food, clothing, and transportation, an arrangement that caused needless suffering among the uprooted Indians. Frequently the contractors' greed led them to buy condemned meat and spoiled flour to feed their charges. For transportation, the contractors rented cheap, untrustworthy boats to get the Indians across major streams, sometimes with disastrous results. One steamboat, jammed to the rails with Creeks, sank in the Mississippi River, and 311 Indians drowned. The Cherokee suffered similar difficulties, and some scholars estimate that nearly four thousand of the fifteen thousand tribesmen who started west at gunpoint died either on what the Indians called the "Trail of Tears" or during their first months in what is now Oklahoma.

Not all of the Indians accepted removal as inevitable. The Cherokee, among the most acculturated of the Eastern tribes, sought to use their acceptance of the white man's ways as the basis for retaining ancestral lands. Hoping to present a unified front to the Georgia legislature, the tribal leaders met during the summer of 1827, drafted a constitution, and formed the Cherokee Republic. Then they elected John Ross as president and prepared to defend themselves. Unfortunately, the act of creating their republic made forced removal inevitable. The United States Constitution prohibits the creation of a new state within any existing state without its permission—something Georgia refused to give. Instead, the officials demanded that the federal government force the Indians to vacate their lands. After the passage of the Indian Removal Act in May 1830, the tribal leaders appealed to the United States Supreme Court. In *The Cherokee Nation v. Georgia* (1831) and the later *Worcester v. Georgia* (1832), the Court ruled in the Indians' favor, but it proved unable to help them. President Andrew Jackson allegedly remarked after the latter ruling, "John Marshall has made his decision. Now let him enforce it."

In addition to showing the Court's inability to stop removal, these decisions had a second long-range impact on the status of Indians. In *The Cherokee Nation v. Georgia* Chief Justice John Marshall described Indian tribes as "domestic dependent nations." This position meant that they must look to the United States "for protection; rely upon its kindness and its power, appeal to it for relief for their wants." A year later, Marshall reiterated this idea in his decision, *Worcester v. Georgia*. His rulings in these two cases strengthened the position that individual tribes were not independent nations. Marshall's views became the basis for the later opinions that depicted Indians as wards of Washington, people who needed the government to take care of them because they could not manage for themselves. These ideas became an important influence followed after the Civil War by the Bureau of Indian Affairs.

The Seminole tribe in Florida also refused to be moved, and in 1835 they started a guerrilla war that cost the United States thousands of casualties and at least $50 million. The army even imported bloodhounds from Cuba to track down its elusive foe, but with little success. Sporadic fighting dragged on until the mid-1840s, when the soldiers captured Indian leaders by treachery. Soon after the Seminole War ended, and the defeated tribesmen were shipped west to Indian Territory. Now the last major group of Indians was gone from the Eastern third of the nation. By the Mexican War only a few scattered remnants of the once numerous and powerful tribes remained. Forced removal had succeeded.

Unwillingly, the tribesmen moved west. A rising tide of settlers followed. Industrialization, agricultural expansion, and mechanization called for acquisition of Indian land and resources. Unlike the immigrants and slaves who helped build the American economy with their hands, backs, and minds, the tribesmen contributed their property to the process. Economic development received a major boost from the involuntary Indian contribution while at the same time nearly destroying the tribes.

As white Americans evolved contradictory policies toward the Indians, they also questioned their attitudes toward slavery. The Quakers, particularly in New England and Pennsylvania, acted first, but even those in the South began to manumit blacks wherever the law permitted it.

Southern Antislavery Falters

The ideology of the Revolutionary era buttressed the cause of those who opposed slavery. Emancipationists frequently used the ideas of the Declaration of Independence, and early state constitutions and laws included sentiments about the rights of man. Critics noted that equality and slavery were incompatible. One Massachusetts judge observed, "The idea of slavery is inconsistent with our own conduct and our constitution.... There can be no such thing as perpetual servitude of a rational creature." Black military participation in the Revolution also encouraged some colonies to consider emancipation. Some northern states granted freedom to black soldiers, but the South rejected such proposals. Lord Dunmore, the British governor of Virginia, also promised freedom for those blacks who had fought with the Loyalists, but the English did little to live up to this promise.

In the South, many planters such as Thomas Jefferson held slavery to be morally wrong. Yet Jefferson owned numerous slaves and depended on them for plantation labor. He was not sure that whites and blacks could live together in freedom, and when he thought of emancipation, he hoped for colonization outside of America. In the end Jefferson, like so many of the South's leading planters, made few concrete proposals to end slavery. Although he cohabited with one of his slaves, Sally Hemings, and upon his death freed the woman along with her children, he carried his ambivalent feelings about slaves to his grave.

Other Southern planters also considered freeing their bondsmen. In the upper regions of the South, Maryland and Delaware enacted laws encouraging manumission. As a result, the number of free blacks in those states increased significantly. Virginia and North Carolina passed similar laws, but fewer individuals released their bondsmen and bondswomen. South Carolina and Georgia, on the other hand, maintained their traditions.

Economic factors largely account for the failure of antislavery in the southern states. The slaveholders depended on their chattels for labor and refused to make a large financial sacrifice in the cause of human freedom. After the Revolution planters hoped that with English control and restrictions gone the West would be open for expansion and foreign trade in tobacco would be more profitable. Yet it was cotton that formed the base for southern expansion and became the cornerstone of the region's economy. Eli Whitney's invention of the cotton gin in 1793 made it economically profitable to grow short staple cotton in much of the South. Americans produced only thirteen thousand bales of cotton before its invention, but by 1860 output had increased to about 4,500,000 bales annually. As the nineteenth century wore on, English and Northern mills became ready consumers of American-grown cotton.

Not everyone raised cotton. In the older states, diversified farming and other staple crops remained important. Substantial production of rice in South Carolina, sugar in Louisiana, and tobacco and hemp in North Carolina, Tennessee, and Kentucky indicates existing dependence on cash-crop agriculture. In addition, farmers also raised cattle, hogs, corn, and other foodstuffs to feed the people.

Some whites urged moving to a more diversified economy, especially manufacturing, and the South did witness the spread of cotton mills, iron works, and other industries before the Civil War. The mining of gold and lead also grew, as did timber and turpentine production. To serve these industries and to help move people and goods more easily, some people earned their living building or operating canals and railroads. Nevertheless, the South lagged behind the rest of the nation in both industry and transportation because it devoted most of its capital to land and slaves for agriculture.

As a result, the South had few major cities before the Civil War. Some towns grew into small cities in the early nineteenth century, but the region could boast of few urban centers when compared with the free states. Of the cities in the future Confederacy, only New Orleans had a population of more than one hundred thousand people, and in 1861 it was the only southern community large enough to rank among the nation's nine largest cities. Although a few southern towns served as important regional centers of trade, banking, and even some manufacturing, the region remained overwhelmingly rural throughout most of the nineteenth century.

Southern Free Blacks

With improved prospects for expansion of cotton-growing areas, many whites grew even more firm in their beliefs about the necessity of retaining slavery. At the same time, however, they felt uncomfortable with free blacks in their midst and sought ways of removing them. One popular notion espoused by many whites, including Abraham Lincoln, had an organization to support it: the American Colonization Society. Formed in 1817, some of its proponents saw it as a way to eradicate slavery; they reasoned that white Americans might favor abolition if the nation could deport all blacks to Haiti or Liberia in Africa. Others ignored slavery and just wanted to rid the nation of free blacks. Even the antislavery Republican Party, founded in 1854, had its share of colonizers. Senator James Doolittle of Wisconsin said it would keep "our Anglo-Saxon institutions as well as our Anglo-Saxon blood pure and uncontaminated," whereas others said it "would relieve us from the curse of free blacks."

Because of its expense and opposition from free blacks, the colonization movement had little success. Instead, whites enacted laws aimed at excluding African Americans. Using charges often leveled at minorities throughout American history, legislators complained that their states would become "an asylum for all the old and decrepit and broken down negroes that may emigrate or be sent to it" or "the Liberia of the North." With voters supporting these attitudes by large majorities, several states in both the North and South barred the entrance of free blacks, and others required them to post bonds guaranteeing good behavior. When legislation failed to keep blacks out of their communities, angry whites sometimes resorted to violence, and periodic race rioting erupted in the antebellum period. Perhaps the worst episode occurred in a city without slaves, Cincinnati, when, in 1829, mobs of whites assaulted blacks, burned their homes, and drove about half of them out of town. Many of the escapees fled north to Canada.

In the South free blacks lived on the margin of society. Virtually "slaves without masters," the 250,000 free African Americans living there in 1860 found themselves with few legal and social rights. They could not vote, except in Tennessee, North Carolina, and parts of Louisiana, and during the 1830s both Tennessee and North Carolina disfranchised them. Through custom and by law the white South heaped restrictions on them, especially after the 1830s. By the Civil War free blacks were banned from the schools, the militia, public places, and some types of employment and were subject to curfews, registration systems, and verbal and physical abuse. They could make contracts, be married, sue, and hold property, but generally they could not testify against whites in the courts or sit on juries. They also faced harsh penalties for criminal offenses.

It is not surprising that blacks lived at the fringes of the economy and that most existed in or near poverty. Only a few managed to become successful planters. Most of those in rural areas barely scratched out a living, and if they owned land, it was usually a small amount. The landless frequently became hired hands or casual laborers. The cities offered more opportunities, but here, too, the former slaves faced discrimination and often found jobs only as unskilled laborers or as domestics. In 1831 Savannah banned blacks from becoming apprentices in the trades of "Carpenter, Mason, Bricklayer, Barber, or any other Mechanical Art or Mystery" and later extended the list. In spite of such discrimination, some free blacks did become skilled workers. The Deep South's most prosperous African Americans lived in New Orleans. There, proportionately more of them than Irish or German immigrants were skilled workers, and some even became successful businessmen and professionals.

Free blacks formed their own social institutions. The church was especially important then, as it is in our own times. African Americans, most of whom are Protestant fundamentalists, have always been especially comfortable in their own churches, and their ministers were, and are, expected to assume leadership positions vis-à-vis white society. Many of the most respected African American leaders of the twentieth century, for example, included the Reverends Martin Luther King Sr. and Jr., the Reverend Jesse Jackson, and Black Muslim minister Louis Farrakhan. In the antebellum South, of course, whites were suspicious of, and passed laws to restrict, black religious life. Blacks also organized schools, clubs, and cultural groups and sought to improve and educate themselves, but none of these competed with their own local churches as places for worship and relaxation and as institutions in which the most important issues facing the community were discussed.

Slavery in the Old South

White Americans tried to ship free blacks back to Africa, but they could not end slavery. Antislavery agitation failed nationally, although the Northern states did abolish the institution. In 1787 the Northwest Ordinance outlawed slavery in what became Ohio, Indiana, Illinois, Michigan, and Wisconsin, but at the same time slave owners could bring their human property into the region south of the Ohio River. The Constitution prevented the banning of the international slave trade for twenty years. Thus until 1808 Americans continued to import blacks legally from Africa or the West Indies. Even after Congress prohibited the trade, smuggling continued for several more decades. These latter-day importations had less effect than the natural increase in the domestic population. By 1860 nearly four million slaves lived and worked in the South.

One of the most repulsive aspects of slavery was the interstate sale of human beings. Planters who occupied the best lands of the Gulf states after Indian removal, and who wanted to purchase slaves, did so from dealers in the Eastern seaboard states or the Upper South. Estimates of the interstate slave trade are not precise, but Virginia, the largest seller, provided roughly three hundred thousand slaves to the Gulf states between 1830 and 1860, and hundreds of thousands more were sent south from more northern slave states such as Maryland and Kentucky. Even defenders of slavery considered public auctions of slaves a necessary evil and sometimes looked down on the dealers. The buyers usually wanted "prime fields" (young healthy males), but women and children were

One of the most horrible aspects of slavery was the slave trade itself. This painting, done in 1853, is of slaves going south after the sale. By Eyre Crowe. (Chicago Historical Society)

Slaves working the cotton fields. From *Harper's Weekly,* 1875. (Library of Congress)

also sold in the marketplace. Occasionally slave owners made some effort to keep marriages intact, but the South did not have legal safeguards to prevent the separation of husbands and wives. Families, as opposed to marriages, were even more vulnerable to the slave trade. Most sellers tried to keep mothers and children together, but once the young ones passed the age of thirteen, they were sold separately without regard for their parents and kin. The traumatic experience of being bought and sold like cattle has been immortalized in black folklore with songs such as "No More Auction Block for Me."

Even if the planter brought slaves with him to the new cotton lands of the Deep South, he was apt to destroy families. Frequently husbands and wives lived on different plantations, and if a planter migrated and took his male slave along, the slave's wife and children on another plantation remained behind. This happened frequently in the antebellum South, as planters seeking new opportunities took hundreds of thousands of slaves with them to the Deep South. Thus, whether by sale or migration, the massive movement of slaves between 1820 and 1860 proved especially difficult for their families.

Whether slaves were sold, carried by the owners, or simply born in the newer regions of the South, slavery expanded rapidly in the Gulf states. At the time of the American Revolution over half the slave population lived in Maryland and Virginia; by 1860, although Virginia still had the largest number of slaves, these two states accounted for only 15 percent of the bond servants. Alabama and Mississippi, two states that did not come into the Union until after the War of 1812, ranked closely behind Virginia. Of the nearly four million slaves in 1860, about half dwelled in the cotton kingdom.

At the time of the Civil War, only about one-quarter of the South's white families owned slaves, and most of these owned only a few. Twelve percent of the owners had more than twenty slaves, and a small minority owned large numbers: three thousand families had more than one hundred slaves and a few families more than five hundred. Some of these large owners held several plantations, using overseers to run them. Most bondsmen and bondswomen lived on plantations having twenty or more slaves. These were usually the large cotton plantations in Alabama, Mississippi, and other cotton-growing regions (where according to the 1850 census, more than two-thirds of the South's 2.5 million slaves worked), rice plantations in South Carolina, and sugar plantations in Louisiana. In the cities such concentrations happened less often than in the countryside, and only a few owners had large numbers of slaves.

Although most slaves lived on cotton plantations, not all toiled in the fields. A minority became skilled workers, such as carpenters and blacksmiths. Some cooked food; others cared for children or were servants in the master's house. Overseers were usually white, but the bulk of the drivers, who supervised the slaves in the fields, were black. Plantations usually grew their own food and raised their own cattle and hogs, and slaves cared for the food crops and raised the livestock. During the off season even the hands who usually worked in the tobacco, rice, sugar, and cotton fields helped with domestic chores and the maintenance of the plantation, including such jobs as construction and repair of fences and buildings. Of course, on those farms having only a few slaves, they engaged in a wide variety of tasks.

Slaves also labored in the Old South's industries. They could be found in iron foundries and tobacco plants in Virginia, hemp factories in Kentucky, sugar mills in Texas and Louisiana, rice mills in Georgia and South Carolina, and even in the fledgling cotton mills, the coal, iron, salt, gold, and lead mines, and the timber and transportation industries. In Charleston about one-quarter of the adult male slaves worked as skilled laborers, and in some cities of the Old South slaves outnumbered the whites in important crafts. It was not unusual for these skilled slaves to hire themselves out for wages and live apart from their masters in quasi-freedom, although in the towns many of them lived in a building behind the master's house.

Obviously slavery provided profits and comforts that owners were reluctant to abandon. Although during the 1780s slave codes and laws restricting manumission were moderated, the invention of the cotton gin in 1793 and the profits that it promised lessened the talk about freeing slaves. During the nineteenth century Southerners again tightened their grip over this "peculiar institution."

By the 1830s fear of slave revolts, such as Nat Turner's in Virginia in 1831, and the rise of abolitionism in the North hardened white attitudes. The South became more militant in defending slavery, increasingly viewing the system as a benefit to both white and black, a blessing sanctioned by God. Southern voices of criticism against slavery became fewer and fainter, while the belief in black inferiority reinforced the white man's view that servitude was an appropriate condition for blacks. "He the negro is but a grown up child, and must be governed as a child," wrote George Fitzhugh, one of the better-known defenders of the institution. "The negro race is inferior to the white race and living in their midst," he continued, "they would be far outstripped or outwitted in the chaos of free competition....The negro slaves of the South are the happiest, and in some senses, the freest people in the world."

In the antebellum South the slave codes became increasingly more repressive to make the slave stand in fear of the white man. As one judge said, "The power of the master must be absolute, to render the submission of the slave perfect." Slaves could not possess firearms or leave the plantation without

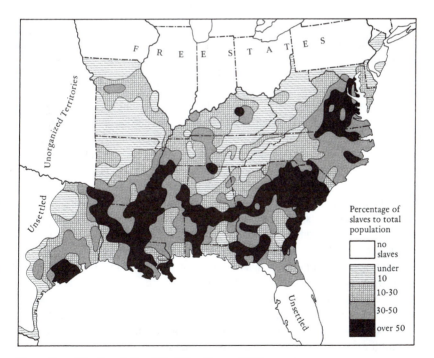

Proportion of the Population Who Were Slaves, 1850.

permission. It was illegal to teach them to read and write. They could not hold meetings without having a white person present, and they could not insult or strike whites or testify against them in trials. Separate laws and courts dealt with slave offenses, and for certain crimes blacks received more severe sentences than white people did. Whipping was the most common form of public punishment for slaves, though South Carolina permitted branding until 1833, and there were cases after that of slaves having their ears chopped off. Alabama permitted up to one hundred lashes on the bare back of a slave for forging a pass. For some offenses death was permissible.

The harshness of the law was somewhat mitigated by the profit motive, by planter paternalism, and in some cases by the slaves' legal status as persons. Slaves were defined as property but considered persons, too. For example, the malicious killing of a slave was considered murder, and some codes regulated the hours of labor and told masters to provide a proper diet. These provisions were partly motivated by self-interest and partly by the fact that white southerners recognized blacks as human beings. The killing of a slave was both the taking of a life and the destruction of a valuable piece of property. When the state executed a slave for a capital crime, it generally compensated the owner for his loss. Occasionally masters discharged overseers who were too brutal; some masters even sued overseers for injuring their slave property; and on occasion the state prosecuted overseers for killing or maiming slaves.

In practice the slaveholders controlled the legal process, and the courts offered meager protection for people in bondage. If the owners' power made for only a slight legal protection as persons, it also enabled masters to disregard such features of the codes as the ban on teaching slaves to read and write. The practice of hiring out and living away, although frowned on and illegal in many places, remained common in the cities. A Savannah grand jury maintained that the practice of slaves being able "to hire their own time or labor for themselves" was "an evile" that "is striking directly at the existence of our institutions." But that same city had slaves who hired out, including one who "hired his time of his master at two hundred and fifty dollars a year, which he paid in monthly installments. He did what he called job work, which consisted of undertaking jobs, and hiring men to work under him" and he had seven or eight other blacks, "all hired to help remove the cotton in wheelbarrows."

The practice continued because masters found it profitable to hire out their bondsmen and because employers needed skilled or even unskilled laborers for short periods. The skills that workers possessed made them valuable enough for owners to overcome their fears about the lack of controls under the hiring-out system. Some city governments rented slaves for municipal projects, such as building streets and removing garbage. Others, however, owned their own workers. One historian has noted that the city of Savannah even used its slaves as firemen, and they were reported to be the pride of the town. "We suppose that there are no more efficient or well managed companies in the United States," boasted the local newspaper.

Evidence exists that urban slaves had better shelter than those living on the plantations in run-down cabins, but usually their housing was crowded, drafty, and dirty and lacked adequate furniture. Some visitors found the slave quarters "in the most decayed and deplorable condition" and "built of logs, with no windows—no opening at all, except the doorway, with a chimney of sticks and mud." Kind and prosperous planters provided their slaves with sturdy white-washed log cabins and privacy.

Diet, medical care, and clothing varied, but they were frequently inadequate. Frederick Douglass said that as a child in slavery he was "kept almost in a state of nudity; no shoes, no stockings, no jacket, no trousers; nothing but coarse sack cloth or town-linen, made into a sort of shirt, reaching down to my knees." Usually adults had better clothes, and many had special attire for holidays. In the cities one could find well-dressed slaves, the household servants of rich townsfolk and planters. Masters tried to provide a healthy diet, but some relied on cornmeal, salt pork, hominy, and fatback. More fortunate slaves had their own gardens and hence ate better food. Because the black population grew rapidly through natural increase in the antebellum South, there must have been a certain minimum standard of living, but the life expectancy of slaves was shorter than that of whites.

Most slaves worked from sunup to sunset. During the harvest season they toiled even longer; in the off season plantation repair and maintenance chores kept them busy. Those working in industries and mining had few seasonal adjustments and seldom got relief. Usually owners allowed their slaves to rest on special occasions, such as Christmas and after the harvest, and some gave Sundays and occasional Saturdays as holidays, too. Pregnant women received time off just before and after the birth of a child, but the young mother had to be back in the fields or at the "Big House" within days after the delivery.

How masters extracted labor from and disciplined their slaves was crucial to the daily life of the individual. Stories about physical cruelty abound. Force characterized the system on the large plantations of the Deep South. One former bondsman recalled, "I have seen slaves whipped and I was whipped myself. I was whipped particularly about a saddle I left in the night after using it during the day. My flesh was cut so bad that the scars are on me to this day." Cruel masters also stingily rationed food and shelter, did not allow slaves to leave the plantations, and used dogs to hunt runaways. A few even maintained jails for the slaves and took care to give public whippings as an example for the others.

Yet many masters tried to avoid brutality, and ex-slaves recalled those who did not use force. An Alabama bondsman recalled, "Us lucky, 'cause Massa

Cole don't whip us." Even some who used the lash urged caution. A Louisiana planter observed, "I object to having the skin cut, or my negroes marked in any way by the lash.... I will most certainly discharge any overseer for striking any of my negroes with a club or the butt of his whip." Others avoided the whip either because they found such brutality repugnant ("The overseer whose constant and only resort is to the lash... is a brute, and deserves the penitentiary") or because they favored different methods of control. Instead of punishment, they offered inducements—better housing, food, and clothing. They allowed slaves to grow and even sell their own food.

Owners and overseers sometimes used their power to take sexual advantage of slave women. At one extreme the sexual bond was accompanied by deep feelings; some men kept mistresses to whom they were strongly attached. In New Orleans the practice was quite open; elsewhere it was done quietly. Sometimes the mixed offspring of these unions were educated and freed. One wealthy Virginia planter made his paramour head of the household. He tutored and freed their four children. When his daughter married a slave, he purchased the husband's freedom and gave them land, and at his death he willed his property to his three sons. This practice was uncommon, but it was not unusual. A large proportion of the free black population had white ancestors.

At the other extreme, masters could force themselves on unwilling slaves, and some looked on blacks as fair game, for, as Frederick Douglass said, the "slave woman is at the mercy of the father, sons or brothers of her master." Nor could the male slave protect his wife, sister, or mother without risking severe punishment. Most interracial sexual unions were of white males and black females. White females and black males sometimes became attached, but such unions were considered taboo in the Old South.

Miscegenation and the lack of legal status of the family did not mean that all slaves lived without families. To be sure, some masters cared little about morality or stable families. In fact, they realized that promiscuous behavior often produced children, increasing the plantation labor force. But most owners wanted reliable workers, and when they thought that monogamy encouraged stability, they promoted such relationships. If they thought that loose arrangements did not upset the routine of the plantation, however, they ignored the slaves' sexual practices. Some whites, of course, were deeply religious and paternalistic and assumed responsibility for slave conduct and morality. These masters insisted on sexual purity, family stability, and monogamy; slaves had their own ideas on these subjects.

Control over family life was part of the general power owners possessed. Masters ruled, and ultimately slaves had to come to grips with that fact. Many appeared cooperative, even passive and docile. Southern whites liked to think that their charges were happy, faithful, and loyal. They frequently saw this

"Sambo" type as the typical plantation "darkie." In his extreme form, "Sambo" had no thoughts of freedom and was willing to sacrifice his life for the beloved master and mistress and their family. Although there were some passive slaves, many hid their true feelings about their hatred of slavery and whites and only appeared to be loyal and contented. When their chance came, many of these supposedly contented slaves fled; or, in the case of the Civil War, they joined the Union army. Even the house servants, often favored and considered more trustworthy, sometimes left their masters when they had the opportunity. Thus slaves could exhibit both a willingness to accept their status and the will to resist it. A few resisted violently, and Nat Turner's 1831 revolt sent chills throughout the South. Literate and skilled, Turner believed that he "was ordained for some great things in the hands of the Almighty." Members of his uprising massacred several white families before armed whites crushed them. Turner and forty followers were either executed or murdered because of the rebellion.

Many slaves were neither Sambos nor rebels. They were sullen and resentful or were alternatively sullen and cooperative. They broke tools, worked slowly and inefficiently, killed livestock, and sometimes made life difficult for their owners. A few even sued, sometimes successfully, for their freedom on the grounds that they were illegally being held in bondage. Most slaves became efficient workers, however, even though they might have yearned for independence, because if they resisted openly they risked punishment. When life became especially unbearable, they ran away. Slave patrols and the long distance to the free states hindered the fugitives' flight. Running away also meant the loss of loved ones who would probably never be seen again. Yet, although the numbers are not known exactly, thousands did break away. Until the United States took Florida, that area offered a haven, especially among the Indians there, but most runaways followed the North Star to either the free states or Canada.

Despite their intense desire for liberty, most slaves obeyed their masters and accommodated themselves to the "peculiar institution." Some even developed close ties with their owners. There were slaves who, when given the chance, did not flee. Some were too old with no place to go; others had relatively kind masters for whom they had feelings of affection. Whites later exaggerated the loyalty of slaves, especially that of the black "mammies" who raised the masters' children, but close bonds often existed between such black women and those whom they nurtured.

Often, household workers and personal attendants received better treatment than the field hands. More privileged slaves sometimes even identified with their oppressors. The black drivers, for example, gained power and status, and household servants received fancy clothes. One slave recalled when he got new clothes: "I had known no comforts, and had been so cowered and broken in spirits by cruel lashings that I really felt lighthearted at this improvement in my personal appearance, although it was merely for the gratification of my master's pride; and I thought I would do all I could to please my Boss." Others received money, gifts, better food, and fewer restrictions.

Like everyone else, not all African Americans possessed sterling character; more than a few informed on others who were also in bondage. They turned fugitives in or reported plots or revolts to the master. Perhaps it was a personal conflict that motivated some to expose others, or perhaps they were seeking special privileges or rewards. Angry slaves called these bondsmen "white folks' servants" because "they are just the same as white men." Having such trusted help, masters were known to leave the plantations under their care and to reward them for work well done when they returned. Yet privileged status did not end their longings for emancipation. If the white South feared their slaves' desire for freedom, they rarely acknowledged it.

The slaves did not organize their lives solely according to white people's dictates. They possessed a rich African heritage, which when combined with New World experiences formed an African American way of life. At the forefront of their American values stood God and a fundamentalist Protestant faith that focused on a Christianity of work and obedience. The slaves harmonized aspects of different African religions with these teachings and blended them into a faith more suitable to their needs. Black spirituals envisioned ultimate redemption and recognition of personal worth. Old Testament themes of the release of the Hebrew children from bondage, of David's triumph over Goliath, and of Daniel's deliverance from the Lion's Den dominated their prayers:

> He delivered Daniel from de lion's den
> Jonah from de belly ob de whale,
> And de Hebrew children from de fiery furnace,
> And why not every man?

In other cases African culture resisted any fusion with Christianity or the white world. African beliefs in magic, voodoo, and conjurers survived into the nineteenth century, and through these media some slaves tried to retaliate against oppressive whites. Owners could control the legal status and much of the physical life of the slave but not necessarily his mind or culture. A conjurer who allegedly could affect whites, as well as blacks, was a powerful person, a supernatural defense against the harshness of slavery. One slave recalled that "I was led to believe that I could do almost as I pleased without being flogged." When threatened by his master with a beating, "I did not believe that he could do it, while I had this root and dust, and as he approached me, I commenced talking saucy to him."

Folktales also played an important part in slave culture. Some of the oral traditions told of the African past and tribal religion, but most were secular, taught a moral, and emphasized survival. The most famous of the narratives concern "Br'er Rabbit," the shrewd bunny who managed to outwit his foes. Scholars have traced these animal trickster stories to Africa, but they were well suited to a slave society. Faced with white power, the blacks, like "Br'er Rabbit," had to be cunning to endure. "De rabbit is de slickest o' all de animals de Lawd ever made. He ain't de biggest, an he ain't de loudest but he sho' am de slickest." Clearly the folktales and other forms of slave culture pointed to ways of dealing with a harsh world. As one scholar observed,

> In their religious songs and sermons slaves sought certainty in a world filled with confusion and anarchy; in their supernatural folk beliefs they sought power and control in a world filled with arbitrary forces greater than themselves; and in their tales they sought understanding of a world in which, for better or worse, they were forced to live. All forms of slave folk culture offered their creators psychic relief and a sense of mastery.

If religion, magic, music, and stories gave slaves a sense of themselves, so did the most important institution of slavery—the family. The power of the master to make and break families should not lead us to minimize their importance. While some masters stressed family life, the bondsmen had their own reasons for doing so and managed to establish rules for courtship, sex, and marriage. Slaves, for example, did not marry their blood cousins. The sexual code among slaves accepted prenuptial sex along with fidelity in marriage.

Most slaves lived in two-parent households. Of course, the master and overseer supervised slave families, but the slaves themselves could and did socialize their children. If the father lived on another plantation, relatives played a more significant role in the life of the mother and her children. Aware of the importance of their family and kin, slaves used family names for their children's first names. But unlike whites they never named children after their mothers. Some slaves even used surnames that differed from those of their masters. The choice of names shows how the bondsmen regarded their families.

Poor Whites

Blacks were not the only poor people in the antebellum South. Many white farmers had neither slaves nor decent land and lived in wretched poverty in the piney-wooded or swampy areas. Unskilled urban workers, as well as those who toiled in the industries of the Old South, also had little wealth. Industrial workers labored long hours for low wages, faced occupational hazards, and lived in crowded housing. The Irish, who toiled on canals and railroads, as well as other white laborers in the mines, were among the lowest paid workers in America. The vast bulk of this white population descended from colonial stock, as few immigrants came to the Old South. In 1860 the slave states possessed about five hundred thousand immigrants, who barely accounted for 13 percent of the nation's foreign-born. The South's major ports, Baltimore and New Orleans, attracted many of these foreigners, and the states of Maryland, Missouri, Louisiana, and Texas contained most of them. Germans, who favored Maryland, Missouri, and Texas, and the Irish, who dwelled in Louisiana and Georgia, constituted most of the foreign-born population, although ethnic enclaves could be found in Alabama and Mississippi as well. About thirty thousand Central European Jews also found their way to the South, and many of the rural hamlets received visits from Jewish peddlers who later became small shopkeepers. Louisiana, with about eight thousand, contained the largest number of Jews in the antebellum period.

Most immigrants chose to settle outside the South because the shipping routes generally took them from Europe to northern ports such as Boston and New York and because they believed that the free states provided more economic opportunities. The newcomers did not want to compete with the plantation system and slave labor. Furthermore, by the time of the mass immigration after 1845, they knew that most of the best cotton land of the Old South had been gobbled up by the old-stock whites. Of course, there were still opportunities in the South. Germans settled in Texas, for example, because land was available there; both the Irish and Germans worked in the cities; and the Irish also found jobs building canals and railroads.

The nativism (hostility to foreigners) of pre-Civil War America, most pronounced in the free states, might have discouraged immigrants from settling there, but the slave states also had their share of bigotry. In some areas southerners detested the Irish because of their Catholicism, and they scorned both the Germans and the Irish because of their clannishness. Some southerners blamed the massive immigration to the North after 1840 with tipping the population balance in favor of the free states to the detriment of regional interests, and many were apprehensive about the immigrants' views toward slavery.

In particular, the antislavery sentiments of German settlers alarmed native whites and caused them to suspect the newcomers. In the 1850s German radicals in Louisville denounced slavery, and in San Antonio another group of Germans called the institution "an evil, the removal of which is absolutely essential according to the principles of democracy." Most Germans in the South, however, accepted the dominant views and denounced Republicans. Generally, Irish and Germans were known to dislike both blacks and abolitionists. If

Germans did not own many slaves, it was not because they abhorred the institution, but rather because they settled in areas unsuitable for cotton production or were urban dwellers.

Whether foreign or native born, urban or rural, rich or poor, controlling southerners had one thing in common—the color of their skin. Even though some poor whites refused to fight for slavery during the Civil War, an overwhelming majority of the region's population still believed in white supremacy, Indian removal, and black slavery.

The differences between the North and South became more pronounced after 1830. Antislavery sentiment rose among the people north of the Mason-Dixon Line, and the growing economies of the two sections diverged. It was the struggle over slavery, however, and especially slavery in the territories, that would eventually split the nation.

3

Forging a New Nation
The North (1776–1840s)

While plantation agriculture spread west across much of the Lower South, the northern economy followed a different path. Although agriculture remained important in almost all regions of the country, in the North commerce and industry developed at a more rapid pace. Commercial and industrial ventures depended on more urban markets and improved transportation facilities, so the northern economy and society became more diversified than the basically rural and agricultural South. As the two sections drifted apart economically, they developed different needs, and they often competed with each other rather than cooperating. Although both faced similar problems in regard to the Indians, the South had a much greater interest in the slave system, whereas the North had to consider ways of accommodating its increasing number of free blacks and, later on, a continuing flood of European immigrants.

Indian Relations

The creation of an independent United States gave the northern Indian tribes few reasons to celebrate. They had fought alongside the British, but the Treaty of Paris, which granted independence to the United States, ignored the tribes' contributions as English allies and gave them no consideration as owners of land in North America. After signing the treaty, the British did not withdraw their troops completely but kept some men stationed at Detroit and other frontier outposts, which they used as bases for a lively trade and propaganda effort among the tribes. Under these circumstances and in response to American claims of sovereignty and efforts to extract land from them, Indian leaders resolved to oppose the "Big Knives" and to drive the pioneers out of their country. From approximately 1776 through 1815 they tried diplomacy, trade alliances, cultural and religious movements, intertribal confederacies, and warfare. Despite their eventual defeat, the tribes demonstrated that they recognized the threat posed by the advancing pioneers, and they used every means at their disposal to thwart and defeat the Americans while they worked to retain their native identities, their particular cultures, their lands, and even their physical independence.

During the mid-1780s American negotiators concluded treaties with groups in the Upper Ohio Valley and New York. Not satisfied with these agreements, representatives of individual states and spokesmen for the trans-Appalachian frontier settlers often ignored the treaties and tried to seize the tribes' ancestral lands. Seeing that their efforts to reach a peaceful agreement with the United States had failed, Indian leaders such as Blue Jacket (Shawnee), Joseph Brant (Mohawk), and Little Turtle (Miami) worked to organize a northwestern confederacy, and in 1786 they rejected the earlier treaties as fraudulent. Instead, they announced that the Ohio River was the boundary, and that all land north or west of that stream belonged to the Indians.

This brought the tribes into direct confrontation with the United States, because in 1787 Congress claimed the same land, calling it the Northwest Territory. Pioneers from Kentucky raided north into Ohio, and Indian war parties retaliated to destroy frontier settlements. Despite an estimated 1,500 pioneer deaths, the Indian raids failed to keep the whites out of Ohio. In 1790 and 1791, after President Washington called for troops to pacify the area, frontier militia armies marched north into Ohio, building forts and destroying Indian villages, but each time large Indian forces under Little Turtle and Blue Jacket crushed the invading white armies and drove them back south of the Ohio River. Finally, in 1794 General Anthony Wayne led a well-trained army of regulars north and defeated the tribes at the Battle of Fallen Timbers. This surrender quieted the northern frontier for the next decade.

Having lost the initiative to the advancing Americans, the tribes turned inward and began to place increasing dependence on their own cultural traditions. Choosing to focus on spiritual values, several Indian prophets offered tribal alternatives to either warfare or surrender. Among the Seneca of New York, Handsome Lake began a native revival movement. By 1800 he was calling on his people to forsake alcohol, to place more reliance on agriculture, and to combine some Christian and some traditional religious ideas if they hoped to survive. His teachings became known as the Long House Religion or the Code of Handsome Lake. They offered renewed hope for immediate survival and future well-being to some Seneca, and his followers proved almost completely resistant to later American demands for tribal land cessions in New York state.

While Handsome Lake preached his code to the Seneca, in 1805 another medicine man, the Shawnee Tenskwatawa, experienced several life-changing visions. These transformed him from a village drunk to a sober, earnest teacher, so that his example and powerful denunciations of the white man's weapons, food, and alcohol appealed to many Shawnee, Delaware, and Miami people living in the Ohio Valley. Urging the villagers to accept his new ideas and ceremonies, he preached that all tribes were a part of a greater Indian nation and that none should cede any more land to the advancing Americans. He promised that if the converts followed his teachings, they would be spared at some future time when a great catastrophe would destroy the whites and unbelieving Indians. Hundreds believed Tenskwatawa's teachings, and many flocked to Prophetstown, a new village in northwestern Indiana.

By 1809–10 Tecumseh, the Prophet's brother, assumed at least joint leadership of the movement. A warrior and diplomat rather than a religious leader, Tecumseh saw the resurgence of tribal pride as yet another chance to forge an Indian confederacy with the British against the Americans south of the Great Lakes. A dynamic speaker and a forceful leader, he stressed that the tribes all had to agree not to sell more land as he strove to turn the Indian cultural and religious movement into a political and military alliance. After the 1809 Fort Wayne treaty talks, Tecumseh and the chief American negotiator, Governor William Henry Harrison of the Indiana Territory, had several angry debates over land cessions. Not only did the Indian leader reject the validity of treaties concluded earlier by any single tribe, but he also demanded that the Americans return lands taken in the recent past. At one point in a meeting between the two men, they sat next to each other on a long bench, and Tecumseh crowded Harrison so that he had to move to the end of the bench. When the governor objected, Tecumseh replied that he was just showing Harrison how the whites had pushed the Indians off their land. Despite the Shawnee brothers' inspirational leadership and organizational skills, the tide of settlement continued. In late 1811, during Tecumseh's visit to the Southeast seeking new recruits for the alliance, Governor Harrison defeated the Indians and destroyed Prophetstown.

Having tried diplomacy, warfare, religious revival, and political confederacies to little avail, many Indians readily joined the British against the United States during the War of 1812. That conflict provided the tribes with their last real chance to halt American expansion—and that only if the British won. In the North, Tecumseh rallied the tribes of the Great Lakes region, joined the British forces in Canada, and engaged in heavy fighting in Ontario. He died in late 1813 during the American victory at the Battle of the Thames. With his death Indian efforts to stem the flood of pioneers into the region ended.

During the next two decades the northern tribes had neither the strength nor the organization to resist the continuing American demands for more land. When the removal program began in earnest, during the late 1820s, they lacked the power still available to the southern tribes. Certainly the Indians objected to being forced off their ancestral homelands, and they tried every available tactic to delay the exodus. For example, they hurriedly planted corn each spring and then insisted on remaining to harvest it—thus making their westward trek more difficult because they were forced to move during the autumn or winter. Despite the delays, removal continued, and the tribes crossed the Mississippi, no matter how reluctantly. Only one group, a splinter of the Sac and Fox tribes, objected enough to cause bloodshed, and that resulted more from misunderstanding than from any conscious decision to fight.

What became known as the Black Hawk War resulted from a long-standing dispute that began in 1804 when Governor Harrison had tricked a few warriors into signing a treaty ceding their lands in Illinois. The tribesmen ignored the agreement because their regular leaders had not participated in the negotiations. Then, because the treaty allowed them to live on the ceded land until it was needed, most of them forgot about the arrangement. In 1831, however, frontier settlers in Illinois forced the Sac and Fox to cross the Mississippi at gunpoint. The villagers spent a miserable winter in Iowa, and in early 1832, led by the aged warrior Black Hawk, about two thousand men, women, and children returned to western Illinois to plant corn in their old fields. This "invasion" caused Illinois Governor John Reynolds to muster the state militia and demand federal troops. The Indians, frightened by the show of force, tried to surrender, but undisciplined Illinois militiamen fired at envoys carrying a white parley flag, causing the rest to retreat. During the summer of 1832, regular troops and militiamen chased the fleeing Indians across northern Illinois and southern Wisconsin before catching them on the east bank of the Mississippi. There, in the so-called Battle of Bad Axe, the soldiers destroyed most of those who had dared to migrate east instead of farther west.

Northern Antislavery Succeeds

In contrast to the unaltered relations with the Indians, American treatment of blacks in the northern states underwent a fundamental change. The assault on slavery predated the Revolutionary era. In the eighteenth century a few religious groups worried about their connection to slavery, and the Quakers took the first steps away from it by withdrawing from the slave trade and freeing their individual slaves. This proved relatively easy to do in the northern colonies, where antislavery sentiments encountered a relatively weak bondage system. Quakers in New England and Pennsylvania acted first, but even those in the South began to manumit blacks wherever the law permitted.

Quaker opposition to slavery received strong support during the Revolutionary era. Spokesmen demanding liberty and equality realized that slavery was incompatible with such concepts. Blacks served in the armies fielded by some northern states, often gaining their freedom as a result. Thus a combination of pressures to end bondage reached its peak in the northern colonies, where court decisions, individual emancipations, and state constitutions and law combined to end slavery. Between 1780, when Pennsylvania passed the first manumission law, and 1804, Rhode Island, Connecticut, New York, and New Jersey provided for the gradual ending of human bondage. In Massachusetts court cases and individual manumissions by owners terminated slavery, and in Vermont the state constitution of 1777 banned it. What happened in New Hampshire is not known precisely, but apparently some owners freed their slaves in return for military service, whereas other blacks simply ran away. In any event New Hampshire had only 674 slaves in 1773 and none by 1810.

Despite the gradual phasing out of slavery in the North and efforts to end or at least limit it in the South, national agitation against it failed. The Northwest Ordinance of 1787 outlawed slavery in the area that eventually became Ohio, Illinois, Indiana, Michigan, and Wisconsin, but there was still ample room for its expansion in the southwestern region, which reached to the Mississippi River and, after the Louisiana Purchase, farther westward. Though slavery was not mentioned by name, the United States Constitution recognized slavery through the fugitive slave clause and the three-fifths compromise, which allowed the South to count each slave as three-fifths of a white person for purposes of taxation and allocation of seats in the United States House of Representatives. The Constitution also specifically prevented Congress from banning the slave trade until 1808. For the most part, southern blacks would have to wait for the Civil War for their deliverance.

Immigration and Assimilation

The years immediately following national independence witnessed a gradual renewal of immigration from Europe, but at a volume much smaller than in earlier decades. Although no official records show the total number of people who entered the United States, scholars estimate that about 250,000 newcomers arrived between 1783 and 1815. Usually the new settlers came from those European nations that had supplied the largest number of emigrants during the late colonial period. Scots-Irish immigrants, 90 percent of whom came as indentured servants, arrived by the boatload, and the British consul in Philadelphia estimated that perhaps twenty thousand of them had left Britain during the 1780s. Fewer people left the German states, either because conditions there had improved or because it had become increasingly difficult to get away.

A renewed influx of French-speaking people entered the country during the era of the French Revolution in the 1790s. In 1791 the black, largely slave population of Santo Domingo in the Caribbean revolted, forcing between ten thousand and twenty thousand white French-speaking islanders to flee. Many of these refugees migrated to the United States, where the public welcomed them and Congress appropriated funds for their aid. The French Revolution, which began in 1789, and wars resulting from it drove thousands of French from their homeland at about the same time. By 1792 small groups of royalists and aristocrats fleeing their enemies reached America. Most of the incoming French settled in eastern cities or towns and remained there as urban workers, entertainers, or professional people. In Philadelphia, at least one hundred French or bilingual publications appeared in the 1790s, seven times as many as a decade earlier. As a group, the upper-middle-class French-speaking immigrants melted into the general population rapidly and with little difficulty.

Because of the relatively small number of immigrants who arrived between the 1780s and 1815, there was little to interrupt the ongoing process of assimilation. By the time the Revolutionary War ended, many former immigrants proudly considered themselves Americans, and even had that not been the case, the small stream of newcomers from their homelands was not enough to sustain feelings of national or ethnic identity in those who had arrived earlier. In particular, the steady decline in the use of languages other than English provided the most obvious measure of assimilation. Dutch and German—the two most widely used foreign languages in the United States at the end of the eighteenth century—both became second languages, local curiosities, and even died out in some areas. In Philadelphia, however, German-speaking Germans looked down on their countrymen who had already adopted English as their preferred language. Without a renewed supply of native-speaking clergymen, churches grudgingly shifted their services to English. In 1794 the General Synod of the Dutch Reformed Church accepted English as its official language. Dutch preaching lingered on in parts of New Jersey and New York, but often as a special service "to gratify the aged, who love to hear the Word in their mother tongue." Much the same story can be told of the German churches. By the turn of the century American-born ministers began replacing those from abroad and began introducing English instead of using German. Congregation after congregation adopted English in their services, although some of the Pennsylvania German churches resisted the trend well into the nineteenth century.

As churches Americanized, so did the foreign language press. During the late eighteenth and early nineteenth centuries, the number of German newspapers declined, and many that tried to keep the language alive lasted only a few years. By the end of the Napoleonic Wars in 1815, the German press survived only in Pennsylvania.

Fear of Foreigners

Many Americans in the new republic thought of their society as a haven for those escaping from oppression and expected the nation to gain strength from the immigrants attracted to its shores. Others feared that the United States might be overrun by the malcontents and dregs of other societies. In the First Congress, Representative James Jackson of Georgia went beyond the prevalent anxieties to call for the exclusion of "the common class of vagrants, paupers and other outcasts of Europe." This and similar statements show the continuing fear of people whose ways differed from Anglo-American traditions. Debate on the issue continued sporadically, but the Naturalization Act of 1790 called for only a two-year waiting period before white immigrants could apply for citizenship. An influx of people during the French Revolution kept the issue alive, and in 1795 Congress increased the waiting time from two to five years.

The nation's two political parties, the Federalists and the Jeffersonian Republicans, agreed that too many foreigners might endanger American institutions but split over which people posed the greatest threat. Conservative Federalists believed that French Jacobins and Irish radicals were the most dangerous, whereas the Jeffersonians welcomed these people while criticizing French royalists and other aristocratically oriented groups. The growing numbers of Irish in the major cities hated the British and supported the Republican party because of its pro-French and anti-British stand. Their influence angered many New England Federalists who feared foreigners—especially those of Republican leanings. Harrison Gray Otis of Massachusetts wanted no foreigners to come, above all no "hordes of wild Irishmen, nor the turbulent and disorderly of all parts of the world, to come here with a view to disturb our tranquility, after having succeeded in the overthrow of their own Governments." Anti-Semitism also reigned strong in Federalist circles during the 1790s.

Not content with verbal outbursts, in 1798 the Federalist-controlled Congress passed a series of laws clearly aimed at cutting Jeffersonian strength by reducing the personal liberties of aliens and other dissenters. A new naturalization law extended the residence period needed for citizenship from five to fourteen years, and an Alien Enemies Act and an Alien Friends Act gave the president authority to arrest and deport resident aliens suspected of subversion. These laws, based on the assumption that the United States and France were on the brink of war, were little used. Nevertheless, they achieved at least part of their goal, because during the year hundreds of French men, women, and children fled the United States.

Still unsatisfied, the Federalists pushed the Sedition Act through Congress. This measure stifled most domestic criticism of the Adams administration, and although not designed exclusively to attack recent immigrants, the government applied it mostly to Irish and French newspapermen. Through this law the Federalists attempted to silence what they called the "pack of imported scribblers." Although the government imprisoned some journalists, newspapers, magazines, and pamphlets continued to attack the Federalists and contributed directly to the Jeffersonian victory in the 1800 presidential election. Jefferson's supporters were less suspicious of aliens, and his administration returned to the earlier five-year residency requirement for citizenship for free whites. Moreover, the rampant bigotry and hostility of the previous decade began to subside.

The Movement West

While Easterners coped with suspected radicals, other Americans streamed across the Appalachians into the Ohio Valley and the Great Lakes area. This flood of settlement had begun just prior to independence and continued with only slight interruption until 1820. In the area south of the Ohio River, Kentucky and Tennessee became states in 1792 and 1796, respectively. To the north, Ohio entered the union in 1803. Economic difficulties related to the War of 1812 slowed western development, but by 1820 all of the territory east of the Mississippi River had been carved into states except for Florida, Michigan, and Wisconsin.

Most of the new westerners were farmers or small businessmen and professional people such as millers, tanners, meat packers, blacksmiths, wagon makers, store operators, and bankers who all owed their livelihood to the farmers. With the exception of a few efforts at large-scale farming or livestock raising in Illinois, the northern settlements had nothing to compare with the plantation agriculture of the South. Northerners invested in large amounts of land more for speculation than for farming.

The western regions, however, did not remain agricultural and rural for long. In fact, towns such as Pittsburgh, Cincinnati, and St. Louis existed before many farmers had arrived in the area. In any case, the early Midwestern settlers needed urban centers nearby, for although they did not resort to plantation agriculture, they were still commercial farmers, and they looked to the towns as markets or at least trading centers for disposal of their crops. Thus the most expensive land usually lay near the avenues of transportation such as rivers, canals, or roads and near the market towns. Even a casual glance at a current map of the Midwest indicates that many of these urban centers remain today.

The rush of western settlement forced Americans to look for better means of transportation. During the colonial era waterways offered the best transportation and communication, and although the mountains separated east from west, rivers continued to be the best way of moving people and goods. At first pioneer families moved down the Ohio River, its tributaries, and the Mississippi on rafts, barges, arks, and keelboats, but the voyage of Robert Fulton's steamboat *New Orleans* from Pittsburgh to New Orleans in 1811 inaugurated a new mode of travel. By 1820 steamboat navigation on many western streams had reduced the costs of transportation by 60 to 80 percent and noticeably speeded travel. It also tied the agricultural Midwest to the port of New Orleans until the 1830s, when the major eastern cities developed better facilities for trade with the West.

Because rivers often flowed in the wrong direction, or were simply too far away for easy use, many Americans depended on the existing roads. These, however, could be as frustrating and difficult to use as the streams, for only a few were actually wide enough for large freight wagons or carts, and they often contained stumps and boulders. Unpaved, most roads became muddy tracks in spring and fall and frozen ruts in winter. Governments at all levels tried to improve the roads with only modest success. In 1806 Congress chartered the Cumberland, or National, Road to connect the Chesapeake region with the Ohio Valley. Unfortunately, work on the road did not start until 1811 and then halted during the war that began the next year. It took until 1818 for the builders to reach Wheeling, Virginia, where work again came to a stop. In 1825 Congress provided more money, and over the next several decades workers inched their way west to Illinois. Private road or turnpike companies built more than ten thousand miles of improved roads, mostly in New England and the middle states. Most of these ventures cost so much that the companies went broke or gave their roads to the individual states.

Clearly something more than roads and rivers was needed. Americans turned to canals during the 1820s with the hope that they would solve the nation's transportation woes. Canals cost more to build and maintain than roads, and so most had to be constructed with public rather than private funds. In 1817 only a handful of canals, with an aggregate total of about a hundred miles in length, existed in the United States. That year New York governor De Witt Clinton convinced the state legislature to authorize a project to connect the Hudson River with Lake Erie by canal. In 1825 this project, known as the Erie Canal, linked New York City by water with the Great Lakes and offered midwestern farmers an alternative to trading with merchants in New Orleans.

Equally important, the Erie's instant financial success stimulated the other major eastern cities to try similar ventures. Boston considered a canal, but the terrain prohibited this, so the city fathers began to build railroads. In 1826 Philadelphia got legislative support for a scheme using canals, railroads, and rivers to tie that city to Pittsburgh beyond the Appalachian Mountains. Baltimore decided to build the Chesapeake and Ohio Canal in its efforts to tap western trade opportunities, but this project never got past the mountains. In 1828 Baltimore changed its plans and ordered work to begin on the Baltimore and Ohio Railroad. Ohio, Michigan, Indiana, and Illinois unsuccessfully tried building canals with state funds. By 1840 some 3,326 miles of canals stretched across the country. Despite their immense cost these could be used only part of the year, and thus they failed to offer cheap, dependable transportation on a regular basis. By the 1840s, public interest shifted to railroads as the best means of transportation for both goods and people.

Urban and Industrial Growth

As better transportation facilitated movement, the West became an increasingly important market for American products. This in turn stimulated the growth of Eastern business and manufacturing. The process of industrialization proceeded slowly during the early decades of national independence. Until the South and West opened as large markets after the Civil War ended, manufacturing remained local and small scale. In 1791 Secretary of the Treasury Alexander Hamilton wrote that "the expediency of encouraging manufactures in the United States... appears at this time to be pretty generally admitted." Yet several more decades would pass before the nation had either surplus labor or capital, and until an adequate transportation system emerged, industrial production remained a minor element in the economy.

Nevertheless, some manufacturing had existed in America since well before independence. Often towns had local forges, flour or sawmills, paper factories, tanneries, and even small textile shops; most of these remained only part-time ventures or lasted but a few years. The first factory of significance was a New England cotton mill directed by Samuel Slater. Begun in Pawtucket, Rhode Island, in 1791, the mill employed children at wages of 12 to 25¢ a day, and it remained a small operation until the Napoleonic Wars limited the supply of European goods available in America. Then, in 1808, at President Jefferson's urging, Congress passed the Embargo Act, which curtailed foreign trade sharply. Thereafter the New England cotton textile mills grew at a fantastic pace. In 1808 there were only fifteen mills in the United States; eighty-seven more had been built by 1809. The number of spindles in the nation increased from eight thousand in 1808 to thirty-one thousand in 1809 and to eighty thousand in 1811. Between 1815 and 1831 the number of spindles in New England alone had tripled, and by 1860 it had tripled again. On the eve of the Civil War the average cotton textile mill in New England had seven thousand spindles, compared with an average of two thousand spindles for mills in the South and West.

At the Boston Manufacturing Company in Waltham, Massachusetts, which built the first integrated cotton mill in the world in 1813, factory workers did everything from unbaling cotton to dyeing the cloth before it was sold. The Lowell mills, as they came to be called, abandoned child labor and chose instead to hire young farm women, aged fifteen to thirty. Despite having to live in closely supervised boarding houses, the women used their years as mill employees to gain some personal freedom from rural and small-town family life and to earn cash wages, often for the first time. By the 1840s the mill owners began to hire Irish immigrant families to whom they paid less money. This led the New England natives at the mills to strike while feeding anti-Irish feelings in the region. The operation at the Lowell mills was both an immediate and a long-run success, stimulating other groups of investors to imitate its methods.

Industrial progress was not limited to the textile mills. The iron industry grew steadily, producing consumer products such as stoves and, later, rails for the railroads and a variety of iron and steel products. The boot and shoe industry, concentrated in New England, lagged behind textiles, but the invention of the sewing machine in 1846 revolutionized the manufacture of boots and shoes.

Economic expansion came at an uneven pace. The nation suffered a major economic panic in 1819, an agricultural depression between 1828 and 1831, a recession from 1833 to 1835, and a near-disastrous economic collapse between 1837 and 1843. These slumps in the economy both retarded economic growth and contributed to social conflict. President Jackson's veto of a bill rechartering the Second Bank of the United States in 1832 and the subsequent withdrawal of federal government funds from that institution precipitated retaliatory action from Nicholas Biddle, its director, who called in loans and contracted credit. This action in turn triggered a near panic in 1834 and 1835 as economic conditions worsened. Coincidentally the number of riots and labor disturbances increased at the very time of the downturn. More than a thousand young women walked off their jobs in Lowell, Massachusetts, in February 1834 to protest a 15 percent cut in wages. The National Trades Union conducted at least 175 strikes between 1834 and its ultimate demise in 1837, when the business collapse crushed the trade movements.

As factories grew, the continuing demand for laborers attracted many to towns and cities. Young people from rural areas and newly arrived immigrants, sought employment in the burgeoning industrial concerns. This growth of manufacturing and the increasing urbanization in the Northeast and Midwest set those areas apart from the more rural South. As Table 3.1 shows, by the 1830s eastern and northern cities had far outpaced all of their counterparts in the future Confederacy except New Orleans.

The northern seaport cities outdistanced all others as centers of commerce, industry, and population. Of these, New York, the nation's largest city, clearly stood out. It benefited from a large hinterland market whose residents transported their produce to and purchased manufactured goods from the city via the Erie Canal, as well as the Hudson and Mohawk rivers. New York's prosperity also rested on its prime location between New England and the middle

TABLE 3.1.   Population of Major Cities, 1830–1860*

	1830	1840	1850	1860
New York	202,589	312,700	515,547	813,669
Philadelphia	80,462	93,665	121,376	565,529
Brooklyn	20,535	47,613	138,882	279,122
Baltimore	80,620	102,313	169,054	212,418
Boston	61,392	93,383	136,881	177,840
New Orleans	46,082	102,190	116,375	168,675
Cincinnati	24,831	46,338	115,436	161,044
St. Louis	4,977	16,469	77,860	160,773
Chicago	—	4,470	29,963	112,172
Charleston	30,289	29,261	42,985	40,522
Richmond	16,000	20,153	27,570	37,910

*Some increases are due to changes in city boundaries.

states; its excellent port; the keenness of its businessmen, who, among other things, had the foresight to build the best warehousing facilities for the transatlantic trade; and the boldness of the Black Ball clipper ship line, which scheduled regular transatlantic crossings regardless of the amount of cargo on board or the nature of the weather.

New York City also had its share of ambitious merchants. Not satisfied with the volume of wheat, flour, fish, and other commodities that they received from the Northeast, they sent their ships to New Orleans, Mobile, and Savannah to pick up cargoes of cotton on their way to Europe. On their return trips to the United States, vessels carried both immigrants and manufactured goods. Thus the shrewdness of its citizens and its favorable location thrust New York into the forefront of American urban industrial development. Philadelphia, Boston, Pittsburgh, Cincinnati, and Chicago also progressed industrially and benefited from their locations, which made them centers for trade and commerce. While northern cities celebrated commercial and industrial expansion, the South remained wedded to agriculture and slavery.

From the start national economic and diplomatic policies had favored commerce and industry over agriculture, thus bolstering the North and West at the expense of the South. The Washington administration's policies encouraged industry through tariffs, and a national banking system laid the foundation for future development. Although the Jeffersonians looked askance at such actions, they failed to repeal them once in office. During Jefferson's presidency, the nation acquired the territory of Louisiana ("Louisiana Purchase"), which extended America's western border from the Mississippi River to the Rocky Mountains and more than doubled the nation's size. This step secured the use of the Mississippi River for Americans and spurred thousands to move west. In 1816 Congress chartered the Second Bank of the United States and adopted the nation's first protective tariff. Three years later the federal government moved to recognize the newly independent republics of South and Central America, partly motivated by the desire to obtain trading rights in those countries. The Monroe Doctrine of 1823, Andrew Jackson's efforts to purchase Texas and the San Francisco region in the 1830s, and the later annexation of Texas and the Oregon country in the 1840s were all part of American economic and territorial expansion during the first half of the nineteenth century.

Free Blacks in the North

As the nation spread west to the Pacific, developed industry, and established growing cities, attitudes toward minorities changed little if at all. Although blacks were free in the North, people there supported the work of the American Colonization Society, established in 1817, to return free blacks to Africa. As did southerners, northern whites thought these people were inferior and wanted them segregated or removed like the Indians. Some states enacted codes to deny African Americans the ballot, to segregate them in schools and public accommodations, and to prohibit them from testifying against whites in the courts. Even in New England and New York, where blacks could vote and where they found some degree of legal and social acceptance, they nevertheless encountered considerable hostility and segregation. Usually they were expected to attend separate churches and schools, and when black and white abolitionists attempted to desegregate the Boston schools in the 1850s, the Primary School Committee refused and declared that racial distinctions were made by the "All-Wise Creator" and that "a promiscuous intermingling in the Public Schools" was harmful to both races. Massachusetts eventually desegregated the Boston schools, but only after heated political battles in the courts and the legislature.

Not all such attempts succeeded. In Canterbury, Connecticut, Prudence Crandall, a Quaker, announced her intention of admitting a black girl to her boarding school. Protests from the white parents and the withdrawals of many white students led her to open the school exclusively to black girls. Whites in the community protested bitterly; one town official vowed that no "nigger school shall ever be allowed in Canterbury, nor in any town in this State." He was certainly right about Canterbury; angry mobs and legal harassments forced Crandall to leave town.

Despised as they were, blacks experienced frequent economic discrimination. One scholar has estimated that about 87 percent of them toiled as servants, dock workers, or common laborers. In 1838 the Pennsylvania Abolition Society said that nearly a quarter of Philadelphia's free black artisans did not practice their crafts because of "prejudice against them," and by the 1850s the percentage of those skilled blacks in Philadelphia not working in their trades rose to 38 percent. Often observers reversed the causes and effects of such discrimination, at least in their minds. One Pennsylvanian, unable to find blacks in high status positions, commented, "We see them engaged in no business that requires even ordinary capacity, [and] in no enterprizes [sic] requiring talents to conduct them. The mass [of them] are improvident, and seek the lowest avocations, and most menial stations." An English traveler to the United States noted that most white men "would rather starve than accept a menial office under a black." Many black women in the North earned their keep by washing white people's clothes.

Despite existing discrimination, however, some African Americans became skilled workers, and a few achieved successes as teachers, ministers, and businessmen. The arrival of immigrants from Ireland and the German states of Europe again made life more difficult for northern black workers. In the 1840s many lost their jobs—especially to the poor Irish—in service positions, along the docks, and in canal and railroad construction. In 1849 one observer in Philadelphia noted that "a few years ago we saw none but blacks" as stevedores and hod-carriers, whereas "we now see nothing but Irish." Northern factory owners also preferred the new Irish immigrants over African Americans. In 1847 less than 0.05 percent of Philadelphia's black males worked in the city's factories.

To help themselves, northern, like southern, African Americans formed their own organizations, and these groups had more freedom than in the South. The first of the all-black groups appeared in the northern states shortly after the American Revolution. Mutual aid and fraternal societies appeared as early as the 1780s to provide funds for burials and schools. Black churches were more important than these societies, and their ministers emerged as leaders in the urban communities. When Richard Allen and his fellow worshipers were made unwelcome in Philadelphia's predominantly white St. George's Methodist Church in the 1780s, they established an all-black congregation that evolved into the African Methodist Episcopal Church. Similar incidents led to the creation of other black churches and eventually black denominations, either Methodist or Baptist.

In the North, African Americans also published their own newspapers, such as former slave Frederick Douglass's *North Star*. They were active in the underground railroad, which assisted fleeing slaves. In addition, they organized groups to agitate for the end of slavery and racial discrimination in the North. Some worked with white abolitionists, but others formed their own groups. Although the emergence of the white abolitionist movement and antislavery parties in the 1830s gave hope that bondage might end, many northern whites greeted abolitionism with fear, hate, and even violence. Even outspoken abolitionists who favored emancipation rarely argued that black people and white people were equally endowed and deserved equal opportunities.

Excluded from the white community, northern blacks created their own world because they had little choice. While protesting against segregation, their organizations generally accepted the values of white America. They urged self-help among their members, stressed education and mobility, pushed for equal rights, and rejected schemes to send them back to Africa. In 1831 one black gathering argued that "the time must come when the Declaration of Independence will be felt in the heart, as well as uttered from the mouth, and when the rights of all shall be properly acknowledged and appreciated.... This is our home, and this is our country."

Yet not all blacks accepted white America's values and desired assimilation. Some said that they would never find equality in the United States and that they must emigrate to Africa or the West Indies. Although such sentiments stemmed largely from despair of winning freedom and equality in white society, a few blacks even began to view Africa and their heritage in a positive light; they rejected the view that Africa was a backward continent. These glimmerings of black nationalism would become stronger in the post-Civil War era as African Americans developed their own institutions and refreshed memories of their African heritage. Pre-Civil War African Americans confronted the issue that all black Americans would face. Decades after the war ended, black leader W. E. B. DuBois remarked: "One ever feels his twoness—an American, a Negro; two souls.... He simply wishes to make it possible for a man to be both a Negro and an American, without being cursed and spit upon by his fellows, without having the doors of opportunity closed roughly in his face."

Renewal of Immigration

Although Americans seemed preoccupied with the fate of the black people, they also recognized the overall needs of their developing industrial society. They needed labor, and over the next two centuries immigrants and their progeny provided it. Between 1819, when Congress mandated the inauguration of a system to keep statistics on the immigrants, and 1840, approximately 743,000 foreigners reached the United States. Of these more than 80 percent came from Ireland (335,000), the German states (155,000), and England, Scotland, and

Wales (103,000). Only smatterings arrived from other places in Europe before the Civil War. Though some of the immigrants left their homes for political and religious reasons, the majority, like foreigners before and since, did so to improve their economic status. Although more than 65 million people would eventually reach the United States, in the 1830s and 1840s fewer than one million arrived.

These newcomers entered a nation fresh from two victories over the world's strongest power, Great Britain, in the War for Independence and the War of 1812. Self-conscious nationalism pervaded the United States after General Andrew Jackson's crushing victory over the British in the Battle of New Orleans in 1815. Not only did that event create a new national hero whose popularity rivaled that enjoyed by George Washington only a few decades earlier, but it also made Americans swell with pride at having won the war. After that, people believed that this country could achieve whatever it desired. And it was at about this time that American science, American art, and American literature all began to flourish. So, too, did a new wave of religious ferment that stirred a good many New Englanders and New Yorkers, but the religious revelations that seemed so real to some Americans seemed bizarre to others.

Group Suppression and the Mormons

At the same time that the majority strove to become more self-consciously "American," a number of religious groups came under increasing public disfavor. Among these were the Roman Catholics, who are discussed in the next chapter, and the Mormons, or members of the Church of Jesus Christ of Latter-day Saints. The Mormons were founded by Joseph Smith of New York after he had a series of visions and visits from the Angel Moroni, from whom he learned of a hidden set of golden plates on which God's revelations were written in hieroglyphics. According to Smith's testimony, he received permission from the angel to remove and translate the plates. The task took two years, and in 1830 Smith published the completed translation of the Book of Mormon, which he claimed was a direct revelation from the Almighty and equal to the Bible. Together with his family and friends, he then organized the Church of Jesus Christ of Latter-day Saints. As a result of Smith's attempts to propagate these beliefs, the Mormons soon became objects of suspicion and derision.

To avoid conflict and further denunciation, Smith and his followers moved west to the small community of Kirtland, Ohio, in 1831. For a few years they attracted new converts, established farms and businesses, and even started a bank. Then the Panic of 1837 struck, ruining their efforts and causing a host of angry creditors to denounce them. Smith and his converts fled farther west to frontier Missouri, where they began the process of resettlement.

People in Missouri proved even less tolerant than those in their previous settlements, and trouble broke out almost immediately. Embittered by their experiences, Smith vowed to his flock: "Our rights shall no more be trampled with impunity." At their July 4, 1838, celebration he told his listeners that "the man, or set of men, who attempt it, does it at the expense of their lives. And that mob which comes on to us to disturb us, it shall be between us and them a war of extermination, for we will follow them till the last drop of their blood is spilled, or else they will have to exterminate us." This declaration did nothing to endear Smith's group to Missourians, and within a few months bands of anti-Mormon guerrillas roamed the countryside, robbing and beating the Latter-day Saints and burning their homes. Smith appealed to Governor Lilburn Boggs for protection, but instead the governor proclaimed that the Mormons "must be exterminated or driven from the state, if necessary, for the public peace." Attacked by frontier ruffians and state officials alike, in early 1839 the Mormons retreated east into Illinois.

There the discouraged members of the Latter-day Saints began to rebuild. Nauvoo, their new community, grew rapidly, and, with fifteen thousand inhabitants, by 1845 it had become the largest city in the state. Despite the envy and distrust of its neighbors, the community might have enjoyed peaceful relations if news that the Mormons were practicing polygamy had not gotten out. Joseph Smith had continued to receive "revelations," and plural marriage was one of these. Few Nauvoo leaders actually practiced polygamy, but it became the issue that tore the community apart. Mormons who objected to the practice published a newspaper attack on Smith in Nauvoo, and church officials ordered the press destroyed. This brought a near riot, and Smith and his brother were arrested and jailed at nearby Carthage. There a mob stormed the jail and killed the brothers. Then, amid increasing raids by gentile mobs, the bulk of the Mormons united under Brigham Young, who negotiated a tenuous peace by agreeing to leave the state in 1846.

Young and other church officials then led the faithful across the Mississippi River into Iowa, and by the end of 1846 thousands of Mormons had settled there. The next year, however, Young himself took his followers farther west, and the group reached the Salt Lake Valley in July 1847. Once in Utah, church leaders worked desperately to create a new home in the desert for their embattled followers. Large-scale irrigation, communal economic practices, and incredible industry secured the region for the Mormon pioneers. But even there they were not entirely free from suspicion and harassment.

The Mormons had gone west to escape the United States and had settled in the Salt Lake Valley, at that time part of Mexico. But after the Mexican War ended in 1848, the entire area was ceded to the United States, which had shortly before acquired Oregon from Great Britain. The acquisition from Mexico posed no immediate threat to the Mormons because they were so far from other American communities, but Salt Lake City lay squarely on one of the main overland routes to California, which had also been obtained as part of the settlement with Mexico. That same year President James K. Polk informed the nation that California's gold mines were "believed to be among the most productive in the world." This announcement led to a stampede, as hundreds of thousands of people from all over the world made their way to California to seek their own fortunes.

Manifest Destiny

It was not only gold that attracted Americans to the West. Ideology and agricultural and commercial needs played even more crucial roles. A desire to acquire western territory in the 1830s and 1840s moved President Andrew Jackson to attempt to purchase Texas and the San Francisco area from Mexico.

"American Progress." This 1873 illustration reflects the nineteenth-century vision Americans had of the westward movement and their belief in the glory of American progress. (Library of Congress)

Missionary reports coming back from Oregon, describing the incredible richness and fertility of the soil in the Willamette Valley, whetted the appetites of American farmers. The agricultural possibilities stimulated an "Oregon fever," and in the 1840s wagon trains from Missouri headed west to the Pacific.

Commercial and manufacturing interests also promoted expansion. The harbors of present-day Seattle, San Francisco, and San Diego lay in territory owned or claimed by Great Britain and Mexico, and Americans coveted these warm-water ports and coaling stations that could serve as springboards for commercial ties with Asia. That foreign powers controlled these lands did not disturb Americans, who genuinely believed, as a later expansionist would write, that "God, with infinite wisdom and skill [was] training the Anglo-Saxon race" for its ultimate destiny. Americans were certain that the Almighty wanted the United States to spread its institutions across the continent to the Pacific, and then "move down upon" Mexico and Latin America and "out upon the islands of the sea, over upon Africa and beyond."

In the 1840s, however, this spirit of "Manifest Destiny" extended mainly to the Pacific and the Caribbean. In 1844, James K. Polk of Tennessee ran for the presidency on an expansionist platform and won support from a majority of voters. During his four years in office he divided the Oregon Territory with Great Britain, ensuring that the United States received all of the valuable agricultural land below the 49th parallel, which included the superb Puget Sound harbor; he also took the country to war with Mexico, ultimately acquiring the present-day Southwest, along with the harbors of San Francisco and San Diego, as part of the spoils of war. This action introduced a new ethnic group of perhaps eighty thousand people, at least partly Indian in blood and mostly Spanish in language and culture, into American society. Prior to the nineteenth century fully 90 percent of these people lived in present New Mexico in towns and villages stretching northward along the Rio Grande from El Paso to Taos. Others lived in small communities from the Texas border west to California. Primarily farmers and ranchers, they encountered almost immediate discrimination from their new neighbors. To many other Americans the Hispanics could not be assimilated easily because they were dark skinned, mixed-race, and Catholic. So other than the merchants involved in the Santa Fe trade, few citizens welcomed them. Even in our own day some Americans still cling to negative stereotypes of Mexicans and Mexican Americans.

Despite existing hostility toward the Mexicans who became Americans after their lands became part of the United States, President Polk described the great benefits that would accrue to the nation from its newly acquired territory. In his 1848 State of the Union address to Congress he reported that no section of our country is more interested or will be more benefited than the commercial, navigating, and manufacturing interests of the Eastern States. Our planting and farming interests in every part of the Union will be greatly benefited by it. As our commerce and navigation are enlarged and extended, our exports of agricultural products and of manufactures will be increased, and in the new markets thus opened they can not fail to command remunerating and profitable prices.

Yet the acquisition of the new territory from Mexico would also lead, indirectly, to the greatest political upheaval in the nation's history. A little-known congressman, David Wilmot of Pennsylvania, arose in the House of Representatives in August 1846 and proposed, as an amendment to an appropriations bill under consideration, that "neither slavery nor involuntary servitude shall ever exist in any part" of the territories that would eventually be annexed to the United States. Although not many recognized its significance at that time, the so-called Wilmot Proviso opened a hornet's nest in American politics. Almost every major piece of domestic legislation considered by the Congress during the next fifteen years would in some way touch on the expansion of slavery, and this issue ultimately led to the Civil War. In the 1840s, however, few people realized that Congressional passage of the Wilmot Proviso marked the beginning of the end of slavery in the United States.

4

Slavery, Civil War, and Immigration
(1840s–1880s)

The acquisition of more than 1,200,000 square miles of territory in the West coincided with the accelerated pace of agricultural and industrial growth in the United States. Practically every segment of the economy mushroomed in the years preceding the Civil War. Production of corn, wheat, and cotton increased rapidly, while the riverboat and port cities quickened the pace of their activities. The total value of imports and exports in the nation rose from $125,250,000 in 1843 to $687,200,000 in 1860. Domestic trade alone multiplied tenfold during these years, and on the eve of the Civil War it exceeded $10 billion. Massachusetts with its textile and shoe factories, Maine with its lumber mills, Pittsburgh with increased iron and coal production, and the Midwest in general reflected the dynamism of the decade. (Most of the increase in railroad trackage, from 8,500 miles in 1850 to 30,000 miles in 1860, connected the agricultural markets and industrial centers with the Atlantic port cities.) The American population grew from twenty-three million in 1850 to thirty-one million ten years later, while during this same period the number of foreign-born practically doubled from two million to over four million. The most dramatic growth occurred in the Midwest; Minnesota, for example, increased its population 2,760 percent in the 1850s. Every section shared in the prosperity. Southern exports of cotton leaped from 2,469,000 bales in 1850 to 4,387,000 bales in 1860, and even the region's manufacturing output showed impressive gains: production of steam engines and machinery rose 387 percent, whereas the production of agricultural tools increased 101 percent and that of boots and shoes 80 percent. California's gold output surpassed the half-billion-dollar mark between 1848 and 1857. The 1850s also saw national production of coal and railroad iron increase by 182 percent and 100 percent, respectively, and the amount of wheat exported from Illinois leap from nine million to twenty-four million bushels. Possibilities for still further expansion in the American economy remained for energetic entrepreneurs who would turn visions into accomplishments.

Americans in the mid-nineteenth century believed that unequaled opportunities awaited the enterprising. A wilderness stood ready for conquest, cities yearned for growth, and industries and mines had barely been developed. Farms had to produce more foodstuffs, but a better system of transportation was needed to move goods and people more quickly from place to place, and workers had to be found to tend the machines and till the soil. Industrialists and state governments therefore made extensive efforts to recruit settlers both at home and in Europe. This expansionist philosophy would grip Americans until World War I. After subduing the continent, visionaries looked abroad in search of sources for raw materials and outlets for agricultural and industrial products. New inventions such as the sewing machine, refrigeration, and incandescent lights would stimulate whole new industries, while industrial geniuses such as John D. Rockefeller, finance capitalists such as J. P. Morgan, and the development of business bureaucracies and scientific management would produce significant growth in employment opportunities for Americans and foreigners alike.

Fortunately for the United States, this industrialization coincided with a similar process in Europe that uprooted millions of people. Famine and poverty, agricultural enclosure movements, and industrial development that drew people from farms but failed to provide enough employment in cities combined to force thousands from their homes. Once people started moving, there were no limits to their search for an ultimate destination. The news of "fortunes" to be made in America, along with real deprivation and unstable governments in Europe, induced more than four million Europeans to cross the Atlantic between 1840 and 1860 (see Table 4.1). Approximately 75 percent of these emigrants came from Ireland and the German states. The overwhelming majority of them sought greater economic opportunities in the United States;

TABLE 4.1. Main Sources of European Immigration
to the United States 1841–1860

	1841–1850	*1851–1860*
Belgium	5,074	4,738
Denmark	539	3,749
France	77,262	76,358
Germany	434,626	951,667
Great Britain		
England	32,092	247,125
Scotland	3,712	38,331
Not specified	229,979	132,199
Ireland	780,719	914,119
Netherlands	8,251	10,789
Norway } Sweden	13,903	20,931
Switzerland	4,644	25,011

only a small percentage left their homes because of religious or political persecution.

Emigrants from Europe frequently endured the most harrowing conditions during their ocean voyages. This was especially true before steamships started replacing sailing vessels in the 1850s, for on the older boats the journey generally lasted more than a month. With the newer ships, the time was cut in half, and then in half again. By the advent of the twentieth century it took less than a week to cross the Atlantic Ocean. The earlier journeys, however, aroused serious criticism from both passengers and humanitarians. Fourteen Norwegians who traveled on an English ship in 1853 later detailed their treatment on board. It was a month, they recalled, "of bruised heads, broken ribs, a broken collarbone, and teeth knocked out as a result of brutal treatment by seamen whose orders, given in English, they could not understand; of food thrown to the emigrants as if they were dogs, and of the emigrants fighting for it like wild animals; of bunks full of lice; of dangers of assault upon wives, sisters, and daughters." The passengers who survived such treatment were quite relieved to reach America.

Settlement Patterns

Practically all of the Europeans landed at one of the five major American ports. As the figures in Table 4.2 indicate, New York City always received the lion's share. Immigrants too poor or too despondent to go farther remained in these cities; the others followed the established transportation patterns inland. From New York City foreigners either sailed up the Hudson River to the Erie Canal and then moved westward or made the journey by rail.

Every region and major city in the United States during the middle of the nineteenth century saw its immigrant population mushroom. By 1860 the foreign-born and their children constituted a majority in New York, San Francisco, New Orleans, and Chicago. Industrial and commercial needs dictated the patterns of settlement. Cities with good harbors increased their trade and needed stevedores and laborers, and fledgling manufacturing communities sought unskilled hands. River ports and railroad depots facilitated development, and territorial and economic growth in turn stimulated the need for additional laborers in the nation's factories and mills.

Immigrants responded by moving to regions and cities where the jobs beckoned. New England attracted many, especially the Irish, who landed at Boston before the Civil War and by the 1880s were in the process of obtaining a solid footing there. French Canadians came south across the border to work in the numerous textile mills and shoe factories of Massachusetts and Rhode Island.

TABLE 4.2. Immigrants Entering American Ports

	Total	New York	Boston	Philadelphia	Baltimore	New Orleans
1846	158,000	98,000	13,000	7,000	9,000	22,000
1851	408,000	294,000	25,000	18,000	8,000	52,000
1855	230,000	161,000	17,000	7,000	6,000	20,000

New York City Percentage of Total Immigrants
1846—62
1851—72
1855—70

The Middle Atlantic states housed the largest number of newcomers. New York City, the nation's premier port, welcomed more immigrants than did all other ports combined, and the city also provided numerous jobs for each succeeding boatload of newcomers. As a result it contained the largest Irish and German populations of any American city in the nineteenth century. Philadelphia also provided opportunities for these groups, especially before the Civil War. The first Midwestern cities to receive large numbers of immigrants, such as Cincinnati and St. Louis, had connections via the Ohio and Mississippi rivers to New Orleans. After the completion of the Erie Canal in 1825 and the transcontinental railroads in the post-Civil War era, the northern Midwestern cities became major immigrant terminals. St. Louis, Cincinnati, and Milwaukee all attracted large German populations, although other groups settled there as well, and Germans and Scandinavians predominated in the upper Midwest. By the outbreak of World War I huge colonies of every European minority lived in most northern cities.

Although the southern states attracted relatively few foreigners, on the eve of the Civil War, foreign-born people constituted 39 percent of the urban white population. In 1858 an observer walking on the streets of Richmond, Virginia, commented, "one might be at a loss to know whether German or English is the language of the country." Forty percent of the population of Charleston, South Carolina, in 1860 was born outside of the United States. It was allegedly the only city in the United States in which German immigrants were not subject to victimization. The Irish, however, constituted most of the foreigners in antebellum Charleston. In the most famous novel about the Civil War, *Gone with the Wind,* author Margaret Mitchell named her heroine "Scarlett O'Hara," suggesting an Irish heritage. In Louisiana, the French, Germans, and Irish contributed to making New Orleans the region's most cosmopolitan city.

After the Civil War a variety of other peoples settled elsewhere in the South. Some southern leaders tried to attract Chinese laborers because they were thought to be more industrious and less costly than African Americans. Italians could be found in Louisiana, Mississippi, and Florida. Cubans who made cigars preferred Georgia as a destination in the 1880s and Florida in the 1890s. Generally, however, the population in the southern states remained overwhelmingly made up of American whites and blacks. At the end of the nineteenth century only 2 percent of white people in the region had been born abroad.

Most of the European immigrants regarded the South's climate as unhealthy and felt more comfortable in the northern Midwest, where the soil and the weather were more akin to what they had been accustomed to in their European homelands. In this area, people of German and Scandinavian stock predominated, and the main occupation was farming. In the late nineteenth century Wisconsin possessed the largest percentage of foreign-born people of any state east of the Mississippi River. Germans constituted a majority of the foreigners in that state. After the Civil War, Germans continued coming to the region, but Scandinavians, especially Norwegians, planted roots in the upper Midwest also. Near the end of the century and in the first decade of the twentieth century, Swedes swelled the region's population. As a result of the availability of good farmland, German and Scandinavian immigrants moved into Iowa, Minnesota, Kansas, Nebraska, and the Dakotas as well. In the Rocky Mountain states, mining for gold, silver, and copper attracted people from all over the world. Europeans, Asians, Canadians, Mexicans, and South Americans expected to find their own wealth beneath the ground. The mining areas of Utah, for example, contained more than twenty-five different nationality groups, which helped to make the Rocky Mountain states the most ethnically diverse section in the nation.

The Germans and the Irish

None of the immigrant groups outnumbered the Germans, equaled their scope of influence, or settled in a larger and more varied number of locations. They went to both urban and rural areas and, except for New England, to every section of the country, working as farmers and laborers, skilled craftsmen, and professionals. By 1900 they constituted the largest single foreign element in thirty states, including Wisconsin, California, Kansas, Missouri, New Jersey, and New York, and they were the most prominent ethnic group in eight of the nation's ten largest cities. Only in Philadelphia and Boston did the Irish outnumber the Germans.

The nineteenth-century German emigrants to the United States represented all classes. They included intellectuals, radicals, and labor union organizers, and their impact was vast. In the early years of the American Federation of

Labor, founded by Samuel Gompers in 1884, both English and German were recognized as official languages. Modern American socialism also had its roots in New York City's *Kleindeutschland* (Little Germany).

The overwhelming majority of Germans who arrived in the United States, however, were not politically oriented but agricultural workers and artisans intent on improving their economic positions. The Germans had a reputation for hard work, thrift, and determination, and they made every effort to maintain their Old World culture. When they relaxed, they did so with verve, and their communities overflowed with beer gardens, breweries, concert and lecture halls, and a variety of theaters, singing societies, and athletic organizations. The German *Gymnasium* stressed the development of both a sound mind and a sound body. In religion Germans were divided among Jews and conservative Catholic, Lutheran, and Reformed churches, with a sprinkling of anticlericalists and freethinkers.

German immigrants also transplanted their traditional Christmas customs of lavish foods, joyous songs, and beautifully decorated trees, which proved so appealing to others in the United States that the dourness of the New England Yankees and the rowdiness of some of the more boisterous Southwestern communities all but disappeared as ways of celebrating Jesus Christ's birth. Although many Germans went into politics, they were not an especially political people. They did not deluge almshouses or charity hospitals, either, and they engaged in few activities outside of their ethnic associations that would bring them into social contact with other peoples.

In contrast to the varied groups, classes, and values of the Germans, the three million Irish who also made their initial impact in American society in the 1840s and 1850s were almost exclusively poor, downtrodden, and Roman Catholic. Their entry into the United States aroused great anxiety and hostility because, aside from the Africans and the newly included Spanish speakers in the Southwest, they were the first major non-Protestant group to arrive in huge numbers. Their Catholicism, at the core of all their values, came into direct conflict with the Protestantism of old-stock Americans and most of the other European immigrants. They believed in the subordination of the state to the church ("Religion overrides all other sovereigns, and has the supreme authority over all the affairs of the world," one of their spokesmen proclaimed) and that Catholicism was the only true faith. Moreover, they subscribed to the related church doctrine that declared "no man has or can have a *religious* or *moral* right to be of any religion but the true religion." These views clashed head on with strongly held majority ideas that the *Protestant* God looked over the United States and that, in theory at least, all men had the right to worship, or not, as they pleased so long as they did not disturb their neighbors.

The Irish, unlike the restless Americans who sought new frontiers to conquer, accepted their station in life. They felt, historian Oscar Handlin tells us, that "they were victims of incalculable influences beyond their control" and therefore resigned themselves to whatever fate had set out for them. These opinions also conflicted with the optimistic strain in American society that preached that anyone could succeed by dint of hard work.

Finally, the Irish included many of the poorest and most degraded of the mid-nineteenth-century immigrants from Europe and apparently worked hard at whatever menial tasks were available. Many had fled Ireland rather than starve during the Great Hunger of the 1840s, and they arrived penniless. Packed into the Eastern ports and industrial cities with little money and few skills, they soon constituted a large part of the working-class population. In many American cities Irish names appeared more frequently than those of any other native- or foreign-born ethnic group on lists of paupers and criminals. These factors alone would have made them unwelcome even had there been no national or religious prejudice against them. Indigent American workers despised the urban Irishmen and complained that by working for low wages they took jobs away from "honest" men. They dominated the ranks of common laborers in most cities but, except for owning saloons, avoided commerce and the skilled crafts. In addition, the Irish thought that their children should contribute to the household rather than waste their time in school. As a result the Irish had the lowest incomes, lived in the worst conditions, and received a disproportionate amount of public charity. Some Irish did succeed in American terms, but in numbers and proportions they lagged behind the Germans, English, and Scandinavians. In a country motivated by material advancement, the Irish turned to the church for salvation and security, and this only increased Protestant opposition.

During the 1850s the Germans and Irish constituted the two major immigrant groups in the United States; their combined numbers approximated two million people. The British ranked a distant third, with about three hundred thousand emigrants reaching the United States during the decade. The massive Irish influx totaled more than a million people for the years 1847–53, whereas the German figure did not exceed one hundred thousand until 1852. By 1854 Irish emigration had begun to wane, but the German totals that year exceeded two hundred thousand for the first time. Thereafter, German immigrants outnumbered all others in every year except three through 1892.

The Mining Frontier

While this continuing flood of Europeans into the United States during the mid-nineteenth century dominated the scene, newcomers from Asia and Latin

America began arriving as well. In January 1848, even before the negotiators trying to end the Mexican War completed writing the Treaty of Guadalupe Hidalgo, workmen found gold near the American River in northern California. Once people realized that the news of the discovery was no hoax, excitement swept through the small California settlements. "The blacksmith dropped his hammer, the carpenter his plane, the mason his trowel, the farmer his sickle, the baker his loaf, and the tapster his bottle. All were off for the mines, some on horses, some on carts, and some on crutches, and one went in a litter." Late in 1848, after people in the rest of the nation read newspaper reports of the gold deposits and had their dreams of wealth supported by President James Polk's announcement of the discovery, gold fever swept the country. From every state and territory in the Union, as well as from a dozen other nations, would-be miners abandoned their pursuits and headed toward California. The population influx happened so quickly that Congress admitted California to statehood in 1850 without requiring it to go through the stages of territorial government.

Although fantasies of untapped riches stimulated the population surge and the California mines produced massive amounts of gold, few individual miners became wealthy. Nevertheless, mining was the first important magnet that attracted settlers to the Far West. Many migrants had no intention of working the mines but recognized that the burgeoning population needed shops and services to provide food, clothing, housing, transportation, and entertainment. In short, economic opportunity beckoned. Exploitation of western mineral wealth fell into several distinct eras. The first occurred from 1848 until 1858 in California, during which miners learned their trade through bitter experience. Using placer or surface mining techniques, the men dug sand and gravel from the creek beds and banks, washed them out with water, and collected whatever gold remained. Placer mining required the least skill, technology, or capital, but was also the least efficient and productive way to extract minerals. During the 1860s prospectors spread placer mining, based on their California experience, throughout the mountain west.

Thousands of adventurers hurriedly set up hundreds of mining camps, stretching from Oregon in the north almost to the Mexican border in the south. Living in tents, caves, or shacks, the gold seekers dug into the stream banks and hillsides with frenzy. When picks and shovels failed to move earth fast enough to suit them, some turned to hydraulic mining, a process by which they cut down entire hillsides with powerful streams of water. However the miners pursued the gold, they came and went in a continuous stream of humanity that left scattered towns and cities throughout the West.

As placer mining diminished in California, quartz and hydraulic mining became increasingly important. Corporations, with their superior resources, moved in to exploit the more valuable and difficult-to-get vein gold. Often buried in quartz and other hard rock deposits, this gold had to be separated from the rest of the ore with rock crushers and other expensive equipment, which left little opportunity for the individual miner still hoping to "strike it rich." As a result, disappointed California miners drifted throughout the mountain West looking for new mineral regions.

From 1869 to 1879 mining investment and technological advances centered largely on the famous Comstock Lode near Virginia City, Nevada, while mineral exploration in the rest of the West remained dormant. During the last decades of the nineteenth century new discoveries and investments in Colorado, Nevada, Montana, South Dakota, and Arizona kept the nation fascinated and the miners moving throughout the West.

Mining discoveries brought people, capital, transportation, and business enterprise to outlying regions, where these assets had barely been present. As early as the 1850s large numbers of Europeans immigrated directly to the mining regions. Their numbers and variety gave camps there an ethnic flavor not often found outside the eastern port cities and the larger Midwestern industrial centers. As in the rest of the nation, many of the most highly skilled came from Ireland and from Cornwall in Britain, where mining had been an important occupation for generations. During the 1860–80 era a severe depression hit the Cornwall mines, and between one-quarter and one-third of the workers there left the country, many coming to the American West.

The mine operators welcomed skilled workers enthusiastically. At the Comstock Lode, for example, the census of 1880 showed that although Americans composed more than half of the population of that community, most of the actual mining was done by the foreign-born. Of the 1,966 miners listed in the census, 691 were Irish, 543 English and Cornish, 394 American, and 132 Canadian; the remaining 206 included smaller numbers of men from several other countries.

Frequently, mineral discoveries proved a mixed blessing, as ore deposits became exhausted or failed to live up to the expectations of miners, business people, and investors. Hundreds of crumbling western ghost towns stand as mute evidence to this difficulty. Nevertheless, when mining became less important in local or regional economies, the inhabitants often turned to other occupations, enabling some settlements to broaden their economic bases and survive. Thus the influx of large groups originally enticed by mining opportunities served to populate many parts of the West.

But the original lure of the West also created many unrealistically high expectations. Thus a sense of betrayal, accompanied by frustration and bitterness, lingered throughout the region. Difficulties arose from disappointed dreams of finding gold in the streets or, at least, in the stream beds. In California men who had earned $15 to $20 a day in 1848 had to be satisfied with wages near $2 to

$3 a day only four years later. Rather than thriving as individual prospectors, most became day laborers working for the newly organized mining companies. This rapid decline in personal status, the sharp reduction in earning power, and the overoptimistic expectations that had lured thousands west in the first place combined to make many miners violence-prone bigots. Beginning in California, a pattern of frequent public antagonism toward blacks, Indians, Mexicans, and Asians soon spread throughout the mining camps of the West.

California led the way in the amount and intensity of this hostility. When the United States acquired that region as part of the Treaty of Guadalupe Hidalgo in 1848, it guaranteed the property rights of all Mexican residents and the retention of their Catholic faith, Spanish language, and cultural traditions. Only about 7,500 Mexicans lived in California at the time, and it appeared as if they could be absorbed easily. However, the continuation of the hatred initially aroused by the war between Mexico and the United States and the discovery of gold in California made such an accommodation practically impossible. News of rich gold deposits attracted at least six thousand more Mexicans to the mining regions, and American miners resented having to share the wealth with their former enemies.

Bitterness grew particularly harsh in the Sonora mines of central California. There the presence of hundreds of Mexican miners aroused so much anxiety among those of European and American birth that in 1850 the latter group pushed a Foreign Miners' Tax through the new state legislature. As a result of this discriminatory law, all foreign miners had to pay a $20 monthly licensing fee for the privilege of mining gold. Aimed at both the newly arrived Mexican miners and their countrymen who were California natives, the tax succeeded in driving most of them from the gold fields. Once they left, the tax was lowered to $20 a year.

Economic frustration alone, however, does not explain the prevalent hostility. Although such woes aggravated latent attitudes, American traditions must also be considered. Racism and prejudice were not indigenous only to the Californians—people brought their feelings with them from other places. The state's first governor, Peter Burnett, had been a prime mover for antiblack legislation in Oregon in the early 1840s. In California he recommended similar action, unsuccessfully urging the framers of the state constitution and then the members of the state legislature to exclude free blacks from residency. The lawmakers, although narrowly spurning his suggestion, nevertheless shared some of his prejudices. Hence California's first state constitution did not allow Indians, blacks, or Asians to testify against white people in the state courts.

On the other hand, the Europeans who arrived in California during the middle of the nineteenth century—and predominant among the earliest newcomers were about seven thousand French—usually did not experience the same difficulties as racial minorities. Americans accepted them and assumed that they would participate in helping the region grow. In San Francisco, however, the French clung together, failed to learn English quickly, and engaged in a "wild glorification of... every thing connected with their beautiful France." As a result, they had more difficulty in assimilating than did immigrants from Great Britain, who spoke English, and from the German states, who tried quickly to adapt to the prevailing customs. Chileans and Chinese also made up significant numbers of the newcomers to California's expanding population, but they did not receive the enthusiastic welcome provided to Caucasians from Western Europe and the eastern sections of the United States.

The Chinese

Nearly a quarter-million Chinese arrived in California between 1849 and the early 1880s. Most of them had come over as indentured or bond servants, having had their passage paid for in return for a promise to work for a stipulated period of time. Throughout the West they worked on the railroads, in the mines, in agriculture, and at domestic chores. They gave Californians no cause for disliking them. During their first few years in the state they encountered little discrimination. A contemporary observer of the Chinese in 1850 commented that "their deportment is grave and dignified. They seem never to meddle or intervene in the affairs of others." Chinese immigrants did tasks that white men considered menial and beneath their dignity, such as washing and ironing clothes or preparing meals. By 1860 they owned laundries, restaurants, and hotels and also monopolized the making of shoes, shirts, underwear, cigars, and tinware in California.

As economic difficulties for the white men in California increased, the Chinese began to experience prejudice. Their numbers, industry, and economic success intensified white hostility. Alone among the immigrants, the Chinese regularly paid the annual $20 tax that California required for foreign miners. The virtues of thrift, hard work, and responsibility, which the Chinese possessed in abundance, and which Americans praised so lavishly when displayed by WASPs (white Anglo-Saxon Protestants), did not mitigate expression of the most outrageous kinds of bigotry. In 1854 California passed legislation forbidding Chinese to testify for or against white people in the state's courts, and in 1857 it established segregated schools for their children. Americans dubbed the Chinese "groveling worms," and accused them of eating rats and dogs and of being a "retrogressive and inferior race." Anti-Chinese spokesmen also denounced the gambling, prostitution, and opium smoking that occurred in the Chinese neighborhoods but said little if those activities occurred elsewhere.

Nineteenth-century drawing depicting Chinese laundry workers. Laundries were one of the few places in which Chinese immigrants could find employment. From *Leslie's Magazine,* 1881. (Library of Congress)

Crowded Chinese housing conditions convinced whites that the filth and disease there would spread into the rest of society. One Caucasian complained: "The Chinese are like a sponge; they absorb and give nothing in return but bad odors and worse morals. They are a standing menace to the women of this country. Their very presence is contaminating. They have sown the seed of vice in every city, town and hamlet in this country. They encourage, aid, and abet the youths of the land to become opium fiends."

Whites' fears and antagonism sprang from a belief that the Asians would never blend into American society. "They are a distinct race," commented one hostile white. "They never assimilate with our people, our manners, tastes, religion, or ideas. With us they have nothing in common." Despite the existing hostility, the Chinese continued migrating to the United States through the 1880s, when the federal government erected barriers against them.

The Railroads

Expansion of the railroads encouraged the growth of the Chinese population. Practically all western railroad building took place after the Civil War, for prior to the 1860s not enough people lived in the West to justify such construction, and sufficient capital was not readily available. To remedy the latter situation Congress had passed the Pacific Railroad Act in 1862. This act authorized federal loans and land grants to the Union Pacific to extend tracks west from Omaha, Nebraska, and to the Central Pacific to lay tracks eastward from California. In May 1869 the work crews of the two railroad companies met near Ogden, Utah, thereby completing America's first transcontinental railroad. By the mid-1890s other lines—the Northern Pacific, Great Northern, Atchison, Topeka and Santa Fe, and Southern Pacific—had been finished. With trunk and connecting lines being built at the same time, track mileage in the nation soared. In 1872 the United States had 57,300 miles of railroad track. A decade later it had increased to 114,400 miles, and by 1900 the rails stretched past two hundred thousand miles. The new track was by no means limited to the West, but the burgeoning railroad network had tied that region firmly to the rest of the nation by the end of the nineteenth century.

As massive construction projects that needed skilled and unskilled laborers, railroads, like the mining camps earlier, attracted people to the West. During the 1860s the Union Pacific hired thousands of Irish workmen, whereas its western competitor, the Central Pacific, imported about ten thousand Chinese laborers. Not only did these newcomers build the two lines mentioned, but also many of them remained in the West to work on other railroad projects.

The majority of the twenty thousand or so Chinese who had come to California in the 1850s found working conditions abhorrent. In 1867 two thousand of them struck against the Central Pacific Railway. They demanded an increase in pay from $30 a month to $40 a month, cuts in the working hours to ten hours a day and eight hours when working in the tunnels, and they called for an end to overseers whipping them. The strike lasted a week, and then they returned to work without having gained any of their demands.

To feed and house their vast work crews, the construction firms provided temporary prefabricated cities—often called "Hell on Wheels" because they were little more than shanties that could be moved from one place to another. Most of the early railroad camps were just that, but some remained as the nuclei of later settlements. Existing towns such as Omaha, Kansas City, Denver, and Salt Lake City, to mention a few, benefited from the railroad boom. Serving as supply bases, sources for labor, and banking centers, these cities prospered because of railroad building and subsequent business operations.

The Coming of the Civil War

Before the Civil War, however, there was little need for transcontinental railroads because so few people lived beyond the Mississippi River. The conflict began in 1861 and precipitated the most serious domestic crisis in American history. The acquisition of the vast region from the Rocky Mountains to the Pacific coast during the 1840s raised the issue of extending slavery into that area. Southerners demanded the right to transport their human property westward, but many Northerners, more responsive to moral and political pressures at home, refused to concur with the southern point of view. The political debates of the 1850s aroused the nation, destroyed political parties, and gave rise to the emergence of new leaders. The Republican Party, founded in 1854, developed out of the resulting political chaos. Dedicated to preventing the expansion of slavery beyond its existing limits, the new party failed in its first effort to win the presidency two years later. In 1860 Republicans broadened their base by promising homesteads, free farms to those wanting them, a protective tariff to encourage business, and a transcontinental railroad to tie the west coast to the rest of the country. Then they turned to a moderate candidate, Abraham Lincoln, who had supported the Fugitive Slave Law, passed in 1850, which called for the return of all runaway slaves to their lawful owners. In addition, Lincoln had promised not to touch slavery in the states in which it existed. He believed in white supremacy and advocated the colonization of blacks abroad. Because of his conservative views on the race issue, some radicals distrusted this "slave hound" from Illinois.

Yet Lincoln opposed the expansion of slavery and had said that a nation could not endure half slave and half free. He thought that industrial progress would be slowed and that the nation would remain divided until the agitation over the expansion of slavery ceased. His election in 1860 frightened militant Southerners, and some states seceded from the Union. Lincoln's decision in April 1861 to reinforce Fort Sumter, an American army base at Charleston, South Carolina, provided the spark to start the Civil War. Despite the president's insistence that the struggle was to save the Union and not abolish slavery, this distinction became blurred as the war progressed.

The war affected the economy. The departure of Southerners from Congress gave free rein to the spokesmen for industrial expansion. Without the presence of Southerners, northern legislators passed measures promoting economic growth. Large-scale demand for food, uniforms, blankets, shoes, weapons, and so on necessitated more laborers. To meet the nation's needs, as well as to propel the economy, Congress raised the tariff, thereby protecting newly established manufacturers, and granted land for railroad expansion, education, and homesteading. The 1862 Homestead Act promised 160 acres to anyone willing to develop the land. European farmers took the challenge and came to the United States to try their fortunes once the war ended in 1865. Generous land grants from Congress also spurred railroad building, which had slowed temporarily when the war began. Once industrial interests gained control of Congress, they never relinquished it. Titans of industry and their allies have been the major forces shaping national economic legislation ever since.

Blacks and the Domestic Crisis

Thus the war that had started to save the Union ended with the triumph of industrial forces, as well as the abolition of slavery. Practical and military concerns certainly had more to do with both of these results than did moral considerations. When the war came, black volunteers rushed to serve the Union cause, but the federal and state governments rejected them. The Providence, Rhode Island, police even declared that they would break up groups of drilling blacks as "disorderly gatherings." When General John C. Fremont declared martial law in Missouri and freed the slaves, Lincoln overruled him. The president worried about public opinion in the North and the reaction of the border slave states, which, despite much pro-Confederate support, had not joined with the states of the Lower South. If freedom were to come, Lincoln wanted compensated emancipation and not unilateral action by military commanders. Radical abolitionist criticism was unable to move the president.

Circumstances, however, and Lincoln's changing attitude gradually pushed the federal government in the direction of employing black troops and ending slavery. At first, the war did not go well for the North. Heavy casualties and military failures made the use of black troops seem more appealing. Then the slaves themselves created a problem for northern generals. Large numbers fled the plantations and poured into the Union lines. Perplexed generals did not know what to do with these "contrabands," as they were called. Some suggested returning them to their masters, others fed and cared for them, and a few wanted to use them against the Confederacy as laborers or soldiers. In the Sea Islands of South Carolina, occupied by the Union, General David Hunter in May 1862 freed the slaves and impressed them into the army. But Lincoln countermanded the order. Although the president declared his opposition to the use of black troops as late as the summer of 1862, he soon allowed northern commanders to recruit them in segregated units.

Lincoln had hoped to compensate slaveholders as an inducement for emancipation and had suggested colonization for the newly freed blacks. Congress abolished slavery in the District of Columbia, granted $300 per slave compensation, and indicated its support for the president's proposals for the border states. By the summer of 1862, however, Lincoln had resolved to end slavery. In September he issued the preliminary Emancipation Proclamation and on January 1, 1863, the final one. The proclamation freed only those slaves under rebel control, and slavery disintegrated as the Union armies pushed south.

Many northern whites did not want to see slavery terminated because they believed that abolitionist movement made the South fight harder and hence prolonged the war. Others simply did not care whether blacks were enslaved. Competition between whites and blacks for jobs did not help, either. On several occasions during the war angry white workers assaulted African Americans and burned their homes. In Buffalo, where blacks labored as longshoremen, white workers killed three of them and severely beat twelve others. Cincinnati, Chicago, Detroit, Cleveland, Boston, and Harrisburg all experienced riots; the worst one occurred in New York City in July 1863. Before 1863 the union armies relied upon volunteers, but there were not enough of them. The federal government then instituted a draft, which the Irish and other workers hated because they believed the war was ending slavery and would leave the Irish to compete with southern blacks who might come north. In protest against conscription, thousands roamed the city, burning and looting. Mobs lynched several African Americans and destroyed the black orphanage; fortunately, attendants managed to get the children out. Not until the draft was temporarily suspended in New York and officials brought in federal troops did the riots cease. All told, perhaps seventy-five people died as a result of the onslaught.

After the riots ended the public again focused on the war, which finally ended in April 1865. Before unity could be attained, however, some efforts had to be made to help the former slaves move productively into the new society. Following the assassination of Lincoln in April 1865, his successor, Andrew Johnson, and the Congress wrangled for three years over the best way to revive the nation.

In 1866 Congress established a Freedmen's Bureau to provide temporary assistance to the former slaves, and the nation later adopted the Thirteenth, Fourteenth, and Fifteenth Amendments to the Constitution, which, respectively, outlawed slavery, defined who an American was for the first time, ostensibly protected civil rights, and prevented black men from being denied the vote. These amendments were intended to help ease the paths of the erstwhile bondsmen (but not women) into the free world. However, insufficient education, an overwhelmingly agrarian background, lack of land redistribution, and racism thwarted the progress of the blacks.

During the Reconstruction era (1865–1877) this racism sometimes erupted into violence. The Ku Klux Klan, for example, attacked African American men, especially when they attempted to vote and exercise their civil rights. Federal authorities helped protect black men's civil rights, and they were able to vote and hold office during the Reconstruction period. But the white South, aided by the Klan, overthrew the Reconstruction governments by 1877. As a result, blacks remained politically powerless and often remained as workers on southern farms. Meanwhile, the region's industries expanded slowly. In Birmingham steel mills developed. Workers in Georgia and Florida made cigarettes and cigars, while cotton mills operated throughout the area. New Orleans continued to serve as a prominent port, and so, for a time, did Galveston, Texas. Despite this, few blacks benefited from these economic developments.

The failure of the attempt to bring a degree of racial democracy to the South eventually ended in a torrent of racism, and after 1890 the Fourteenth and Fifteenth Amendments became dead letters for the next half century. To be sure, most white southerners suffered economically as well, but many members of the old planter class and their descendants landed on their feet. Those planters who survived and the new industrialists, who exploited white and black workers alike, ruled the South.

Although African Americans failed to win equality, the Reconstruction period and its aftermath did see the growth of black institutional life in the American South. First, the black family, which had no legal status under slavery, received the sanction of law. Thousands of freedmen took advantage of the new situation to legalize their unions. "My husband and I have lived together fifteen years and we wants to be married over again," explained one wife. Many who were parted from their mates and children during slavery now searched for their loved ones. Some took to the roads seeking their families; others advertised in the newspapers. A white correspondent for a northern journal reported encountering one freedman who had walked nearly six hundred miles in two months in search of his wife. Not all spouses could be reunited, but the Reconstruction era did see the stabilization of the black family in ways impossible under slavery.

Removed along with the legal restrictions against the black family were the restrictions against southern black churches. After the Civil War thousands of freedmen and women left the slave galleries in the churches of their former masters and flocked to their own Baptist, Methodist, and Holiness churches that grew substantially in the aftermath of slavery. Their own churches were important to blacks, for here they could be free from the watchful eyes of whites. No wonder that a number of black politicians and other leaders were clergymen. After the elimination of blacks from southern politics in the 1890s, they functioned politically by determining policy and choosing leaders in their churches.

The churches also provided an outlet for their culture. Through African American religious music and the services themselves, blacks expressed their own experiences and longings for the future. The singing of African American spirituals and the shouting characteristic of services in the slave era continued, but they declined among the educated elite, who preferred to forget connections to slavery. In a later era the spirituals were replaced by gospels. Whereas the former emphasized the Hebrew children and deliverance from slavery, the latter recognized the sorrows of this world but, as the following song suggests, also promised hope for the future:

> The Lord will provide,
> The Lord will provide,
> Sometimes another, the Lord will provide.

> It may not be in my time,
> It may not be in yours,
> But Sometimes another, the Lord will provide.

Not all African American culture was expressed in religion. Southern blacks used songs as well as humor and other oral traditions. The songs were sung by black workers to provide a rhythm for work, but they also talked of love and life. In the late nineteenth century African Americans produced jazz and later blues; these musical forms spread to the North and became popular in the twentieth century.

The Mormons

While the former slaves sought new lives, in the late 1840s the refugee Mormons had migrated to Utah with the same goal. Because many other Americans considered their distinctive religious ideas heretical, they endured continuing persecution. So they fled into Mexican territory. When the United States acquired vast territories in the West in 1848, they found themselves back in this country. During the next two decades thousands of the Latter-day Saints abandoned their homes and property in the East and Midwest and gathered near the shores of the Great Salt Lake. When they first tried to plow the bricklike desert soil, their plows broke in the stubborn ground. Within a few months, however, Brigham Young had organized work parties that dug irrigation ditches and diverted mountain streams into them. With water to help, the plows did their work. The Mormons were the first Anglo-Saxons to use large-scale irrigation in North America. Within a few decades irrigation spread into many parts of the West, and in 1902 Congress passed the Newlands Reclamation Act. This spurred the spread of other western irrigation projects and the development of cotton and fruit farms from Texas to California.

When they first moved to Utah, church leaders hoped to achieve political and economic independence. They established a string of settlements in parts of what are now southeastern Oregon, southern Idaho, southwestern Wyoming, and northern Arizona. Mormon families considered it an honor to help start new communities, and they sent their missionaries to the eastern United States and western Europe to recruit converts who could then be sent to the new western Zion. By 1856 some twenty-two thousand Saints lived near the Great Salt Lake or along this great "Mormon Corridor," which, shaped like a banana, curved from southeastern Oregon down through Ogden, Utah, and then south and southwest into San Bernardino, California.

While settlement took place, church leaders also hoped to achieve immediate statehood so that they could protect their community from federal interference. Accordingly, in March 1849 Brigham Young called a constitutional convention, and this body adopted a constitution for the would-be state of Deseret. The Mormons, claiming all of Utah, most of Arizona and Nevada, and parts of California, Idaho, Wyoming, and Colorado, sent a delegation to Washington to lobby for statehood. There they met widespread opposition, and in 1850 they had to settle for the creation of Utah Territory, with much reduced boundaries. Fortunately for the Mormons, federal authorities appointed Brigham Young governor and four other high church officers to administrative positions in the government. Church leaders thus continued to make nearly all political decisions for the territory.

Their insistence on retaining polygamy and the quarrels between church officials and non-Mormon federal officials in 1857 brought a major crisis. That year one of the federal territorial judges fled Utah and returned east, claiming that the church ran the government and that Brigham Young was a dictator who used a group of "destroying angels" to crush all opposition. With little effort to investigate, President James Buchanan dispatched an army of 2,500 men to subdue the supposedly rebellious Mormons. Frantically the Saints evacuated the women and children, prepared to burn their homes and farms rather than submit to federal occupation, and launched raids against the army supply columns. These succeeded so well that the troops failed to reach Utah that year, and the conflict ended without major fighting. Despite continuing anti-Mormon bitterness in some parts of the country, the Saints continued to attract converts, and a steady stream of them populated dozens of towns and rural areas throughout the West. Thousands of Scandinavian Mormons migrated to Utah; by 1900 they made up 34 percent of the state's foreign-born and, with their children, 16 percent of Utah's population.

Postwar Immigration

Mormons were only one of the immigrant groups to arrive before and during the Civil War. Once that conflict ended, newcomers continued entering the country from the German states, Ireland, and England. After 1865, increasing numbers came from Scandinavia, where a series of crop failures provided a spur. Whereas before 1860 annual immigration from Scandinavia exceeded four thousand only twice, after the Civil War a great surge ensued. More than two hundred thousand people from Sweden, Norway, and Denmark arrived in the United States between 1866 and 1874, over a million came between 1880 and 1892, and another five hundred thousand or so landed on our shores in the decade preceding the outbreak of World War I in 1914. Altogether, after 1860 more than two million Swedes, Norwegians, and Danes moved to America.

Swedes and Norwegians constituted nearly 90 percent of the total Scandinavian migration, with the former outnumbering the latter by a ratio of approximately two to one. Most of these people settled in the upper Midwest. The Swedes were the most urban of the Scandinavians; in the twentieth century, census tracts regularly found 60 percent or more of them concentrated in cities. Chicago housed the largest Swedish contingent in the world outside of Sweden, and

TABLE 4.3.   Main Sources of Immigration to the United States, 1861–1890

	1861–1870	*1871–1880*	*1881–1890*
Europe			
Austria-Hungary	7,800	72,969	353,719
Denmark	17,094	31,771	88,132
France	35,986	72,206	50,464
Germany	787,468	718,182	1,452,970
Great Britain			
England	222,277	437,706	644,680
Scotland	38,769	87,564	149,869
Ireland	435,778	436,871	655,482
Italy	11,725	55,759	307,309
Norway	71,631	95,323	176,586
Sweden	37,667	115,922	391,776
Switzerland	23,286	28,293	81,988
Russia	2,512	39,284	213,282
Asia			
China	64,301	123,201	61,711
America			
Canada and Newfoundland	153,878	383,640	393,304

sizable groups of Norwegians took advantage of job opportunities there, as well as in New York, Cleveland, Minneapolis, and San Francisco.

Less noticed than the large numbers of Germans, Irish, and Scandinavians, a continuing stream of people from England, Scotland, and Wales entered the country during the last half of the nineteenth century. At first many of the immigrants came as part of the gold and later mineral rushes in the West. Miners from Cornwall worked in the underground hard-rock mines, earning praises for their skills and knowledge, and the Welsh often worked in the coal mines. So many Welsh came that, by 1851, 7 percent of British immigrants worked as miners. Later, between 1870 and 1900, 1,600,000 more people migrated from Britain. Unlike many foreigners, these newcomers spoke English as a native tongue and did not feel as strange in the United States as did those from other lands. Many moved directly to the Midwest to begin farming and soon sent for their families. The married women often worked in textile mills or on farms, whereas single women quickly became domestic servants, an occupation that offered plenty of jobs. Immigrants from the United Kingdom were often welcome in America because they had valuable skills, especially for the iron and steel industry, textiles, and mining. A few industries, such as pottery, relied almost totally on British skilled workers. Even in growing cities experienced English workers soon found themselves at the top of the working class.

Finding Employment

Whatever nation the foreigners came from, the first task they confronted was finding jobs. Whether they stopped in a city or moved into rural areas in search of farmlands, no other aspect of their lives was of greater concern. Those who did not work did not eat and could not support their families. To be sure, even many of those employed earned insufficient sums to maintain a decent life for either themselves or their families. The immigrants usually arrived with little capital and few skills, and so employers took advantage of them. Although industry and commerce were booming, thereby providing millions of new jobs, there were always more people willing to work than jobs available for them. The reservoir of cheap unskilled laborers frustrated the attempts of unions to raise wages and improve working conditions. Real wages did improve in the late nineteenth century, but they still remained low. Almost every account of workers in these years details their pitiful salaries. In an era when $500 to $600 a year was considered the minimum necessary to support a family of five, most laborers earned less. Women received even lower wages, while working longer hours than men. In New York City a skilled tailor might make $6 to $10 working fourteen hours a day, six days a week; however, a seamstress rarely took

The arrival of immigrants at Castle Garden, allegedly to take the place of American strikers. Castle Garden at the tip of Manhattan was the point of arrival for many immigrants before Ellis Island opened. A persistent fear of Americans was that immigrants took jobs from native-born workers. From *Leslie's Magazine,* 1882. (Library of Congress)

home as much as $3 in her good weeks! Maids and other domestics, whose daily toil totaled upward of sixteen hours, had the opportunity of earning $4 to $10 a month plus a basement or attic room and board.

The abundant supply of foreign laborers contributed to the growth of cities and accelerated transportation development in the United States. Many immigrants, especially the Irish, were collected in the Eastern port cities and taken to distant construction sites to build railroads, bridges, tunnels, and canals. In Philadelphia, Chicago, and New York—but not Boston—the Irish were represented in various aspects of the construction business aside from common labor. The industries of some cities soon became identified with particular ethnic groups. Hence the Germans in Milwaukee and Cincinnati were thought of in connection with brewing and wine making, whereas in Boston the Irish operated 900 of the city's 1,500 liquor stores in 1850. In Ohio, one historian tells us, drugstores with German proprietors were thought of as "a guarantee of reliability, for only German pharmacists had been trained in the fundamentals of chemistry."

Overall the Germans had a smaller percentage of common workingmen than the Irish and a larger number of skilled craftsmen in most of the cities where they lived. German tailors, cabinetmakers, and small shopkeepers abounded in every section of the country except New England and the Far West. Some Germans were domestics and unskilled laborers, but these categories are more frequently associated with the Irish. For example, one-third to one-half of all Irish immigrants were classified as domestics or unskilled workers in New York City in 1855, whereas only 15 percent of the Germans appeared in those occupations. In Boston in 1860, the Irish constituted 7,000 of the city's 8,500 laborers. In New Orleans the Irish who arrived in the 1840s and 1850s (more prosperous Irish had come earlier in the century) also worked in the most menial positions. They frequently toiled outdoors in subtropical sun and muddy swamps laying out streets and digging canals.

But immigrant experiences varied from city to city. Philadelphia, which was a textile center, a port city, and the hub of a wide railroad network, had a variety of economic enterprises—one wit noted that everything from battleships to bonbons was manufactured there—and greater opportunities for advancement existed. The Irish thus progressed more rapidly in Philadelphia than they did in Boston or New York. In Savannah, Georgia, in 1860, foreigners owned most of the dry goods and clothing establishments, retail groceries, saloons, cigar and tobacco shops, barber and hairdressing salons, bakeries, confectioneries, hotels, and expensive stores. Almost half of the city's population was foreign born, and six of its nine banks had foreign-born directors. In the 1850s a Frenchman opened the first bakery in Dallas, Texas. And in cities such as New York, Philadelphia, Boston, and Cincinnati, German Jews utilized the newly developed sewing machines in setting up factories for mass-produced clothing.

Artisans from Great Britain used their skills in the manufacturing of textiles. When the United States increased its duties on silk after the Civil War, owners of British factories took their machines and workmen to America to begin anew, virtually destroying the industry in England. English skills were also evident in mining. As news of better wages in American mines spread in Great Britain, many left to seek a new way of life. English miners worked in the coal fields of eastern Pennsylvania, and Welsh miners found jobs elsewhere. Among the most famous of the British miners were those from Cornwall. The Cornish immigrants put their knowledge to good use in such places as Wisconsin and the hard-rock mines of the American West. In the nineteenth century Britain made many improvements in metallurgy, and English workers brought knowledge of these advances with them to the New World. Although the British immigrants included a high percentage of skilled craftsmen, many of them also had to work for low wages in unskilled jobs.

Not all immigrants found employment in industrial and urban America. Few Irish, but large numbers of Germans and Scandinavians, took up farming in Pennsylvania, Wisconsin, Ohio, Illinois, Texas, and other states. Life was not easy in rural America. Clearing the land and enduring inclement weather, which included freezing blizzards and blistering droughts, discouraged alien and native-born farmers alike. Often they had little money and so had trouble starting a farm. Although free land was available under the Homestead Act, others often owned the best lots, and there were tools and supplies to purchase. The long hours of toil and loneliness added to the tribulations of farm families. Many children, accustomed to workdays lasting from 4 A.M. to 10 P.M. and long winters of virtual isolation from friends and relatives, had no desire to spend their adult lives in similar circumstances. The twelve-hour workdays in industry and the opportunities for social intercourse that urban areas provided seemed to offer a much more stimulating existence. Hence many of the new city dwellers were migrants from rural areas.

Living Conditions

The type of work the breadwinners did and the amount of their earnings determined the family's living conditions. Most frequently the workers' homes were inadequate and unhealthy. On the frontiers and in rapidly growing new towns, families often made do with badly built facilities. A Dutch emigrant recalled constructing his sixteen-foot cabin in Milwaukee in 1846 "out of rough common lumber. The boards were lapped and nailed on like siding, without anything else being added inside or out, and the roof was of the same material. There was also a so-called upstairs which was reached by climbing a homemade ladder. Not much of a manse this—and it was certainly an uncomfortable dwelling during a storm or in weather below zero." Irish workers who helped build Illinois canals lived in log huts and mud cabins.

The majority of newcomers suffered in pestilential tenements in the nation's largest cities. They got off the boats, found work, and then sought homes nearby. To cope with this influx of people speculators converted old mansions and factory lofts into housing units, while others hastily built cheap tenements. As a result, rents were high, and the living units lacked essential features. Often they had no floors—just dirt, feathers, or patches of straw. Air and light were luxuries, and sewage accumulated both inside and outside of the dwellings in New York and other cities, where dwellings for the poor had no indoor toilets and backyard privies overflowed frequently. In 1850 three-quarters of the houses in New York City had no sewers, and water overflowed into the streets. The first bathtub in the United States appeared in Cincinnati in 1842. Some newspapers called it a plaything of the rich; Philadelphia prohibited its use between November 1 and February 28; and Boston banned the bathtub unless prescribed by a physician. "Men of medicine and men of God," one chronicler tells us, warned that the practice of bathing "would wash away a man's virility and a woman's virginity."

Under these circumstances diseases and epidemics abounded in the major cities. Cholera, smallpox, malaria, tuberculosis, pneumonia, typhus, and typhoid were common afflictions of the poor, and especially of the Irish. In New Orleans twelve thousand people died during the summer of 1853; among them were four thousand Irish, and St. Patrick's cemetery reported a shortage of gravediggers. Epidemics hit the new immigrants more severely than the Americans because they were already physically debilitated from their ocean crossing and also because a greater percentage of them congregated in the stifling and unhealthful urban ghettos.

Immigrants also crowded into the inadequate public facilities, and from the 1830s on, they consistently totaled more than 50 percent of the inmates of the almshouses, insane asylums, and jails. Picked up as vagrants, drunks, or general nuisances, they were also victimized by unjust administration of the laws. Young immigrant women were looked on as fair prey by their employers or "gay blades" about town. A far too typical example of exploitation was the case of a New Orleans woman plied with liquor by several men, who then seduced her. She was sentenced to jail for public drunkenness whereas her abusers went free.

Insensitive community officials failed to make constructive criticism. Instead, they condemned the victims and blamed them for the ills of society. "The Irish suffered the most," one New York City Board of Health official concluded in 1832, because they were "exceedingly dirty in their habits, much addicted to intemperance and crowded together in the worst portion of cities." In the 1858 annual report of the New York Association for Improving Conditions of the Poor, the author noted: "Our city, operating like a sieve, lets through the enterprising and industrious, while it retains the indolent, the aged, and infirm, who can earn their subsistence nowhere, to become a burden and often because of their vices, a nuisance to the community."

This type of prejudice gave the newcomers all the more reason for clinging to one another for support. The Americans, who would not associate with the immigrants in any case, then assailed them for their clannishness. More important, however, the foreigners felt more comfortable with those of similar backgrounds and experiences. The enclaves where they clustered constituted the beginnings of the urban immigrant communities. These have been the places in which recent immigrants and their children felt comfortable and coddled and the places that second- and third-generation adults left, having been given in their earlier years the support and protection that would ease their paths into the dominant society at the appropriate time. The advent of the Irish and the Germans marked the beginning of the large neighborhoods of the foreign born. In New York, Cincinnati, St. Louis, Chicago, and Milwaukee, to name but a few communities, one found *kleindeutschlands* (Little Germanies), where all of the shopkeepers spoke German, where the daily life almost duplicated that of the old country, and where traditional customs prevailed. In the 1850s Milwaukee had its "German market," a shopping center and a clearinghouse for local gossip. When American women from "Yankee Hill" patronized the shops, one could hear the Germans calling out, *"Da kommt die englische Dame!"* or *"Die Dame von Yankeberg!"* Lutheran church services conducted in German and parochial schools perpetuated the language among the children.

Almost every ethnic group had its own benevolent society to assist immigrants at the dock. Frequently these provided food, shelter for a night or two, travel assistance, and job information. The Irish Emigrant Society of New York and *Die Deutsche Gesellschaft* were among the busiest in the middle of the nineteenth century, but also active were the Scots' St. Andrew's Society, the Hebrew Immigrant Benevolent Society, and the French Benevolent Society.

Other associations and organizations, ranging from benevolent to quasimilitary to special interest, also arose. To some extent these were established to promote group solidarity and continuity, but another factor, sometimes overlooked by observers, concerned immigrant disdain for the apparent lack of culture and refinement in the United States. Many Germans, for example, who had a rich heritage of music, art, and literature, as well as a standard for civilized behavior, regarded the Americans as uncouth and bizarre. One historian of the German Americans, Carl Wittke, tells us that some of them

> ridiculed such American habits as rocking in chairs, chewing and spitting tobacco, standing up to a bar to down a drink, getting "eye-openers" each morning, wearing hats crooked, and sticking feet on tables and window sills. They were not impressed by the "anarchical noise" of Fourth of July or firemen's parades, or by the muddy streets, the corrupt shirt-sleeve, tobacco-cud politics of the cities, and the "human bull fighting" known as pugilism. They preferred sausage and sauerkraut to pie and pork and beans. They were shocked to find slavery firmly established and nativism rampant in a free republic. They hated American Sabbatarianism, blue laws, and "the temperance swindle," and the more radical ridiculed what they called the religious superstitions of the American people. They were determined to preserve their language and customs and to resist assimilation to an inferior culture.

Hence the restricted social contacts involved in community athletic groups, picnics, dances, lectures, and intellectual meetings served the dual purpose of providing recreational outlets while still preserving a valuable heritage. The

An early Norwegian Lutheran church in Crawford County, Wisconsin, about the mid-1880s. (State Historical Society of Wisconsin)

songfests of one group of German organizations, the *Sangerbunds* or singing societies, proved so popular that national meetings of German *Sangerbunds* were held in cities such as St. Louis and Cincinnati.

Some groups, especially the Irish, established fire and militia companies. In 1846 an observer commented, "There is scarcely a city of any note in the United States in which an Irish volunteer corps is not to be found, clothed in the national colour and ornamented with the harp, shamrock, and other national emblems." For the Irish St. Patrick's Day dictated a massive turnout for fun, parties, and parades of militia companies in full and colorful regalia.

Immigrants from Great Britain also formed their own groups. Although fluency in the language and Protestant background gave them an entry into American society, they too felt different from Americans and sought each other out. The Welsh had their own style of Protestantism and loved to attend their *eisteddfod,* a festival of singing and literature. The Scots also had their associations. The various groups from Great Britain, like other foreigners, also published their own newspapers. One factor that unified the newcomers from the United Kingdom was hatred of the Irish, and not a few joined the ranks of the growing anti-Catholic, anti-Irish movements of the nineteenth century.

Animosity toward Foreigners

The hostility expressed toward the Catholics seemed, to some extent, to be generally applicable to all foreigners. Although immigrants aided American industrial growth, old-stock Americans resented them. They were regarded as unsavory and inferior beings merely because of their European heritage. "What has annoyed me most in my associations with the Americans," one Norwegian wrote back home,

> is their prejudice against Europe, which they regard as hopelessly lost in slavery and wretchedness. Three fourths of the people in the East and ninety-nine hundredths of the people in the West are fully convinced that the other side of the Atlantic is nothing but a heap of medieval feudal states, which, indeed, show some slight indications of reform here and there, but have not made much political progress and have not enough vitality to rise from the abyss of misery and corruption into which they have fallen as the result of centuries of ignorance and despotism; their doom is inevitable.

Americans regarded themselves, on the other hand, as privileged and generous people who were willing to share their destiny with the less fortunate Europeans who chose to leave their homelands. In return for this "generosity," however, they expected recent arrivals to relinquish their old ways and values. And "until they have become morally acclimated to our institutions," Horace Mann, the Boston educator, declared, they were simply unfit for participation in American society. One of the ways that Mann and others expected the foreigners to "become morally acclimated" to American customs was through the common school, which would instill among all youth the values and outlook of "real" Americans. To some, however, the very idea that Europeans could adapt seemed absurd. "Our Celtic fellow citizens," a New Yorker confided to his diary, "are almost as remote from us in temperament and constitution as the Chinese." A New Englander expressed still another attitude toward the foreigners. He did not much mind them, but he found them somewhat amusing. In verse he mocked the habits and accents of the Germans he saw about him:

> Mine cracious! mine cracious! shust look here and see
> A Deutscher so habby as habby can pe!
> Der beoples dink dot no prains I haf got;
> Vas grazy mit trinking, or someding like dot.

Animosity toward foreigners probably developed out of discontent with national economic adversity. The late Jacksonian era may have been a time of great opportunity for the "common man," but it was also one of economic dislocation. Increased emigration from Europe, which started in the 1820s, contributed not only large numbers to the ranks of the unemployed but also, according to the estimates of one scholar, "came close to creating a permanent semi-pauperized working class." In cities such as New York, Philadelphia, Baltimore, Cincinnati, and Washington, this led to an increase in poverty-stricken people, crime, and public disorder. The periods of economic difficulty coincided with the increase in riots and labor disturbances. "Americans in the nineteenth century," one scholar tells us, "engaged in economic conflicts with their employers as fierce as any known to the industrial world." This was certainly true of the Jacksonian era.

More significant in regard to ethnic relations, however, was the increased number of racial and religious conflicts. Instead of venting their wrath on the entrepreneurs who owned the factories and the government and courts that supported capitalists and suppressed labor organizations, the working people blamed foreigners and minorities for their woes. Throughout America's history the majority has unquestioningly followed the patterns set in an Anglo-dominated colonial America. Thereafter Americans have been suspicious and resentful of those who failed to adapt rapidly to the prevalent customs. During times of contentment and prosperity, immigrants who did not conform were usually left to fend for themselves, but in eras of emotional or economic

Cartoonist Thomas Nast's view of St. Patrick's Day, 1867. Nast—along with many other Americans—viewed the Irish as ugly, brawling drunkards. From *Harper's Weekly,* 1867.

adversity they have been victimized by both verbal and physical attacks. Sometimes immigrants and minorities have been labeled as the causes of the national difficulties; in other instances they have stood in for elite groups as a more socially acceptable outlet for the release of high tensions.

In Jacksonian America a contracting economy precipitated the battles. Whereas there had been only some twenty-odd riots between 1828 and 1833, the number increased to sixteen in 1834 alone and thirty-seven in 1835. Abolitionists who wished to end human bondage, free blacks, and the Irish served as targets for the rowdies, who were often unemployed, underemployed, or on the brink of poverty. Sometimes skilled Protestant workers fought with unskilled Catholics, and both persecuted free blacks. Labor troubles preceded the burning of a black church and other violence perpetrated on abolitionists and African Americans in New York City in 1834. In 1835 and 1839 economic hardship led to attacks on blacks in Washington and Cincinnati, respectively. In Philadelphia five major riots against blacks broke out between 1829 and 1850, and a notorious struggle in 1844 between Protestant and Catholic workers continued for four days in the streets of the Kensington section of the city.

The Kensington riot occurred not only because of economic discontent but also because Protestant Americans were incensed that school authorities had succumbed to Catholic pressures to allow the Catholic Bible to be read in the public schools, along with the King James version. Before three thousand troops entered the fray to restore order, the rioters had burned more than thirty buildings and had injured or killed at least fourteen people. In spite of the militia's arrival, Protestants set fire to two Catholic churches and several other buildings. The Kensington riot, and many others as well, happened during a spell when a combination of heat, humidity, and stench frustrated people of the lower classes beyond endurance. In "the city of brotherly love," however, it took more than the weather to incite such aggression. Problems during the Jacksonian era were so severe that one historian has observed, "By any measure, the period from 1835 to 1850 was the most violent in Philadelphia's history."

Anti-Catholicism

Important as economics and race were in the development of American hostility toward minorities, the outstanding ingredient in pre-Civil War nativism was the vehement fear and dislike of Catholicism, and particularly the Irish Catholics. Boston erupted with numerous anti-Catholic demonstrations in 1823, 1826, and 1829, and local roughnecks burned the Ursuline Convent at Charlestown, Massachusetts, in 1834. The convent stood as a symbol of growing Irish competition for jobs and was a little-understood institution in the community. Rumors of dungeons and torture chambers there inflamed the prejudices of the local rowdies, who vandalized the building. The general public disavowed the violence, the governor offered a $500 reward for evidence leading to the capture of the perpetrators, and thirteen men were arrested. Of these, eight were tried but only one was convicted; he received a life sentence. It is difficult to know how much this particular incident reflected local problems, but it certainly was not an isolated example of hostility toward Catholics.

There were several other indications of anti-Catholicism during the pre-Civil War decades. The Protestant Association in New York City leveled a continuous stream of attacks at Irish Catholics, and the *New York Protestant* printed these items regularly. In 1834 Samuel F. B. Morse, now famous as the inventor of the telegraph, published a series of letters entitled *A Foreign Conspiracy against the Liberties of the United States*. In it he denounced an Austrian Catholic missionary society for sending men and money to America. The next year the Reverend Lyman Beecher followed Morse's epistle with *A Plea for the West,* in which he accused the Pope of plotting to dominate the American West by sending hordes of Catholic settlers there. Although others may not have been as specific in their charges as were Morse and Beecher, the truth was that most American Protestants believed Catholicism to be incompatible with American ways. The Irish are "our natural enemies," claimed one editor, "not because they are Irishmen, but because they are the truest guards of the Papacy." Prominent Catholics in the United States did little to assuage existing fears; instead, their actions encouraged Protestant hysteria.

Archbishop John Hughes, the leading spokesman for the American Roman Catholic Church in the 1840s and 1850s, tried unsuccessfully to obtain state aid in New York for Catholic parochial schools. Similar efforts by Catholics in Detroit also failed. Catholics objected particularly to the use of the Protestant Bible in the public schools, but they also wanted to isolate their children from non-Catholic influences. Of course, in a nation of true religious freedom, no child would have been required to engage in religious practices in the public schools that their parents found objectionable, but the church's objections merely confirmed the views of American Protestants that Catholics were subversive elements in society. After all, Protestants regarded the public schools as one of the best ways of assimilating foreign children into the dominant culture. The *Minnesota Chronicle and Register* observed in 1850 that the common school

> takes the child of the exile of Hungary, of the half-starved emigrant from the Emerald Isle, and of the hardy Norwegian, and places them on the same bench with the offspring of those whose ancestors' bones bleached upon the fields of Lexington.... As the child of the foreigner plays with his school fellow, he learns to whistle "Yankee Doodle" and sing "Hail Columbia," and before he leaves the

school-desk for the plough, the anvil or the trowel, he is as sturdy a little republican as can be found in the land.

But the Roman Catholics did not want that kind of assimilation. Archbishop Hughes frightened American Protestants when he announced: "Everyone should know that we have for our mission to convert the world." This was exactly what the Protestants in the United States feared; it squarely opposed their beliefs that it was the *American* mission to convert others to the American way of life. The 1853 annual report of the Boston School Committee summarized the Protestant argument: "The ends of government...require that religious instruction should be given in our Public Schools.... The whole character of the instruction given must be such and such only as will tend to make the pupils thereof American citizens, and ardent supporters of American institutions."

Catholic school children who attended public schools were often victimized by Yankee schoolmarms who incorporated society's views into their instruction. Boston's Cardinal O'Connell later recalled how those "good women" barely concealed the bitter antipathy they "felt toward those of us who had Catholic faith and Irish names. For any slight pretext we were severely punished. We were made to feel the slur against our faith and race, which hurt us to our very hearts' core." It did not help Irish Catholics either that in a reform era they opposed temperance, abolition, and public education while they supported slavery and the Fugitive Slave Law.

Political Nativism

Battles over the public schools were not the only signs of nativism. Anti-Catholic feeling had been manifesting itself in violence for decades before the Civil War. No doubt these episodes of public disturbances were partly triggered by books, newspapers, and pamphlets warning of the Catholic "menace" to American civilization; such accusations not only flourished from the 1830s through the 1850s but also surfaced once again at the end of the nineteenth century and would reappear more strikingly for a third time during the 1920s. On each occasion the anti-Catholic paranoia would be reflected in the political arena.

The Know-Nothing Party of the 1850s was the largest of a variety of local nativist groups emerging during the 1840s and 1850s. Nativism in American politics was not unusual; hostility toward Germans, Quakers, Scots-Irish, and other ethnic minorities had cropped up during the colonial era, and hostility toward foreigners had resulted in the passage of the Alien and Sedition Acts in 1798. But a nativist political party was a product of the 1840s. The acquisition of western lands, the forceful removal of the Indians beyond the frontier, and the organization of Nebraska territory in 1854 exacerbated the anxieties of those people who feared Catholic encroachment. "Everyone knew," the authors of one American history observed with tongue in cheek, "that the Pope had his eye on America, for who would dwell in decaying Rome when he could live in the Mississippi Valley?" Obviously the United States had to protect itself. Some of the bigots joined openly hostile organizations, but many preferred the secretive Know-Nothings. (When members were questioned about the goals of their party they would respond, "I know nothing.")

Under the banner of anti-Catholicism and antiforeignism the Know-Nothings achieved some success at the polls, especially in the elections of 1854 and 1855, when they won impressive victories in a few Northeastern states and sent sixty-four men to Congress. By the election of 1856, however, many of the party's members had already switched to the new Republican Party, but those who remained loyal gave their votes to the American Party, as the Know-Nothings then called themselves. The party collapsed after 1856 because southerners had gained control of the organization, passed proslavery resolutions, and failed to give anti-Catholicism the prominence many northern Protestants thought it deserved. As a result the political aspects of northern bigotry achieved little, and the Know-Nothing movement disintegrated in the late 1850s, when the slavery controversy overshadowed American concerns about immigration and Catholicism. Besides, the Crimean War between the Russians and the British improved economic conditions in Europe, and the conflict over slavery in the United States resulted in lower immigration totals after 1854. During the Civil War, immigration fell still farther, and anxiety about immigration lessened considerably.

For a time in the 1860s, the war distracted people, so that fear of immigrants and hatred of different ethnic groups waned somewhat. In fact, some citizens welcomed the newcomers' arrival. Industrialists, railroad builders, and other businessmen needed cheap immigrant labor for the nation's factories, mines, and fields. At the same time, more people meant higher sales of goods and services and a stimulus to the national economy. Others besides business people also welcomed Europeans into their communities. The nineteenth-century ideas of growth and progress meant that state, territorial, and even city governments worked to attract people. More than a score of states, including Michigan and Wisconsin, opened offices in New York to lure immigrants west as they disembarked from their ships. Finally, Americans believed that their nation offered a home to the politically and religiously oppressed and that America had a unique world mission to aid those seeking asylum.

5

Burgeoning Industrialism and a Massive Movement of Peoples

(1880s–1930s)

Industrial Expansion

The industrial expansion of the mid-nineteenth century stimulated further economic growth in subsequent decades. Although the Panic of 1873, the recession in the middle of the 1880s, and the terrible depression in 1893–94 punctuated the advances, the aggregate accomplishments are impressive. New industries such as oil refining and iron and steel, new processes of economic organization such as trusts, and new overseas markets all led to greater manpower needs. Whereas in 1860 total investment in United States industry approximated $1 billion, by 1890 it had increased to $6.5 billion, and by 1910 the figure exceeded $13 billion. National wealth practically doubled in the first decade of the twentieth century, and the worth of foreign investments multiplied fivefold between 1897 and 1914. The nonagricultural work force jumped 300 percent between 1860 and 1890, when the numbers employed in factories, mines, construction, and transportation topped eight million. Twenty years later, in 1910, these same industries recorded almost fifteen million employees. The native birthrate and the movement from farms to cities simply could not provide the labor demanded by this fantastic economic explosion.

Besides labor, the United States needed capital, technological developments, and natural resources before embarking on further industrial expansion. The first, capital, came from wealthy Europeans, especially the English, who invested heavily in railroads and mining. The United States government assisted the railroads with loans and generous grants of land. The Homestead Act of 1862 enabled farmers to get free land, and other federal laws and policies permitted timber and mining interests to purchase valuable tracts at bargain prices. Federal concern showed itself further in the passage of protective tariffs and banking laws to help many businesses. The government also refrained from intervening in contractual relations between employers and employees or demanding safety and sanitary precautions. State and local authorities provided tax abatement for industry while minimizing their efforts to regulate working conditions.

The lack of governmental support for the laborers maximized profits and allowed the increased accumulation of capital. Recessions during the 1870s and 1890s and the Great Depression of the 1930s hurt business, but generally profits remained high enough to feed the growing industrial plants and generate new capital. A good example is the Pullman Company. For the year ending July 31, 1893, wages paid out came to $7,223,719, whereas dividends to stockholders totaled $2,520,000. Because of a severe depression that ensued the following year, sales and total income fell, and wages were reduced to $4,471,701. Nevertheless, the business slump did not affect the dividends, which increased to $2,880,000.

Industrial society also benefited from an abundance of natural resources. The Ohio, Mississippi, and Missouri rivers spanned much of the continent and connected with the Gulf of Mexico and the Atlantic coast. Excellent harbors in New York City, Philadelphia, Boston, Baltimore, New Orleans, Charleston, Tampa, San Diego, San Francisco, and Seattle further stimulated manufacturing and commerce. The fertile lands of the southern states yielded cotton for the textile industry, while farm production increased sufficiently to feed the industrial and urban populations and to generate surplus food for export. The rich coal and iron-ore lands were crucial to the growth of the steel industry, and the western states contained enormous deposits of gold, lead, silver, copper, and other valuable minerals. As new materials were required in the twentieth century, the nation found them. Oil production, so important for economic development in the twentieth century, first occurred in Pennsylvania, but drillers later discovered larger deposits in Texas and Oklahoma and off the shores of California and the Gulf Coast states.

In technology the United States also rose to the occasion, at first borrowing heavily from abroad and then producing its own practical scientists. A nation that counted such people as Thomas Edison, Alexander Graham Bell, and Henry Ford among its inventors had no shortage of creative ideas. The incandescent light, the telephone, the automobile, and similar developments propelled industrial society. Technology transformed farming, too. Machines such as thrashers, reapers, and cotton and corn pickers, along with irrigation, new strains of seeds, various fertilizers, and ways of controlling crop and animal diseases, all stimulated agricultural production.

An energetic labor force proved as important as capital, resources, and technology to the industrial transformation. Many white farmers moved to the cities in search of work, but there were not enough of them. A few businessmen suggested hiring blacks, but most employers preferred to use whites, at least until World War I. Fortunately, the United States had another source of labor: between 1880 and the onset of a worldwide depression in 1930, more than twenty-five million immigrants came to the United States (see Table 5.1).

TABLE 5.1.   Immigration to the
United States by Decade, 1881–1930

1881–1890	5,246,613
1891–1900	3,687,564
1901–1910	8,795,386
1911–1920	5,735,811
1921–1930	4,107,209

In so doing these people made a vital contribution to the building of our modern society.

Uprooted Peoples

The process of industrial expansion occurred throughout the world. In the 1890s the Russian economy was perhaps the fastest growing one in Europe, but other nations on that continent and in Latin America, Asia, and Africa also experienced the impact of industrial upheaval. Innumerable technological changes affected millions of people. Industrialism uprooted many from their traditional ways of life while presenting heretofore unanticipated opportunities for movement. At best, the changes offered possibilities for a more prosperous and secure life; at worst, they meant exchanging agricultural desperation for industrial drudgery.

Europeans and Asians went to the United States, Africa, and Latin America; freed slaves and their children moved north; and American Indians, after near annihilation, clung to reservations in the north central and southwestern states. Many of these population movements overlapped. Europeans and Asians arrived in the United States throughout the nineteenth century, but their numbers soared dramatically between the 1880s and World War I, and then again in the 1920s. Blacks tried to fend for themselves in the South during the late nineteenth century, but several hundred thousand moved north during the Progressive era (1900–1917)—and continued to migrate in the 1920s—primarily to fill a labor shortage created by the curtailment of European immigration during World War I. Starting in the twentieth century, hundreds of thousands of Mexicans crossed the American border in search of a better way of life.

A diversity of peoples came to, or moved through, the United States seeking economic opportunity. The state immigration bureaus eagerly recruited Europeans, and railroads sent agents to Europe and the American port cities

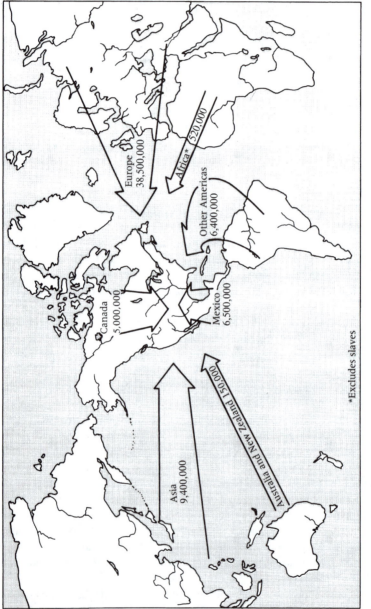

Immigration to the United States, 1820–2007 (Excludes slaves and undocumented immigrants)

Europe
38,500,000

Africa* 520,000

Other Americas
6,400,000

Canada
5,000,000

Mexico
6,500,000

Asia
9,400,000

Australia and New Zealand 150,000

*Excludes slaves

Immigrants on the deck of an Atlantic liner in 1906. (Library of Congress)

with promises to people of free or cheap land and passage. Steamship lines, hungry for the profits of the passenger trade, actively sought immigrants to sail on their ships. During the Civil War Congress enacted a contract labor law that enabled agents to scour the European countryside for workers, but in 1885 it repealed this law. Yet illegal labor agents operated for many years in Europe.

Many northern and western Europeans succumbed to the inducements, but by the end of the nineteenth century the sources of labor changed as the bulk of the population movement shifted to southern and eastern Europe, while a revolution in Mexico led to an influx of people fleeing that troubled society. The most numerous of the twentieth-century arrivals in the United States included more than three million Italians, three million or more of the various Slavic peoples, two million eastern European Jews, more than one million Mexicans, and hundreds of thousands of Asians, Hungarians, Greeks, Armenians, Syrians, Turks, Christian Arabs, Bulgarians, Latin Americans, Portuguese, and French Canadians.

An exact count of the immigrants from that era is impossible. Slavic groups from the German and Austro-Hungarian empires were frequently mislabeled by American immigration inspectors as Germans, Austrians, or Hungarians,

Immigrants lining up to be processed at Ellis Island, about 1900. (United States Immigration and Naturalization Service)

although they might have been Serbs, Slovenes, Croatians, Czechs, or Montenegrins. (Europeans also had problems with identification. One Slovak writer complained in 1915: "The Magyars say we are Magyars, the Czechs that we are Czechs. But we are Slovaks!") Italians who lived in the Austrian Tyrol were recorded as Austrians, whereas Poles were not listed separately between 1899 and 1918. Mexicans who arrived in the Southwest by land were not counted until 1907, and even after that hundreds of thousands merely crossed the border at places other than official immigration stations. Jews came in classified only according to nation of birth, so one can only estimate their numbers from Russia, Austria, and Rumania. Therefore, figures used in immigration statistics and census tracts only approximate the numbers of different peoples who arrived in the United States.

Immigrant Settlement

The patterns of settlement remained similar to those of the mid-nineteenth century. The Middle Atlantic region housed more newcomers than any other section. New York City continued to be the nation's premier port for immigration, and the city's population swelled. In 1930, some 75 percent of New Yorkers consisted of foreigners and their children. Italians and eastern European Jews predominated, but enclaves of almost every other ethnic group, ranging from Arabs to Yugoslavs, lived there. The city's overflow population gravitated

A newly arrived immigrant, about 1900. (National Archives)

toward Connecticut and New Jersey factories and Pennsylvania manufacturing
and mining communities. The Slavs in particular found that the Pennsylvania
mines provided the best paying unskilled jobs, and many of them went to the
Pittsburgh area. Buffalo, a port on the Great Lakes connected to New York City
via railroad, as well as the Hudson River and the Erie Canal, received many
Poles and Italians. It also served as one of the gateways to the Midwest, where
Chicago attracted just about everyone.

A Lake Michigan port, the nation's railroad hub, a center for the grain and
lumber trades, livestock processing, and meat packing, and the home of breweries and iron and steel mills and the Midwestern garment and financial center,
Chicago almost always needed labor. Successive waves of foreigners and
blacks filled its needs. By 1900 those of German stock constituted 35 percent
of the city's population; Irish, 17 percent; and Scandinavians, 14 percent. As

the century progressed, an extraordinarily diverse number of peoples found their way to the "Windy City." In the 1920s Chicago included the largest colonies of Scandinavians, Persians, Poles, Czechs, Serbo-Croatians, and Lithuanians in the nation; it ranked second in numbers of Germans, Greeks, Slovaks, Jews, and African Americans.

Other midwestern cities also attracted migrants from Europe and the American South. Detroit, Cleveland, and Milwaukee proved particularly attractive to Slavs from the Austro-Hungarian Empire. Cleveland's prosperity rested on its Lake Erie location and on its iron and steel foundries, blast furnaces, and rolling mills. In 1906 it was estimated that one of every five Cleveland inhabitants was German or Jewish, and one of every six of Slavic background. Detroit, the nation's most important point of entry for both English- and French-speaking

Eastern European immigrants in the marketplace of Stevens Point, Wisconsin, about the turn of the twentieth century. Although most eastern Europeans migrated to the industrial centers of the Northeast and Midwest, they could be found in smaller towns like Stevens Point as well. (State Historical Society of Wisconsin)

Canadians, also claimed a polyglot population. In the mid-nineteenth century the city's early settlers mingled with French Canadians, Germans, and Irish, but by the 1890s eastern European Jews and Poles started coming. Within the next few decades Detroit witnessed the growth of black, Rumanian, Greek, Armenian, Lebanese, Bulgarian, and Macedonian colonies. Milwaukee, Omaha, Duluth, and Minneapolis-St. Paul grew originally as centers for Germans and Scandinavians, but after the 1880s immigrants from southern and eastern Europe settled there. The "Head of the Lakes" region in northern Minnesota, Wisconsin, and Michigan housed the largest concentration of Finns anywhere in the world outside of Finland.

The South was even less hospitable to the new immigrants than it had been to the old, but foreign-born workers and their enclaves appeared throughout that region. New Orleans remained an ethnically diverse city, and the state of Florida had contingents of Cubans, Spaniards, Greeks, and Hungarians. Prior to 1905 Florida had even sought people of Italian, Chinese, and Japanese descent because of a desperate labor shortage. There were also Italian agricultural colonies, as in the sugar cane fields of Louisiana, and scattered pockets of foreigners in cities such as Atlanta, Richmond, and Memphis.

The New Immigrants

The Italians were the most numerous of the new immigrants. More than three million of them arrived in the United States between the 1880s and 1930s; about one-third, however, returned to Europe. Mostly poverty-stricken people from southern Italy, more than 75 percent settled in New York, Pennsylvania, and New England, but significant numbers went to every section of the country, with colonies in Detroit, Chicago, New Orleans, Denver, and San Francisco. Many of the Italian men came for temporary work and then returned home during the slack season. From 1908 to 1916 more than one million Italians went back to Italy, but World War I and the immigration restriction legislation of the 1920s halted their commuting.

Italian peasants left southern Italy to seek a better life in the United States. Their reasons for leaving their homeland varied. Poverty gripped their land, and between 1884 and 1887 cholera epidemics killed more than 55,000 people, while frightening tens of thousands of others. Beginning in the late 1880s increased citrus production in California and Florida cut American imports of southern Italian lemons and oranges, ruining the export market of farmers there, and France put a high tariff on imported wines that also hurt the Italian economy. Conditions became so bad that some peasants dwelled in hovels of wattle and daub or straw. Those Italians who had gone to America told friends in the old country of plentiful jobs and high wages. Such news from the United States, received at a time when conditions were so bad, swept through southern Italy. "Once this movement got under way," notes one historian, "it seemed like an avalanche to gather momentum and carry all before it until whole districts had been depopulated of their males." Sometimes entire villages left together and, once in the United States, settled in the same neighborhoods. Calabrese, Venetians, Abruzzese, and Sicilians isolated themselves in separate areas. Americans may have lumped them together as Italians, but their group identification did not extend beyond their village associations. In America they discovered that they were all regarded as one people!

Once in the United States, the Italians worked in construction and heavy industry, on the railroads, and in the mining camps. Soon they gained a near monopoly of the fruit and vegetable business in New York City and New Orleans and engaged in truck farming on both East and West coasts. In California they often prospered more than in other sections, and many of their vineyards and fruit orchards became quite successful. Despite the fact that some prospered, most worked as common laborers.

Italian street market in New York City, about the time of World War I. (New York Community Service Society)

Two million Jews constituted the second largest body of immigrants arriving in the late nineteenth and early twentieth centuries; like the Italians, they could be found throughout the country. Also like the Italians, their largest contingent (over 75 percent) remained in New York City, New Jersey, Pennsylvania, and New England. The Jews made up at least half of all Russians entering the United States between 1890 and 1914, and perhaps 90 percent in some of those years. Ninety-five percent of the emigration from Poland in 1920 was Jewish. Victimized by the industrial transformation, the rise of Pan-Slavism with its nationalistic emphasis, and the rampant pogroms in Russia, Poland, and Rumania, Jews cherished a desire to fit in the United States.

For centuries Jews had been a minority group in other nations, and this experience helped them to settle in this country. Although most of the men were skilled or semiskilled laborers, their meager earnings in the United States still kept them near the brink of poverty. Jews worked in New York City's garment district, as well as in cigar and toy factories and printing plants in a number of cities, but many prospered as retail tradesmen, accountants, lawyers, and doctors. In the United States they pioneered in the manufacturing of ready-to-wear clothing; they started the film industry in New York City and later in Hollywood; and they achieved prominence as major department store merchants in New York City, Philadelphia, Chicago, Atlanta, Dallas, Birmingham, and elsewhere. Because so many Jews have become prosperous since the end of World War II, it is often overlooked that a majority of their forebears arrived impoverished. Only a few made spectacular successes, and it took two to three generations before most Jewish families found a niche in the middle class. As a result of the massive Jewish movement from Russia, Austrian Galicia, and Rumania, American Jewish life changed from a predominantly German to an overwhelmingly eastern European style.

The third major group arriving in the twentieth century, the Slavs, settled mainly in an area stretching from Connecticut to Minnesota (see Table 5.2). The term *Slav* includes Poles, Bohemians (Czechs), Ruthenians (Ukrainians), Slovaks, Russians (but not Russian Jews), Bulgarians, Serbs, Croatians, Montenegrins, and Slovenians. The western division of Slavs includes Bohemians, Slovaks, and Poles; the eastern and southern Slavs comprise the Russians, Ruthenians, Bulgarians, Serbs, Croatians, and Slovenians. The last three, along with the Montenegrins, are also the groups that live in the area that used to be Yugoslavia.

The United States possibly received more than four million Slavs, a figure that is an uncertain estimate at best. One difficulty in calculating the number of Slavs in the United States is the fact that so many of them returned to Europe. Some estimates indicate that 50 percent or more of the Slovaks, Slovenes, and Croatians went home, and figures for the other Slavs are problematic. The

Czechs, who came with their families and included a goodly proportion of professional and skilled workers, artisans, and small businessmen, were more likely to remain in America than the Serbs or Poles, who came singly, intent on saving their money before returning home to buy property and settle down. The outbreak of World War I in 1914 altered the future of hundreds of thousands who had originally planned on returning to Europe.

One cannot discuss the Slavic immigrants without indicating the significant cultural, linguistic, historical, political, and religious differences among them.

TABLE 5.2.   Slavic Groups

	Religion	Language	Alphabet	Major Regions of Settlement in the United States (1880–1930)
Poles	Roman Catholic	Polish	Latin	Chicago, New York, Detroit, Milwaukee, Pittsburgh, Buffalo, Cleveland
Slovenes	Roman Catholic	Slovenian	Latin	Cleveland, Milwaukee, Chicago, Joliet (Ill.), Pennsylvania
Croatians	Roman Catholic	Serbo-Croatian	Latin	Chicago, Pittsburgh (New York City after 1945)
Serbs	Serbian Orthodox	Serbo-Croatian	Cyrillic	Chicago and Detroit
Montenegrins	Serbian Orthodox	Serbo-Croatian	Cyrillic	
Macedonians	[a]	[b]	Cyrillic	Detroit
Russians	Russian Orthodox	Russian	Cyrillic	New York and Pennsylvania
Bulgarians	Bulgarian Orthodox	Bulgarian	Cyrillic	Detroit
Slovaks	Roman Catholic	Slovak	Latin	Pennsylvania (mostly Pittsburgh area); also Illinois, New York, Ohio, New Jersey, Michigan, Wisconsin, Minnesota
Czechs	Roman Catholic	Czech	Latin	Chicago, Cleveland, New York City
Ukrainians	Ukrainian Orthodox	Ukrainian	Cyrillic	Pennsylvania, New England, Chicago

[a] Macedonians were from Yugoslavia, Greece, and Bulgaria. They belonged to the Serbian Orthodox, Greek Orthodox, or Bulgarian Orthodox church, depending on the country in which they lived.

[b] In Yugoslavia they spoke Serbo-Croatian; in Greece, Greek; in Bulgaria, Bulgarian. In the recent past efforts have been made to use the Macedonian language.

Although belonging to the Indo-European peoples, each group had a different cultural and historical experience. The Poles, Croatians, Slovenes, and Slovaks were Roman Catholics; the Serbs and Montenegrins, Greek Orthodox; the Russians, Russian Orthodox; and the Czechs were divided between Roman Catholics and atheistic freethinkers. The groups came from different, although often contiguous, regions of Europe and frequently regarded one another with suspicion. The Poles and Czechs started going to the United States in the nineteenth century and had already established some colonies before the Civil War. The Croatians from Dalmatia also had some settlements in America as early as 1820. They pioneered in the oyster industry in New Orleans and southern Louisiana and in the tuna industry in San Pedro, which is about twenty-five miles south of Los Angeles, California. Most of the Dalmatians in California live in this area and work in fishing or related industries. One of the characteristics of many of the Slavic peoples, and of the eastern and southern Europeans in general, except for the Jews, is that a large percentage regarded the United States as a place to earn some money before returning to their native countries and settling down. The Jews, who really had no homeland to return to, did not think in these terms, and only about 5 percent of them went back to Europe. The non-Jews, though, roughly 70 to 80 percent of whom came over as single men, thought otherwise, and something like 60 to 80 percent, depending on the individual ethnic group, returned to their homes after a stay in the United States.

Hungarians, Greeks, Lithuanians, Dutch, Portuguese, Armenians, Middle Easterners, and French Canadians also came in large numbers. Almost all came for greater economic opportunities, but some, like the Armenians, sought to escape annihilation.

The Hungarians may be cited as among those people who planned to stay only temporarily in the United States. Between the 1880s and World War I, 1.8 million of them arrived. Nonetheless, so many had already returned home that the 1910 census recorded only five hundred thousand or so in the country. The records for the years 1908–14 indicate, however, that 64 percent of those who immigrated to the United States from Hungary subsequently returned. Hungarian enclaves could be found in New York City, as well as in the mine and steel furnace regions of Ohio, Pennsylvania, New Jersey, and West Virginia. The cities of Cleveland, Chicago, and Detroit, which housed numerous colonies of Slavs, also developed sizable Hungarian populations. Before leaving Europe Hungarian immigrants were for the most part members of the peasant class and had been quite devoted to their church. Most of those in Cleveland were Roman Catholic, but other Hungarians could be found of the Reformed, Lutheran, Baptist, and Greek Orthodox faiths.

The Greeks also came to the United States with the intention of "making a killing" and returning home. As with so many others, however, they changed their minds once they arrived, or else circumstances altered their plans, and less than half made it back to their homeland. The Greek exodus, about 10 percent of that nation's population between 1900 and 1925, occurred primarily because of the curtailment of the overseas currant market in the 1890s and the 1907 failure of that crop. Families scraped together whatever they could to send their young men to America to make some money that could be sent home. The men came alone with "their families' pool of silver coins sewed to their rough goatskin underclothing." Tied to their lapels were identification tags indicating their destination in America and the name of the relative or labor agent who would receive them and help them find work. The Greek immigrants, like so many others, looked outlandish with their tags, carrying bundles or straw suitcases; once in America, however, they worked with the fervor of zealots.

Most of the five hundred thousand or so Greeks went to New England, Chicago, New York City, Detroit, and San Francisco, but they could also be found in Milwaukee, Atlanta, and Salt Lake City, in the mines and mills of Colorado and Wyoming, in the copper pits of Butte, Montana, and on the railroad track gangs in the Far West. Some even cleared sagebrush in Idaho, and others prospered as sheep men in the Rocky Mountain area. The Greeks despised working for others and, as soon as they could, sought to establish their own businesses. By the 1920s they owned more than 2,000 restaurants, 150 grocery stores, several hundred shoe-shining and hat-cleaning parlors, and numerous flower shops. They dominated the manufacturing and sale of candy in Chicago and were well represented in the sweets business throughout America. Whenever they could they also purchased buildings and properties. During the 1920s about 50 percent of the Greeks in Atlanta owned their own businesses, even though many had been in the United States less than five years. Ninety-five percent of the Greek immigration to the United States originally consisted of men; those who wished to remain in America often went home to choose a bride. The immigration restriction acts of the 1920s made this more difficult, so the custom of "picture brides" developed. These were young women who had never seen their husbands before they disembarked in the continental United States. The depression of the 1930s affected the Greeks in the United States like everyone else, and many returned to their homeland during that decade.

The Lithuanians, Portuguese, and Dutch are among the other European groups who participated in the massive movement from Europe to the United States. The Lithuanians, often mislabeled as Russians, Poles, and Germans, sent hundreds of thousands of people to America between 1870 and 1930, but somehow the census bureau and Lithuanian spokesmen reached outrageously different figures. In 1918 Lithuanians estimated that at least 750,000 of their countrymen were in the United States, but the 1920 census takers found only 135,000 of them! In the 1930s Chicago housed a colony of about 100,000 Lithuanians, probably the largest concentration in this country. Most of them were of the Roman Catholic faith. Originally blue-collar workers, their respect for education and ambition to advance in society stimulated their children to seek other endeavors.

The Dutch, famed for their settlement of colonial New Amsterdam, now New York City, came in much greater numbers during the industrial era than they had in the colonial period. On the eve of the twentieth century there were over one hundred thousand Hollanders in the United States. Thirty thousand lived in Michigan; Illinois housed about twenty-two thousand; and Iowa, ten thousand. In the hundred years between 1820 and 1920 more than three hundred thousand Dutch immigrants reached the United States, but as stern Calvinists who settled for the most part in farming communities away from urban centers, they attracted considerably less attention than those who engaged in industrial pursuits.

Fewer than one hundred thousand Portuguese, 98 percent of whom were Roman Catholic, came to the United States, but those who did gravitated mainly to New Bedford, Massachusetts, where the whaling fleets are docked, and to Rhode Island and California. In fact, about one-third actually settled in the Golden State. Their focal point originally was the San Francisco Bay area, but they spread out from there to the Sacramento and San Joaquin valleys, and a number planted roots in Oakland. Many of those who were not seafarers became successful farmers. By 1950 most of those of Portuguese stock were in the rural areas of the state, and in southern California they ranked second only to the Dutch in the dairy industry. One Portuguese immigrant, J. B. Avida, a native of the Azores, arrived in the United States sorely missing one of his favorite vegetables. In 1888 he bought acreage near Merced, California, and started cultivating it. His crop grew well, and he sold it to restaurants wherever he could. The San Francisco restaurants served it first, but then it made an impact throughout America. Soon Avida was known as the "Father of the Sweet Potato Industry." Another group of Portuguese immigrants came from Portugal's colony, the Cape Verde Islands, which is located off the northwest coast of Africa. The exact number of Cape Verdeans in the United States is not known because they were counted as Portuguese or missed by American immigration authorities. Cape Verdeans are dark-skinned people of mixed ancestry, chiefly Portuguese and African. Mostly male, they settled in southeastern Massachusetts and northeastern Rhode Island, where the men found employment as sailors, and both sexes worked in the cranberry bogs.

Like the Portuguese, the Armenians also numbered fewer than one hundred thousand immigrants and, also like them, settled in Massachusetts and California.

But there the similarities end. Armenians, who also found homes in New York, Pennsylvania, Illinois, Wisconsin, and Michigan, were mostly peasants and unskilled laborers, and they escaped not only from poverty but also from the brutalities of the Turks, who massacred them the way whites slaughtered bison on the western plains in the United States. Armenians found work in New England textile mills and shoe factories, in the Pennsylvania foundries, and on the farms or in the packing houses, canneries, or cement works of California. In 1915 more than eight thousand Armenians lived in Fresno, California.

Often overlooked among those who chose to come to the United States are the approximately 450,000 Middle Easterners, mostly from Syria and Lebanon, but also from Yemen, Iraq, Arab Palestine, and other sections of the region. Over 125,000 were Lebanese Maronites (affiliated with the Roman Catholic Church); there were also 100,000 Greek Orthodox, 50,000 Melkites (a combination of Roman Catholic and Greek Orthodox), 25,000 Moslems, 10,000 Protestants, and 140,000 unaffiliated or members of smaller Christian sects. Turkish persecution of Syrians had led to their exodus from the Middle East. Some arrived as early as the middle of the nineteenth century, but the majority came after the 1890s. They formed colonies in New England, New York, Pennsylvania, Michigan, and Ohio, making every effort to blend with the American churches of their respective sects. As Christians in the Ottoman Empire, they owed no allegiance to a secular state, region, or culture, and they were neither Arabs nor Turks, neither Asians nor Assyrians. They were usually shopkeeping and lower-middle-class Semitic Christians influenced by economic difficulties and persecution to seek a better life in the United States. Once here, they obtained whatever work they could but made every effort to improve their situations. They disliked working for others and started their own businesses as soon as they could. Some became peddlers, others merchants; some owned grocery stores; and a number owned and operated large trucking, clothing, amusement, and food enterprises. Many adopted American- or French-sounding names and attended local American churches.

French Canadians, or Franco-Americans as they prefer to be called, are associated with a particular region in the United States, even though they established settlements in Illinois, Wisconsin, Louisiana, and New York. Nonetheless, one thinks of them in connection with New England, where over a quarter of a million were firmly entrenched by 1900, mostly in textile and industrial towns. The French Canadians left economically distressed Quebec because agriculture presented such a dismal future and because of the comparatively high wages available in the United States; however, once in America, they worked for sums that others disdained. The French Canadians were of the Roman Catholic faith, and only the Irish, among ethnic groups, outnumbered them in New England.

Ranching

Not all of the people pouring into the United States during the late nineteenth and early twentieth centuries came to take industrial jobs or to live in its sprawling cities. Many headed west, seeking work on the farms and ranches there. The almost limitless Plains had plenty of grass for either sheep or cattle, and even much of the arid region beyond the Rockies could sustain large herds. Little ranching occurred in the West until after the Civil War, for until then the Indians and buffalo dominated the Plains region, and the railroads had not extended their tracks far enough to enable cattle grazers to ship their animals to Eastern markets. By the 1870s Indian wars, destruction of the buffalo herds, and construction of the first transcontinental railroads changed these circumstances. With most buffalo gone, cowboys drove massive cattle herds north from the Texas Plains to regions as far as Wyoming and Montana. Most, however, stopped at places such as Dodge City and Abilene, the railhead towns in Kansas.

Although most Americans picture all cowboys as white, at least one-quarter of them were black, and possibly another quarter were Mexicans. A typical crew on the Long Drive that took cattle north to the railroad towns included eight men, three or four of whom might be African American or Mexican. The foreman was almost always white, but the wrangler and cook could be of any background—black, white, Mexican, or, as the cowboys said, "Portugee." As long as the individuals performed their tasks well, they got along with the others to some degree, but color determined the choice of leadership. One black cowboy, renowned as a rider, roper, and trail cook, lamented, "If it weren't for my damned old black face, I'd have been a boss long ago," and whites who knew him agreed. The life of the cowboys was often brutal—branding, roping, and castrating animals—and this carried over to personal relationships, as well. Frequently they fought and quarreled with one another because of their bigotry. "The way to handle Mexicans," one Texan asserted, "is to kick 'em in the ribs." Yet despite the prejudice and conflict, the men accomplished their goals, and they brought eastern and foreign investment to the West, encouraged railroad building, and provided limited markets for merchants and farmers who lived near the cattle trails and towns.

By the late 1880s overgrazing, low Eastern prices, and disastrous weather ended the open range and the long cattle drives. The sudden collapse began in the summer of 1886, one of the hottest and dustiest on record. Water holes dried up, grass turned brown, and by the end of July many streams had run low or had stopped running completely. Following that summer came the worst winter ever recorded on the northern ranges. Temperatures fell to as low as forty-five degrees below zero, and some animals froze to death. Thousands of cattle died—estimates range up to 75 percent of some of the herds. After that the demoralized ranchers also had to contend with homesteaders, sheep grazers, and barbed-wire enclosures as an increased population started demarcating property lines and erecting barriers. Although the old style of ranching would not be the same again, it nevertheless remained part of the western economy.

Sheep raising is less well known or celebrated than cattle ranching, but it was of almost equal importance to the western economy. Practiced from Montana and Idaho in the north through Colorado and south into Arizona, as well as west in Oregon and Nevada, this industry brought hatred and violence to the West for decades. Usually sheepmen hired Indian or Mexican herders, and most white Americans did not accept either group well. A foreign group, the Basques, many of whom originally went to California in search of gold, gravitated to the sheep regions after the Civil War, and later compatriots from Europe joined them. As a group, they were uniquely successful.

Sheepherding is a lonely endeavor. It requires great patience and fortitude and the ability to cope with intense boredom. The attraction that the occupation had for the Basques was probably the opportunity it afforded to be free, autonomous, and yet gainfully employed. In Europe the Basques had been fishermen, carpenters, shipbuilders, and masons, but not sheepmen. Yet in the United States they had no difficulty in adapting to the new life. Historically Basques have been independent and have maintained their separateness from other groups near whom they lived. The Basque country of the Iberian peninsula in Europe was divided and incorporated into France and Spain in the early part of the nineteenth century, but the Basques always favored their own culture and never quite fit in with either the French or the Spanish. The number of Basques in the United States probably never exceeded fifteen thousand, but this figure fails to reflect their importance as sheepmen in the mountain ranges and deserts of the West after the 1870s.

Farmers

Other European groups, such as the Germans, Scandinavians, and Czechs, migrated to farming regions in Kansas, Nebraska, the Dakotas, Texas, and, to a lesser extent, Colorado, Washington, Oregon, and California, where many prospered. Nevertheless, as general rule agriculture was a risky venture in much of the West. Unaware of this, in 1854 Congress opened both Kansas and Nebraska to settlement. This brought a rush of pioneers into those territories, but the continuing difficulties with the Indians, and the conflict between transplanted northerners and southerners, prevented widespread settlement. In 1862 Congress passed the famous Homestead Act, which offered a 160-acre plot of land to any adult who would live on it for five years and make minimal improvements on the property. Meant to help pioneer farmers, this legislation came at a time when the existing technology and agricultural techniques were inadequate for the challenges posed by the Plains environment. As a result, thousands of homesteaders moved west, only to encounter crop failures and other disasters. There is no question that eventually the Homestead Act helped to populate much of the West, but the first few decades of its operation brought misery and heartache to thousands.

It took new varieties of seeds, increased knowledge about agriculture in arid and semiarid regions, and the introduction of better equipment before farmers succeeded in much of the West. In 1862, the same year it passed the Homestead Act, Congress adopted the Morrill Land Grant Act, which provided federal land subsidies for each state and territory to use in creating or strengthening its engineering and agricultural colleges. The agricultural experiment stations, in conjunction with public agriculture schools, introduced drought-resistant varieties of seed, as well as dry farming and crop rotation. County and state agricultural societies and dozens of agricultural magazines and newsletters helped spread these new ideas and techniques. By the early twentieth century they were widely known.

Efforts by the major western railroads to attract customers for their land, generous federal land laws that made it cheap and easy for individuals to get western land, and a boom psychology among farmers produced several land rushes during the late nineteenth century. During the 1870s farmers occupied land in Minnesota, South Dakota, western Iowa, Nebraska, Kansas, and Texas. After the depression of the mid-1870s ended, a new current of optimism swept thousands more west. Several wetter-than-average years convinced would-be farmers that they could gain large profits if only they bought enough land. By the 1880s farmers had claimed or bought millions of more acres of federal and railroad lands in the Dakotas, western Nebraska, Kansas, and eastern Colorado, an area erroneously described as the "rainbelt of the Plains." A series of droughts in 1889, 1890, and 1894, followed by the depression of the mid-1890s and the return of the grasshopper swarms to the Plains in 1894, combined to push many farmers into bankruptcy. Tens of thousands fled east or moved into western towns to try other occupations. Others became tenant farmers on land they once had expected to own. For example, in 1900 Nebraska had nearly fifteen thousand fewer people and six thousand fewer farms than a decade earlier.

Although real obstacles slowed agricultural development in much of the West, farmers continued moving into the region until the Great Depression of the 1930s, and minority groups played an important role in western agriculture throughout the period. Even though many blacks had agricultural experience in the Southeast, relatively small numbers of them joined the surge west. Homesteading, at least for former slaves, was a new experience. In addition, court decisions and some legislation denied blacks equal access to the public lands open to whites. Still, some blacks did become western farmers. In fact, during the 1870s and 1880s substantial numbers of them migrated west into Kansas and Nebraska. Often called Exodusters, they met racial antagonism, as well as some property and voting restrictions, but these difficulties failed to halt their trek. For example, it has been estimated that between fifteen and twenty thousand black farmers settled in Kansas in the year 1880. Also, several entire black communities, such as the settlers at Nicodemus, Kansas, moved from the South to the West.

The Japanese

On the Pacific Coast the Chinese provided most of the stoop, or squat, labor in agriculture. A significant element in the population since the gold rush, most Chinese never earned enough money as miners or on the railroads to return to their native land. As a result many of these workers shifted to manufacturing jobs and agriculture. By the 1880s Chinese constituted about half of the farm laborers in California. However, in 1882 anti-Chinese feeling on the West Coast and elsewhere induced Congress to pass the Exclusion Act, which suspended Chinese immigration for ten years. It was made permanent in 1902. Because the Chinese did much of the state's menial labor, substitutes had to be found.

The growing demand for labor in the Far West and the need to replace the Chinese in the 1880s led to the influx and temporary acceptance of Japanese immigrants. Immigration from Japan to the United States, though, was unique in several regards. Unlike practically all other groups, who came solely to improve their own and their families' welfare, the Japanese exodus resulted in part from Japan's expansionist philosophy. A significant portion of that nation's ruling class perceived immigration as part of their imperial and colonial policies. Japanese rulers believed that they, along with the white race, had an aptitude for colonization, and they sought every opportunity to expand their interests abroad. Thus they encouraged surplus laborers to leave the country, believing that their departure would contribute to the planting of Japanese culture overseas and provide a market for Japan's exports. They also assumed that these laborers would enrich the nation's coffers by returning a part of their foreign earnings to relatives in Japan. In addition, the workingmen remaining at home would have less competition, thereby raising their chances for higher wages. As a result of these views and the opportunities available to individuals who left, large numbers of Japanese ventured to Korea, Taiwan, and the United States. Although some of these émigrés hoped to return to Japan, many took their families with them. Until 1890 fewer than one thousand Japanese had entered the United States in any single year. After that date their numbers increased gradually until 1898, when Hawaii was annexed to the United States. In the next five years more than sixty thousand Japanese moved from those islands to the mainland. Many of them had gone to Hawaii to work on sugar plantations and in canning plants; on the mainland most continued to do agricultural work, but others toiled on the railroads, in the mines, and as domestics. By the 1920s more than 120,000 people of Japanese ancestry lived in the United States.

Unlike the Chinese, whose center in California was San Francisco, the Japanese went mainly to the Los Angeles area. In California and elsewhere on the West Coast, they became prime factors in the raising and distribution of fruits and vegetables, eventually producing 99 percent of the celery and 95 percent of the strawberries in Los Angeles County. Many Japanese who settled in Oregon and Washington also engaged in truck farming and, like their compatriots in California, wanted to become independent entrepreneurs. To achieve their goals, they worked eleven to fourteen hours a day, almost starved themselves, and saved whatever they could to buy their own property. One immigrant recalled how difficult life was in the early 1900s: "In those days a stray jackrabbit meant a feast and a cow killed by a passing train was a Godsent banquet."

The Koreans

Until recently migrants from Korea have received little attention in American or ethnic history textbooks. Repressive conditions at home, where the Japanese imposed a harsh colonial policy in the late nineteenth and early twentieth centuries, forced Koreans to escape poverty and seek jobs elsewhere. At the beginning of the twentieth century the Hawaiian Sugar Planter's Association sent a representative to Korea to woo young men who sought opportunities elsewhere. His visit paid off handsomely, as between 1903 and 1905 about seven thousand Koreans went to Hawaii to work on the plantations. Others went to Mexico, but soon word got back to the homeland that Mexicans brutalized the newcomers. This news, combined with pressure from the Japanese on the Korean government to halt the exodus, slowed the flow of those still looking elsewhere for employment. The migration halted quickly when, as a concomitant to the 1907 "Gentlemen's Agreement" with Japan, laborers from Korea, then still a Japanese colony, were also excluded from the United States.

Like newcomers from other ethnic backgrounds, most of the Koreans who sought their fortunes elsewhere were young men. Like the Japanese, these men also sought "picture brides" to join them; together they formed family units. Some of the women were shocked to discover that their new husbands were much older than they had appeared in their pictures. Nonetheless, the women had committed themselves to marriage, and they went through with their bargains. Korean women, like those of many other ethnic groups, were expected not only to engage in traditional female chores at home but also to seek wage-based labor outside of it as well.

Korean families in the United States established the usual churches, organizations, and ethnic associations characteristic of minority communities. They included the Korean Women's Association, founded in 1908, and the New People's Association, which worked to rid the homeland of its Japanese conquerors. Because of existing prejudices in the United States, few educational or business opportunities were available to Koreans, whose opportunities for social mobility were significantly curtailed. Not until the 1950s did most Koreans begin to have opportunities generally available earlier only to Caucasians.

The Mexicans

While public attention focused on the antagonism toward Asians on the West Coast, in the early twentieth century Mexican immigrants began moving north into the United States. There were several reasons for this migration. First, in 1902 Congress passed the Newlands National Reclamation Act, which stimulated irrigated agriculture in the Southwest. The law set aside nearly all money that the federal government received from the sale of public land in sixteen western and southwestern states in a revolving fund for building and maintaining irrigation projects. Within a decade farms with newly irrigated fields offered jobs to thousands of unskilled workers. Irrigation aided cultivation in Texas, Arizona, and California and transformed the San Joaquin, Sacramento, and Imperial valleys into veritable Gardens of Eden. The number of irrigated acres more than doubled, from 1,004,233 in 1889 to 2,664,104 in 1909, and then increased to 4,219,040 in 1919. Cotton acreage in California's San Joaquin Valley jumped from 5,500 in 1919 to 172,400 in 1931. By 1929 California farms were producing between 300,000 and 500,000 caseloads of vegetables, fruits, and truck crops, almost 40 percent of the nation's total for these items. It was therefore fortunate for the Americans that the 1910 Mexican Revolution created a vast upheaval that sent as much as 10 percent of that nation's northern population to the United States. The number of farm laborers in the Golden State increased from 59,145 in 1890 to 196,812 in 1930, and Mexicans made up a majority of those workers in several areas of the state.

Official immigration figures list over seven hundred thousand Mexican arrivals between 1901 and 1930, but the totals were at least twice that number. There were no border guards before 1924 to prevent illegal entry, and before 1907 no one counted Mexicans who arrived by land. Like most other immigrants, these people came for jobs. In the early decades of the twentieth century El Paso, Texas, served as the major distributing point for Mexican immigrants, in some months processing more than five thousand people. Three major railroad lines passed through the city and facilitated the placement of the newcomers on farms, in mines and smelters, and on the railroads. Like the farms and mines, the railroads employed thousands of unskilled foreigners, who could be hired at lower wages than the American-born workers would accept. As a result the newest immigrants generally occupied the lowest rung on the economic ladder. On the western railroads a variety of foreigners had been employed as section hands on the track gangs, but within twenty years of the Mexican Revolution, as the figures in Table 5.3 show, Mexicans dominated the field.

The Mexicans worked wherever they were needed. As World War I and the immigration restriction acts of the 1920s curtailed emigration from Europe and Asia, the southwestern mines, the sugar beet fields of Colorado, and the steel foundries in Illinois, Ohio, and Pennsylvania had difficulty finding sufficient help. Again the Mexicans benefited. They did not have to travel far to cross the border; labor agents helped transport those who went to the Midwest and east to Pennsylvania; and in the Southwest they were familiar with the terrain and the increasing number of Mexican *colonias* that had developed. San Antonio and El Paso, Texas, had the largest number of Spanish-speaking people in that state, whereas in California El Centro, Calipatria, Calexico, and Los Angeles served as major Mexican dwelling places. So many Mexicans moved north that in 1925 Los Angeles had a larger Spanish-speaking population than any other city in North America except Mexico City. In Los Angeles Mexicans were not rigidly segregated but lived chiefly throughout central and eastern sections of the city. As they held mostly unskilled and poorly paying jobs, their homes were among the most run-down in the growing city. Yet they found better economic opportunities here than in rural America, and some worked in skilled employment and owned their own homes.

TABLE 5.3.   Ethnic Groups on Nine Western Railroads
(Percentage of each working as track men)

	1909	1928–1929
Greeks	21.9	2.0
Italians	17.0	3.5
Japanese and Koreans	11.2	1.0
Mexicans	17.1	59.5

During the 1920s economic conditions in the United States varied widely. A postwar recession hit in 1920 and lasted two or three years in some industries. This resulted in widespread industrial layoffs of Mexican workers. For example, the Ford Motor Company in Detroit sent three thousand Mexican employees back to their homeland at its own expense. In the Southwest cotton prices fell sharply, in some cases from $3.80 to $1.80 a pound, and disgruntled workers were laid off, found themselves unable to collect unpaid wages, or went on strike to protest pay cuts. Most of the strikes failed, as strikers and their leaders were deported. During the last half of the decade demands for cheap agricultural labor increased the need for Mexican workers, particularly in California, and despite growing anti-Mexican feelings, these workers continued to migrate north toward the jobs.

Continuing efforts to restrict this immigration failed during the 1920s because of pressure from the railroads and the farming groups of the Southwest. The stock market crash of 1929 and the depression that followed not only ended the era of huge immigration but also actually reversed the tide, as thousands of Mexicans returned to their homeland. Repatriation, or sending the aliens home, seemed a simple answer to the growing unemployment caused by the depression. Some were deported by United States immigration officials; others returned voluntarily. However, state, local, or federal agencies forced most of them, and their American-born children, to repatriate. Many of these people went without any financial assistance, but the Mexican government helped about 5 percent of them to settle in special colonies.

The Filipinos

At the same time that Mexican workers entered the country, smaller numbers of other immigrant groups joined the western work force. Once the United States annexed the Philippine Islands in 1898, the islanders could move freely to the mainland. The first who arrived consisted of several hundred students chosen by the federal government to be educated in this country before returning home, where later they held government positions. This program lasted only from 1903 to 1907.

Most of the Filipinos arrived, however, after the Hawaiian sugar planters and pineapple growers had recruited over 100,000 of them in 1907–08, as soon as the "Gentlemen's Agreement" curtailed the flow of cheap labor from Japan and Korea. With a chance to earn wages from four to ten times as much in the United States as at home, Filipinos came eagerly, although numerous Americans objected to their presence. In the 1920s, when Congress considered restricting Mexican immigrants, as well as Europeans and most Asians, California farmers sought Filipino workers. During that decade at least thirty thousand came from Hawaii and the Philippines. By 1930 estimates placed anywhere from thirty to one hundred thousand Filipinos in the country. During the depression in that decade, many of these workers lost their jobs to white refugees from Texas, Arkansas, and Oklahoma and soon returned to their homeland. Those who remained established colonies in or near Seattle, Portland, San Francisco, and Stockton, California.

Between 1924 and 1943 the Filipinos constituted a unique group in the United States. They were the only Asian laborers allowed into the country because the United States owned the Philippine Islands. Yet as Asians they could not become citizens. However, those born in either Hawaii or on the continent were citizens by birth. In 1934 Congress finally curtailed Filipino immigration to 50 persons a year. The United States also promised to grant the islands their independence in ten years. Because World War II ended in 1945, the Philippines did not receive independence until 1946.

Filipinos cutting lettuce in Salinas, California, 1935. Filipinos, Japanese, and Mexicans were often the main performers of the backbreaking work required of farm laborers in the Southwest. By Dorothea Lange. (Library of Congress)

Other Immigrants

Several other immigrant groups also helped populate the West. Italians moved to California, where they engaged in truck farming. Some succeeded as operators of vineyards and fruit orchards. Of the one hundred thousand Portuguese who immigrated, nearly one-third settled in California. Their focal point originally was the San Francisco Bay area, but they later spread to the Sacramento and San Joaquin valleys. As had the Italians, the Portuguese entered agriculture, and in southern California they ranked second only to the Dutch in the dairy industry. The Armenians who settled on the West Coast found work on California farms, in packing houses, canneries, and cement works. By 1915 more than eight thousand of them lived in Fresno. Greeks settled throughout the mountain west. The so-called Czar of the Greeks, Leonidas G. Skliris, stationed himself in Salt Lake City and there acted as the agent for the Utah Copper Company, the Western Pacific Railroad, the Carbon County mines, and other employers. He found jobs for most of the Greeks. More than 8,500 Asian Indians, mostly Sikhs, also immigrated to the West Coast between 1900 and 1930; five thousand of them landed at San Francisco in the first decade of the century. They worked on the railroads and in the lumbering centers of the Northwest. One group of these Asian Indians, placed in the sawmills at Bellingham, Washington, was attacked and beaten in 1907 by about five hundred whites. The local newspaper explained two days after the assault that the Indians "are repulsive in appearance and disgusting in their manners.... Their actions and customs are so different from ours that there can never be tolerance of them."

All of those who immigrated to the American West during the last half of the nineteenth century or the first third of the twentieth did so hoping for a better life. Miners, farmers, ranchers, railroad workers, or city folk all expected economic improvement, and much opportunity, in fact, existed. For most, however, the myth of western abundance and opportunity exceeded the reality. Instead of the pot of gold at the end of the rainbow, they found hard work, low wages, and poor living conditions, as well as ethnic tensions that developed along much the same lines as in the rest of the nation.

Black Migration North

Foreigners may have contributed the largest numbers to the movement of people within the United States, but after 1880, and especially after 1910, American blacks from the South engaged in a major migration of their own as they left their homes for jobs in the North (see Table 5.4). The failure of the Reconstruction

Congress to provide the freedmen with land precluded them from developing a solid economic base, and this ultimately caused the black exodus. Sharecropping emerged as a common arrangement for black farmers during the Reconstruction era. Under this system blacks, and many whites as well, contracted to work on someone else's land and pay the owner a share of the proceeds after the harvest. The planter would advance money for tools, seed, food, and other supplies that the cropper might need; he, in turn, would pay for these advances at high interest rates after the crop, usually cotton, was harvested and marketed. The sharecropper could also raise his own food, and if he had a successful crop and got a good price for the cotton, he could pay his debts and perhaps have enough left over to purchase some land. Yet few made profits when the accounts were settled. Indeed, most remained in debt after the annual reckoning, because the planter kept the books, and the illiterate cropper was sometimes cheated outright or left confused by the financial settlement.

Many blacks, wanting money to buy their own land, preferred this arrangement to its chief alternative, gang labor for wages, which reminded them of slavery. Others did not engage in sharecropping but hired themselves out instead; still others rented and tilled the soil. These systems, however, left the capital-short black farmer at a disadvantage; all that he could sell was his labor, and that went cheap.

Staying on the land did not inevitably mean that blacks remained on the plantations of their former masters. Even before the Civil War ended, blacks were on the move. Afterward, a considerable migration of freedmen took place from the seaboard to states further inland. They poured into cities such as New Orleans, where they were wretchedly poor, hungry, and ill-housed. Some of the skilled, who had learned their trades as slaves or as free blacks before the war, found work and little discrimination in wages, but many of the unskilled and those newly arrived from the plantations either had to accept exceptionally low-paying menial and servile positions or else did not work.

Some former slaves learned a trade and earned higher wages, but other skilled workers lost their hold on some crafts or were paid less than whites for

TABLE 5.4.   Black Population of Selected Northern Cities

City	1880	1890*	1900	1910	1920
Boston	5,873	8,590	11,591	13,564	16,350
Chicago	6,480	14,852	30,150	44,103	109,458
Detroit	2,821	3,454	4,111	5,741	40,838
New York	19,663	25,674	60,666	91,709	152,467
Philadelphia	31,699	40,374	62,613	84,459	134,229

*Includes Chinese, Japanese, and Indian.

Black sharecroppers in Alabama, 1937. (Library of Congress)

the same work. With few exceptions white unions shunned black workers. At the beginning of the twentieth century only forty thousand of the nation's 1,200,000 union members were black, and in many cases white unions barred black members or insisted on racially segregated locals. Although unions such as the United Federation of Miners in Alabama resisted segregation, in other instances white workers went on strike to protest the hiring of blacks. Moving north or west allowed some African Americans to escape this situation. After the end of the Reconstruction era in 1877, thousands found new homes in Kansas, while still others drifted to New York City and Philadelphia. Yet most black Americans remained in the South, relentlessly trying to sustain themselves as farmers. As a result of World War I, which began in Europe in August 1914, immigration from the continent declined precipitously. Then blacks streamed into the northern cities to take the unskilled jobs. From 1910 to 1920 more than 500,000, and in the next decade nearly 750,000, blacks moved north. In those years they generally followed the railroad routes to New York City, Philadelphia, Chicago, and, to a lesser degree, Detroit, Cleveland, and Pittsburgh. Most

African Americans moving to the cities preferred the North, but the nation's capital, Washington, D.C., also received a sizable influx, as did southern cities such as Atlanta, New Orleans, and Birmingham. In the West, Colorado housed 8,000 African Americans in 1900—more than any other state west of the Rockies.

Like the European, Asian, and Latin American minorities, economic conditions drew African Americans to the cities. Other factors also contributed to their move. Southern racism, especially acute from 1890 to 1920, made the North seem like the Promised Land. Chronic southern poverty, always worse for the blacks, was the push factor, and the lure of jobs in the cities was the pull. Also affecting blacks' decision to leave was the advent of the boll weevil, which swept north from Mexico across Texas and other states, ravaging cotton crops and financially ruining farmers, both black and white. In some counties virtually the entire planting was destroyed in a single season. In 1915 floods ruined thousands of farm acres in Alabama and Mississippi. With a labor shortage in the North during World War I, industries that had relied on European immigrants had to recruit African Americans. Black newspapers, such as the *Chicago Defender,* also urged their readers to come north, where the wages were good and discrimination less onerous. Letters from those in the north often repeated the message.

With millions of people moving about the country and communities continually expanding and having to make room for and adjustments to newcomers, it is no wonder that massive tensions existed. Periodically these stresses resulted in strains too difficult for the changing communities to cope with peacefully.

6

The Process of Adjustment

(1880s–1930s)

The process of adjustment for the immigrants and urban blacks varied widely. The degree of prejudice encountered, the education available, and family values all contributed to the individual experiences. Most blacks and immigrants, regardless of cultural background, never moved beyond working-class status. The big differences occurred among the immigrants' children and grandchildren, with many factors contributing to mobility. Rampant bigotry made progress for African Americans especially slow. The immigrants and migrating blacks usually moved with the desire of improving their economic conditions. A better life meant jobs that paid well—or at least more than could have been earned in their home countries or made in the rural South. During the rapid pace of industrialization in the United States in the late nineteenth and early twentieth centuries, positions for the unskilled existed in every section of the country. As one Greek wrote home, "Work is everywhere. Your two hands are all you need." When immigration fell off at the start of World War I in 1914, blacks found greater opportunities.

Wages and Working Conditions

Although some people knew exactly where they wanted to go, others relied on labor agents to help them. Among the Italians, Greeks, and Syrians, *padroni* assumed that responsibility. Some *padroni* traveled to Europe to recruit workers; others made the initial contact in the United States. They negotiated deals with employers, sent the workers off to their destinations, and collected and distributed the men's salaries after deducting their service fees. Some *padroni* also provided housing, wrote letters, and interpreted the American scene for their innocent charges. If the immigrants were lucky, the *padrone* was honest; if not, they had few options. No matter what the character of any individual *padrone,* he served the purpose of bringing laborers to jobs in a day when public employment bureaus were few. In the East, where most of the immigrants first touched American soil, a network of American labor agents supplemented the *padroni.* Often these agents also engaged in practices that many today might consider reprehensible. For example, their letterheads included phrases such as "Strike Orders Handled on Cost Plus Basis," indicating that they provided strikebreakers for industrial firms.

It would be impossible to discuss in detail the destinations and occupations of the more than twenty-five million immigrants who reached American shores between 1880 and 1930, but certain generalizations can be made. Most people knew where they wanted, or could, go and what kinds of work they would accept. Unskilled foreigners and blacks obtained most of the menial jobs on the railroads and in every mining and manufacturing center of the nation; they also dominated the ranks of toilers in American agriculture. The Irish and Poles considered peddling and needlecrafts either beneath their dignity or occupations for women, but both of these groups regarded as "manly" heavy work calling for physical strength and prowess. As a result many Irishmen went into construction during the middle of the nineteenth century, and many relatives and friends joined them later. There was a good deal of truth to the jocular remark of that fictional Irish humorist, "Mr. Dooley," who claimed that on entering the United States, "a shovel was thrust into me hand and I was pushed into a street excyvatin' as though I'd been born here." By the end of the nineteenth century and into the twentieth, the steel mills and mines throughout the country were desperate for brawny males, and so they recruited Poles and other Slavs, who accepted the long hours and low pay without much protest.

In many industries the social composition of the work force changed with the passage of time. On the railroads, for example, after 1880 Italians, Greeks, and Japanese replaced the earlier Chinese and Irish laborers, and they in turn gave way to Mexicans in the twentieth century. New York City's garment district at one time employed Germans and Irish, later Jews and Italians, and more recently blacks, Hispanics, and Chinese. On the West Coast after 1910 Mexicans and Filipinos practically ousted the Chinese and Japanese from many areas of agricultural production. A number of Mexicans and blacks also moved into Midwestern industry in the 1920s, as the Slavs moved up to supervisory positions. It did not always work out well for the minorities. As one steel foreman put it, "We have Negroes and Mexicans in a sort of competition with each other. It is a dirty trick."

Although immigrants and blacks often had no difficulty finding unskilled jobs, few worked a full fifty-two-week year or earned decent wages. Every industry had its periods of unemployment. In New England's textile towns, most immigrants could count on no more than a forty-week year. In 1889 a survey of a quarter of a million railroad laborers disclosed that 70 percent had worked fewer than two hundred days during that year and that 40 percent of those people had an annual income of less than $100. Wages in other industries were also insufficient to meet family needs, and job security was just as

TABLE 6.1.   Wages of Immigrants

Armenians	$730
Jews	$685
North Italians	$657
Lithuanians	$636
Greeks	$632
Poles	$595
Syrians	$594
Slovaks	$582
Ruthenians (Ukrainians)	$569
South Italians	$569
Russians (non-Jewish)	$494
Serbs	$462

uncertain. By 1910, when $900 a year was considered necessary for a family of five to maintain a modest standard of living, only one out of seven of the foreign born earned that much. The average annual *family* incomes of immigrant groups, according to one survey taken before World War I, are shown in Table 6.1.

Wages, although four to ten times higher than they were in Europe, were nevertheless wretched, as prices were high. Adult males sometimes earned $2 or more a day but rarely averaged $455 for the year. Blacks fared worse than immigrants, earning the lowest wages for the most menial and degrading work. Discrimination by trade unions also diminished the chances of blacks getting skilled work. Given the low wages of the era, it is no wonder that people from all over the world flocked to Detroit following Henry Ford's 1912 announcement that he would pay assembly-line workers $5 a day.

Although Ford may have done something for the auto workers, the situation in other industries remained deplorable. In the ring-spinning and carding room of the New England textile mills, for example, dust, dried sputum, heat, moisture, poor air and light, and carbon monoxide produced conditions that cut years from the weavers' lives. A third of the spinners in Lawrence, Massachusetts, died before having worked ten years, half of them before they were twenty-five years old. For some, death came instantly, as accidents were common during the making of industrial America. Working in the mines and on the railroads was particularly hazardous. In 1910, for example, approximately three thousand railroad workers were killed and more than ninety-five thousand injured.

Working and safety conditions were especially bad for women and children. "At the bottom of the industrial system," we are told, "was a body of sweated, underpaid women, of overworked children, and of hard-driven day-laborers whose lot often seemed worse than that of dumb beasts." There are tales of Polish children earning $2.68 for a sixty-hour week in the Shenandoah coal mines and of a fifteen-year-old girl in Chicago taking home $27 for 245 days of labor. Slavic women and boys earned less than $1 a day in Pittsburgh's spike, nut and bolt, and steel wire factories. Women also sweated for ten hours daily, at wages of $.10 an hour, in the city's steam laundries. They stood continuously in pools of water with their shirts soaking from the steam. One worker complained of the hot manglers and washing machines: "The work's too hard, and you simply can't stand the heat."

In Chicago and New York City Italian females just about monopolized the home finishing of cloaks in the garment trades. One factory paid girls as high as $1.20 for a finished garment, each of which usually took one and a half hours, but 50 to 70¢ per coat was a more common figure. When one scans salaries, sums such as $1.35 for a full week's work and $9.37 for thirteen weeks' labor crop up frequently. Most unbelievable is that many Italian women continued working fifteen- and sixteen-hour days in which all they received for their efforts was 50 or 60¢. One explanation, perhaps, is that they had no choice. A contemporary observer wrote that their husbands and fathers were desperately anxious to bring money into the home and that women were regarded as instruments to advance this end.

Most black and many immigrant families could not have survived without the wages of wives and children: the 1910 census recorded over two million child laborers. The cultural background, as well as the poverty, of each group dictated who would and who would not be allowed to seek gainful employment. Italian children were pulled out of school as early as possible. Boys went out to seek jobs; some girls did so, as well, but most remained at home to help mothers with their domestic chores. Italian women usually worked at home or in a family business, but in cities such as New York, Buffalo, and Chicago some husbands and fathers encouraged them to get paying jobs. The Irish, Poles, and French Canadians thought that everyone should contribute to the family coffers, and they, too, saw no point in an extended education. Dutch and Greek women did not work outside of the home unless it was in a family business. Greek males believed it was humiliating not to be able to support their wives, mothers, daughters, or sisters. French Canadian women worked in factories but not as domestics. Irish, German, Bohemian, Scandinavian, and Slavic women did both factory and domestic work. Mexican women could work in fields but not in factories or someone else's home. Polish women worked wherever they could find jobs; marriage and family were not necessarily valid reasons for ending their wage earning.

Child laborers working in the mines. The utilization of child laborers reached its peak in the early twentieth century. (Library of Congress)

There is the story of a Polish woman in a West Virginia mining community who, although pregnant, did not let her delicate condition interfere with her duties as mistress of a boarding house. One evening the woman retired to her bed, gave birth at three o'clock in the morning, and then was up at six o'clock preparing breakfast for her thirteen ravenous boarders and fixing lunches for their dinner buckets. At the beginning of the twentieth century black urban women had little choice because their husbands earned so little. In New York City nearly 60 percent of black women worked, compared with 27 percent of foreign-born and 24 percent of native-born white women. Mostly they found jobs as domestics or in other low-paid occupations. For black women to work was nothing new; during slavery they had traditionally worked on the plantations of the South.

Low wages for long hours in abysmal surroundings were thus the common experience of immigrants and blacks, both male and female. The miserable factory and mining conditions stimulated the development of labor unions, but because of the overabundance of labor, discrimination, employer opposition, and public and governmental indifference or hostility, unions were not very successful in the late nineteenth century. In the 1870s the Knights of Labor sought to organize nearly all American workers into one big union. The Knights were identified with radicalism and were divided and poorly managed. Thus, after losing some key strikes, the organization collapsed. On the other hand, the American Federation of Labor (AFL), led by Samuel Gompers, emerged as the most successful labor union at the end of the nineteenth century. The AFL concentrated on organizing skilled craftsmen and negotiating benefits from employers, but most workers, especially the immigrants and blacks, were left out. From 1870 to World War I working and safety conditions gradually improved, and during the Progressive reform years after 1900 unions won more acceptance. During World War I the government urged business to recognize unions and union contracts to avoid strikes and stimulate war production. As a result, trade union membership grew to over five million by the end of the Great War, only to suffer serious reversals during the antiunion climate of the 1920s.

Members of almost all the immigrant nationalities and some of the blacks participated in union activities at one time or another, but their experiences were not uniform. In the nineteenth century Germans dominated the labor movement among the skilled craftsmen; in the 1880s, after the formation of the AFL, the Irish ranked high among the second and third echelon of leaders. The newer groups from southern and eastern Europe had a reputation for shunning union activities, although the Pennsylvania anthracite coal strike of 1897 was dominated by Poles, Lithuanians, Slovaks, and Ukrainians. In that strike even the women participated and the *Wilkes-Barre Times* editorialized that their presence was "a novelty of a not very pleasing nature." In the twentieth century, eastern European Jews figured prominently among the founders and leaders of the International Ladies' Garment Workers' Union and the Amalgamated Clothing Workers' Union. Most immigrants, however, did not at first join unions and were willing to allow employers to co-opt their services regardless of circumstances.

Employers in every part of the country used immigrants as strikebreakers. A North Adams, Massachusetts, shoe factory hired seventy-five Chinese to replace striking employees in 1870; packing plants in Omaha brought Japanese and Greek strikebreakers there in 1904; and Mexicans went to Chicago for the same purpose a generation later. In the Carbon County, Utah, mines, Italians and Slavs replaced English strikers in the late nineteenth century; Greeks replaced the Italians and Slavs, who went on strike in 1903; and Mexicans were used when the Greeks walked off the job in the 1920s. Foreign-born minorities who appeared as strikebreakers in one place often led strikers elsewhere.

Mexicans were prominent among the railroad, copper mine, and agricultural strikers in the twentieth-century west, whereas Italians, who were often discriminated against and refused admission to some unions that they wanted to join, such as the stonecutters, provided the backbone of the Lawrence, Massachusetts, textile strike in 1912.

For blacks the situation was somewhat different. Unions usually excluded them or else segregated them into separate locals. Hence a number of blacks showed no hesitation crossing picket lines. African Americans were employed to break strikes along the waterfront as early as 1855 in New York City, and the practice continued for decades. In 1903 New York City subway contractors replaced protesting employees with imported black workers, and at about the same time meat packers in Chicago did the same.

Hostility to African American laborers kept them out of numerous industries, except as strikebreakers or convict laborers. In the late nineteenth and early twentieth centuries many states in the South leased out some of their prisoners to industrial and agricultural entrepreneurs and received payment for their services. The firms guarded these individuals carefully and did not hesitate to use chains or inflict corporal punishment when they believed that the workers had committed some infraction. In some southern industries, however, blacks were hired as paid laborers. They worked in the bituminous coal fields of West Virginia and Alabama, and in 1907 the Immigration Commission reported that blacks, concentrated in Alabama and Maryland and to a lesser extent in Virginia, Tennessee, and Kentucky, made up approximately 40 percent of the southern steel workers. By 1910 some 350,000 southern blacks were factory workers. In the cities blacks also managed to find jobs as longshoremen and in some of the skilled crafts and building trades. Others worked for the railroads. In nearly all of these jobs, however, black workers faced considerable discrimination. They usually were common laborers in the industries in which they were employed and were paid less than whites. Immigrant workers competed with them for some of the better jobs, forcing many blacks to seek employment as menials or as domestic servants in the homes of white folks.

A number of industries preferred not to use blacks at all. Those southern proponents of a New South, which was to be based on industries and cities, attempted to recruit immigrant labor. State governments, railroads, industrialists, and even planters tried to entice foreigners to the South. South Carolina set up the first southern state immigration agency in 1866, and other states followed. The Southern Immigration Association of America was organized in Louisville in 1883 and held its first annual meeting in 1884. Although the organization lasted only a few years, other groups also tried to promote immigration to the South.

Planters wanted Chinese laborers because they allegedly worked better for lower wages than Europeans would accept. But few came, and other southerners expressed reservations about bringing another racial group to the region. Several state immigration bureaus actually contracted to bring in Poles, Greeks, Italians, and Portuguese, but not in large numbers. Federal law prohibited contract labor, but more important was the reputation of the South among foreign workers. Some did come, lured by labor agents in the North, but on arrival they often found wages lower than had been stipulated. Furthermore, for those immigrants interested in farming, better lands were available in other sections of the United States. Immigrants, often shrewd about the economic opportunities available, accurately believed that the South offered less than other regions.

Thousands of immigrants and blacks in the South were also victimized by one of the most oppressive systems of labor imaginable—peonage, a form of involuntary servitude. Peonage existed in practically every state of the Union but was centered in the southern cotton belt from the Carolinas to Texas, in the turpentine areas concentrated along the contiguous borders of Florida, Georgia, and Alabama, and in the railroad construction camps, the sawmills, and the mines of the South. The peons included unsuspecting immigrants who had been promised good pay and working conditions and southerners who had been fined or imprisoned for some petty offense. The system offered large employers of labor low unit costs of production and enormous profits. No one with any moral scruples would have exploited workers in such a cruel fashion, for peonage was in many respects worse than slavery had been. Whereas in antebellum days slaves had some monetary value and their illnesses and deaths resulted in pecuniary losses, peons required no investment and only minimal expenditures for food and shelter. Hence they were kept only as long as they could toil and then dispensed with in a variety of notorious ways, including murder.

The brutality of life for the peons knew no bounds. Many blacks, often illiterate, were made to sign contracts that gave planters "the right to use such force as he or his agents may deem necessary to require me to remain on his farm and perform good and satisfactory services" and "the right to lock me up for safe keeping." With or without such documents, those who used peons employed armed guards, who did not hesitate to threaten, maim, or shoot their charges. When laborers ran away, they were searched for with bloodhounds and, when caught, severely whipped, often chained, and then brought back. An escaped immigrant peon kept in jail with a vagrant while awaiting trial asked her, "Do they flog men everywhere in this country?" "No," she replied, "just down here in the South where they used to flog niggers." Locked and barred stockades, which were sometimes converted chicken coops or horse stalls, provided shelter during the workers' off hours. In some railroad camps locked boxcars without cots or even straw housed the laborers at night. "In the woods," one peon later recalled, "they can do anything they please, and no one can see them but God."

The institution of peonage, begun sometime after slavery ended, continued into the twentieth century. It attracted nationwide attention in 1906 when the federal government began an investigation in Florida and found conditions resembling "slave-labor" camps. In the 1920s, after heavy floods in Mississippi, over five thousand blacks were retained in refugee camps behind barbed wire until someone would come and promise to give them a home and a job and prevent them from becoming "a public charge." No one knows how long peonage continued or how many blacks and immigrants were impressed, but between 1958 and 1963 the federal Justice Department received more than 170 complaints concerning involuntary servitude from thirty states, including California (home for many Mexican migrants), Florida, Georgia, Alabama, Mississippi, Texas, and Arkansas.

As a result of the abominable treatment so many workers received in the South, especially in the late nineteenth and early twentieth centuries, as well as misrepresentation by labor agents and entrepreneurs, foreigners shunned most of the former Confederate states, and the region could not even hold on to the relatively few immigrants who were enticed there. The 1900 census showed more than 620,000 foreign-born inhabitants in the South; ten years later the figure had declined to half a million. That was only 2 percent of the region's population, compared with 20 percent for the rest of the country. New South industrialists, therefore, sought laborers among the old-stock Southerners. English, Scottish, and Scots-Irish names, seemingly of the "purest" Anglo-Saxon heritage, were found on the payrolls of Southern mills and in the iron, tobacco, and other industries. Southern industrialists could recruit these workers for the mills and factories because rural conditions were so miserable and afforded limited opportunities for poor whites.

These native-born whites in the South fared only slightly better than blacks and immigrants. Workers in the New South's industries were among the worst paid and most exploited laborers in America. Especially appalling were the cotton mills, which employed women and children. Youngsters of eight and nine years toiled twelve hours a day for pitiful wages. The southern states claimed more than half of all of the child laborers in the nation, and in 1900 the census found more than one million employees under the age of sixteen in the South. Whereas northern states were beginning to outlaw child labor, southerners were reluctant to do so. One Mississippi senator branded such legislation "part of a hellish scheme laid in foreign countries," and another politician insisted the elimination of child labor "would destroy the home. It would destroy a civilization based on the Bible." The use of child labor declined after 1920, but conditions in the company-run mill towns remained shocking. One critic of such towns said that the boss:

owns the community and he regulates the life that goes on there after the day's work is over in his mill. He has the power to discharge the worker at the mill, to refuse him credit at his store, to dump a worker's furniture out of a house, to have him expelled from church, to bar his child from school, and to withhold the service of a doctor or hospital.

A mill manager spoke more succinctly: "We govern like the Czar of Russia." Conditions of a similar but less extreme nature existed in parts of the North as well. Public sentiment was sharply hostile to lower-class workers before the 1930s, and especially to laborers who were also ethnic minorities. Bosses hired thugs to beat strikers, and law officers often helped the roughnecks or watched in amusement. During the Chicago garment workers' strike of 1910, Irish policemen "cracked the heads of 'Kikes,' 'Dagoes,' and 'Polacks.' " One observer saw "mounted policemen plunging over the sidewalks and trampeling [sic] peaceful workers." Five years later the mayor of Chicago defended similar episodes of police brutality. When a citizens' delegation came to protest such incivilities, Mayor "Big Bill" Thompson told them, "With these Poles and other foreigners, one cannot do anything else."

The abuses perpetrated against immigrants and blacks did not go unnoticed. Many concerned citizens tried, in a variety of ways, to improve their lot in the United States. Muckraking journalists in the Progressive era, during the early years of the twentieth century, wrote about some of the worst evils, and, along with other middle- and upper-middle-class reformers, sought to better the conditions of working-class Americans through legislation by the local, state, and federal governments. Beginning in the 1870s, and reaching a peak in the years before World War I, states enacted laws curbing child labor, improving factory safety and working conditions, giving greater protection to women, providing some pensions for needy widows with small children, and generally improving the quality of life for those most severely affected by the abuses of the industrial system.

The Tenement Districts

Among those in the forefront of the fight to improve the laborers' lots were the social workers. Jane Addams, the most famous of those dedicated and well-educated Americans who opened up settlement houses in the immigrant communities, established Hull House in Chicago in 1889. No tasks were too menial or too insurmountable for the settlement-house workers. Whatever they felt the community needed, they fought for. Jane Addams had herself appointed garbage inspector so that she could legally require landlords to clean up their houses. The most important function of the settlement houses and leaders, though, was to provide a refuge from the harshness of the outside world. A variety of educational and recreational facilities, such as libraries, arts and crafts classes, social clubs, music and theater groups, gymnasiums, playgrounds, and day nurseries, were available to those who lived in the community. Emotional succor, often the most necessary form of assistance, also ranked high among settlement-house offerings. The settlement workers did not restrict their activities to the local community, though their goals almost always reflected community needs. They petitioned government officials at all levels to help alleviate the worst abuses of factory and city life. One of their main objectives was to improve the physical environment in which they and the immigrants both worked and lived. They succeeded, to some extent, when a state such as New York passed new housing laws requiring windows in every bedroom and plumbing facilities in each tenement apartment, but such new legislation took effect gradually, while the dwellings that already existed remained in use.

Tenement housing may be described, but the full impact of its wretchedness cannot be conveyed in words. New York City, the mecca for most of the immigrants, had, according to a knowledgeable reformer of the Progressive era, "the worst housing conditions in the world." Tenements were overcrowded, with an average of 15.6 persons per dwelling unit in 1910, compared with 9.1 in Boston and 8.9 in Chicago. Sometimes it is difficult to imagine how bad New York must have been when one hears about conditions in other cities. In Philadelphia an investigator discovered thirty Italian families with 123 persons living in 34 rooms; in Chicago the Polish district averaged 339.8 people per acre; and a physician in Los Angeles found 23 Mexicans sleeping in one room.

In Pittsburgh one reporter described the dwellings of Slavic laborers as "so noisome and repulsive that one must visit the lower quarters of Canton to meet their like." The Polish district in Chicago was reputedly "nothing more than an infested wall-to-wall carpet of rotted wood and crumbling concrete." Tenements in city after city were without indoor plumbing, and the outdoor toilets overflowed into basement flats during heavy rains. In 1903 the floors of many Chinese homes in San Francisco were found to be rotting away because the broken sewer pipes and cesspools that lay underneath them had saturated the lots with human excrement. In most cities the stench from piles of outdoor garbage and horse droppings and the presence of chickens, goats, and cows housed along with horses in buildings adjoining residential dwellings was too pungent to describe.

Child laborers stripping tobacco in a tenement house. Not only was the employment of children in violation of the law, but the odor of tobacco that permeated the tenements made life unbearable. (Library of Congress)

The worst housing in the cities, though, was reserved for the black migrants coming from the South. Owners preferred to rent to white immigrants rather than to blacks, and black families sometimes encountered violence when they tried to move outside their growing ghettos. Black renters usually found quarters in dilapidated older buildings left by whites, and the growth in the northern urban black population during the Great Migration of 1910–20 strained available facilities. To pay their rent regularly, blacks, even more than most immigrants, had to take in boarders. Various studies reveal that in northern ghettos in the early twentieth century about one-third of black families took in boarders or lodgers. In the Pittsburgh ghetto half of the single black men lived three or four to a room, and less than 40 percent had a bed to themselves. Half slept two in a bed, and sometimes three and even four shared a bed. No wonder, then, that the health of black Americans was worse than that of others. Blacks were more likely than whites to suffer pneumonia, as well as tuberculosis and other crippling diseases. In 1910 the black death rate was 21.7 per 1,000, whereas the white death rate was 14.5 per 1,000, and between 1915 and 1920 the infant mortality rate of blacks was 50 percent higher than that of whites.

Voluntary Associations

One is often amazed that the immigrants and black migrants managed to survive their experiences in urban America, but they did. Social reforms and a gradually rising standard of living helped, but perhaps the main reason for their ability to overcome the day-to-day difficulties in their lives was the enormous aid and support that they received from their own people, their churches, and the numerous organizations that had been set up to sustain them during their transition period. Blacks and members of almost every immigrant group participated in some of the activities of an organized and cohesive ethnic community, and this helped their own adaptation, as well as providing their children with the strength to go out into the dominant society. As one sociologist observed, "The highly organized community life was ... the means by which the minority group met the problems of adjustment with which it was confronted."

Most of the immigrant groups desired to retain their traditional culture for themselves and their children while at the same time adjusting to life in the United States. They made every effort to transmit the Old World traditions intact to succeeding generations. Language was held on to tenaciously, community newspapers proliferated, and parochial schools were established. Traditional holidays were marked with appropriate festivities, and organizations were formed to keep members of the group together. At the same time, however, thousands of voluntary associations, societies, lodges, benevolent groups, cultural clubs, *Gymnasiums,* literary guilds, choirs, and theatrical circles stood ready to help the newcomer bridge the gap between the Old World and the New. In part these organizations were indispensable to those in a bewildering society who needed security, but immigrants also designed these groups to thwart complete assimilation into the dominant society. A perceptive scholar noted recently that the popular notion that immigrants came to the United States ready to assimilate "is a myth. The specter of 'Americanization,'" he continued, "troubled more immigrants than historians have been willing to admit."

Immigrant associations anticipated subsequent governmental welfare agencies in helping some to find jobs and homes and others to obtain transportation to distant cities. Some groups provided relief, others sustenance. A number gave unemployment insurance; most offered some kind of death benefits. The Irish Benevolent Society of Lawrence, Massachusetts proclaimed, "We visit our sick, and bury our dead." In 1914 the largest of such societies, the *Deutsch-Amerikanischer Nationalbund,* counted over two million members. Women's organizations, mainly devoted to charitable activities and the promotion of the traditional culture, also proliferated. Among the most active were the Polish

Women's Alliance, the *Jednota Ceskyck Dam* (Society of Czech Women), and the National Council of Jewish Women.

Although it would be impossible to discuss all of the myriad minority societies, one might look at the Polish National Alliance (PNA), founded in 1880, and the Polish Roman Catholic Union (PRCU), founded a few months later, as prototypes. Both organizations began on the eve of the great migrations from Poland. They helped the immigrants on their arrival, published newsletters, provided insurance, organized libraries, established museums, maintained youth programs, sponsored trips back to Poland, promoted education, and were influential in getting monuments built in American cities celebrating the past glories of Americans of Polish descent such as Tadeusz Kosciuszko and General Kazimierz Pulaski, who fought in the American Revolution. The PNA's annual calendars, replete with useful information and Polish proverbs, were avidly sought by American Poles. But the two organizations differed in their emphasis. The PNA's main goals were to develop support for an independent Poland while at the same time instilling loyalty to the United States in Polish Americans. The PRCU, on the other hand, dominated by Catholic priests, emphasized the separateness of Poles from other Americans and

Baseball team of the Polish National Alliance, 1939. (Immigration History Archives)

discouraged participation in non-Polish Catholic activities. Like all such groups that refused to recognize that the Old World culture could not be transplanted intact and that American-reared children could not be kept in complete ethnic isolation, the PRCU fought a losing battle. In 1935 when the PNA claimed a membership of over 280,000 people, the PRCU had only about 150,000.

Black Associations

The two most well-known black organizations founded in the early twentieth century, the National Urban League and the National Association for the Advancement of Colored People (NAACP), stressed the need for full equality and better living conditions for blacks. The NAACP called for immediate civil rights and combated racism in the courts and legislatures. During World War I the Association, while reluctantly accepting a Jim Crow army, tried to get more black officers and improved training and social facilities for black troops. In the 1920s the NAACP unsuccessfully lobbied for the enactment of a federal antilynching law. The Urban League was less political and concentrated on helping rural migrants adjust to city life by getting decent housing and jobs.

Whereas both the NAACP and the Urban League tried to integrate blacks into the mainstream of American life, other groups and individual blacks promoted black culture. In the late nineteenth century a few blacks, such as Methodist Bishop Henry Turner, rejected the notion that blacks could become part of American culture and urged instead emigration to Africa. In 1892 Turner wrote from Liberia, "One thing the black man has here, that is manhood, freedom, and the fullest liberty; and he feels as a lord and walks the same way." Few blacks went to Africa, but some began to study their African and African American heritages. Black authors began to collect materials about the experiences of blacks in America. The most influential group was the Association for the Study of Negro Life and History, founded in 1915, which published the *Journal of Negro History*. Other organizations, like the Society for the Collection of Negro Folk Lore, gathered materials about black culture.

The most spectacular leader urging black pride and concern about Africa was Jamaica-born Marcus Garvey, founder of the Universal Negro Improvement Association, who arrived in New York just before World War I. With fervent oratory Garvey urged freedom for Africans, a back-to-Africa movement, and pride in being black and chided those who advocated social equality and assimilation. He told blacks to start their own businesses and organizations, and he built a national black movement with a special appeal to the masses who had recently moved to the cities. In the 1920s this flamboyant leader ran afoul of the law, and his black shipping business ran into financial difficulties.

Following his conviction and deportation his movement fell apart, but he was the first black in America to build a genuine nationalist movement.

Cultural and Recreational Activities

Numerous cultural endeavors also afforded outlets for social intercourse in an ethnic setting. Many minorities formed marching bands that led parades to Sunday picnics. For some groups, such as the Greeks, national identification was so strong that they took their flags along with them. Other recreational opportunities were made possible by the coffee houses, saloons, beer gardens, musical organizations, athletic teams, and drama societies that proliferated within most of the immigrant communities. The Swedes, Poles, and Czechs had an ethnic theater, as did the Germans, whose earliest performances were staged in local taverns without props. The Italians, who had a profound love of opera, also participated in other dramatic and musical productions. Antonietta

Sauk City Wisconsin Dramatic Company, a German American group, in 1904. The immigrant theater helped many groups to maintain their own cultures. (State Historical Society of Wisconsin)

Pisanelli Alessandro organized one of the better-known Italian American theatrical companies in San Francisco in 1904. The Yiddish (Jewish) theater, the most famous of the ethnic drama groups, originated in the 1880s in New York City and lasted for more than half a century. The theater was the "great cultural passion" of the Jews, and acting provided a release for a good deal of their creativity. Eventually a large number of actors, writers, and directors from the Yiddish theater achieved fame in New York City's commercial theater, as well as in the motion picture industry in Hollywood. In the 1920s and 1930s several American theater critics upheld aspects of the Yiddish theater as models of accomplishment and seriousness.

Blacks also produced important cultural works. During the 1920s the success of a group of novelists, poets, and dramatists asserted the presence of "the New Negro." Writers of what was known as the "Harlem Renaissance" explored folk themes and black identity and rejected white standards. Yet it was in the area of music that black culture made its most original and major contribution. Some black groups studied and sang spirituals while other black

A traditional New Orleans funeral procession. Mourners, accompanied by a jazz band, march from the funeral parlor to the cemetery. (Louisiana Tourist Development Commission)

musicians composed the black musical revues so popular after 1910. Coming up from the South were jazz and blues musicians. "Jelly Roll" Morton recalled that around the turn of the century in New Orleans, "music was pouring into the streets from every house.... Little boys and grown-ups would walk along the avenues, swaying and whistling jazz tunes." Many of the great black musicians, such as Louis Armstrong and Ethel Waters, had little formal training, but they grew up in the black musical tradition, and their genius and creative styles found eager audiences in the growing urban ghettos. By 1910 a black theater had opened in Harlem, and it began to feature blues singers. Records made the blues popular in the 1920s and 1930s. A creation of black society, the blues, with their themes of pathos, was relevant to the black condition. Whereas the writers associated with the Harlem Renaissance appealed to an elite group, the blues were popular among both the rural and urban black masses. From 1920 to 1940 more than five thousand blues records were issued featuring over one thousand black musicians. These records were mainly purchased by blacks.

The Churches and Parochial Education

Of all the ethnic institutions, none was more important than the church. Whether black or white, Protestant, Catholic, or Jewish, religious bodies exerted an influence far greater than any of the other community organizations. The Lutherans were strong among the Scandinavians and the Germans, but many of the former later became Baptists and Methodists. The lives of the eastern European Jews were at first almost totally circumscribed by religious dictums. Roman Catholicism contained by far the largest number of immigrant adherents and had more parishioners than all the other immigrant churches combined. The faithful included an overwhelming majority of Irish, Poles, French Canadians, Lithuanians, Croatians, Slovaks, and Slovenes, as well as a goodly number of Germans and Czechs. Mexicans and Italians were also Catholic, but the former followed practices that were unfamiliar to those of European descent, whereas the latter, especially the men, did not have much respect for the church or its hierarchy. Blacks were mostly Protestants, usually Methodists or Baptists.

Black Protestants usually attended segregated churches. Whites had not welcomed them to their services even when they were few and continued to exclude them as a large number of southern blacks began pouring into the cities. When a neighborhood became predominantly black, whites abandoned their churches to the African Americans. Older established black churches witnessed a big growth in membership, and they and some of the newer congregations

The congregation of a Polish Catholic church in St. Paul, Minnesota, 1918.
(Immigration History Archives)

developed social programs for the immigrants. The Reverend Reverdy
Ransom's church in Chicago, for example, ran a day nursery and an employment office. Perhaps equally important among the religious institutions were
the numerous storefront churches that appeared in the expanding urban ghettos. These evangelical groups had great appeal to the poor, less educated rural
blacks, who found in their services a similarity to the emotional worship of the
rural black churches. There the service would be fervent with the traditional
shouts and music; it was a bit of home in the city.

Just as the black churches adapted to the needs of their parishioners, so, too, did
those organizations serving the immigrants. The Catholic hierarchy in the United
States, dominated by those of Irish ancestry, established thousands of parallel
social, educational, and athletic groupings designed to keep Catholics separated
from non-Catholics and free of assimilationist influence. Most Catholics were
willing to go along with this policy, and some, notably Germans, French Canadians,
and Poles, isolated themselves still further on national bases. The Italians also
wished to remain by themselves, but the church played little role in their lives.

No groups were more devoted to or involved with the Roman Catholic
Church than the Irish and the Poles. It was the center of their world, and the

priest was the authority in the community. The Irish, of course, had come first, and in the church they found the only American institution both familiar and willing to accept them. As Archbishop Hughes remarked about Irishman in the middle of the nineteenth century:

> It is only when he has the consolation of his religion, that he feels comparatively happy in his new position. If on the Sunday he can be present at the holy sacrifice of Mass, if he can only see the minister of his religion at the altar and hear the word of God in the language to which his ear was accustomed from childhood, he forgets that he is among strangers in a strange country.

The church was no less important for the Poles. As one wrote, "Without the Church we would have lost our identity." Polish children were educated in the parish school, which was conducted in the Polish language and taught by Polish nuns and priests. Poles needed to preserve their culture, but nationalism and Catholicism were so intertwined that they could not separate one from the other. For Germans and French Canadians the parish school, conducted in the familiar tongue, was also important. One Milwaukee priest observed in 1852, "German Catholic schools are the crying need in this country because German children, if Anglicized, by some strange fate generally become alienated from Catholic life."

In fact, many ethnic groups conceived of education as the means with which to preserve the Old World language and culture. In spite of their poverty, Jews, Greeks, Swedes, Japanese, and Chinese, to mention a few, either set up day schools for instruction in traditional ways or else had afternoon or summer schools for that purpose. The tenacity with which the immigrant groups held on to their schools can be observed from the eruptions in 1889 and 1890, when lawmakers in Illinois and Wisconsin required public schools to provide some subjects in the English language. In Wisconsin both Catholics and Lutherans united in opposition. They both saw the law as an attempt to destroy parochial education. As one German put it, his children had to be educated in the "language of Luther." In both states strong opposition to the enactments led to their repeal.

Public Education

No amount of devotion to the Old World and its needs, however, could counteract the "baneful" effects of an American education on the children and grandchildren of immigrants. Not that this education was consciously destructive to Old World ties—although in many cases it certainly weakened them—but for children born and reared in the United States, attachment to the Old World culture came to consist only of their love for their parents and for the traditions in which they were raised. To a certain extent, of course, parochial schools still promoted the history and culture of the old country. In the major urban centers, where most children attended the public schools, educators also had to acknowledge the presence of the immigrants. In the nineteenth century eight Midwestern states allowed German to be used as the language of instruction where there was a sufficient demand. This policy continued in some of the states until the United States entered World War I in 1917. Kansas counties in the 1890s had schools conducted in German, Swedish, Danish, Norwegian, and Czech; some San Francisco elementary schools provided Italian, German, French, or Spanish; and practically every state in the country at one time or another offered elective courses in a variety of foreign languages.

But in an American urban setting, the children came in contact with numerous divisive influences. Moreover, children growing up in the United States thought of themselves as, and wanted to be, Americans. This was not done to spite their parents but out of a real conviction that, regardless of their backgrounds, their destinies lay in America, and the faster they achieved the status of "American," the better off they would be. Nevertheless, the path to becoming American was fraught with anxiety. One woman recalled that when she started school in Texas around 1915, "I could not talk English. Not one word. We spoke German. When I went to school I had to speak English. But I couldn't talk English. I was so scared."

Parents and ethnic leaders alike recognized the Americanizing influences of the public school, but members of different groups did not have a uniform response to the threat. Some, however reluctantly, accepted the fact that their offspring would become Americans; they valued education too much to deprive their children of it. The determining factor in a child's future success in the United States often hinged on whether the child's culture prized education for its own value or because of what it could do for the individual. Armenians, Asians, Bulgarians, Czechs, Dutch, Germans, Greeks, Jews, Lithuanians, Macedonians, and Rumanians thought that their sons should be well educated and were willing to make sacrifices to help them along. Other groups, mostly Roman Catholics such as the French Canadians, Irish, Italians, Mexicans, Poles, and Slovaks, saw little advantage in education aside from learning the rudiments of reading and writing or as a necessary aspect of inculcating the faith, and they pulled their children out of school and sent them to work as soon as the law allowed or the children could get jobs. All groups had different expectations for their sons than they had for their daughters. While education may have been prized by several ethnic groups, the need to educate daughters never ranked as high on parents' priorities lists. In fact, some groups merely wanted their daughters to read and write (and not all thought even this was necessary), and to prepare themselves for marriage and motherhood.

Many immigrant parents subscribed to the views expressed by a Catholic prelate, Father Rene Holaind, that "all the child is entitled to is to receive the education necessary to live in comfort in the condition of his parents." A number of Catholics also saw the public schools as "a huge conspiracy against religion, individual liberty and enterprise, and parental rights." Poles regarded public schools as "unchristian, pagan and demoralizing institutions" that would rob their children of a priceless heritage. One scholar tells us that the Irish had no respect for intellect and possessed a "contempt for learning." Some southern Italians had unique ideas about education. The offspring of one wrote, "Mother believed you would go mad if you read too many books, and Father was of the opinion that too much school makes children lazy and opens the mind for unhealthy dreams." Another Italian American, who attended college, recalls friends and relatives pointing out to his father that it was a "scandal" for the healthy son of a packing-house worker to get so much education.

Not to be overlooked is the fact that many school systems were not supportive of those immigrants who wished to get ahead through education. One historian reported about schools for Mexican children in Houston: "Most educators viewed Mexican children as racially or culturally inferior. They also demeaned and denigrated their linguistic and cultural heritage." When Houston's Mexicans sought better education, authorities generally sent them to segregated schools.

Many blacks who moved north wanted their children to get an education, but they found conditions inhospitable for schooling. Whereas educators were eager to get the children of immigrants into the schools to "Americanize" them, they were frequently indifferent to black youngsters. Hence school boards spent much less money to educate them. In the South, where fewer than 40 percent of all children regularly attended schools before World War I, fewer than one in seventy African American youths reached the eighth grade. Black schools remained apart because of segregated housing, and school boards even used gerrymandering to make the racial lines more rigid. In Indianapolis in the early 1920s, white parents, despite black protests, induced the school board to build a separate high school for blacks. The few African Americans who escaped the ghettos and were admitted into the public universities of the North also found segregation and discrimination in their dormitories and other facilities.

Indian Education

While military actions against the tribes ended late in the nineteenth century, the government continued its long-term efforts to acculturate the indians, and education played a major role in this process. Beginning in 1870, the government earmarked funds specifically for Indian education, and reservation and boarding schools competed for money and the chance to "civilize" their charges. From the late 1890s to the 1930s thousands of Indian children were legally kidnaped and forced to attend school far from home. When their parents could not pay for their transportation home during vacations, the youngsters remained at school. The government curriculum, designed to eradicate all signs of Indianness, made no concession to the children's cultures. As a general policy the school's staff cut off the boys' long hair, punished children for speaking their native languages, and replaced their clothes with ill-fitting hand-me-downs. Bureau of Indian Affairs employees cooperated with zealous Christian missionaries to prohibit the children from holding tribal dances or ceremonies, which they considered pagan rites that had to be abolished.

Stifling regulation of all aspects of student life turned the schools into virtual prisons. Continuing shortages of funds led superintendents to cut their costs, often by reducing the food budget for the children. A major investigation showed that the schools fed their charges at a per capita cost of 12¢ to 14¢ a day at a time when the army spent 52¢ per day for each soldier's food. At the same time, the field matrons who worked with the children encouraged the students to consume dairy products. Unfortunately some of the Indian children suffered stomach disorders because they had trouble digesting the milk and cheese. The effort to alter their diets caused another serious problem, ill health: many dairy cattle then carried tuberculosis, which spread quickly throughout the Indian schools. The problem became so bad that even government officials admitted widespread malaise among the children. According to investigators, "malnutrition was evident. They [the children] were indolent and when they had a chance to play, they merely sat about on the ground showing no exuberance of health youth." The poor diet and crowded living conditions spread disease, and only when the authorities feared that a child was dying would they voluntarily send him or her back to the reservation.

Despite these circumstances, not all of the students looked back on their school days with anger. Some remembered the friendships they made with members of other tribes and residents of other reservations. This contact led to a growing pan-Indian movement a few years later. The academic training and vocational skills they received pleased others, while their participation in athletic events, marching bands, and military-style units brought satisfaction as well. By the turn of the century graduates of schools such as Carlisle and Hampton secured permanent jobs as a part of the growing Indian service bureaucracy. Although a small number of them worked for the government and a few even went to college, most Indian school students returned home, often with few skills for that environment. Certainly the use of education to weaken tribal cultures succeeded, and only rarely did the schools offer anything to replace the values they tried to destroy. Yet they did prepare a group of young Indians for leadership roles.

Physical brutality also took its toll. At the Ogalala boarding school near Pine Ridge, South Dakota, two runaway boys were captured, returned, and beaten. "Their heads were shaved, though it was winter. One of the boys had a ball and chain locked onto his leg and was locked to the bed at night." There were tales of other cruelties. One Bureau employee reported having seen Indian children "thrown in cellars under the building.... I have seen their shoes taken away from them and they then [were] forced to walk through the snow to the barn to help milk. I have seen them whipped with a hemp rope, also a water hose."

For those who remained at home the situation was also bad. Few reservations included good farmland, and even if the Indians had chosen to till their acreage, religious beliefs about Mother Earth prevented many of them from farming. For those who tried, however, poor soil and repeated droughts brought discouraging crop failures. With no economic base and little opportunity for employment, the reservations became pens of misery and despair. By the 1920s most Indians lived in dirt-floored shacks or tents with no water or plumbing and little heat. Usually the entire family ate, sat, and slept in a single room with only a table, a couple of boxes for chairs, and a single bed. Their food consisted of whatever rations they got from the agency office, a few vegetables they raised, and fruit berries they gathered. Often dogs and horses had to be eaten to prevent starvation.

By the early decades of the twentieth century the condition of Indians seemed hopeless. Using almost any standard of measure—family income, infant mortality, life expectancy, unemployment, alcoholism, or suicide— American Indians stood firmly mired at the bottom of the social and economic ladder. Whether by accident or by design, most Indian tribes had ceased to function or had been reduced to ineffectiveness. As their culture disappeared Indian despair mounted, but they tried to retain control of their reservations and lives. In 1878, when Congress created the agency police, young men seeking relief from enforced inactivity volunteered to serve as policemen and army scouts. Both positions incorporated the traditional duties of a warrior, and both brought some cultural satisfaction. On the other hand, Indian police had to serve as models for cultural change by wearing white men's clothing, cutting their hair, and having only one wife. Present on at least forty-six reservations, these men enforced the Bureau of Indian Affairs agent's will, which often pitted them against others of the tribe. When Congress established the Courts of Indian Offenses to deal with outlawed religious ceremonies and dances, healers and medicine men, and plural marriage, some leaders served as judges. This brought those who sought to control the pace and direction of accommodation to the white demands into conflict with traditionalists, who opposed any cultural transformation of Indian society.

Tom Torlino, a Navajo, photographed about 1886. (Arizona Historical Society)

By the 1880s some Indians turned to pan-Indian rather than tribal or reservation efforts to improve their situation. On the southern plains the Native American Church evolved out of a new combination of peyote use and Christian practices and ideas. Peyote, a cactus fruit long used in the Southwest to produce visions among its users, fit well into the long-held practices of inducing dreams through fasting. By the 1890s ritual use of peyote had spread through many Oklahoma tribes; a decade later it appeared in the Missouri and Mississippi valleys too. The new religion merged Indian and Christian beliefs reaching beyond any single tribe or reservation. Although actively opposed by the Bureau of Indian Affairs and by Christian missionaries, adherents persisted; in 1918 groups in Oklahoma incorporated the Native American Church, which continues to unify Indian people today.

Tom Torlino after three years at the Carlisle Indian School. (Arizona Historical Society)

Off-reservation Indians took some initiatives too. By 1900 many young Indians had met young people from other tribes at the boarding schools. They came to realize that they shared difficulties, and a growing sense of Indianness began to replace local identities. A small group of college-educated people called for a national organization to speak for all tribes, and in 1911 they founded the Society of American Indians. Although divided over goals and methods, prominent Indians such as Carlos Montezuma, Gertrude Bonnin, Thomas L. Sloan, and Charles Eastman organized to bring tribal difficulties to public notice.

Little would have been done to improve the situation had not the public become involved. In 1922 a major congressional fight erupted over the Bursum

Pueblo Land Bill, which sought to strip the New Mexico tribes of most of their remaining lands. This focused public attention on the plight of the Indians. Alarmed humanitarians awoke to the desperate conditions on the reservations and demands for change became widespread. Long-established groups such as the Indian Rights Association, as well as the newly organized American Indian Defense Association, began a muckraking campaign against the federal government—and in particular the Bureau of Indian Affairs (BIA). Articles blasting incompetent and dishonest bureaucrats appeared in the *New York Times*, *The Nation*, *Good Housekeeping*, and the *Literary Digest* in the East as well as *Sunset* magazine in the West. These publications described the Indians as being "shamelessly and openly robbed" by local officials who seemed to consider Indian property as "legitimate game."

The government took two actions. It appointed a Committee of One Hundred to investigate and make recommendations. Then in 1924 Congress passed, and President Calvin Coolidge signed, the Indian Citizenship Bill. This act gave all Indians full citizenship in theory but not in fact. The BIA still regulated many areas of Indians' lives, and both federal and local laws prevented tribesmen from voting in public elections or from legally buying alcoholic beverages. The Committee of One Hundred called for a further investigation, and in 1928 the Institute for Government Research published the Merriam Report. This publication documented in painful detail what reformers had only suspected about wretched conditions on the reservations and at the Bureau schools. More important, it questioned the entire effort to force assimilation on the Indians.

The crisis of the Great Depression gave the nation a chance to overhaul long-range policies toward the Indians. In 1933 President Franklin D. Roosevelt appointed John Collier, a longtime vociferous advocate of Indian rights, as the new commissioner of Indian affairs. The next year Collier lobbied successfully for the passage of the Indian Reorganization Act or the Wheeler-Howard Act. Under this law the government encouraged Indians to reconstruct their tribes, adopt tribal constitutions, elect their own leaders, and form tribal corporations to work for economic progress. Proposed as a return to traditional Indian ways, the idea of elected leaders ran counter to existing Indian practices, and many objected strenuously. Nevertheless, fifty-eight tribes chose to follow this new path that same year, and most of the tribal governments existing today got their start under the 1934 Reorganization Act. At least for a time, after two centuries of trying to destroy Indian societies and to force tribal people into the national mainstream, the government accepted the idea that the tribesmen did not have to surrender their unique cultures to be loyal Americans.

The Minority Press

Foreign-language and black newspapers supplemented the education offered in the schools and exercised a considerable influence on their readers. Next to the church and the school, they frequently served as the single most important social and educational institution in the minority communities. People who had never read anything in Europe or on southern farms accustomed themselves to reading the daily or weekly newspaper. In fact, the first newspaper published in the Lithuanian language appeared in the United States, not in Europe. These newspapers helped people develop a sense of group pride and group awareness among those who may never before have thought of anyone as "kin" if they had not lived in the same village. Some of the papers helped foreigners adjust to the United States as they instructed their readers in how to register to vote, how to take out citizenship papers, and how to conform to American modes of behavior. In many ways the foreign-language press exerted a powerful influence in the immigrant communities. In Cleveland, we are told, "no movement whether social or political could succeed among the immigrant groups without the approval of their press. To be ignored or 'teased' by these papers meant failure for any business or political venture." Gradually, the immigrants became sophisticated in their use of the newspapers. In Pittsburgh, Croatian leaders organized several meetings with local journalists to explain to them who the Croatians were and what they wanted. Blacks in the cities also discovered the virtues of their own press because white newspapers printed derogatory news or else ignored them. In addition to discussions about items of group interest, newspapers such as the *Chicago Defender* provided lists of "do's and don't's" in city life for recently arrived Southern blacks.

Maintaining Old World Ties

Newspapers also kept readers informed about events in their native lands and tried in numerous ways to preserve involvement with and love of the old country. Special organizations sent money back for various good causes and encouraged individuals to make contributions, as well. Between $5 million and $10 million annually went to Mexico in the 1920s; Greeks sent $121 million home in 1921; and the amount that went back, over the years, to Ireland and Germany probably exceeded $1 billion. Even the groups with relatively few immigrants in America contributed to the fatherland. In 1910, for example, Finns in the United States donated $3,500 to the "Fight for Finland's Freedom Fund." Raising such money was never very hard. As one commentator noted, "Who was there with soul so dead he would not say a prayer, shed a tear and give a dollar for the cause of old Ireland?"

The greatest outpouring of feeling occurred during wartime. Immigrants raised money for relief and frequently returned home to fight for the cause. During the Balkan wars in 1912, Serbs and Greeks went back to Europe to battle the Turks, and Serbs, Croatians, and Slovenes participated in World War I The Bohemian National Alliance in the United States even influenced Congress to amend the immigration laws so that Americans of Czech descent who joined the French legions during the war would be allowed to return to this country without difficulty.

World War I also stimulated intensified efforts by American immigrants to obtain independence for their homelands. Irish nationalism had been strong in the United States for decades, but during and after the war the Irish put great pressure on President Woodrow Wilson to support an independent Ireland. American Poles, with better results, applied similar tactics to create a united Poland free of German, Austrian, or Russian political control. Some groups used their influence to create new states. Croatians, Slovenes, and Serbs held numerous rallies promoting the establishment of Yugoslavia; some Jews hoped

Czechs and Slovaks demonstrate their loyalty to the American cause in World War I. From the U.S. War Department General Staff. (National Archives)

to obtain a homeland in Palestine; and Czechs and Slovaks launched a drive for the formation of the state of Czechoslovakia.

During the 1930s and World War II, Greek, Polish, and Jewish groups, to name but three, helped compatriots and lobbied in Washington for the benefit of friends and relatives in Europe. The Poles protested the new boundaries for Poland determined at the Yalta Conference in 1945, and American Jews tried to obtain favorable interpretations of immigration legislation, as well as new laws to help refugees after World War II. They also used their influence after World War II to win American support for the establishment of the state of Israel in 1948.

Politics

Ethnic minorities could exert influence on the United States government because they had learned how to function in the American political system. No group proved more sophisticated or adroit in manipulating the system to its own needs than the Irish, who had a keen understanding of political power and how to use it. Having experienced what they saw as centuries of oppression by the English in Ireland, they had learned how Anglo-Saxon law could be used to obtain desired goals. As the only major immigrant group to arrive in the United States with this knowledge, they had an advantage over the other newcomers. Their initial experiences in the United States further convinced them that they would have little control over their own destiny unless they obtained political power. Because within their community positions of political importance carried high status, group approval coincided with practicality.

One aspect of their heritage that helped the Irish when they entered politics was their allegiance to the Roman Catholic Church. From this attachment they knew how a disciplined and cohesive organization functioned and how much could be accomplished when each member of the group accepted the guidance of established authorities. The urban political machine, set up according to hierarchical principles, may be likened to the church organization, with the political ward being equated with the local parish and the powers of the urban boss being similar to those of the archbishop. The members of the party, like the parishioners in the church, gave undeviating loyalty to the institution. In return, those who exercised authority could forgive almost any human foible except disloyalty and could also dispense favors to those deserving them.

When the Irish first came to the United States in large numbers, they found the Democratic Party more congenial than the Whigs. The latter included a large percentage of Protestant bigots, whereas the former seemed to have a much more tolerant and broader-based constituency. Once in the party, the

Irish helped to fashion it into the group that appealed to most of the immigrants who came after them. Not every Irish immigrant became a Democrat; many in Philadelphia and Rochester, New York, for example, joined the ranks of the Republicans after the Civil War. Nor did every immigrant follow the Irish in their allegiance—the Swedes, for example, were prominent Republicans—but over the next century or so the overwhelming majority of immigrants, and blacks after 1933, found the Democratic, rather than the Republican, Party more attuned to their needs.

Irish politicians understood the immigrant ethos, which facilitated their dealings with the newcomers. Unlike the Republicans, many of whom wanted "to civilize, to Christianize and Americanize these people," Irish Democrats wanted only to exercise political influence in the choice of elected candidates. As a result, by the end of the nineteenth century the Irish came to dominate the Democratic Party and the local political scene throughout most of urban America, including Boston, Chicago, New Orleans, New York City, and San Francisco.

The Irish political boss may be likened to a modern social welfare agency. He helped his constituents from the moment of their arrival in America, and he remembered those who remained loyal to him. One Boston ward leader had agents stationed at the pier waiting to assist the immigrants coming down the gangplank; thereafter, he did not have to worry about obtaining their support when he needed it. Ward bosses also provided jobs on the public payroll, posted bond for those held on criminal charges, obtained exemptions from city ordinances, speeded the process for those who wanted peddling licenses, sent food baskets at holiday times, appeared at social gatherings, and served as friends during any emergency. The Irish boss knew that his position depended on the votes of his ward or precinct. He tried not to show favoritism to any ethnic group. As one New York City politician put it, "it makes no difference to me whether I take my hat off in a church or put it on again in a synagogue." Chicago politicos often boasted of putting various southern and eastern Europeans on the public payroll. Moreover, while "Big Bill" Thompson was mayor of the city in the 1920s he hired so many African Americans as "temporary employees" that cynics referred to City Hall as "Uncle Tom's Cabin."

One of the most colorful of the Irish bosses, Boston's Jim Curley, was especially good at providing jobs. His administration fixed the streets, built hospitals, and laid out playgrounds and beaches. Although he had his faults and his administrations handled their funds carelessly, one historian reminds us that "much of what he did needed to be done." The cost would be excessive, the payrolls padded, and corruption ignored—yet "without him most of these projects would never have been undertaken."

Irish bosses, like many others who obtain power and positions of prominence, also aroused opposition. They angered those who envied their power, and their use of influence for personal gain frequently bordered the thin line between immorality and illegality. Rarely did they reject bribes or "favors" from those who received their largesse. They also had to protect their flanks, sometimes in ruthless and despicable ways, from others who wanted to obtain the power that they possessed.

In Chicago in the 1920s, one man of Czech ancestry, Anton Cermak, successfully battled the Irish machine within the Democratic Party, and between 1927 and 1933 he enjoyed the powers and prestige that Irish mayors had both before and after his administration. Like the Irish, the Czechs in Chicago put a premium on political power, and through Cermak they saw the chance to obtain the recognition they coveted. Enraged at being lumped together in the public mind with southern and eastern European immigrants, the Czechs longed for separate—and favorable—appraisal. They were sufficiently literate, cohesive, and stable to work together to achieve their goals.

Cermak, at first a ward boss, fulfilled his own ambitions and at the same time capitalized on Czech aspirations. In the 1920s, as other Democrats began to resent Irish domination of the political scene, he took advantage of this discontent. One of the main gripes against Irish political domination was that the choicest political plums, and sometimes two-thirds of the elected positions, went to fellow Irishmen. Once Cermak, who had proclaimed himself a leader of all of the foreign-born, achieved his goal of becoming mayor, Irish domination ceased as he distributed good jobs to members of other ethnic groups equitably. During his tenure in office, Slavs, Italians, and Scandinavians received greater recognition than they had previously. His boldest stroke occurred in 1932 when he chose a Jew to head the state Democratic ticket; the candidate won the election and became governor of Illinois. In 1933 an assassin's bullet, aimed at President-elect Franklin D. Roosevelt, killed the mayor, who rode in the same automobile, and soon the Irish regained control of Chicago's City Hall. They held on to it until the death of Mayor Richard Daley in 1976.

Like any leader, the political boss could retain his constituents' loyalties only so long as he moved in the direction that his followers wished to go. During the Progressive era, the immigrants supported most of the political and economic changes proposed. They backed, for the most part, reforms such as a federal income tax amendment to the United States Constitution, laws to regulate business, workman's compensation, mothers' pensions, safety legislation, the establishment of bureaus of labor statistics, and regulation of wages and hours, especially for women. Some, but certainly not all, even came around to accepting women's suffrage, although many regarded women in politics as a degrading thing and a threat to the family structure.

But the one "reform" that evoked almost unanimous opposition from every immigrant group except the Swedes was Prohibition. Many minorities, especially Irish, Germans, Czechs, Poles, and Yugoslavs, saw the saloon or beer parlor as a place to meet friends, exchange tales and jokes, read newspapers, and imbibe a few drinks. Most immigrants attached no stigma to these places and, in fact, considered them to be indispensable social institutions. But most WASP Americans believed that the consumption of alcoholic beverages led to poverty and moral degradation and, galvanized by the Anti-Saloon League and the Women's Christian Temperance Union, fought ferociously to outlaw it. The successful campaign climaxed with the passage of the Eighteenth Amendment to the Constitution in 1918 during the patriotic fervor aroused by American entry into World War I. The president of one German American group had proclaimed earlier that "Prohibitionism is a fight against Germans," and many Americans later interpreted it that way, also. German Americans had assumed, and correctly so, that the approval of Prohibition would be only the first step in the path of future xenophobic legislation. And so the Germans, as well as most other immigrant groups, battled to preserve their liquid pleasures. But the moral commitment that erupted during World War I overrode their objections.

Social Mobility

In spite of the many hardships that immigrants faced, they nonetheless improved their lot. They did not go from rags to riches, but often they moved up from being unskilled laborers to becoming skilled workers with higher pay. Moreover, real wages increased in the late nineteenth century, and working hours were reduced from the 1880s to World War I. With increased leisure and higher pay, the immigrants were able to become part of the emerging consumer culture. Immigrants especially enjoyed the movies, which, before the arrival of the talkies in the late 1920s, did not require knowledge of English. Important, too, was the desire to own their homes. By World War I one-quarter of the newcomers bought their own dwellings. And they had enough funds left over to support the many organizations that served their needs and to purchase newspapers in their own languages. Finally, too, immigrants were able to send money home, which could be used by those left behind or for tickets (mostly prepaid) to follow the immigrants to America. The culture that the immigrants tried so hard to maintain and the values that they strove to preserve dissipated with each succeeding generation. Their children, and to a lesser extent their grandchildren and great-grandchildren, clung to some traditions, but the "pull" of American society proved too strong. Most immigrants came to America for economic reasons, and they instilled the drive for success in their children. To succeed in American society, however, meant that the English language had to be mastered and spoken and that American customs had to be followed.

For some groups, cultural needs and values coincided with American goals, and therefore their children progressed quickly. The Greeks, for example, placed a high emphasis on work, status, and achievement. Parents wanted their children to move to a higher station in life than the one to which they were born, and they stimulated them to advance. The professions, especially law and medicine, were considered attractive positions. Germans regarded work as a necessary concomitant to life, and they instilled that idea in their children. Parents expected their offspring to master their tasks and accepted only first-rate performances from them. The following accomplishments of the children and grandchildren of one immigrant German family suggest their cultural values:

> Of the five sons and one daughter of Max and Anna Goettsch, two received M.D. degrees, three received Ph.D. degrees, and one received a degree in engineering. The daughter was not allowed to go to high school. Of Max's seven grandchildren, five received M.D. degrees, one received a Ph.D. degree, and one received an A.B.
>
> The most striking feature of the second generation is the educational attainments of the women. Five of the seven grandchildren were female. Of these five, three earned M.D. degrees, one earned a Ph.D., and one earned an A.B.

Of the groups that prized education, none achieved as much, or moved as quickly out of the working class, as the Jews. The traditional culture weighed heavily in Jewish accomplishment. Eastern European Jews considered a life devoted to study as the social ideal, and the most respected members in the community were the men who pursued that goal. No one else, no matter how wealthy or skilled, could compare in status with the Talmudic scholar. He received the greatest deference in the ghetto regardless of his economic status, and parents sought learned men as husbands for their daughters. In the United States, Jewish immigrants did not exalt their rabbis and scholars as much as they had in Europe, but the tradition of respect for learning continued. Jews encouraged their sons to achieve intellectually, and many of their daughters resented not being favored in the same fashion. A higher percentage of the children of eastern European Jewish descent graduated from high school and college, when given the opportunity to do so, than did the scions of any other ethnic background. A 1911 survey of New York City, where large numbers of both Jews and Italians lived, revealed that 16 percent of Jewish children were finishing high school. This was the highest proportion among immigrant groups. Practically no Italians finished high school. Five years later Jewish enrollment constituted 13 percent of the student body of Columbia University, 44 percent of that of Hunter College, 73 percent of that of City College, and 21 percent of that of Fordham University, a Roman Catholic institution. With one exception all of these schools were for men only. Hunter College enrolled only women. In his studies of social mobility in Boston, Stephan Thernstrom found that 75 percent of the children of eastern European Jewish immigrants entered the middle class after starting out in the working class. This percentage was higher than for any other immigrant group.

It is impossible to pinpoint which cultural characteristics stimulate mobility and which do not, but education, family values, and religious affiliation seem to make a difference. Offspring of Protestant and Jewish immigrants, therefore, progressed faster in American society than the children of other Europeans. The groups with the slowest economic achievement included those with a strong attachment to the Catholic Church, or groups in which parents equated American education with the destruction of family values. Thernstrom's study found that the Irish and Italians in Boston had the least mobility, and he suggests that parochial education in some way failed to stimulate the necessary ambition. In Chicago, Poles moved up the socioeconomic ladder slowly. Perhaps Robert Cross's study of the Catholic Church at the end of the nineteenth and early part of the twentieth centuries reveals the reason for this lack of mobility. He notes that "to the Catholic conservatives, the only proper response to social difficulties was devout passivity." We also know that not only did the Poles and Irish invest much of their resources in their churches, but they also insisted that their priests provide guidance on the most crucial matters they faced. And most of the Catholic priests subscribed to the view that only within the Catholic community, and only by accepting Catholic doctrines and outlook, could salvation be achieved. The descendants of Catholic immigrants gradually came to accept the value of social mobility, but the immigrant church did not emphasize this goal, as did many Protestants and Jews.

Another retarding factor in mobility has to do with family attitudes toward individual achievement. Mexicans, French Canadians, Poles, and Italians cherished views that would scarcely induce their offspring to surpass them in attainments. Often they taught children that individual accomplishment had to be subordinated to family needs; that education in itself had little value; and that gainful employment at the earliest age was a positive good. Mobility, children learned, took one away from one's family and threatened traditions. None of these groups stressed the advantages of learning English. Hungarian women in Detroit, for example, could be in this country for fifteen or twenty years without speaking English. "Why should I learn this funny English language when

I do not have to?" one woman asked. "None of my neighbors know how to talk English. If these American people want to talk to us so badly, why don't they learn our language?"

Each of these groups found change somewhat threatening; hence they failed to encourage their children to stray from what they already knew and believed. Among the Mexicans, for example, the culture dictated that an individual refrain from trying to do something he could not master. One sociologist tells us that for them, it would be better "not to try to reach a goal barred by serious obstacles than to pursue a goal at the risk of failure. Not to try does not reflect negatively on their manliness and honor but to try and fail does." Finally, individuals from these groups who moved up in American society were regarded negatively. As one Polish American historian writes, "Members of Polonia feel bitter toward their educated class, resent its attitude, and consider it ungrateful."

Gradually, these differences among the varied immigrant cultures blurred with the passage of time. Succeeding generations, exposed to the nationalizing influences of the public school and, increasingly after the 1920s, to the media, grew to adulthood with shared ideas about life in the United States. Their goals, their heroes, and their attitudes toward success showed a greater resemblance to a homogenized Americanism than to the foreign cultures that had been so supportive for their parents. They were on the path to assimilation.

It makes a great difference, of course, whether children grow up in a culture that encourages them to achieve in American terms or one that does not. Members of both categories have been successful in the United States, but the numbers coming from the former group are much greater than those coming from the latter. In Los Angeles, for example, the Mexican American Movement (1934–1950) emphasized the importance of education for socioeconomic advancement, but only a minority of adolescents heeded that advice. For a variety of reasons, including family finances, family values, inappropriate school curricula, and widespread bigotry, a 1930s study found that 53.7 percent of the girls and 43.7 percent of the boys quit high school before graduation. As a result of this failure to strive for greater accomplishments, most Mexicans before World War II did not achieve a status significantly higher than that of their parents.

At the same time, most children of other immigrant groups showed progress in social mobility from one generation to another, but the pace of that progress depended in large part on the values the children learned at home. Of course, even children with a desire to achieve cannot easily overcome institutionalized bigotry. Nor can they be oblivious to or remain untouched by a worldwide depression such as occurred during the 1930s. And finally, despite group influences and emphases, not every individual conforms to the stereotypical behavior of the minority to which he or she belongs. Nevertheless, most of the ethnic offspring did move to a class above that of their parents.

Whereas the children of immigrants progressed socially and economically, blacks rarely did. Their standard of living rose, but no matter how hard their families pushed them or how much education they had, racial discrimination prior to World War II proved an almost insurmountable obstacle. The small black business and professional elite catered largely to the poor crowded into the growing urban ghettos. Just as the Irish had competed with blacks for certain jobs in the mid-nineteenth century, immigrants from southern and eastern Europe competed with them in the twentieth.

Assimilation

With mobility came assimilation. The higher one's income and the more prestigious one's position, the more likely it was for the ethnic ties to be loosened. In fact, the factors promoting assimilation became so powerful that the descendants of the immigrants could scarcely resist them. American society, despite its rhetoric of tolerance, demanded conformity, and the immigrant children and grandchildren hastened to meet the dominant standards. Organizations set up to aid those in need, such as the Illinois Immigrants' Protective League and the North American Civic League for Immigrants, focused primarily on integrating their charges into American society. Employers such as Henry Ford in Detroit, and cities throughout the country, instituted English classes and "Americanization" programs for foreigners. At the Ford Motor Company school, the first thing immigrants learned to say was "I am an American." One prominent educator in New York City enunciated the prevailing sentiments when she said that the immigrants "must be made to realize that in forsaking the land of their birth, they were also forsaking the customs and traditions of that land; and they must be made to realize an obligation, in adopting a new country, to adopt the language and customs of that country."

The dominant elements in the Catholic Church hierarchy in America, mostly Irish, also came to promote "Americanization." The babble of tongues in the ethnic parishes hindered unity, and so they tried to assimilate all of the newcomers into one large American Catholic Church. But Germans, Poles, Lithuanians, and French Canadians, loyal Catholics though they might be, resented Irish control and the attempts to promote uniformity. Most of the immigrants rejected calls for them to relinquish their heritage. They wanted priests who spoke their languages and services that reflected the flavor of the Old World. Many Poles, for example, equated Americanization with the hated German and Russian attempts to impose their values on them in the regions where those European powers ruled at the end of the nineteenth century. To Poles a free country meant the freedom to retain their Polish customs and remain Polish Catholics. These conflicting views led to bickering among the various national groups and with the hierarchy in the American Catholic church well into the twentieth century.

Members of the second and third generations, however, did not share their parents' and grandparents' commitments to Old World values and felt more comfortable with the Americanized Roman Catholic Church. When they were young they had no choice but to conform to their parents' standards, but as they grew to adulthood, they rebelled. As one Polish American tells it, the traditional culture never had a chance to succeed with him or with his peers: "this generation, of which I am a part, never had to face the problem of pulling away from Polonia. We had never properly belonged to it. To us it was a slowly decaying world of aged folks living largely in a dream. One day it would pass and then there would remain only Americans whose forebears had once been Poles."

Immigrant adult-education class, about 1920. Governments and voluntary agencies ran thousands of classes and programs for immigrants in an effort to Americanize them and prepare them for citizenship. (Library of Congress)

The signs of Americanization are readily apparent. Many foreigners changed their names. The Dutch "Kok" became "Cook," the Jewish "Greenberg" became "Green," and the Greek "Kiriacopoulis" became "Campbell." Intermarriage, the most destructive element to survival of ethnic culture, took more time to achieve. At first children feared ostracism from their communities, so they were wary of marital partners who did not have family approval. Also, some parents found ingenious ways to keep their children within the fold. There is a story of a Jewish immigrant woman in Fargo, North Dakota, which housed a tiny Jewish community. To find eligible mates for her several daughters, she opened a boarding house for Jewish bachelors. A granddaughter recalled, "She got husbands for all her daughters." Over time, religious barriers broke down. Today about one-half of Catholics and Jews marry individuals of another faith. For most third- and fourth-generation Americans, national heritage has practically disappeared as a concern in selecting a mate.

The process of adjustment and Americanization varied from group to group. For some of the immigrants' children and grandchildren, American bigotry accelerated the pace. Their parents had been forced to bear the burden of foreignism, but the children did not necessarily care to carry the culture of their ancestors forward—especially when to do so bore such a stigma in the United States. Perhaps cultural pluralism could have developed in the United States had there been a real spirit of tolerance. But as the next chapters show, "difference" was not considered in neutral terms. *Different* meant "inferior," and few people growing up in American society consciously chose to be attacked or ostracized in the land of their birth.

7

Ethnic Tensions and Conflicts

(1880s–1945)

Throughout our history many Americans looked on outsiders as strange, inferior, or potentially disloyal. Those attitudes proved so strong that frequently the descendants of assimilated immigrant groups accepted them, too. As a result they viewed the new waves of foreigners as necessary sources of menial labor and approved the annihilation of Indians because allegedly they blocked the progress of the white man's civilization. Contempt for American Indians and the belief in black inferiority grew steadily in the nineteenth century. As for the foreign masses coming to American shores in the late nineteenth and early twentieth centuries, the voices of bigotry became louder. Prejudices found expression both in elaborate "scientific" theories that "proved" the innate superiority of old-stock white Americans and in crude ethnic slurs. Intolerance also manifested itself in violence as well as in social, legal, and economic discrimination.

Rapid changes in American society and the economy after the Civil War reinforced intolerance. In the 1890s American nativists began noting with alarm the shifting patterns of immigration that brought so many Jews and Catholics from southern and eastern Europe. Labor violence highlighted by the national railroad strike of 1877, the 1886 Haymarket riot in Chicago, and crowded slums in the nation's fastest growing cities, also created uneasiness about the stability of American society. Nativists blamed foreign radicals and agitators for the unrest. During the Progressive era, many Americans singled out the newcomers as the cause of corrupt urban political machines. Reformers who opposed saloons and alcoholic beverages saw a connection between corruption and drinking. They believed that curbing immigration would curtail the sordid aspects of American urban politics. A considerable number of Progressive reformers accepted that idea.

Others feared the economic impacts of massive immigration. When depression drove wages down and threw people out of work, they blamed the immigrants for lowering the American standard of living. Often the newcomers, themselves prisoners of peasant ignorance and superstition, came with traditional hatreds and suspicions of one another, and they did not lose these feelings quickly when they arrived in the United States. All of these factors contributed to the widespread intolerance and bigotry that flourished in the United States during the late nineteenth and well into the twentieth centuries.

Pseudoscientific Racism

Pseudoscientific racism provided the intellectual foundation for the nation's intolerance. Often, society held new immigrants to Anglo-Saxon standards. One sociologist enunciated the views of many Americans when he described the immigrants to the United States. northern Europeans, he believed, were most desirable because they possessed—and surpassed everyone else in— "innate ethical endowment." Southern and eastern Europeans, on the other hand, were "beaten men of beaten breeds," and some of them clearly belonged in "skins, in wattled huts at the close of the Great Ice Age."

Such ideas found wide acceptance. Some people in every region or section of the United States detested the minority peoples in their midst. Nor were there any states in which blacks or immigrants could feel secure. Throughout the nation the only major difference was which group would bear the brunt of local prejudice. Usually the largest minority in an area attracted the most unfavorable attention, but even small groups failed to escape the widespread bigotry.

Despite the viciousness and muddled thinking that was directed at immigrants, the bigotry was even more intense when directed against racial minorities, especially black Americans. Whites stereotyped them in newspapers, speeches, and on the stage as lazy, shiftless, and childlike, as beasts and rapists. They called blacks "niggers," "darkies," and "coons." Politician Tom Watson of Georgia, who early in his career courted their votes, later wrote that the black man has "no comprehension of virtue, honesty, truth, gratitude and principle." And he insisted that the white South had to "lynch him occasionally, and flog him now and then, to keep him from blaspheming the Almighty, by his conduct, on account of his smell and his color." A few racists likened blacks to apes and scarcely considered them as human beings at all. One book, entitled *The Negro a Beast,* had wide circulation in the early twentieth century.

A variety of "learned" opinions buttressed such diatribes. Blacks allegedly ranked lowest on a "scale" of human worth, falling below the southern and eastern Europeans. Proponents of the Darwinian notions popular in the late nineteenth century, who saw life as a jungle where the fittest survived, claimed that blacks were losing out in the competition among races, and some even saw them as slipping backward into a morass of vice and immorality. At the very least, the argument ran, whites had to rule the racially inferior people. Even many of those who demanded better treatment for black Americans believed in their inferiority.

Cover for a piece of sheet music, 1899. (State Historical Society of Wisconsin)

Not all Americans succumbed to the dominant ethnic ideologies of the era. Presidents Grover Cleveland, William Howard Taft, and Woodrow Wilson, who may or may not have harbored similar views, nevertheless vetoed immigration-restriction legislation that discriminated against southern and eastern Europeans. In Wilson's case, at least, his veto marked a reversal of a position enunciated in earlier years when he indicated that many of the newer immigrants consisted of "multitudes of men of lowest class from the south of Italy, and men of the meaner sort out of Hungary and Poland, men out of the ranks where there was neither skill nor energy nor any initiative of quick intelligence....The Chinese were more to be desired, as workmen if not as citizens, than most of the coarse crew that came crowding in every year at the eastern ports."

Not until World War I did these antiforeign feelings have enough strength to curb immigration. Various reformers cautioned against slurring foreigners and urged acceptance of pluralism. Some helped organize the Immigrants' Protective League, and others, such as Jane Addams, lived and worked in the urban ethnic neighborhoods. Probably the major reason for the failure of immigration restriction prior to the 1920s was economic; the nation had a seemingly endless need for the labor the newcomers brought. When workers began to saturate the industrial employment market and the fears of further immigration became overwhelming, Congress passed legislation to restrict European and Asian entry into the United States.

As for blacks, few whites after 1890 could be found to speak in their behalf. Racial demagogy peaked around the turn of the century, and its expressions pervaded even the highest levels of government. In 1902 one of Alabama's United States senators, John T. Morgan, ranted on the Senate floor about how "negro suffrage...has been one unbroken line of political, social, and industrial obstruction to progress, and a constant disturbance of the peace in a vast region of the United States." Senator Francis G. Newlands of Nevada, born in Natchez, Mississippi, and reared in southern Illinois, offered specific suggestions for change. At the Democratic National Convention in 1912 he called for the repeal of the Fifteenth Amendment to the Constitution, which forbids the denial or abridgment of the vote "on account of race, color, or previous condition of servitude," and asked for a national prohibition against black suffrage. Even President Theodore Roosevelt expressed shallow and bigoted opinions. In 1906 he wrote to one correspondent: "Now as to the Negroes! I entirely agree with you that as a race and in the mass [they] are altogether inferior to the whites."

Some reformers challenged these outbursts. In 1905, when a South Carolina psychologist concluded that the IQ test proved innate black inferiority, Oswald Garrison Villard, editor of the *New York Evening Post,* disproved and debunked his findings. Some liberal whites, such as Mary White Ovington, defended the black man's right to vote. Along with others, she tried to help through organizations such as the National Urban League, founded in 1911, which had a social work approach. More militant whites joined with blacks and founded the National Association for the Advancement of Colored People (NAACP) in 1909.

Triumph of Jim Crowism

These voices against bigotry remained a minority, however, after the 1880s. The prevalent views, along with the weariness most Americans felt about the crusade to aid the freedman, helped end Radical Reconstruction of the South in 1877. However, even though the overthrow of southern Radical Republicans did not halt all of the achievements of the Reconstruction era, by the 1890s a torrent of racism engulfed southern blacks. Almost every area of human contact became subject to state and municipal regulations segregating the races. Collectively known as "Jim Crow" legislation, these laws proliferated throughout the region. The "grandfather clauses" (which allowed men to vote if their grandfathers had been eligible to vote) came first, followed by literacy tests, poll taxes, and white primaries to eliminate blacks from the electoral process. Then communities segregated railroads, streetcars, schools, steamboats, restrooms, drinking fountains, and other public facilities and enacted ordinances requiring separate neighborhoods for blacks and whites.

Lynching, or at least the threat of it, became the most brutal method of chastising the blacks. This incredible means of dispensing "justice" occurred in several regions of the country, but most frequently in the South. At times mobs left the bodies of whites and Asians dangling from trees, but overwhelmingly most victims were blacks. By the late nineteenth century southern lynchings averaged more than two per week, although most took place during the warm months between April and October. On occasion large mobs witnessed the hanging and torturing of helpless blacks, some of whom the crowds burned alive. In 1893 a few men gouged out the eyes of a black man with a hot poker before setting fire to him; in 1921, after a particularly vicious group burned a black male, the onlookers waited for the fire to subside before scrambling for the man's bones, which they took home as souvenirs.

Most victims of lynching were men. So were the victims of the previously mentioned convict lease system. Historian Douglas A. Blackmon described this practice using twenty-two-year-old Green Cottenham as an example. In 1908 an Alabama judge found him guilty of vagrancy, and sentenced him to one year at hard labor. The state then leased him to the Tennessee Coal, Iron, and Railroad Company, a subsidiary of the United States Steel Corporation. He found himself toiling under the lash in a coal mine with working conditions that resembled slavery "in all but name." Some women were caught up in this system. Blackmon also found cases of women living in virtual slavery after having been sentenced without any fair trial. Cornelia Hammock's experience provides a vivid example of how the system operated in Georgia. The town mayor convicted her on a charge of larceny despite her not-guilty plea. Sentenced to join other convict laborers doing farm work, she died only two days later. State authorities never investigated her death.

For a number of angry Americans, individual assaults did not suffice. Many an attack focused on large minority groups of people. Between the 1870s and 1890s the Chinese in the West suffered from massive outbursts in Los Angeles,

San Francisco, Seattle, Reno, and Denver. Of the last attack, one Chinese scholar lecturing in Chicago observed, "If a single American was treated in China as were the victims of the anti-Chinese riots at Denver, the United States would send 100,000 missionaries to civilize the heathen." In Nebraska mobs beat Greeks; Slavs endured similar assaults in Utah. Italians were gunned down or strung up in places as diverse as Florida, Colorado, and Illinois. An 1891 incident in New Orleans, which had international repercussions, resulted in the lynching of eleven Italians after a local jury had acquitted them of murder.

Despite widespread antipathy toward immigrants, the worst demonstrations focused on African Americans. In Atlanta in 1906, newspaper suggestions that some black men had raped white women set off one of the bloodiest racial assaults since the 1890 massacre at Wounded Knee. African American flight to the North also triggered demonstrations there. The Great Migration, between 1910 and 1920, resulted in more than five hundred thousand blacks leaving the South and going to northern cities. Competition there between blacks and whites for jobs, housing, and recreational facilities also caused trouble. In 1917, in East St. Louis, Illinois, tension between black and white workers erupted into a full-scale race riot. Two years later a similar outburst rocked the nation's capital, and in July 1919 Chicagoans witnessed an even bloodier episode. Chicago had experienced decades of racial tensions before the Great Migration heightened the competition for jobs and homes, and even before the riot, blacks who purchased or rented housing in white areas were the targets of bomb throwers. The Chicago riot itself began when whites threw rocks at a black youth who swam across the supposed line separating the "white" from the "black" swimming area of the city's beaches. When the youth drowned, violence erupted into a race war, and the city experienced a week of terror and bloodshed; twenty-three whites and twenty-five blacks died and over five hundred persons were injured before the state militia restored order.

Treatment of Indians

The nation's oldest minority, the Indians, experienced no race riots only because few of them lived close to large numbers of whites. Despite this, the tribal people suffered from violence and bigotry throughout the nineteenth century. The decades after the Civil War saw the federal government accelerate its policy of racial segregation by forcing the last western tribes onto ever-contracting reservations. Then, whenever restless tribesmen fled from their captivity, columns of blue-clad troops pursued them. Thus the violence against Indians seemed to come from the government rather than individual citizens, but this was not so. Widespread civilian antipathy toward the reservation dwellers made it impossible for any government policy to help much, and often the army campaigns resulted from popular hatred rather than military necessity. Particularly in the West, whites considered the tribal people as pests at best and as dangerous enemies at worst. One Nevada newspaperman claimed that the only way to end Indian hostilities was through the "total extermination of every red-skin from the [Canadian] to the Mexican frontier." Several years later another western spokesman claimed that the life of a single pioneer was worth more than hundreds "of the best red devils that ever scalped a white person." A third editor recommended welcoming the Indians when they asked for peace and then slaughtering them "as though they were as many nests of rattlesnakes." With such views prevalent in much of the West, it is not surprising that the white population generally welcomed violence against their Indian neighbors.

As rails laced the countryside together and mines, smelters, and towns came to dot much of the West, the Indians there had few, if any, reasons for wanting to join American society. Often they considered the pioneers to be greedy, dishonest, and dangerous. At the same time Caucasian newcomers feared the tribal people as physically dangerous. Even more important, they considered Indians as a major obstacle to regional development. Most of the approximately 175,000 tribesmen on the West Coast lived in areas heavily overrun by prospectors: the northern coastal mountains and along the Sierra foothills. Although population statistics are vague and often inaccurate, it seems likely that as late as 1850–51 nearly one hundred thousand Indians lived in the mining regions of California. As gold seekers, teamsters, lumbermen, and farmers poured into the state, the Indian population plummeted. Thousands died from measles, typhoid, smallpox, and malaria, as well as from tuberculosis and venereal disease, all brought in by the newcomers.

Homicide and starvation also destroyed many others. Americans who crossed the plains and Rockies brought a hatred and fear of Indians with them. They rarely bothered to differentiate between peaceful and hostile villagers. Often an Indian was considered "a cruel, cowardly vagabond, giving to thieving, gambling, drunkenness, and all that is vicious, without one redeeming trait." As such his life was worth little, and usually those who killed Indians escaped punishment. If the tribesmen dared protect themselves or avenge wrongs at the hands of the whites, vigilante groups pursued them. Whenever possible, miners destroyed Indians' food and shelters and forced them to move out. Such campaigns and individual acts of violence so reduced their numbers that by 1880 no more than twenty thousand Indians survived in California. In only thirty years the influx of whites had engulfed and destroyed nearly 80 percent of the resident Indians.

Although the pioneers caused rapid destruction for the California natives, there were exceptions. The Plains tribes, in particular, had achieved a blending of native and European resources that strengthened their material cultures. These groups, which included the Sioux, Cheyenne, and Crow in the north and the Arapaho, Pawnee, Kiowa, and Comanche farther south, had acquired horses from the Spanish in the Southwest a few generations earlier, giving them mobility for hunting and warfare.

By the time white Americans reached them, their mobile culture, sophisticated use of the environment, large numbers, and skill as hunters and fighters meant that the Plains tribes could not be taken lightly. Nevertheless, between 1849 and the end of the century, a seemingly unending stream of pioneer miners, lumbermen, ranchers, and settlers flooded the land. These developments

Late-nineteenth-century view of Indians. Many whites believed that it was impossible to "civilize" the Indians and that they were shiftless or hopeless drunkards. (Library of Congress)

made it increasingly difficult for whites and Indians to live in peace, particularly as the large buffalo herds of the Plains dwindled rapidly. In the twenty years following the Civil War, commercial hunters killed millions of animals to feed construction crews building the transcontinental railroads and to provide leather hides for the rest of the nation. From 1872 to 1874 the hide hunters alone killed more than 3,500,000 buffaloes; during those same years the Indians killed a mere 150,000 for their food. In 1874 Secretary of the Interior Columbus Delano noted that "the buffalo are disappearing rapidly, but not faster than I desire." The federal government's policy toward the Indians of "destroying their hunting habitats, coercing them on reservations, and compelling them to begin to adopt the habits of civilization" would have a better chance for success, officials believed, if the warriors could no longer hunt.

As early as 1851, Congress had appropriated $100,000 to negotiate with the Plains and Mountain tribes in order to secure safe travel routes to the Pacific. That same year government diplomats and Indians met at Fort Laramie and concluded treaties that called for the Indians to vacate certain areas while promising payments of goods and supplies to the tribes and peace for both groups. Tribal leaders realized that each land cession only temporarily slackened white demands for more land. The Cherokee newspaper predicted that once white settlement extended to the Indian country, the government would send a negotiator "with a pocket full of money and his mouth full of lies." The government agent would use flattery, bribery, and alcohol to extract "something that will be called a treaty." Leaders of the northern tribes also objected to repeated calls for treaties, each of which promised the Indian that this move would be his last. The oft-quoted question of Sioux Chief Spotted Tail, "Why does not the Great Father put his red children on wheels, so he can move them as he will?" showed their bitterness.

However, not all Indians felt either overwhelmed or threatened by the advancing whites. Many leaders negotiated skillfully with government personnel as they sought to enrich their tribes. Some chiefs preferred withdrawal to signing more treaties. Others, including the followers of Sitting Bull, fled to Canada for a time, and a group of the Kickapoo migrated to Mexico, where some of their descendants remain today. A few prominent leaders, such as the Comanche Quanah Parker and Sioux Red Cloud, urged their followers to come to terms with the advancing Americans, as distasteful as that seemed at the time.

Despite this range of Indian responses, interracial violence racked the West for an entire generation, as some groups chose warfare as the best response to the continuing white invasion. When called on to pacify the Indians, most of the time the army failed to catch its elusive foes. When it did, better organization and heavier firepower usually triumphed. Yet Indian warriors won victories even if they lost the wars. During the summer of 1862 Little Crow led angry Sioux on a rampage across frontier Minnesota, in which at least five hundred settlers and soldiers died before the fighting ended. Just four years later the Sioux destroyed Captain William J. Fetterman's command of eighty men while trying to drive the army from its forts along the Bozeman Trail, which stretched through the heart of the tribal hunting grounds. This victory stunned the government. Quickly it agreed to withdraw the soldiers, and the Indians burned the empty forts.

In 1876 Cheyenne and Sioux warriors annihilated five companies of the 7th Cavalry under Lieutenant Colonel George A. Custer and sent a shock wave through the nation then busily celebrating its centennial. The next year, Chief Joseph led several hundred Nez Percé Indians in a masterful flight from eastern Oregon into Montana. During the several-month 1,600-mile trek, the Indians completely outfought and outmaneuvered many of the best units the army could bring against them. But this campaign ended as did all the others. The fugitives ran out of food, horses, ammunition, and the will to fight, whereas the army brought fresh men and supplies against them. The Ute War of 1879, the Apache wars of the 1880s, and the destruction of Big Foot's band of Sioux at Wounded Knee in 1890 ended open warfare.

Having tried treaty negotiations, physical withdrawal, and armed resistance in response to the continuing flood of whites moving into the West, some Indians turned their attention to religion to ensure survival. By the 1870s a few shamans began offering new advice, and many Indians accepted their teachings with enthusiasm. The most important religious movement, the Ghost Dance, began among the Paiute tribe of Nevada. There, during the 1880s, a shaman named Wovoka dreamed of meeting the Great Spirit and then began preaching to his neighbors. He claimed that a number of natural disasters would destroy the whites, and that the ancestors of the Indians would return and repopulate the West. To achieve this, the Indians had to accept the prophet's message, which included a modified circle dance, accompanied by a group of special songs Wovoka claimed he had learned through his visions. The prophet cautioned his followers to remain at peace, to avoid alcohol, to be just to others, but also to shun dealings with the whites whenever possible.

Nevertheless, the Ghost Dance led to disaster when it swept through the poverty-stricken Sioux at Pine Ridge. There, when the local Indian agent panicked and forbade any further dancing, Chief Big Foot and several hundred followers fled the reservation to continue the ceremonies. Units of the 7th Cavalry followed, and in December 1890, when the troopers sought to disarm the Sioux and return them to the reservations, fighting broke out, resulting in the massacre at Wounded Knee. Thus, although the Ghost Dance and other religious movements offered some consolation to the tribes, they ultimately failed to help overcome the daily problems.

Sioux Indian Camp on the River Brule near Pine Ridge, South Dakota. The photograph was taken about 1891, shortly after the "Battle" of Wounded Knee, in which army troops killed two hundred Sioux, including women and children. (Library of Congress)

While Indians tried to retain their culture, the government continued long-term efforts to destroy tribal identities. Beginning in the 1870s agents from the Bureau of Indian Affairs (BIA) recruited young warriors to serve as scouts and auxiliaries for the army. In 1878 Congress appropriated the first funds to operate Indian police forces on the reservations. The men who took these jobs had to cut their hair, wear the white man's clothes, speak English, and enforce reservation regulations. By 1883 the government had established a system of Courts of Indian Offenses, which struck at the heart of village life. Presided over by some former chiefs, as well as would-be leaders, these courts enforced reservation rules against plural marriage and participation in traditional religious observances such as the Sundance. Both the reservation police and the courts undermined customary leaders and traditions, weakened tribal unity, and provided models for those few individuals who wanted to adopt white customs.

In addition to disrupting tribal society, the reformers and government alike sought to turn all Indians into sedentary farmers. To accomplish this, the whites suggested that giving each adult Indian his or her parcel of land would encourage the tribal people to become individually oriented. It would also leave much "surplus" land on the reservations for frontier whites to acquire.

Even those who considered themselves friends of the Indians favored allotting land on an individual basis. Such pressures to force land ownership on the tribesmen led to the passage of a so-called Indian Homestead Act in 1875. This legislation extended to some Indians the provisions of the 1862 Homestead Act if they asked for the land. The optional provisions of this law failed to satisfy the proponents of allotment, however, and after an extended campaign in 1887 they succeeded in getting Congress to pass the Dawes Severalty Act. It assigned a specific plot of land to each adult Indian, hoping to disrupt tribal use of land in common. Many tribes and individual Indians objected, but the people of the Indian Territory were able to delay the loss of their land for only a temporary period. In a few cases local Indian leaders subverted the policy by claiming allotments as a bloc and maintaining their communal economic practices. Nevertheless, partitioning tribal reservations proved the most successful of several methods used to weaken Indian societies.

Should these pressures to force individual land ownership fail, the bureaucrats hoped that education in the ways of the dominant culture might make Indians less unique. Schools such as the Carlisle Institute and the Haskell Institute in Kansas served as training grounds for young Indians. Upon graduation from these institutions the young men and women were to return to their reservations and convince fellow tribesmen to adopt the white man's "superior" customs.

At the end of the nineteenth century the techniques used to destroy tribal culture, such as individual landholding, white man's education, and continuing pressures to forget old Indian customs, had taken their toll. In some instances tribal identity became vague, but at the same time the Indians refused to become mere imitations of the white majority. Crowding tribal remnants together in even smaller areas increased intertribal exchanges of customs and ideas. The mixing of children from many groups at boarding schools planted the seeds for the later pan-Indian movement, which grew steadily in the twentieth century.

By the first decade of the twentieth century, those citizens who believed "the only good Indian is a dead one" should have been happy. Poverty, malnutrition, disease, and death stalked the shrinking reservations. By 1900 only two hundred thousand Indians dwelled on or near the reservations, most living in wretched conditions. Although the policy of assimilation had failed to get them into the mainstream of American life, it had succeeded in the other half of its objective, as Indians seemed to be disappearing rapidly as a distinct group. Throughout the nineteenth century many white Americans believed the "inferior" or "primitive" groups had to give way before more "civilized" ones. These people saw the steady decline of the Indian population as the proper result of this process and concluded that the tribesmen would not long remain an identifiable part of American society.

Attitudes toward Asians

Whereas the Indians had been placed on barren reservations, other groups in the West, needed for their labor, could not be shunted aside so easily. The Chinese experiences there created too much interracial friction to encourage further immigration. In fact, by 1875 the riots and bitter hostility had resulted in congressional legislation banning prostitutes, especially Chinese ones. Then in 1882 Congress enacted the Chinese Exclusion Act. This prohibited laborers from China from entering the country for ten years although the time frame kept being extended. The 1882 law marked the beginning of concerted efforts by the federal government to refuse admittance to specific groups. That same year another law barred persons likely to become public charges and others thought to be undesirable. To enforce these acts, the federal government took control of immigration and gradually created a bureaucracy to carry out the laws. In 1910 the federal government began requiring Chinese immigrants to be admitted by officials at Angel Island in San Francisco harbor, whereas most Europeans had to enter at Ellis Island in New York. (Angel Island closed in 1990; Ellis Island screened its last immigrant in 1954.)

Nativists repeatedly insisted that Japanese workers lowered the American standard of living. These nativists also argued that the Japanese could not be assimilated into national life because they constituted an alien race with inferior customs. At first the warning about Japanese immigrants attracted little support, but by 1900 the situation in California had changed. Newspapers carrying headlines such as "Brown Man an Evil in the Public Schools" and "The Yellow Peril—How the Japanese Crowd Out the White Race" fanned public hysteria. In 1905 anti-Japanese agitators met to form the Asiatic Exclusion League. This group drew its support from labor organizations and patriotic societies because it insisted that Japanese workers labored for lower wages and were undesirable citizens. In addition, League spokesmen saw the growing power of Japan in the Pacific as a threat to American security. Some racists claimed that Japanese immigrants might be agents of a dangerous foreign power.

Opposition to the Japanese led to an international incident in 1906, when the San Francisco School Board announced that it was going to segregate Japanese schoolchildren, who numbered fewer than one hundred students. The personal intervention of President Theodore Roosevelt and negotiations with Japan led to a rescinding of the order and the forming of the "Gentlemen's Agreement," which limited emigration from Japan. As immigration subsided, anti-Japanese opposition declined somewhat in California, although the legislature enacted laws to prohibit most Asians from owning land. Nonetheless, politicians and patriots continued assailing them. Social and economic discrimination also persisted.

Asian Indians, though few in number, also witnessed calls for keeping them out of America. Authorities banned some, claiming that they might become wards of the state. Therefore, a general immigration law enacted in 1917 barred Asian Indians from entry. A few years later Congress halted the admission of "picture brides." As a result of these acts, Asians could no longer bring their families to America. Many of the single men remained bachelors, but others, including a number of Sikhs, married Mexican women and saw their children raised as Catholics.

To some extent hostility toward Asian minorities shifted to the Filipinos, who replaced the Japanese as agricultural workers, especially during the 1920s. Although not American citizens, Filipinos could immigrate freely to the United States because they lived in an American possession. Their arrival in Hawaii and California led to antagonism, discrimination, and even violence in those places. Patriotic and labor groups believed that they took jobs from Americans and demanded their exclusion. In 1934 Congress settled the issue by passing a law that granted an immigration quota of fifty per year to the Philippine Islands until independence was achieved ten years later. In 1946 the Philippines became self-governing, and its citizens then became subject to American immigration laws.

Attitudes toward Europeans

European entrants, who constituted by far the largest numbers of minorities in America, also encountered continued hostility in the United States. In general, however—although there certainly were exceptions—they received better treatment than Asians, Mexicans, African Americans, and Indians. As the Europeans acculturated into American society they became, except for religious preferences, indistinguishable from other whites. But until they assimilated, they did not enjoy the privileges of equal status.

Germans and Scandinavians, greeted at times with much suspicion, gradually received more cordial treatment, although World War I resulted in a torrent of abuse directed at the Germans. The Irish, on the other hand, had a much more difficult time, as many Americans continued to dislike them. One commonly used textbook in the nineteenth century warned that unless this country curbed immigration, the United States would become "the common sewer of Ireland."

The coming of the southern and eastern Europeans after the 1880s somewhat muted the prejudices toward the earlier immigrants, now seen in some quarters as substantial citizens, frugal, hardworking, industrious, and capable of assimilation into American society. The venom heaped on Jews, Italians, Greeks, and other southern and eastern Europeans rivaled the worst epithets borne by the Irish decades before them. The Italians, dismissed as "the Chinese of Europe," symbolized those southern and eastern Europeans who "blotted the native landscape." The poorest and worst neighborhoods in Chicago were described as teeming "with negroes, Jews of the lowest class, and 'dagoes,' which term, as everyone knows, is applied indiscriminately to Italians, Sicilians, Corsicans, and Greeks." Called "wop" or "Dago" or "Guinea," the Italian was assumed to be a criminal and an inferior being not fit to associate with "white" Americans. In many areas of the South, Italian American children had to attend the segregated black schools, and a common saying on the New York docks was, "One white man is as good as two or three Italians." Other Europeans met similar hostility. The Greeks became known as "the scum of Europe." A California restaurateur summarized his feelings toward them in a pithy advertisement: "John's Restaurant. Pure American. No Rats. No Greeks."

Many old-stock Americans questioned the "whiteness" of southern and Eastern Europeans, but by law they were white. They could become citizens and vote, and they did not face the vicious Jim Crow practices that diminished southern blacks. Early in the twentieth century the Bureau of Immigration announced that forty-five races or peoples were entering the country, including thirty-six "indigenous to Europe." These newcomers were nationality or linguistic groups, not distinct races, but those wanting to exclude these immigrants considered them to be inferior people. E. A. Ross, a well-known and respected progressive and professor at the University of Wisconsin, wrote that "the Mediterranean peoples are morally below the races of northern Europe is as certain as any social fact. . . . Immigration officials find that different peoples are as day and night in point of veracity, and report vast trouble in extracting the truth from certain brunet nationalities."

Europeans were sometimes blamed for the ills and conflicts of the cities and rapid industrialization. When strikes and labor-management disagreements led to violence in the late nineteenth century, old-stock Americans said that foreigners brought radical and alien ideas to America and that the immigrants, not working conditions, caused the troubles. Following the assassination of President William McKinley, Congress banned anarchists. Americans blamed foreigners for labor problems and also castigated the newcomers for supporting corrupt political machines in the nation's growing cities.

Interethnic Conflict

With all of this rancor displayed toward ethnic groups, one might assume that the minorities would have banded together to protect themselves. Just the opposite sometimes occurred. Immigrants of different backgrounds shunned or even fought each other. Sometimes rivalries emerged because competing groups sought the same jobs; at other times conflicts resulted from historical squabbles brought from Europe or served as a way for foreigners to take on the coloration of "real" Americans. Also important, however, were their American experiences, which so brutalized hundreds of thousands of lower-class immigrants that one of the few socially acceptable ways for them to vent their frustrations was to attack members of other ethnic groups.

Of the early entrants, the Irish seemed to have had great animosity toward others. At first they even looked on Irish from different sections of the old country with malice, and American observers regarded them as "involved in continual internecine strife." Rivalries of "Corkonians," "Far-Downs," and "Connaught-Men" (representing different counties in Ireland) often produced bloody brawls. Later they abandoned such quarrels, joined together, and battled Czechs, French Canadians, Greeks, Poles, Italians, and Jews.

The Germans divided not only along religious lines between Catholics and Protestants but also according to regional backgrounds. High Germans dissociated themselves from Low Germans, Swabians shunned Bavarians, Württembergers disliked Prussians, and so it went. Together the Germans snickered at the Poles and sneered at the "wops." In one Nebraska county a sort of "iron curtain" separated Germans from Danes until the 1950s.

The Czechs got on with the Germans but not with the Magyars, Italians, or Irish. They frequently attributed personal misfortunes to the antagonism from the Irish that they incurred in Chicago. The Czechs and Slovaks, who united to push for their own country in Europe, still were not completely at home with one another in America. Among the Slovaks themselves, Catholics and Lutherans kept their distance; both remained wary of the secularists. Croatians and Serbs in the United States engaged in numerous bouts of name-calling and fist-fighting when circumstances brought them together. In the Pennsylvania mines Hungarians, Swedes, Italians, and Irishmen battled one another; in cities all over America there was little intermingling among the residents of the many "Greektowns," "Corktowns" (Irish), "Dutchtowns" (German), "Dago Hills," or "Sauerkraut Rows."

In many communities Greeks from Crete did not like mainland Greeks, and both of them hated Italians, Turks, and Slavs. Finns did not get on with Swedes or Montenegrins, and in some sections of the United States French and German barroom brawls became major concerns to the local populace. Like the Irish, the Poles had a reputation for being "constant troublemakers." They fought everyone they came near, including Italians, Syrians, Greeks, Slovaks, and Czechs, and they despised Jews.

Religious Bigotry

Anti-Semitism, in fact, was the one prejudice common to most of the European immigrants, and it surfaced among Americans as well. Jews long resident in the United States also harbored animosity toward their brethren from eastern Europe. The older American Jewish community, originally populated by emigrants from the Iberian Peninsula and central Europe, feared the entry of the strange-garbed Orthodox Jews. American Jews worried that with the arrival of coreligionists from Russia, Poland, and Rumania the latent anti-Semitism in this country would erupt, and events proved them to be correct. Once the eastern Europeans arrived, however, the Americanized Jews did everything they could to ease their adjustment to the New World. They set up numerous educational and charitable institutions and provided community leadership in affairs touching Jews in general. The gentile majority, on the other hand, responded to the influx by increasing its discriminatory practices, barring Jews from clubs and resorts, from jobs, and from certain residential areas. Most vicious, however, was the frequent harassment from street thugs and bullies who beat up Jewish children, pulled old men's beards, and hurled epithets. This hostility prevailed among Protestants and Catholics, old-line Americans, and immigrants.

Nevertheless, antipathy toward Jews lacked the same virulence or organization in the United States as antagonism to Roman Catholics. The death of the Know-Nothing Party in the 1850s ended organized opposition to them until 1887, when a new anti-Catholic group, the American Protective Association (APA), was formed in Clinton, Iowa. Dedicated to preserving public schools and aiming to eliminate Catholics from what it perceived as their growing "political control" of the nation, the APA won the support of more than two and one-half million Protestant Americans, mostly in the Midwest and the Rocky Mountain states. It reached its zenith during the terrible depression years of 1893–94 and then, as one historian of the movement wrote, died after 1896 "for no apparent reason other than that the times were not ripe for it to flourish."

The demise of the APA, however, did not mean the end of anti-Catholicism; it waxed especially strong in the areas in which the largest number of Catholics lived, as well as in the Southern and Midwestern "Bible belts," where Baptist and Methodist fundamentalists dwelled and where frustrated politicians such

A demonstration by the Ku Klux Klan in Beckley, West Virginia. The revived
Klan reached a peak membership, estimated by some at around four million,
in the early 1920s. (Library of Congress)

as Tom Watson of Georgia stirred interethnic hatred. From 1910 to 1917
Watson conducted an anti-Catholic crusade in his newspaper, the *Jeffersonian*.
He considered the Roman Catholic hierarchy "the Deadliest Menace to Our
Liberties and Our Civilization" and characterized the Roman Catholic religion
as a "jackassical faith." Thanks in part to Watson's outrageous diatribes (particularly against Leo Frank, a Jew who had been found guilty of murder in
Atlanta in 1913 but whose guilt was questioned by people throughout the country), in 1915 a new Ku Klux Klan formed in Georgia. During the next decade
it went on to become one of the most powerful anti-Catholic, as well as antiforeign, organizations in the history of the country.

World War I

In addition Watson's fulminations and the Klan's bigotry, World War I
unleashed still more ethnic tensions. President Woodrow Wilson asked
Americans to remain neutral, but naturally, with so many allegiances to the Old

World and its constituent peoples, they did not. Ethnic Americans had ties to those they left behind in Europe, and they tried to help compatriots there. But once the United States entered the war in 1917, Americans came to view anyone or anything that smacked of Germany and Germans with great distrust. The American involvement in the war lasted only from April 1917 until November 1918, but the nativist feelings aroused during the conflagration did not die quickly. Americanization drives during the war led to both silly and dangerous antiforeign campaigns. In Cincinnati sauerkraut became "liberty cabbage," and elsewhere in the Midwest fierce anti-German opinion forced other changes. Personal names such as "Mueller" and "Schmidt" became Miller and Smith, respectively, and German-speaking Lutherans and Catholics shifted their church services into English. Continuing hysteria after the war ended brought proponents of immigration restriction enough support to get new legislation through Congress.

Immigration Restriction

Wartime fears intensified American xenophobia and contributed to Congressional determination to override President Wilson's second veto of a literacy bill. Its framers designed this act to exclude from the United States those over age sixteen unable to read a short passage in English or another language, to keep southern and eastern Europeans from entering the country. The 1917 triumph of the Bolsheviks in Russia created pressure for additional restrictions, as many feared that foreign radicals would attempt to carry their revolution to America. Furthermore, strong anti-Semitism and anti-Catholicism in the 1920s increased support for limiting immigration. American workers also worried that a flood of newcomers would depress wages and take their jobs.

The years following World War I saw drastic changes enacted in immigration policy. In 1921, and again in 1924, Congress passed laws to curb the influx from abroad. In the first bill each European nation received a quota based on its proportion of the foreign-born population in 1910. The total was set at 3 percent of the foreign-born population. Three years later the legislators reduced the figure to 2 percent and the base year to 1890, thereby favoring members of ethnic groups that had arrived before that date. The 1924 act excluded further Asian immigration, except for Filipinos who lived in an American-controlled country, and provided for the establishment of a commission to set permanent quotas. In 1929 yet another immigration policy went into effect. Each European group was apportioned a percentage in relation to its total population in the United States in 1920, as well as to an overall annual immigrant ceiling of 153,714. The legislation had been designed to favor northern Europeans; consequently, the British, the Germans, and the Irish received more than 65 percent of the allotted places.

Immigration restriction cut the flow of manual laborers to America, but the nation's economy no longer needed so many unskilled workers for its mines and mills. Even before the 1920s, white-collar employment had begun to grow faster than blue-collar employment, and women took many of the new clerical jobs. Of course, the nation still needed some untrained and low-paid workers for agricultural, manufacturing, and service industries, but rural native whites and, after 1910, African Americans, Mexicans, and Filipinos joined Greeks

"You cannot come in. The quota for 1620 is filled." Cartoonist's view of the national origins quota. By Hendrik W. Van Loon. From the *Survey,* 1924.

and Italians in these occupations. During periods of labor shortages, such as World War I, the government made special arrangements to recruit Mexicans. Whereas restriction drastically reduced immigration, it neither ended nor curbed American prejudices. The period between the end of World War I and the end of World War II witnessed some of the most blatant discrimination ever seen in the United States. Part of the prejudice remained as a carryover from the Americanization drives inaugurated during World War I; part was aggravated by the propaganda of the Ku Klux Klan and other leaders of bigotry such as Henry Ford in the 1920s and Father Charles Coughlin of Detroit in the 1930s. Part of it, no doubt, resulted from the economic woes that visited most Americans in the 1920s, and especially during the Great Depression of the 1930s. But we must also emphasize that discrimination and hostility to minorities existed among the rich as well as the poor, the educated as well as the ill informed, the old-line Americans as well as the recent immigrants. Much of the bigotry also grew out of religious teachings, education or the lack thereof, and economic deprivation, or frustration with life in general. Nor should one ignore the prevalent American view that had existed for centuries: America should remain a white, Protestant nation. Blacks and Asians were considered of lower status. Europeans, Latin Americans, and their offspring would not be acceptable until they shed their foreign ways and adapted themselves to the dominant culture.

The Mexican Experience

During the height of American nativism in the 1920s, hundreds of thousands of Mexicans migrated to the American West to work in agriculture and on the railroads. Their experience resembled that of the Asians with one major exception—there was no significant movement to exclude them. In fact, southwestern growers and railroad magnates made great efforts to prevent any quota restrictions against Latin Americans. Agricultural production could not expand without the Mexican field hands, and the western railroads found Mexicans to be ideal replacements for Greeks, Poles, Italians, Japanese, and other former menials who now moved up the economic ladder. Once again, however, just as with other groups, economic needs did not lead to tolerance or social acceptance. Americans denounced Mexicans, even as the Mexicans worked long hours every day, as immoral, irresponsible, and lazy "greasers" who had to be kept in their place.

By 1930 Mexicans constituted the largest minority in California and the second largest in Texas. Many residents of the Golden State believed, in the words of one educator, that they were "a menace to the health and morals of the rest of the community." Texas, however, included many southerners with strong negative attitudes about other races. Mexicans suffered more there than in any other state. Theaters segregated them, food shops refused them service, and many public facilities barred their presence. One Texan called them "dirty as hogs"; another concluded, "They're just a dumb-bell people.... They drink too much, fight too much."

Economic Depression and Increased Tensions

During the depression decade of the 1930s, many Mexicans could not get jobs, and others lost theirs to make room for other Americans, such as the refugees escaping the poverty of the Dust Bowl in Kansas and Oklahoma. As a result, a mass exodus occurred, with the encouragement and financial support of both the Mexican and local American governments. The returning flow to Mexico in the 1930s was much greater than the traffic north.

For those either unable or unwilling to return to their home countries, the depression years were particularly difficult. As in the past, rampant job discrimination continued against Catholics and Jews. With a surplus of laborers, employers could specify "WPX" (the acronym for white Protestant Christian) in job orders to employment agencies and in advertisements. Statistics on employment barriers against white groups are difficult to find, but some are available for Jews. In New York City more than 90 percent of the gentile firms refused to hire them for white collar positions; in Minneapolis more than 60 percent of the city's retail and manufacturing concerns refused to consider Jews; on the West Coast and the rest of the nation, most Jews who did not work for a government agency were either self-employed or unemployed.

Anxieties and fears of foreigners and bolshevism that appeared during World War I also intensified hostility and discrimination against Jews that continued to grow stronger through the mid-1940s. In the 1920s many colleges and professional schools, especially in the "Ivy League," established Jewish quotas; Ku Klux Klan chapters spread hate; and Henry Ford started a campaign alleging a Jewish plot to establish a world dictatorship. Los Angeles, where Jews had participated in civic and political life until that decade, systematically excluded them from elective office and leadership in community and cultural affairs despite (or because of?) their dominant position in the Hollywood film industry. In the 1930s Detroit's Father Charles Coughlin succeeded Henry Ford as the nation's best-known anti-Semite. Not until World War II, when the federal government importuned the archbishop of Detroit to silence the bigoted priest because his ravings undermined the war effort, did the Catholic Church curtail Coughlin's diatribes. But in Boston, where, according to one writer, the

Roman Catholic Church "could do more than any other single agency or institution" to curb attacks on Jews, it did little. Boston toughs regularly beat up Jews, desecrated their cemeteries, and destroyed their property. One organization tallied 611 anti-Jewish incidents in Boston during the years 1942–43, and it took a New York City newspaper exposé to force the governor of Massachusetts to appoint a committee to investigate the charges.

The attacks on Jews, vicious as they were, did not compare with the difficulties encountered by some other groups during World War II. African Americans made economic gains during the war due to the labor shortage but still encountered prejudice and discrimination in the nation's defense plants, housing, and recreational facilities. In the armed forces, also, existing policies dictated segregating African Americans and generally using them in areas that required the fewest skills. In 1943 both Harlem and Detroit experienced ugly riots. In Detroit white workers resented the black arrivals and were egged on by white supremacists to assail blacks. Tensions over jobs, housing, and amusement areas led to a riot in June, when whites and blacks battled on Belle Isle, a recreational spot in the city. Whites then attacked blacks in the ghetto, who in turn fought back. Before federal troops restored order, twenty-five African Americans and nine whites were dead.

Mexican Americans also encountered injustice and rioting during the war. Seventeen Mexican youths were unjustifiably arrested in Los Angeles in 1942, and nine of them were convicted of murder by a bigoted prosecuting attorney, judge, and jury. It took two years before a state court of appeals overturned the conviction for lack of sufficient evidence, but in the meantime the Mexican American youths had spent two years in San Quentin prison. Sailors rioting at Los Angeles in 1943 focused their wrath on Mexican Americans they met in what later became known as the "Zoot Suit" riots, so named for the mode of dress many of the Mexican American youths favored. The worst atrocity during the war years, however, was perpetuated against West Coast Japanese Americans, their parents, and their children, whom the government rounded up and sent to relocation centers simply because of their ancestry.

"Concentration Camps U.S.A."

The experience of the Japanese Americans on the West Coast during World War II is one of the sorrier chapters in American history. Japanese Americans were frugal, careful, and excellent workers who caused no "social problems," yet racial antipathy conditioned American responses to them. Alien land laws curtailed their opportunities for purchasing property in the West, and business firms refused to hire them in any but menial positions. Despite their high scholastic attainments, educated Japanese Americans often spent their lives selling fruit from sidewalk stands or working for other Japanese businessmen. The law that supposedly protected all Americans worked against those of Japanese ancestry. On San Francisco streets those who tried to defend themselves from wanton assaults were arrested for disturbing the peace. An Arizona vegetable farmer summarized the feelings of many Americans when he said, "One person of Japanese descent was worse than one thousand rattlesnakes."

The accumulated venom toward Japanese Americans, who accounted for only 2 percent of the West Coast's population in 1940, broke loose after the December 1941 Japanese attack on Pearl Harbor. Although the nation had been drifting toward war in 1940 and 1941, the government had made no plans for military control of civilians, nor did the FBI have an overall internal security plan. In the early days of fighting the war went badly for the United States, and a demand arose for internment of Japanese Americans.

Californians feared sabotage by West Coast Japanese Americans. Although no sabotage occurred, the military commander of the army's West Coast forces concluded that the Japanese Americans were probably still plotting. Many white people, caught up in a hysterical wartime atmosphere in which little was known and much was feared, thought something should be done about the "menace" these people represented. Thus in early 1942, in seeming violation of all constitutional guarantees, the federal government rounded up 110,000 Americans of Japanese ancestry on the West Coast, together with their foreign-born parents and grandparents, and sent them to "relocation centers," or "concentration camps," as many critics labeled them. They had to abandon their homes and most of their possessions; after the war the federal government inadequately compensated them for what their property had been worth. The rationale for isolating these people was, according to the army commanding general on the West Coast, that "the Japanese race is an enemy race and while many second and third generation Japanese born on United States soil, possessed of United States citizenship, have become 'Americanized' the racial strains are undiluted."

Wartime fears of espionage also led the federal government to pressure authorities in several Latin American countries to arrest, intern, and then deport to the United States more than 3,000 Japanese, Germans, and Italians living in those nations. More than 2,200 of these "forced immigrants" were Japanese, and soon they occupied an internment camp at Crystal City, Texas. Most of them had been sent from Peru, and when the war ended that nation refused to repatriate them. So hundreds of Japanese languished in Crystal City and other camps, legally unable to remain in the United States, unable to return to their former homes in Peru, or even to immigrate to Japan. It took at least until the mid-1950s before the American government resolved their status. Until then they continued as detainees.

Japanese Americans, young and old, awaiting removal from their West Coast homes to the relocation camps during World War II. From the War Relocation Authority. (National Archives)

The areas selected for the internment camps for Japanese Americans included some of the bleakest parts of California, Arizona, and other western states. One evacuee recalled her first experience in Utah:

> As I stepped on the ground, the dust came up in my face. This was Topaz! We had a hard time to find our home for the barracks were all alike. Topaz looked so big, so enormous to us. It made me feel like an ant. The dust gets in our hair. Every place we go we cannot escape the dust. Inside of our houses, in the laundry, in the latrines, in the mess halls, dust and more dust everywhere.

The other camps were not much better, and some were worse. Another woman told of her experience: "We had to shower in the horses' showers, and the floors were filthy."

The Japanese Americans remained locked up for more than two years. In 1944, the government began to release them. In the interim many of the internees left the camps to take specific jobs where labor shortages existed; those eligible for the armed forces could enlist, and many did. The Japanese American 442nd Combat Team compiled an outstanding record fighting in Italy and

France. In intense and bloody fighting, the unit suffered heavy casualties and won more than eighteen thousand individual decorations for valor. After the camps closed in 1945 the internees scattered to different parts of the United States; a few moved to Asia, but most returned to California to begin life anew.

The devastating psychological effects of internment left lifetime scars. Many of those who had been in the camps refused to talk about what had happened to them behind barbed-wire fences—even with their children and close friends. Then, in the 1970s, a movement began for the United States government to make amends—if any, indeed, could be made—for what had been done to the Japanese Americans during World War II. The efforts culminated in the summer of 1988, when Congress passed legislation offering some financial restitution (about $20,000 per person) to the survivors and their immediate families, along with a formal apology from the government for what it had done.

The end of World War II marked the close of one of the most intense periods of American bigotry. Afterward, with the continuation of wartime prosperity and the end of wartime pressures, some changes occurred. States passed anti-discrimination statutes, schools and employers lessened their quotas and tried to change established patterns, and the federal government began to act to end discriminatory practices. The changes away from traditional prejudice and Anglo dominance marked a major shift in historic ethnic relations in America toward a growing tolerance and a greater acceptance of pluralism.

8

Movement, Mobility, and Cultural Adaptation

(1941–2010)

Since 1941 both the role and the status of American minorities have altered. People already here saw changes that they perhaps had never expected to witness. To the surprise of almost all Americans alive in 1940, not only did the flow of people in and to this country accelerate over the pace of the 1930s, but its nature and character differed as well. Moreover, the commitment made to civil rights and equality of opportunity for all groups and individuals has transformed the United States from a WASP-dominated society into one in which merit and previous discrimination and handicaps are taken into consideration in helping those seeking to improve the quality of their lives. Added to this is an immigration influx since 1970 that exceeds the totals recorded in the first three decades of the twentieth century. All of these events are discussed in this and succeeding chapters, but the focus in this one is primarily on the growth of the suburbs, the expansion of the Sun Belt and the West, new immigration from Europe, and the lives of the descendants of European immigration. Subsequent chapters discuss the struggle for equality by minority groups and the changing social fabric of American society due to the mass immigration into the United States since the 1970s.

The Impact of World War II

World War II, with its need for military manpower and increased production, changed an economically depressed nation into one desperately seeking more hands. Those who had been underemployed got a chance to utilize their skills; those who had been unemployed found jobs; and those who sought expanded opportunities in other sections of the country were encouraged to do so. The war reduced the number of emigrants from Europe, and American immigration laws barred Asians; thus the new workers had to be obtained elsewhere. Defense plants in cities such as Los Angeles and Detroit recruited Mexicans in their midst and sought blacks from the rural South (although 55 of the 185 war plants in the Detroit area hired virtually no blacks). Agricultural growers in twenty-one states, mostly in the South and West, induced the federal government to recruit Mexican agricultural workers (*braceros*) to handle the increased workload. At the same time the descendants of Europeans found greater opportunity as skilled workers in defense plants, in private businesses, and in the lower ranks of the American corporate world. The war, in fact, acted as the catalyst that pushed most of the children and grandchildren of early-twentieth-century immigrants into the mainstream of American society.

Wartime prosperity continued in the United States even after the conflict ended. In general, the labor force needed more skilled workers. Professionals and managerial personnel also found greater opportunities than they had had earlier. As a result, returning servicemen, encouraged by new career possibilities and the GI Bill of Rights, which helped them go to college, either acquired more education and went into the ranks of corporate America or, if they moved into blue-collar jobs, received credit for seniority based on their military service. These factors helped many climb from the lowest levels on the economic ladder, leaving menial jobs in manufacturing and the expanding service industries to be filled by others. Women had been heavily recruited during the early 1940s, when an estimated six million worked in defense industries promoting the war effort. Afterward, most returned home, but soon they moved back into the labor market, usually in low-paying, low-status jobs. In many cases they became clerks or secretaries in the nation's offices. Also, as in the war years, the lowest level positions often went to African Americans leaving southern farms; to Mexican migrants, both legal and illegal; and to a new group, the Puerto Ricans, who as American citizens could take a flight from San Juan to New York City and start a new life there.

The war also influenced the descendants of the great immigration of 1880 to 1930 in still another way. Many children of immigrants came of age during the Great Depression and found dim employment prospects. They took what jobs were available and largely lived in their local neighborhoods. During the war, however, nearly fifteen million young men and several hundred thousand young women left their homes and communities when they were drafted or enlisted in the armed services. There they met people who differed from themselves and were exposed to new regions both in the United States and abroad. When the war ended, they had little desire to return to their former homes. Discussing American Jews, one historian noted that 1945 marked a "turning point." The war disrupted their ties to the past and propelled many of them to seek new lives in other areas of the country. Mario Puzo, author of *The Godfather,* added that the military service saved him from an existence in New York City's Hell's Kitchen, where he grew up.

Southerners Move North

During World War II, just as they did before and during World War I, rural blacks and whites eagerly moved to the northern and western industrial regions. The booming defense plants lured them to such cities as Philadelphia, New York, Chicago, Detroit, and Los Angeles. Factory work paid better than farm labor, and urban slums, miserable as they were, nevertheless provided better shelter than rural shacks.

Moreover, after 1940, previous New Deal advances in the mechanization of southern agriculture started uprooting farm labor. Demographically speaking, it resulted in the greatest displacement of one segment of the population— farmers—in the history of the nation: between 1940 and 1970, twenty million Americans, a figure comparable in scope to the thirty million immigrants who entered the United States between 1880 and 1930, sought new homes. About sixteen million of these people were white; four million were black. Planters simply tore down the shacks of their tenants as the tractor, bulldozer, and cotton picker forced poor workers and their families off the farms and into the cities. Mississippi had nearly three hundred thousand farms in 1940, but only seventy-two thousand thirty years later. Moving offered the only choice most farm workers had; they were too poor to buy machines. Not even legislation helped; the New Deal farm subsidies of the 1930s went mostly to the larger landholders.

Overall the movement of blacks was striking. Over 1.5 million left the South during the 1940s and, although the rate slowed after 1950, more than 2.5 million more left between 1950 and 1970. The statistics on blacks in Boston and Philadelphia, two representative northern cities, tell the tale (Table 8.1).

Mechanization and poverty in rural areas were color blind. Although rural poverty afflicted proportionately more black than white farmers, numerically more poor whites in the South were driven off the land. These descendants of the old-stock English and Scots-Irish also went north and west to defense plants during World War II and afterward moved into the automobile factories

TABLE 8.1. African Americans in Two Northern Cities

	Number of African Americans			Percentage of African Americans in Total Population		
	1940	1970	1980	1940	1970	1980
Boston	23,679	104,596	126,673	3.1	16.3	22.5
Philadelphia	250,000	653,000	638,230	13.1	33.6	37.6

of Detroit, the rubber plants of Akron, and the many industries of Chicago, Kansas City, and Los Angeles. Many from the Appalachians lost their jobs as the coal mines shut down or utilized machines instead of men. Miners then left the region to seek employment elsewhere. Yet they did not always go to the big cities; frequently they found places in smaller communities nearer their homes.

After 1940, however, the American South began to modernize at a fast pace. New industries sprang up, diversification and mechanization came to agriculture, and cities grew rapidly. By 1960 Atlanta, Dallas, and Houston were among the nation's major urban areas. The 1970 census reported that about three out of every four Americans lived in an urban or suburban region, but in the South only two out of three did. Thus a gap in urbanization still existed; by 2010 it had almost closed.

Suburbs and the Rise of the Sun Belt and the West

During the past half-century millions of Americans moved from cities to the suburbs. They could do this because of post-World War II prosperity and the building of the interstate highways, which dramatically cut travel time from suburban communities to urban centers. Older cities such as Detroit, Chicago, St. Louis, and Cleveland lost population, while their surrounding suburbs—and exurbs—mushroomed. In the 1990s, however, New York City, part of the trend in former decades, witnessed a growth revival in which more people entered than left. For the first time in its history the "Big Apple" recorded a gross total of more than eight million people in the 2000 census.

The postwar migration of Americans often entailed movement across the continent. Much of the new growth has taken place in the "Sun Belt," the South, the Southwest, and the Rocky Mountain areas. California surpassed all of its sister states, however, as it became the great mecca for discontented Americans and anxious immigrants who sought a beautiful climate and an expanding economy. In agriculture, in defense, and in the new high-technology processes, California ranked highest in terms of wealth produced and jobs provided. The thriving economy of the Sun Belt states altered the political power in the nation as well. Whereas New York, Pennsylvania, Ohio, and Illinois had been the most populous states in the nation in 1940, seventy years later California ranked first, Texas second, and New York third; Florida was fourth, poised to surpass the Empire State's population in the next census.

In 2009, on the other hand, the fastest growing states—Utah and Arizona —were in the mountains and deserts of the Rocky Mountains. They have become the most recent additions to a region referred to loosely as the Sun

Belt. At various times the label has described the coastal and border states stretching south from Virginia to Florida, then west to California, and occasionally even north to Oregon and Washington, although the western parts of the last two usually see more rain than sun. During the past forty years these states have grown faster than most other parts of the nation. Many people have moved for jobs or for the salubrious climate in California, but the advent of air conditioning and its growing use, especially in the Southwest, since the 1960s have contributed significantly to shifts of population centers from the East to the West and the North to the South. With the exception of California, citizens in regions with somewhat milder climates generally have more conservative values about the rights of labor, their unions, and government assistance to the poor. (Why this is so we do not know.) As populations in the fastest growing states have surged, bitter disputes between preservationists and prodevelopment groups have become more potent. As a result, debates on these topics have also increased in Congress and have become issues of significance in political campaigns.

Three streams of people have contributed to the continuing growth of the West, and of California in particular. Descendants of earlier European immigrant groups have moved there in large numbers. In fact, more Americans of German, Irish, English, French, Dutch, Scots, Scots-Irish, Swedish, Welsh, Danish, Portuguese, and Swiss backgrounds reside in California than in any other state. Despite this fact, the migration of Asians and Latin Americans into the Golden State has changed the population mix dramatically. At least 25 percent of all Californians are foreign-born, and for the first time since statehood was achieved in 1850, a majority of California's population hails from either Latin America or Asia. The current trend in new residents is likely to continue for the foreseeable future.

American Indian Migration

Like other minority groups, the Indians moved to the cities during the twentieth century. During the 1920s veterans of World War I and a few thousand other reservation dwellers who had job skills began moving into the towns and cities of eastern Oklahoma. This migration continued during the Depression as the Bureau of Indian Affairs (BIA) increased its off-reservation employment efforts. World War II brought a marked upsurge in the Indian movement away from the reservations as an estimated 150,000 Native Americans joined the military, took defense industry jobs, or found other employment.

Shortly after the war a terrible blizzard in the Southwest brought the federal government into the process of off-reservation migration on a large scale.

In 1948 the BIA opened placement offices in Denver, Los Angeles, and Salt Lake City for Navajo young people. Within a few years this modest effort expanded into the relocation program, a part of Congress's policy of terminating its involvement in Indian affairs. The idea was to cut federal expenditures by getting people off the reservations and into the cities. By the 1960s twelve cities, including Los Angeles, Chicago, and Minneapolis, had relocation centers, and about two hundred thousand Indians left the reservations on their own or as part of this program. This migration produced a dramatic shift in Indian population. In 1950 only about 56,000 Indians lived in urban areas, but by 1980 that number had surpassed 740,000. Although many experienced major social and economic difficulties in the cities, by 1980 the census bureau reported that over half of the nearly 1.4 million Indians lived off the reservations. In 2000 the Census Bureau reported that the reservations included fewer than 20 percent of the total Indian, Aleut, and Inuit populations.

For people from rural or small-town backgrounds, life in the major urban centers proved difficult at best. In theory the BIA job training and placement programs would ease the Indian transition from reservation to city, and for some this happened. For others, city life proved impersonal, crowded, noisy, and unsatisfying. As a result many despondent, lonely, or unemployed Indians returned home after a few months in town. Rarely did they have the education or job skills to compete successfully. Of the thousands who remained in or returned to the cities for another try, many encountered the same problems as blacks or Spanish-speaking people—lack of housing, bad schools, high local crime rates, and low-paying jobs. In addition, however, the tribal people suffered from a sense of personal alienation and a loss of the family and community ties many had treasured while on the reservation. Despite such difficulties the movement to off-reservation towns and cities continues.

Renewed European Immigration

Whereas internal movements explain much of American development since 1941, immigration increased in the decades that followed. Until 1970 Europeans made up most of the newcomers, as they had done in the past. However, before new groups of immigrants could enter the country, the government had to change its existing restrictive immigration laws and policies. The first breakthrough occurred in 1943 when Congress, as a gesture of friendship to its wartime ally, China, repealed the Chinese exclusion acts and granted China a small immigration quota of 105 people a year. In addition, Congress permitted Chinese immigrants to become American citizens. Three years later the legislators granted the Philippines independence and gave that country, as well as

Immigrant Flows to America

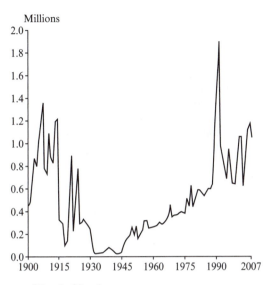

Millions

Source: U.S. Department of Homeland Security

India, small annual quotas. In 1952 the McCarran-Walter Immigration Act gave all nations minimum annual quotas of one hundred persons. It also eliminated the 1924 ban on Asian immigration.

Europeans, however, still fared better. The arrival of these immigrants caused less fuss than had the coming of their compatriots and relatives in earlier years. Few people publicly denounced the survivors of World War II who sought admission to the United States outside of the quota limits, but at the same time Congress moved slowly before making any special effort to assist those Europeans displaced by the war. When it passed the Displaced Persons Act in 1948, the legislation favored the displaced *volksdeutsche* who had been expelled as collaborators by the eastern European nations after the war and limited the number of slots available to the Jews who had survived the Holocaust. In 1950, after Israel had become an independent nation and had opened its doors to the entire world's Jews, Congress amended the 1948 act and eliminated most of its discriminatory and administratively cumbersome provisions. As a result of the two Displaced Persons acts, about four hundred thousand Europeans, mostly Germans, Balts, Poles, and Jews from eastern Europe, reached the United States. When broken down according to religious affiliation, 47 percent of these people were Roman Catholic, 35 percent Protestant and Greek Orthodox, and 17 percent Jewish.

Another two hundred thousand people entered our country because of refugee legislation passed in 1953. We were in the midst of the cold war between the communist-dominated Soviet Union and the "freedom-loving" people of the West. As a gesture that reflected our political attitudes, the United States government made special provision for eastern Europeans fleeing "communist tyranny" to find a home in our country. Following the abortive Hungarian Revolution of 1956, the United States admitted roughly forty thousand Magyars, many of whom settled among other Hungarians in New Jersey, Cleveland, or New York City.

Congress also enacted laws to permit Asian refugees to settle in the United States. In 1961 President John F. Kennedy, using authority granted to the president by Congress, admitted fourteen thousand more Chinese immigrants into the country. This action, and the special refugee laws for eastern Europeans, eroded the national-origins system that had been enacted in the 1920s and reaffirmed in the McCarran-Walter Immigration Act. These moves set the stage for a thorough overhaul of American immigration policy.

In the more liberal climate of the 1960s, Congress scrapped national-origins quotas entirely and created a new system. The 1965 amendments at first divided the world into an Eastern Hemisphere and Western Hemisphere immigration policy, but in 1978 the legislators created a uniform worldwide system. In place of national-origins quotas, each nation received twenty thousand places, excluding immediate family members of United States citizens. Visas were to be determined by a preference system, with most places (74 percent) reserved for family unification. Twenty percent of the visas went to persons with skills and professions needed in the United States and the remainder to refugees. With total immigration pegged at 290,000, excluding immediate family members of United States citizens, immigration was not expected to increase significantly.

It had not been foreseen in 1965, when a major changes occurred in American immigration policies, how the patterns or immigration would change. The Immigration Act of 1965 and its subsequent modifications led to the development of an even greater multicultural society than had already existed. At first Europeans dominated the flow. Between 1960 and 1975 more than twenty thousand Italians arrived annually and settled in places where other Italians had gone, such as New York and New Jersey. In the Red Hook section of Brooklyn, they found not only friends and relatives to help them secure jobs and housing but also churches, stores, and community organizations with familiar names. On the streets they heard their native tongue.

Like Italians, the Portuguese benefited from the 1965 Immigration Act. After the Italians, the Portuguese constituted the largest group from continental

Europe to come to the United States. From 1965 until the early1970s more than one hundred thousand Portuguese people settled near New Bedford, Massachusetts; Oakland, California; and Newark, New Jersey, where they developed significant communities. Newark, New Jersey's largest city, housed forty thousand Portuguese immigrants in 1980. Most had been long-time residents of Portugal, but a few traced their roots to Angola and Mozambique in Africa. In Newark the newcomers formed a distinct community built around their churches, stores, homes, and social activities.

The Greeks were a third European beneficiary of the 1965 Immigration Act's provisions. Under the Johnson-Reed Act of 1924 and the McCarran-Walter Act, Greece had an annual a quota of only 307 people each year, but from 1966 to 1971 about fifteen thousand Greeks came annually, mostly under the new provisions favoring family unification. During the 1970s tens of thousands more arrived. Although they settled nearly everywhere, most went to Greek communities in Chicago and New York. In the Big Apple, they generally found homes in the Astoria section of Queens, and about twenty to thirty thousand located in Chicago's Greektown. In New York other Greeks aided them, and in 1972 they founded a Hellenic American Neighborhood Action Committee (HANAC) to help Greek American causes. Most of the more recent immigrants took jobs working for others, in factories, restaurants, and in construction. A few went into business for themselves, some becoming street vendors in New York City. During the summer of 1980, *Newsweek* reported that the Greeks "have all but taken over the coffee shops" in New York City. By the 1980s the backlogs in both Italy and Greece eased, and emigration to America dropped significantly.

By the late 1970s economic conditions on the continent had improved and the numbers of Europeans seeking entry into the United States had declined. Nonetheless, there were still problems in the region that prompted more people to seek a new life across the ocean. The Irish, for example, faced a deteriorating economic situation after 1970, and many left home. One publisher there observed, "This country has denied a young generation of their right to dream in Ireland, and over 1,000,000 have now hawked their dream to America like millions of Irish before them." When they were unable to acquire legal immigrant visas to America, they came anyway, often on visitors' visas, and then stayed and worked as illegal immigrants. Diversity visas, passed in 1986 and made part of the basic immigration policy in 1990, were based on a lottery system and enabled many of these undocumented Irish to legalize their status and others in Ireland to secure immigrant visas. These men and women mostly settled in or near Irish American communities in Boston, New York City, and Chicago. One Irish American commented about his New York neighborhood: "You go into a diner and it doesn't take 10 seconds before you hear the brogue,

New wave of an old immigration, Astoria, Queens, New York: Greek community
business clearly directed at the Greek immigrants (1980s). (Photo by Elliott
Barkan)

which you wouldn't have heard around here 10 years ago except occasionally."
Mostly better educated than prior waves of Irish immigrants, the men usually
took jobs in construction and the women as nannies.

Ironically, just as the new visas for the Irish became available in the 1990s,
the economy picked up in Ireland. Unemployment dropped, and emigration
practically ceased. From 1990 to 1995 Ireland sent 51,415 people to this country, an average of over 8,000 annually. In the past eight to ten years, however,
their numbers have declined drastically, and many of their former emigrants
are returning to the homeland.

But conditions in eastern Europe have not reversed themselves as quickly,
and there still exists an exodus of Russians coming to the United States. Until
the communist government fell in 1989, it was difficult for Soviets to leave, but
afterward things changed. Nonetheless, it remained difficult for them to get
into the United States because few of the Russians had close relatives who
could sponsor them. However, the diversity visas helped many from eastern
Europe to get to the United States.

The largest of the communist groups came from the former Soviet Union.
They had begun to enter this country during the 1970s when unfavorable economic conditions prevailed in their homeland. Jews, in particular, wanted to

escape the anti-Semitism they experienced. When political animosity between the United States and the Soviet Union thawed somewhat in the 1970s, the authorities allowed more Jews to leave. However, relations between the Soviets and Americans cooled during Ronald Reagan's early years in the White House, and the Soviets again tightened emigration restrictions. The situation changed once again in the late 1980s and especially after the 1989 collapse of communism and the disintegration of the Soviet Union. Hundreds of thousands of Jews again emigrated to both the United States and Israel. Special legislation enacted by Congress in 1989 permitted nearly three hundred thousand persons from the former Soviet Union to enter the country. Most of the people who benefited from the enlarged number were Jews.

They settled primarily in New York City's "Little Odessa" (a section of Brighton Beach along the Atlantic coast in Brooklyn) and in Los Angeles. The latest Russians were generally well educated, knew some English, and had relatives already in the United States. *Science* magazine estimated that 15 percent of those arriving at the end of the 1980s and the beginning of the 1990s possessed Ph.D.s or equivalent degrees in science and engineering. They were often secular, with little knowledge of their religious heritage. Jewish organizations helped many cope with American society and exposed them to Judaism, but in spite of their educations, many could not easily use their skills in finding jobs; communism had not prepared them for living in an open society. They nonetheless built vibrant communities in which they opened restaurants, established groceries selling Russian specialties, and founded nightclubs and organizations to aid other Russian immigrants.

Prosperity and Mobility

The social status and economic progress of so many of the groups who came to America in the late nineteenth and early twentieth centuries improved steadily over the generations. Some immigrants and their children were in the process of moving ahead when the Depression of the 1930s devastated many families and groups. The American entry into World War II in December, 1941, ended unemployment as everyone mobilized for the war effort. At the end of the war in 1945 prosperity returned. Jobs were plentiful, a housing boom began, and so, too, did a "baby boom." People needed everything: houses, cars, household good, clothing, and diapers. Economic mobility for whites resumed. Even Asians, who had been victimized by the Depression as well as by racial prejudice, found wider opportunities.

One group that benefited enormously from the changed conditions was the Jews. Anti-Semitism in the United States peaked in 1945–46, and then began to subside. A popular Hollywood film, *The House I Live In,* in which Frank Sinatra made a plea for tolerance in 1945; the publication of books such as Laura Z. Hobson's *Gentleman's Agreement* (as well as the 1946 movie) and Carey McWilliams's *A Mask for Privilege,* which exposed the depths of anti-Semitic feelings in this country; the Supreme Court's decision to outlaw restrictive covenants in housing; President Harry S Truman's 1948 proposal for a civil rights program; increased American prosperity—all contributed to a decline in prejudice.

Postwar public opinion polls, for example, indicated that fewer Christians believed Jews to be greedy, dishonest, or unscrupulous; and overt anti-Semitism, so common in the 1930s, became less frequent and less respectable. Accompanying the drop in prejudicial attitudes toward Jews was the decline of social and economic discrimination. Universities and professional schools eliminated Jewish quotas, and business firms that had been averse to hiring Jews and Catholics modified their policies. Changes in major corporations and law firms, however, came slowly. A symbolic landmark was established in December 1973, when E. I. du Pont, the world's largest chemical company, chose Irving S. Shapiro, the son of eastern European Jewish immigrants, as its president and chief executive officer.

Another persistent theme in American history, anti-Catholicism, also subsided after World War II. Conflict between Protestants and Catholics continued over aid to parochial schools, a proposed American ambassador to the Vatican, the relations of church and state, publicly sponsored birth control clinics, and abortion. But the deep emotional strife of the past declined sharply. In 1960 John F. Kennedy became the first Roman Catholic elected to the presidency. The ecumenical movement of the postwar society brought Protestants, Catholics, and Jews together in new areas of cooperation. In this same spirit Pope Paul VI visited the United States in 1965, conducted a prayer service before seventy thousand people in New York's Yankee Stadium, and received a warm welcome. In 1979 and 1987 the charismatic Pope John Paul II made similar tours and met with even more enthusiastic receptions. His special 1993 visit to Denver, Colorado, to appeal to American youth was no less successful. In October 1995 he repeated these triumphs with a visit to New York City. Then in 2008 Pope Benedict XVI toured several East Coast cities. When in New York, he, too, prayed in Yankee Stadium. When in Washington, D.C., he and President Bush issued a joint statement urging humane treatment for immigrants and the importance of keeping families together. That same day federal agents raided five chicken plants that employed illegal immigrants. They were all rounded up and arrested, separating the workers from their spouses and children.

However, many legal immigrants, especially those from Europe, over the past half century have been treated with much greater respect than had those who came from overseas in the nineteenth and early twentieth centuries. This reflects the decline in intensity of prejudice in the United States. Greater tolerance can be explained by several factors. The fear of divided ethnic loyalties that was so potent in World War I and to a lesser extent in World War II did not materialize during the Cold War. Prejudice is also strongly, but not exclusively, correlated with levels of income, religious intensity, and education. As incomes and education increased and as religion became less of a commitment and more of a social identification, tolerance grew. Education did not guarantee the end of prejudice, but there is no doubt that the rising levels of education served to dampen the fires of bigotry. A highly educated public seemed more willing to accept ethnic differences. At the same time as they went through the public schools, state colleges, and universities, minority members were absorbing the dominant values of society. Finally, as a result of the immigration laws of the 1920s, the nation had achieved a general balance of ethnic groups. Old-stock Americans no longer feared being overrun by hordes of aliens who might undermine their traditions and destroy their institutions. The foreign-born percentage of the population declined steadily, from about one-seventh in the 1920s to less than one-twentieth by 1970. America was becoming a more homogenized nation as the grandchildren of European immigrants came to be indistinguishable from one another or, indeed, from those whose ancestors came here before the American Revolution. Since the 1970s the foreign born have become a larger part of the American population, and by 2009 they constituted 12 percent of the total population.

As the numbers of newcomers increased in the 1970s, Americans witnessed slow economic growth but high rates of mobility. Opportunities for white ethnics, African Americans, and Asian Americans increased. Plant expansions, especially in the South, Southwest, and West, in industries such as textiles, chemicals, aeronautics, food processing, and oil created many new jobs. In the 1990s more Americans held white-collar jobs than blue-collar ones, and by the end of the twentieth century job opportunities in high tech had gone through the roof.

The children and grandchildren of the immigrants saw these opportunities, and they also realized that education was necessary for mobility. So they flocked to the schools and especially to the growing colleges and universities. By the 1970s more than 40 percent of the college-age population attended some institution of higher education, and many of these students were the descendants of the newer immigrants. By the 1980s groups such as the Jews and Japanese sent about 90 percent of their children to college. Others, such as the Italians and Poles, lagged behind. In 1969 the United States government reported that only 5.9 percent of Italian Americans aged thirty-five and over had completed college, compared with the national average of 9.8 percent.

Among Polish Americans the figure was 7.2 percent. Yet it was clear by the 1970s and 1980s that the descendants of these ethnic minorities attended colleges and universities in large numbers, determined to get an education and better jobs. By 2009 many college and university students from the more recent ethnic groups in the United States were born in, or had parents who hailed from, what used to be called 'third world' countries. The phrase "third world" derived from the Cold War in the 1950s between the Soviet Union and the United States. The first "world" included the United States and its allies; the Communist orbit constituted the second world; practically all other nations were regarded as being in the "third world."

As white ethnic groups, Asians, and African Americans improved their educations and jobs, they began to move from the margins of the business world to its center. In 2009 the President of Pfizer, the largest drug company in the world, admitted at a public meeting of shareholders that "the last time I was sitting at a table like this, in a room like this, was my Bar Mitzvah." In 1940 no one who admitted that he was a Jew would have found an executive position in the firm except, perhaps, in sales where the "pitch" usually worked better with members of the same ethnic group. In the 1950s that same man might have been in Pfizer's employ but certainly would not have highlighted his religious heritage. In the 1970s, the man might have been employed by Pfizer but would not have been its president. By the end of the twentieth century, however, that man might have been a woman, an Asian, or an African American and no one would have raised their eyebrows.

After World War II one noticed an increased movement of people from urban areas to the suburbs and then to the exurbs. One reason for this has been attributed to the flight of middle-class white people who did not want to live near the poorer minorities then moving into the older urban neighborhoods. Blacks and Puerto Ricans, for example, replaced southern and eastern Europeans in the ghettos of the Eastern and Midwestern cities, whereas blacks, Mexicans, and newer arrivals from Asia found their homes in older neighborhoods throughout the country. However, in our own day, people of every ethnic background live in both urban and suburban areas. Those who consider themselves members of the dominant culture rarely, if ever, take a public stance indicating that the newcomers are unwelcome because of their heritage.

Retaining Ethnic Ties

At the same time that newer elements joined American society, older groups engaged in the dual process of moving away from and yet trying to retain their ethnic heritage, regardless of where they lived, where they worked, or how much money they earned. Many immigrants of yesteryear, frequently their children, and sometimes the grandchildren could still be found in urban neighborhoods across the United States. Some lacked the financial means to move; for others a strong sense of ethnic identity kept their communities alive as the people there preferred to live and work among others of similar background. The forces for assimilation had not overwhelmed these residents, especially the older ones, and the familiar shops, churches, clubs, and streets provided welcome signs and sources of comfort amid the pressures of a mass society. As one retired Polish auto worker, who had reached the United States in 1913, said of Hamtramck, Michigan, "You feel better here. I know every stone in the sidewalk. I could go to Florida, but everything would be strange. You feel at home here."

In 2009 fewer members of the immigrants of yesteryear remain behind in the older neighborhoods. Also, these people were less likely to be assimilated into the mainstream of American society. Thus the process of assimilation and movement, like the process of adjustment for the immigrants, was an uneven one. The older colonial peoples were largely assimilated by the early nineteenth century, and by the 1870s the Dutch, English, Scots, Welsh, Scots-Irish, and Germans who came both before and after the Napoleonic Wars in the early nineteenth century lost most of their national heritage. Although many of the first and second generation of the post-1840 mass immigration waves had lived in ghettos, which sometimes contained inhabitants of diverse backgrounds, they associated with and married their own peoples. Hence the Germans, Irish, and Scandinavians retained much of their parents' identity well into the twentieth century. Yet they, too, began to merge with one another, especially after World War I. For some this was a gradual process in which the children and grandchildren went through the schools and found jobs, homes, and even friends and mates outside their own groups. For others, such as the Irish, Italians, Slovenes and Slovaks, it took generations of struggle to obtain respectability and acceptance into American life. Nevertheless, by 1960, men of Irish extraction were well represented in the executive levels of major American corporations, and John F. Kennedy, a descendant of Irish immigrants, won election to the White House.

Almost paradoxical movements have shown the decline of the immigrant church, alongside the revival of religious devotion among some Americans. The ethnic churches, once the keystone of community involvement, disappeared gradually among European immigrants, except for a few in decaying areas of some cities. Moreover, both the major Christian and Jewish religions have diversified in their views; some have become more modern and ecumenical, less intolerant and defensive, and more Americanized. Since the 1970s, however, there have been increased signs that young Jews want to increase their identity with their heritage. In the first decade of the twenty-first century there are signals from the Vatican that Pope Benedict XVI wants Catholics throughout the world to become more traditional and less ecumenical. Jews and Catholics, of course, are not the only people whose signs of heightened religious consciousness have been noticed. With the growth of the Muslim population in the United States it becomes much clearer than there are some groups, including religious women, who have embraced the teachings of their ancestors and have not automatically found the "modern" world with its permissiveness, opportunities, and freedom traditional restraints to their liking.

Many of those who have moved away from their ethnic neighborhoods and who are indistinguishable to outsiders by their work, dress, or manner find emotional comfort by retaining some aspects of their heritage. In the Maine cities of Brunswick and Lewiston French Canadians are still a presence. One can find Scandinavian settlements in such Midwestern cities as Chicago, St. Paul, and Minneapolis. Large colonies of Norwegians, Greeks, and Armenians live in places as diverse as New York, Chicago, and Seattle. In Pittsburgh's Squirrel Hill district, eastern European Jews and their descendants still retain the flavor of an identifiable urban ethnic enclave, whereas in the "Polish Hill" section of the same city residents rejected a Model Cities proposal in 1968 because they specifically did not want to "rejuvenate" their neighborhood. Italians and Mexicans often move to more upscale neighborhoods where several generations live close to one another. Moreover they join societies such as the Sons of Norway Lodges, the Japanese American Citizens League, or the American Jewish Committee. To census interviewers they proudly announce, as did 4.2 million Americans in 1969, that they are "ethnically Polish." They promote ethnic festivals and celebrations; more perhaps as a reminder of days gone by than because of a strong present commitment. Every year Denver holds an Oktoberfest; Basques meet for a weekend in Elko, Nevada; Hungarians have their harvest festivals; Swiss Americans enjoy *Bundesfeier;* and Greeks orchestrate local festivities across the country. In the early 1970s New York City changed the name of one of the streets in which Italians hold an annual San Gennaro festival from "Mulberry" to "Via San Gennaro." Many Americans, even those who do not have an Irish background, celebrate St. Patrick's Day. In Savannah, Georgia, the city closes its schools on March 17, the local dairy puts out mint-flavored milk, and restaurants offer green whipped cream, green drinking water, and green beer. About half of Savannah's 130,000 people turn out for the annual St. Patrick's Day parade, which is second in size only to that of New York City.

While the celebration of Old World holidays pleased ethnics of both older and newer vintage, the European newcomers were still in the process of building social institutions and adjusting to American society. Two groups that illustrate this phenomenon are the "New Irish" and the Russian Jews. Unlike the famine, or poor, Irish who came to America during the nineteenth century, the "New Irish" of the 1980s and 1990s were mostly high school graduates. Although most had "green cards," which gave them legal status and allowed them to seek gainful employment, some did not have appropriate legal documents and actively avoided contact with public authorities and institutions. They did not join Irish American clubs and associations. In New York City, however, they published their own newspaper, *The Irish Voice,* to speak about their concerns. The more recent arrivals from Ireland generally socialized with one another and were considered "clannish" by the descendants of earlier Irish immigrants.

On the other hand, although Russian Jews affiliated with established American Jewish organizations that helped them adapt to American culture and American Judaism, most of them were not especially religious and found American society difficult to understand. For those who lacked English, there was little choice but to join organizations and take part in activities in which the language was Russian. They sought support from companions who kept themselves close to one another by establishing clubs and restaurants similar to those that existed in the former Soviet Union. Russian Jews settled in many different parts of the country but they are particularly united in Brooklyn, New York.

Also in the twenty-first century, American Indians continue to celebrate their traditions. Many who live on or near the reservations, as well as those residing in the Indian communities in the larger cities, now strive openly to retain their Indian heritage. In the past, isolation from the rest of society, particularly for the reservation dwellers, made this easy, but since the mid-1960s young Indians have overcome earlier feelings of inferiority about their culture. Thus from places as varied as the small Stockbridge community in central Wisconsin and the sprawling Navajo reservation in Arizona to Indian settlements in Los Angeles and Baltimore, the stress is now on cultural pride. In language, art, handicraft skills, medicine, and religious practices this determination to retain much of the old Indian way is growing. In major cities Indian cultural centers now offer tribal language classes or a place to learn music, dancing, or traditional lore, serving the same purposes that a German American club might in any large city. The Native American Church also provides cross-tribal bonds for Indian people throughout the country. Indians now share their cultural pride with the rest of society through regional powwows and rodeos, as well as a professional dance group and the work of artisans who offer a wide variety of regional styles and traditions.

Ethnic Groups and Politics

Descendants of various ethnic groups also like to see signs recognizing their accomplishments, status, and worth. One of the most common of these is political recognition. In the late nineteenth and early twentieth centuries, the Irish had a stronghold on most of the urban political machines. After World War II noticeable changes occurred. The Italians became the single largest voting bloc in Rhode Island and promptly elected the nation's first governor, and then United States senator, of Italian origin. Buffalo, New York, chose the first mayor of Polish heritage in 1949, and Maine sent another man of Polish extraction, Edmund Muskie, first to the governorship, then to the United States Senate. Since the 1950s Italians have also received what they considered their political due: the mayoralty of New York City and governorships in Massachusetts, Connecticut, New York, and Washington. In 2007 Louisiana elected as governor a man of Asian Indian ancestry.

Since World War II the ethnically "balanced ticket" has become a political necessity in many states, reflecting the strength of the groups that live there. One story, possibly apocryphal but nevertheless reflecting the thoughts of so many politicos, circulated in 1962 concerning the desperate need of John Bailey, the Democratic political "boss" in Connecticut, for a Polish-speaking Catholic candidate to run as congressman-at-large. Legend has it that in interviewing prospective nominees Bailey asked each only three questions: (1) Are you Polish? (2) Are you Catholic? and (3) Do you speak Polish? He finally settled on Bernard F. Grabowski after eliminating another possibility, Frank Kowalski. The ethnically identifiable name is crucial, of course. Bailey once chose a woman, Elizabeth Zdunczyk, as a candidate for Connecticut's secretary of state. She was of Irish ancestry but had married a man of Polish extraction, and as the politicos said, "the last name was what counted." In 1972 the first Cuban American received appointment as a commissioner on Miami's City Commission. The *New York Times* reported that the "local power brokers [thought] that for the purpose of racial balance there ought to be a 'Cuban seat' on Miami's City Commission. The existence of a 'black seat' and a 'Jewish seat' on different elective bodies [in the city] had been taken for granted for many years." In 1975 one political observer found eighteen Jews, eleven Italians, seven Irish, four blacks, two Puerto Ricans, and one "other" on the forty-three-person New York City Council. The "other," Robert F. Wagner III, son of a former mayor and grandson of a United States senator, was listed as being of "German, English, and Irish" background. By 2009 Hispanics and African Americans constituted the majority of the New York City Council.

In some regions of the country what is demanded in political appointments is recognition, regardless of balance. From 1925 through 1976 every governor of Minnesota (Christianson, Olson, Benson, Stassen, Thye, Youngdahl, and Anderson) was of Scandinavian background. When Wendell R. Anderson resigned in December 1976 to take the seat that Walter Mondale, the vice president-elect, had vacated in the United States Senate, Rudolph G. Perpich, son of a Croatian immigrant, replaced him. Perpich regarded his elevation to the governorship as a political Horatio Alger story. He recalled that he was so much a part of an ethnic community in his earliest years that he spoke no English in 1933 when he entered kindergarten.

By the 1980s ethnic entrants into the political arena usually received a good deal of press attention. In 1982 Mario Cuomo became the first Italian American to be elected governor of New York (his son was elected Attorney-General of New York in 2006); and when Walter Mondale, the Democratic candidate for president in 1984, picked a running mate, he chose an Italian American congresswoman, Geraldine Ferraro. Two years later the voters of Maryland reelected a Polish American, Barbara Mikulski, to the United States Senate. In 2008 President-elect Obama chose an Hispanic woman as Secretary of Labor and a person of Japanese ancestry to head the Department of Veterans Affairs. Jewish Americans have won election to the United States Senate from states with relatively small Jewish populations such as Wisconsin and Nevada. By 2009 Jews in the Senate represented a variety of states, including New York, New Jersey, Wisconsin, California, and Connecticut. In fact, in 2000, Senator Joseph Lieberman of Connecticut became the first Jew to run on a presidential ticket of a major party when Al Gore, the Democratic choice for president of the United States, selected Lieberman as his running mate. Even more startling, however, was the 2002 political scene in Texas. There, Democrats nominated two minorities to head the ticket in that year's election. Tony Sanchez, of Mexican heritage, won the party's nomination for governor, and Ron Kirk, an African American, ran for the United States Senate. Neither, however, was elected.

Since 1961 all of the presidents of the United States have appointed members of minority groups to their cabinets. Kennedy chose two Jews, a man of Polish heritage, and the first Italian American. Lyndon Johnson chose the first African American and also the first African American to sit on the United States Supreme Court. The tradition has continued. In 2001, George W. Bush became the first President to appoint African Americans to the most important foreign policy positions in the administration: Colin Powell as Secretary of State and Condoleezza Rice as National Security Adviser. When Powell resigned in 2005, Bush appointed Rice to replace him. Today, and probably in the future, it would be politically unwise and unthinkable for any president to construct a cabinet with just WASP males.

In closing this section we are reminded of the French expression that, roughly translated, means "the more things change, the more they remain the same."

Even as our country matures and older generations of immigrants blend in and assimilate with others in this country, waves of foreigners are always on the horizon to redo what others have done before them and to suffer the consequences of being the new kids on the block. Individual friendliness can be found throughout the United States, but suspicions of what the future portends because of the arrival of one group or another continue as the descendants of the earlier immigrants and current minorities forget the reception and treatment of their forebears and themselves. Bigotry and xenophobia wax and wane—the groups of victims and the assumptions Americans make about them are the things that change. But as we said at the beginning of this chapter, there is one major difference in immigrant and minority reception and treatment. That is that both our government and most members of society, despite their prejudices, are committed to helping the newcomers "make it" in America in a way that had not been true before 1965. We say that we want the minorities to be "like us" and to retain their heritage as well. A paradox? Of course. Only the future will tell if such opposite goals are both compatible and obtainable.

9

The Struggle for Equality

(1945–2010)

Despite current media reports highlighting discontent with and anger toward members of many minority groups, the past sixty-five years have witnessed the greatest decline of prejudice and bigotry in the history of our country. Fewer people have negative thoughts about individuals from other groups, and certainly there is less discrimination than existed before 1945. Supreme Court decisions and federal legislation have forced all Americans to reexamine their thoughts about those who are different from themselves. Thus Jews, Poles, Irish, Italians, Asians, African Americans, American Indians, and others who had been scorned, excluded, and victimized by prejudice in yesteryear found bigotry on the wane in this country. The growth of tolerance, however, neither brought about a cultural utopia in which all groups enjoyed equal respect nor meant that the nation had at long last achieved its famous melting pot. Nevertheless, the hostility so characteristic of American group relations earlier lost much of its intensity. Economic prosperity, higher degrees of education, lessening insecurities and tensions among religious bodies, growing contacts between various peoples, and the long-term efforts of those who had struggled to bring equality to America all helped to bring an acceptance of others to a higher level than had been customary in the past. No doubt the fact that the descendants of so many immigrants had become Americanized helped to increase toleration because they no longer seemed so different.

Before the mid-1960s, however, a majority of Americans did not or would not publicly support programs designed to ensure equal rights for all citizens. Nevertheless, changes came. California abolished legal school segregation in 1947; Arizona granted Indians the right to vote in 1948; and in 1952 Asian immigrants became eligible for citizenship. In a dramatic and significant move in 1945, the Brooklyn Dodgers baseball team broke the color line in major league baseball by signing Jackie Robinson to a minor league contract; the following year he joined the Dodgers. These actions seemed quite sufficient to most Americans in the late 1940s and early 1950s, but discrimination still continued, although not always in as crude a form as existed in the 1920s and 1930s. Robinson, for example, could not stay in all of the hotels that his white teammates were booked into around the country. Detroit had more than six hundred Jewish teachers in its school system but no Jewish principals. In California Mexicans could no longer be forced to go to separate schools, but Anglo attitudes did not change easily. On the national level, President Harry S Truman in 1948 urged Congress to pass civil rights legislation that would ban discrimination on interstate transportation facilities, provide federal penalties for lynching, outlaw the poll tax, and otherwise protect the black minority in this country, but the legislators rejected these proposals.

Groups such as the NAACP, B'nai B'rith's Anti-Defamation League, and the Japanese American Citizens League challenged discrimination in the courts, lobbied for laws prohibiting distinctions among people solely because of race, religion, or national origin, and brought pressure on the media for favorable images of diverse minorities. At the same time, social scientists refuted the notion that one group was inherently superior to another. Yet progress came slowly. For a number of minorities, especially blacks, Indians, and Mexicans, the changes that occurred demonstrated how much longer a road they had to travel than did the descendants of the European and Asian immigrants of another era.

The Deprived Minorities

Although European immigrants and their descendants make up the largest percentage of ethnic groups, in recent decades blacks, Hispanics, and Asians have become the most visible of the minority groups. In fact, the term *ethnic minority* has often been used to denote these people rather than any specific Caucasians. Along with the American Indians, members of these groups have constituted some of the most deprived members in American society. There is hardly a major urban area without its black or Spanish-speaking ghetto.

When immigrants of yesteryear moved, they abandoned their rat-infested abodes with falling plaster, broken windows, and malfunctioning heating units to the poorer, newer immigrants, blacks, and Hispanics. Since the 1930s the federal government has embarked on programs to improve the nation's housing and tried to arrest urban decay. It achieved only limited success. In the postwar period the Federal Housing Administration and the Veterans Administration have aided millions in purchasing their own homes. Unfortunately, the vast majority of these houses were constructed in suburbs, and many were too expensive for the poorest minorities. Nevertheless, when blacks and Hispanics who could afford the prices asked, they encountered discrimination from banks, mortgage companies, or realtors. For many years the federal government tacitly allowed these practices.

Slum-clearance programs, sometimes called urban renewal, had a more direct impact on the nation's ghettos. Beginning modestly in the 1930s, the federal bulldozer tore down many old, decaying neighborhoods and replaced them with public housing projects. But it also cleared the way for expressways and municipal projects such as Lincoln Center in New York City and the Tucson Community Center, whose cultural programs focused on the tastes of the more affluent members of society. After 1949 the federal government tore down more housing for the poor than it built.

The ghetto-dwelling black and Spanish-speaking Americans also suffered from poor health, high crime rates, and drug addiction. Blacks made gains in health in the 1940s and 1950s, but they still used fewer medical services than whites and visited physicians and dentists less frequently. Living in areas such as the rural South, migrant camps, or the inner cities, where treatment facilities were lacking or often inferior, African Americans and Hispanic Americans were at a disadvantage. Better facilities existed in the cities than in rural America, but in the cities medical care often cost too much for the poor.

The Biddle Alley district of the black ghetto of Baltimore, 1910. (State Historical Society of Wisconsin)

If receiving adequate medical care was a problem, so, too, was crime. Assaults occurred more frequently in the inner-city black and Spanish-speaking neighborhoods than elsewhere. Increasing police patrols failed to halt the growth of crime, and the presence of the police, important as they were for fighting crime, proved a source of difficulty. Relations between these ethnic minorities and the law officers brought misunderstandings and conflicts to many neighborhoods. Charges of police brutality and the breakdown of communications between the police and the community triggered more than one riot in the 1960s. Similarly, a ghastly act that received worldwide notoriety occurred in Los Angeles in 1992 when a video camera captured scenes of policemen beating and kicking a black suspect. Narcotics addiction, like the indexes of crime, was also higher in the ghettos than in other neighborhoods.

Between 1970 and 2000 the income gap between black and white families widened. In 1970 the median income for black families had reached 61 percent of white figures, but the percentage dropped to 58 percent twenty years later. The booming economy of the 1990s aided blacks, even those with low incomes, in the last few years of the decade. But as the twenty-first century dawned, black family incomes amounted to only about 60 percent of those of white families. Part of the reason for the gap was the fact that many black families

The black ghetto of Milwaukee, 1968–1969. *(Milwaukee Journal,* State Historical Society of Wisconsin)

were headed by women who depended on welfare programs or held low-wage jobs. The parents of almost one-half of black children had incomes at or near poverty levels in 2001. The median income of African Americans was somewhat better. In 2006 the black median income was two-thirds of that of whites. In addition, about one-quarter of African Americans lived below the poverty line compared with only 8 percent of whites. Many African Americans achieved high status and pay in professional sports, the movies, and popular culture. Still others turned their attention to academic achievement. In 1970 only 5 percent of blacks were college graduates. By 2004 the figure was 17 percent. However, this compared unfavorably with the more than 30 percent of whites who were college graduates in that year, and Asians had an even higher percentage of college graduates. It must also be pointed out that blacks who came to the United States in the twentieth or twenty-first century from Africa or the Caribbean have significantly higher incomes than blacks whose ancestors were slaves in the United States. Just as with whites, different groups of blacks have different cultures and goals. In fact, the only county in the United States where blacks have a higher average income than whites is Queens County in New York City. That borough is like a mini United Nations because so many different ethnic groups reside there including a thriving middle class black community whose members come mostly from the Caribbean.

The poorest of all ethnic groups were American Indians. Although their life expectancy had improved after World War II, reservation dwellers had high unemployment, low incomes, and poor health. Many Central Americans and Mexicans had better lives than American Indians, but the census bureau reported that roughly one-fourth of Central American immigrants lived in poverty in 2000, more than double the rate of native-born whites.

Yet not all members of minority groups lived in need. Many of the new Asian immigrants arrived with skills and educations that enabled them to earn large incomes. Asian Indians, for example, had an especially high level of education, with many men and women entering the medical fields. Many Latinos had pulled themselves into the middle class. The Cubans, especially those who arrived in Florida and other places on the East Coast before 1980, were the most successful of the Hispanics. Roberto Goizueta was born in Cuba but educated at Yale University. He then returned to Cuba to work for the Coca-Cola Company. When he fled the revolutionary regime of Fidel Castro, he rejoined Coca-Cola and rose to the top. As chief executive and chairman of the board, he became one of the wealthiest Americans before his death in 1997. Other Cuban refugees made rapid strides after living for a few months on welfare in Florida. They ascended the economic ladder in Miami and soon became proprietors of shops,

TABLE 9.1.   Largest Cities with African American Populations

	2000			
	Total population		Black or African American	
Place	Rank	Number	Rank	Number
New York, NY	1	8,008,278	1	2,129,762
Los Angeles, CA	2	3,694,820	7	415,195
Chicago, IL	3	2,896,016	2	1,065,009
Houston, TX	4	1,953.631	5	494,496
Philadelphia, PA	5	1,517,550	4	655,824
Phoenix, AZ	6	1,321,045	60	67,416
San Diego, CA	7	1,223,400	36	96,216
Dallas, TX	8	1,188,580	11	307,957
San Antonio, TX	9	1,144,646	48	78,120
Detroit, MI	10	951,270	3	775,772
Baltimore, MD	17	651,154	6	418,951
Memphis, TN	18	650,100	8	399,208
Washington, DC	21	572,059	9	343,312
New Orleans, LA	31	484,674	10	325,947

Source: U.S. Census Bureau, Census Redistricting Data (Public Law 94–171)

construction workers, and even successful bankers. The second generation excelled in school and pursued education with great enthusiasm.

Toward Civil Rights

It was the gap between the descendants of Europeans and their own status that connected African Americans, Latinos, Indians, and some Asian Americans. Looking at the progress of these earlier immigrants made many blacks, and later Latinos and Indians, eager to increase their standards of living. To achieve similar goals, they took to the streets, the courts, and the halls of Congress and state legislatures. The conflicts began as soon as World War II ended but escalated in the 1950s and 1960s, making those two decades an era of struggle for equality.

African Americans had protested against discrimination and segregation long before then. At the turn of the century they mounted local boycotts against segregated schools and southern transportation facilities, but these efforts failed. The NAACP has fought racism since its inception in 1909. It lobbied for an antilynching bill in Congress during the 1920s and 1930s but failed to get the legislators' votes or presidential support. Blacks won some gains during the

New Deal, as many of them received recognition and appointments from the federal government, but President Franklin D. Roosevelt did not include a civil rights program in his agenda. During World War II, though, African Americans threatened public protests. A. Philip Randolph, head of the Brotherhood of Sleeping Car Porters, warned the president that he would lead a massive march on Washington unless federal action was taken to prevent discrimination in the nation's defense industries. Roosevelt, fearing wartime disunity, ordered the creation of a Fair Employment Practices Commission (FEPC) to prevent job discrimination. The FEPC proved more symbolic than effective, as it lacked real power.

In the 1940s and even before, some white Americans had become more receptive to the concept of equality. Sociologists, anthropologists, and psychologists increasingly stressed the role of environment—the schools, the home, the neighborhood, and racial discrimination—in explaining differences in IQ test results and academic achievement. Historians also rediscovered the black past, in both Africa and the United States, and noted the many contributions that blacks had made to the growth of America. These notions, which slowly made their way into the media, the schools, popular journals, and political and religious rhetoric, were perhaps best exemplified in Gunnar Myrdal's *An American Dilemma* (1944). In this classic study the author painted a picture of blacks caught in a vicious circle. Whites used black poverty to argue that they were inferior and therefore justified fewer opportunities for them, which in turn guaranteed the cycle of poverty. Books such as *An American Dilemma* demonstrated that segregation and poverty had devastating effects, but most white Americans neither knew nor cared about how outrageous conditions had become for blacks.

After World War II ended the NAACP, the Congress of Racial Equality (CORE), and the National Urban League became more vigorous in lobbying and legal actions to achieve their goals. They were joined in this battle by several other ethnic organizations that shared similar goals, such as the Japanese American Citizens' League, the American Jewish Committee, the American Jewish Congress, and the Anti-Defamation League of B'nai B'rith.

The first major breakthrough came from the Supreme Court. In 1938 it forced the state of Missouri to admit a black citizen of that state into its law school; in 1944 the Court outlawed the whites-only primary in Texas; in 1948 it said that restrictive covenants barring certain racial and/or ethnic groups from purchasing or renting dwellings in the neighborhood or building could not be enforced in courts of law. In 1950 it proclaimed that graduate and professional schools could not be segregated.

The most significant, as well as the most famous, of the many victories was the 1954 school desegregation case, *Brown v. Board of Education*. In that decision the United States Supreme Court found the "separate-but-equal" facilities in public schools inherently unequal and therefore in violation of the Fourteenth Amendment to the Constitution, which guarantees each citizen "equal protection of the laws." The importance of the *Brown* ruling cannot be overstated, but it had little meaning until enforced. Most southern states refused to comply with that decision, and in 1957–58 President Dwight D. Eisenhower had to use federal troops to ensure the security of nine African American students in an integrated high school in Little Rock, Arkansas. The Court had urged desegregation with "all deliberate speed," but ten years later few southern schools had complied.

School desegregation, furthermore, was only one of the changes needed to achieve social and economic equality. A. Philip Randolph's announced march on Washington had demonstrated the power of a threat of disruptive action, but in 1955 the arrest of a black woman for refusing to relinquish her bus seat to a white man in Montgomery, Alabama, pointed the way to a new strategy for combating racism. A newcomer to the community, the Reverend Martin Luther King Jr., galvanized the blacks and organized a boycott of all of Montgomery's public buses. After a year the protest succeeded, the city desegregated its buses, and King became a hero in the civil rights movement. The Montgomery bus boycott also resulted in the organization of the Southern Christian Leadership Conference (SCLC) and King's rise to national prominence.

In their efforts to pursue nonviolent demonstrations against segregation in the spring of 1960, African American students staged sit-ins at whites-only lunch counters throughout the South. They maintained that they would not leave until served. As the sit-ins spread and local police arrested demonstrators, southern college students formed the Student Nonviolent Coordinating Committee (SNCC) to coordinate their activities. The sit-ins captured the imagination of the black community even more than had the bus boycott, and thus they opened a decade of intense activity to desegregate America.

Through the 1960s blacks held demonstrations against existing inequalities. In 1961 college youths went on integrated buses, popularly known as "Freedom Rides," to protest segregated facilities in interstate transportation. Their actions brought violence from southern whites and national media coverage. Increasing numbers of Americans began to believe federal legislation was necessary to prevent outbursts of violence during peaceful demonstrations: the protesters had to be protected. The wrath of southern whites came to the fore again in May 1963 when, with massive demonstrations, SNCC and King protested segregation in Birmingham, Alabama. There local police responded with fire-hoses, sharp-fanged German shepherds, and arrests of peaceful participants.

National and international television news reported the brutality in Birmingham, thereby forcing President John F. Kennedy, who had previously been reluctant to take a strong stand in the area of civil rights, to go before Congress with a proposal guaranteeing equal protection of the laws for all Americans. Civil rights laws had been enacted in 1957 and 1960, but their provisions were limited. Congress did not immediately respond to the president's request, but after his assassination on November 22, 1963, and under the forceful prodding of President Lyndon B. Johnson, it enacted the 1964 Civil Rights Act. This law banned discrimination in public accommodations, created a federal fair employment practices agency, protected the right of all adult Americans to vote, and gave the executive branch the power to cut off funds to state and local agencies that practiced racial discrimination.

The new law did not end racial discrimination, for there still remained the issue of enforcement. Within the next decade, however, the United States Supreme Court, in a series of individual cases, outlawed discrimination in housing, transportation facilities, and recreational areas. Then the southern states began to integrate public facilities, although some communities chose to close their beaches or swimming pools rather than accommodate both races together. Yet African Americans still faced the problems of poor housing, inadequate employment opportunities, and lack of political power.

Voting registration drives, spearheaded by SNCC and SCLC and supported by white liberals, led to an increase in black suffrage. Actually, the number of southern blacks exercising the franchise had grown considerably since the end of World War II. But the proportion voting in the mid-1960s in Alabama, Mississippi, Louisiana, Georgia, and South Carolina was considerably less than it was for whites. It took direct federal intervention to ensure minority suffrage. Some blacks concentrated on community action, whereas others tried to work through the Democratic Party and Congress. Martin Luther King Jr. dramatized the problem at Selma, Alabama, in 1965. Once again Congress responded by passing a more effective voting rights law.

Ultimately, although the civil rights movement forced legal accommodations throughout the nation, it did little to improve economic opportunities for those in need of jobs and training. For these people, President Johnson embarked on the War on Poverty, which was intended to eradicate the problems of the poorest Americans. Programs such as Model Cities, Job Corps Training, Operation Head Start, and the various activities of the Office of Economic Opportunity aimed to help those with the fewest opportunities. The War on Poverty failed, however, as many programs shut down in the 1970s and 1980s, casualties of inadequate funding and the war in Vietnam. But other governmental policies, such as the Social Security program with its expanded benefits, the Veterans Administration programs, the food stamp program, and welfare, all aided lower-income Americans. These benefits grew in the late 1960s and 1970s, but a less generous philosophy and a concern about how much money the federal government was spending on these programs led to declines in federal support in the 1980s and 1990s.

In cases in which presidents could act alone, however, changes occurred. President Truman used an executive order in 1948 to desegregate the military. Nonetheless, total integration came slowly. The Korean and Vietnam wars hastened military desegregation, yet problems remained. In the post-Vietnam volunteer army of the 1970s, although blacks constituted about one-quarter of the soldiers, they made up only 6 percent of the officer corps. One black major complained, "Folks talk about the new, modern Army but black men still get lousy efficiency reports because they're black, they still get jobs that are not exactly career-enhancing. In order to be competitive you have to do twice as well, have to be a 'super spade.'" Complaints about promotions and assignments continued, and racial tensions from time to time erupted into violence. In the late 1970s and 1980s the army embarked on race relations programs to improve conditions and to promote blacks more rapidly.

The Movement for Black Power

Neither the federal government nor its programs eliminated poverty. Consequently, many blacks began to lose faith in the legalistic and nonviolent approach to solving their problems. The laws mandating equality of opportunity and treatment did not feed the hungry, educate the poor, or provide jobs. At the Democratic Party's national convention in 1964, furthermore, the majority refused to seat the racially integrated and democratically chosen members of the Mississippi Freedom Party. Instead, convention delegates recognized the group that had been chosen by a "lily white" gathering in the state.

That single action, and experiences with white liberals who tried to "uplift" southern blacks by taking over "tasks, conversations, meetings, and publicity that should have been handled by Negroes," convinced many to reject the goal of desegregation. Now they insisted on equality and the preservation of black culture and values under the guidance of black leadership. During the 1960s African American leaders certainly knew of the racial stirrings in Africa and the rise of Third World consciousness. Stokely Carmichael, the leader of SNCC, perhaps expressed the group's views best when he said that what was needed was "black power." The expression signified different things to different blacks, but it conveyed to all of them what they wanted but lacked—power!

Many white liberals thereafter either became preoccupied with the Vietnam War or lost interest in the civil rights movement because they felt pushed aside by the burgeoning black nationalism. White ethnic minorities, who had supported some of the civil rights goals, increasingly felt threatened by people who wanted absolute equality in housing, schooling, jobs, and leadership positions in society. Thus, just at the moment of its greatest legislative achievements in the mid-1960s, the civil rights movement began to disintegrate. Old-line civil rights groups such as the National Urban League and the NAACP continued their activities, but the main thrust of the movement was blunted by the end of the decade.

Militants took over SNCC and CORE, an interracial group founded in the 1940s, but these two organizations had few members. The Nation of Islam, a black religious body that rejected Christianity and looked to the Middle East instead for inspiration, gained new influence. Founded in the 1930s, the Nation grew slowly at first, then became stronger in the 1960s under the leadership of Elijah Muhammad and the dynamic Malcolm X. The Nation had only a small following, but it proved effective in ghetto work among lower-class blacks. It emphasized strict moral conduct and the building of an economic foundation in the local community. Even though the nationalist groups lacked massive numbers, they signified the weakening of civil rights approaches and the divisions among blacks. Other manifestations of nationalism included emphasis on African history and African American music and arts and a desire for separation among black students on college campuses. Some nationalists were more directly political and urged the building of a black power base in the cities and rural South. Although the Muslims had talked of resisting whites with violence and saw the white man as the devil, they later modified their line.

The Black Panthers, a small revolutionary organization, urged a Marxist approach. Individual blacks also called for violence against whites and guerrilla warfare in the cities. Some organized themselves in unusual associations. One, the Revolutionary Action Movement, saw two of its members convicted for conspiracy to murder NAACP leader Roy Wilkins and Whitney Young of the National Urban League. Calls for revolutionary resistance and warfare, like appeals to nationalism, were not new, and like their forerunners, they had little support during the 1960s. But the anger and despair of these appeals struck a responsive chord.

The Post Civil Rights Era

The black power movement achieved little. Nor did the civil rights movement bring instant success. As a result in addition to street marches, demonstrations, and court cases, African Americans began to use their newly won voting rights to gain equality. Southern blacks began to vote in record numbers after enactment of the Voting Rights Act of 1965. Those in the north also marshaled their strength at the polls. At the end of World War II, only two African

Americans sat in Congress. However, by 2008 the Black Caucus in Congress numbered 42, from both the North and the South. Thousands of blacks had been elected to local offices by then, and there is scarcely a major city in the United States with a large black population that has not elected an African American to the position of mayor. Yet blacks were clearly underrepresented. Only three African Americans had been sent by voters to the United States Senate from the end of World War II to 2008. Several had been elected to governor, and by 2008 African Americans were governors of Massachusetts and New York.

A new era in African-American politics seemed to open up in 2007, when Barack Obama, a senator from Illinois, announced his intention to run for the Democratic Party's presidential election in 2008. Obama had been born in Hawaii to a white mother from Kansas and a black father from Kenya. After a series of hard-fought primaries in 2008, Obama emerged as the winner and was nominated by his party to make a bid for the presidency in the November election. This was the first time in American history that an African American had been chosen by a major political party to run for the presidency.

In November that year Obama decisively defeated his Republican opponent, Senator John McCain of Arizona. The newly elected President gathered the overwhelming majority of black voters, a solid majority of Hispanics, and most of the votes from people under 40 and/or from the most educated. Forty-three percent of white voters, a higher figure than that of John Kerry in 2004 and Al Gore in 2000 supported him. Obama ran virtually neck and neck with McCain among whites outside of the South. Such a large percentage of white votes for a Democrat seemed part of a trend. During the previous two decades a growing number of African American office holders were winning election in white majority districts. In 2008 about 45 percent of black office holders came from districts in which blacks made up between 35 and 45 percent of the population. And others were winning elections in areas in which blacks made up only 20 percent of the population. In 2008 roughly two hundred African American state office holders hailed from white majority districts. New Hampshire State Representative Melanie Levesque, an African American, won an impressive victory in a district in which blacks constituted less than one percent of the population.

Obama's election was an indication of growing tolerance among white Americans. At the same time, political observers pointed out that the campaign of John McCain and its increasing negative tone turned off many voters. The crashing economy in the autumn of 2008 also caught McCain with little to say about economics, especially because he was a Republican whose votes in the Senate were tied to the unpopular President George W. Bush. Although Obama's victory pointed in the direction of increased acceptance by whites of African Americans, there can be no doubt that the new president faced huge problems dealing with the recession and two wars in Iraq and Afghanistan.

At the same time that the civil rights movement failed to achieve equality, the expectations of African Americans rose, thus contributing to increasing anger and frustration in the nation's racial ghettos. On August 11, 1965, during a Los Angeles heat wave, a highway patrolman's arrest of a black youth for speeding and being intoxicated led to one of the worst urban riots in American history. For five days angry blacks firebombed buildings, threw rocks at cars, and looted and burned white-owned property in the Watts ghetto. Before the National Guard quelled the demonstrations, thirty-four persons were killed, and an estimated $35 million in property had been damaged.

There were other riots that year, and still more in 1966, 1967, and 1968 after the assassination of Martin Luther King Jr. in a Memphis motel. The riots in the summer of 1967 were especially destructive. Those in Newark claimed twenty-three lives; all but two victims were black. About the same number died in upheavals in Detroit, where the damage cost an estimated $50 million. All of the riots served notice that the blacks were fed up with what they saw as abuse from white Americans. In 1967 H. Rap Brown, a spokesman for one of the more militant black organizations, warned, "America, you'd better repent and straighten up or we'll burn you down."

Partly in response to the uprisings and partly because of the pressure of the civil rights movement, economic discrimination began to wane. American business firms not only started hiring blacks for executive and professional positions but they also embarked on affirmative action campaigns, seeking out talented members of various minority groups. Those who lacked training and education still had rough going after the riots, but for the young people who had marketable skills new doors sprang open.

By the 1970s nearly half of the nation's schools had desegregated legally. This happened most rapidly in the South. Indeed, by then northern schools remained the most segregated. As important conflicts erupted over busing and school integration in both regions and after 1990, many public schools began a process of renewed segregation. In higher education black enrollment grew substantially after 1960, but it remained underrepresented for the next forty years. In fact, several states, including California and Texas, curtailed controversial affirmative action programs. The courts limited some of these efforts, and as a result African American enrollment dropped at branches of the University of California in Berkeley and Los Angeles, the two most prestigious universities in that state.

Civil rights groups, the Black Caucus, and white liberals continued to push for more programs to aid African Americans, such as Affirmative Action, but after 1990 the mood of the courts turned more conservative. Congress responded similarly and in 1996 passed a law aimed at limiting welfare aid, a disproportionate number of whose recipients were women, mostly African Americans. In addition, in 2008 fewer white Americans believed that society and the federal government should assume major responsibility for helping the disadvantaged.

By the end of the first decade of the twenty-first century, it was obvious that the civil rights and black power movements had failed to achieve the kind of racial equality envisioned in the United States in the 1960s and 1970s. When two black Chief Executive Officers (CEOs), Stan O'Neal and Richard Parsons, stepped down from their positions in early 2008, it left only four blacks in charge of Fortune 500 companies. Parsons did not remain unemployed for long, however. In January, 2009 he became chairman of Citigroup, one of the world's largest banks.

Blacks had been catching up to whites in education and income after the 1970s, but the movement toward equality stalled by the first decade of the twentieth-first century. The most alarming fact was that many young black males were either in jail or otherwise in trouble with the law. In 2007 they were seven times as likely to be in prison as white males. Their unemployment rate remained double that of whites. Salaries for black women reached a near parity with those for white women by 2008, but both groups of women earned less than white males.

One hopeful sign was the opening of top Wall Street employment. After 1980 a few law firms began to hire black lawyers and make them partners. When Gordon Davis was made partner of a "white-shoe" firm (a firm known for hiring upper status white Protestant men) in 1983, he was one of only five African American partners among the major firms. Others followed after 1990, and a few blacks opened their own financial businesses. These prominent African Americans joined the campaign to elect Barack Obama, and they accounted for fifty-seven of the three hundred members of Senator Obama's national finance committee, each member of which had to be responsible for raising $250,000. Yet their limited presence indicated the great difference between white elites and blacks.

The alarming wealth gap between black and white Americans had important implications for the future. Most well-off white families outside of New York City owned their own homes and lived in suburbs that offered good public schools. Although elite jobs had opened for blacks after 1980, at the same time many African Americans lived in the inner cities where they faced high crime rates, poor housing, and low-quality schools. Many whites could afford to send their children to colleges or universities, whereas poorer blacks could not.

The Hispanics

With much of the nation's attention focused on the difficulties of African Americans, groups of young Mexican Americans began to stir. By early in the first decade of the twenty-first century Hispanics passed blacks as the nation's largest minority group. In 2005 the Bureau of the Census reported that Hispanics numbered approximately 42 million to the African American population of roughly 34 million. The militants believed that they should develop their own culture and coexist with everyone else on an equal basis. No large subgroup has ever done this before, and there was little reason to believe that Chicanos could succeed in their effort. The major problems for Mexican Americans were much the same as for African Americans and revolved around bread-and-butter issues: satisfying jobs, higher incomes, and good educational facilities for children. The 1974 report of the United States Civil Rights Commission on the education of Mexican American children in the Southwest (Arizona, California, Colorado, New Mexico, and Texas) concluded that facilities for them were poorer than for Anglos, that their teachers ought to have more practical training for dealing with minority children, and that a pressing need for bilingual classes existed. The commission's study focused on the plight of the Mexican Americans, many of whom believe that current federal programs have been directed toward the welfare of urban blacks. They are not incorrect, because not until the mid-1960s did the national media, centered in New York and Washington, pay much attention to Mexican Americans in the Southwest. As a result this group considered itself "the most overlooked minority in the United States."

Although Mexican American protest organizations date to the turn of the twentieth century, the first organization to have any influence was the League of United Latin American Citizens (LULAC), formed in Texas in 1929. It was composed of middle-class and mostly second-generation Mexican Americans. LULAC had some success in its programs, which concentrated on getting Mexican Americans to vote and on improving their educational opportunities. Another group, which appeared after World War II, was the GI Forum, formed in 1948 by returning veterans. The GI Forum received national attention when a Texas cemetery denied burial to a highly decorated Mexican American veteran who had been killed in the Philippines. However, then Senator Lyndon B. Johnson arranged for the fallen soldier to be buried in Arlington National Cemetery.

The middle-class bias of LULAC limited its outlook and goals, and the GI Forum included few others than veterans and concentrated on issues that they considered to be important. As a result many Mexican Americans wanted to address issues that affected all Mexicanos, and they organized new campaigns.

TABLE 9.2.   Detailed Hispanic Origin, 2006 (Hispanic populations
are listed in descending order of population size)

	Number	Percent
Mexican	28,395,997	64.1
Puerto Rican	3,985,058	9.0
All Other Spanish/Hispanic/Latino	3,044,659	6.9
Cuban	1,517,028	3.4
Salvadoran	1,363,726	3.1
Dominican	1,217,160	2.7
Guatemalan	896,780	2.0
Colombian	793,682	1.8
Honduran	486,026	1.1
Ecuadorian	478,957	1.1
Peruvian	430,009	1.0
Spaniard	372,632	0.8
Nicaraguan	298,928	0.7
Venezuelan	176,451	0.4
Argentinean	175,944	0.4
Panamanian	124,138	0.3
Other Central American	115,064	0.3
Costa Rican	111,678	0.3
Chilean	93,465	0.2
Bolivian	86,465	0.2
Other South American	72,541	0.2
Uruguayan	46,836	0.1
Paraguayan	15,751	0.0
Total	44,298,975	100.0

Universe: 2006 Hispanic resident population
Source: Pew Hispanic Center tabulations of 2006 American Community Survey (1% IPUMS)

Their first effort to receive significant national attention occurred in the 1960s when César Chávez led a grape pickers' strike in California. *La Huelga,* as it was called, attracted Senator Robert F. Kennedy's notice in 1965, and his interest resulted both in national media coverage and a subsequent national boycott of grapes that lasted five years before reaching a partially successful conclusion. The national prominence Chávez achieved far exceeded the monetary benefits to the workers, for never before had any Mexican American received such recognition. As a result he stood as both a symbol and an inspiration to all Chicanos in their quest for social justice. In New Mexico, Reies López Tijerina organized the *Alianza Federal de Mercedes* in 1963 to regain Mexican American lands that he claimed had been "stolen" in 1848, when the United States took the territory from Mexico. Next door in southwest Texas Angel Guitiérrez established *La Raza Unida* party in 1970 because he thought that the only way for Chicanos to achieve social and economic improvement was by gaining political control of their counties. In Colorado, Rudolph "Corky" Gonzales promoted his Crusade for Justice with the intention of improving social and economic opportunities for all Mexican Americans.

Through the efforts of these emerging leaders, by the late 1960s Chicanos had developed a keen sense of group awareness, and the term *La Raza* connoted their dedication to promoting the Mexican American culture, welfare, and lifestyle on a par with that of the Anglos. *La Causa,* the term used to denote the need for overall advancement of Chicanos, seems in effect to have been translated into traditional ethnic goals of recognition and opportunity.

Puerto Ricans, located mainly in the New York City area, are the second poorest Hispanic group, only slightly above Dominicans. They have high rates of unemployment and poor standards of health care, and they live in inadequate housing. Although they made gains in the 1950s and 1960s, conditions did not improve much after 1970, and in 2008 they remained at the bottom of the economic ladder. Only Dominicans were below Puerto Ricans in income and poverty. At the end of the first decade of the twentieth first century whites were twice as likely as Puerto Ricans to be college graduates, and Puerto Ricans had an income that was only two thirds of that of whites. Some mainland Puerto Ricans returned to their home island after 1970, but economic conditions there were not good, either, even though Puerto Ricans on the island did better than those on the mainland.

Like the Chicanos, the Puerto Ricans have organized to secure a share of government programs in housing, education, health, and jobs. For example, in New York City during the late 1960s a Puerto Rican youth group, the Young Lords, took over a neighborhood church to demonstrate the need for a free children's breakfast program. Another organization, the Puerto Rican Association for Community Affairs, founded ASPIRA to encourage their young people to get more education, but it had only limited success. Because they are American citizens, Puerto Ricans are eligible to vote, but they have yet to win their proportional share of New York City's political offices, which would give them more say in receiving government benefits.

As for income and education, Hispanic income and education lagged behind those of non-Hispanic whites. Hispanics made about two-thirds as much as non-Hispanic whites in 2008, and they were considerably less represented among college graduates. There were variations among Hispanics, with Cubans and South Americans having higher levels of income and education than those from Central America and Mexico. In 1988, Henry Cisneros, then San Antonio mayor and himself a Harvard graduate, suggested an explanation for the differences. "Hispanics are predominantly poor," he said. "They come from rural areas where there's no tradition of higher education, and their social patterns and mores are a disincentive. Fathers are very protective of their daughters and don't want them to leave home. The males are supposed to go to work to help the family or into the military." Twenty years later trends indicated that young Hispanics were pursing education in higher numbers. The second and third generations were more apt than their parents and grandparents to attend and graduate from colleges and universities and hence have higher incomes. In 2006 native-born Hispanics reported incomes of more than $30,000 compared with only $23,000 for the immigrant generation.

Like African Americans, Latinos turned to the ballot box to achieve their aims. Hispanics had been elected to national office from New Mexico, but no Hispanics had been elected from other states until Henry González was sent to Congress by the state of Texas at the same time that John F. Kennedy was elected to the presidency in 1960. Others followed, and González, taking his cue from members of other ethnic groups, organized the Hispanic Caucus in 1976, when it had five members. After the 2006 election it claimed twenty-four members. Although Hispanics had passed African Americans as the nation's largest minority, the Hispanic Caucus's size was considerably smaller than the Black Caucus.

Many Hispanics had been appointed to national office, and politicians began to woo voters. Cubans tended to vote Republican, but Mexicans, the largest Latino group, usually cast their ballots for Democrats. Nonetheless, both polit-

TABLE 9.3.   Median Personal Earnings for Full-Time,
Year-Round Workers by Race and Ethnicity, 2006

	Median earnings ($)
Hispanic	26,161
Native born	30,689
Foreign born	23,545
White alone, not Hispanic	40,248
Black alone, not Hispanic	30,789
Asian alone, not Hispanic	43,266
Other, not Hispanic	32,198
All	37,229

Universe: 2006 resident population defined for persons who worked at least 35 hours per week and at least 48 weeks in the past year.
Note: Due to the way in which the IPUMS adjusts annual incomes, these data will differ from those that might be provided by the U.S. Census Bureau.
Source: Pew Hispanic Center tabulations of 2006 American Community Survey (1% IPUMS).

ical parties began to court Hispanic voters. These voters were especially important in Florida, California, Texas, New Jersey, New Mexico, and Arizona. The Pew Hispanic Center estimated that in 2008 nearly 9 percent of American voters were Latinos.

The Asians

At first glance it does not appear that South and East Asians faced major handicaps in finding high-paying jobs, attending schools and universities, or living in safe and comfortable neighborhoods. They had higher incomes and better education than Latinos and African Americans, and they were more apt to locate in suburban communities. When affirmative action programs for blacks and Latinos at the University of California were curtailed, the number of Asians increased at the Berkeley and Los Angeles campuses.

But they, too, faced hostility and even violence. The United States Civil Rights Commission reported a number of violent episodes concerning Asian Americans. One incident in particular alarmed them. In 1992 Vincent Chin, the son of Chinese immigrants, was beaten to death by two unemployed auto workers in Detroit who thought he was Japanese and that imported Japanese cars were responsible for unemployment in the American auto industry. What bothered Asian American groups was the verdict following the two auto workers' convictions. They were fined but received only suspended sentences. Thus, despite their convictions of beating Chin to death with baseball bats, the two men escaped serving any time in jail.

Asian American organizations and individuals also believed that elite universities limited enrollment of Asian students through admissions quotas and that business firms had a "glass ceiling" and refused to promote Asians to top positions. Studies of these issues brought mixed results, and discrimination was hard to prove. However, in two areas, pressure from the Japanese American Citizens' League (JACL) led to Congressional action. JACL conducted a successful campaign in 1952 that persuaded Congress to make all races eligible for naturalization and to accept small numbers of immigrants from each Asian nation. The outstanding military record of Japanese American soldiers in World War II was a factor in winning Congressional support. In 1965 all nations of the Eastern Hemisphere received the same quotas.

Japanese Americans also succeeded in persuading several presidents and Congress that the World War II internment of Japanese immigrants and their children was a grave mistake and deserved some redress. In 1982 a federal government commission pointed out the injustice of internment, saying that "race prejudice, war hysteria, and the failure of political leadership," and not military necessity, caused the internment. The commission recommended that

Congress appropriate funds for reparations to the survivors. After President Ronald Reagan apologized for the treatment of Japanese Americans, Congress finally appropriated $20,000 for each survivor of the camps, beginning in 1990. About sixty thousand persons received this modest sum.

When Hawaii was made a state in 1959, Hiram Fong, a Harvard graduate and Chinese American, became the first Asian senator in the United States, but it was the Japanese Americans who began to dominate Hawaiian politics and accounted for the bulk of senators and representatives. As memories of the war years faded, and as the second-generation Japanese Americans grew up and turned to politics, they won victories in Hawaii, where they made up about 30 percent of the population, and in California the center of historic hostility to these people. Hawaii sent Japanese Americans to the United States Senate and the House of Representatives, and in 1976 Californian voters elected a Japanese American, S, I, Hayakawa, as United States senator. In 1995 one Japanese American, Daniel K. Inouye, and one native Hawaiian, Daniel K. Akaka, served as sentators from our fiftieth state, and three men of Asian heritage, Norman Minetta and Robert Matusui, both of Japanese ancestry, and Jay C, Kim, of Korean background, belonged to California's congressional delegation. Minetta also accomplished the unusual feat of serving in the cabinet of two successive presidents, Democrat Bill Clinton and Republican George W. Bush. He was Clinton's last Secretary of Commerce in the 1990s, and in 2001 Bush's choice for Secretary of Transportation.

The Indians

Along with African Americans and Spanish-speaking Americans, Indians also struggled for equality. World War II had a major impact on them; about twenty-five thousand men left the reservations to serve in the armed forces, and another fifty thousand, young men and women, left to work in defense industries. When these people returned home, they brought new ideas with them. Unhappy veterans criticized the BIA for meddling in tribal affairs, and in particular they objected to the ban on alcohol, which remained federal law until 1953. The young men looked at some tribal matters from a perspective that differed from that of reservation leaders, thus causing friction. Their experiences of having left the reservation, traveling, and occasionally meeting other Indians fostered a broader outlook, and a growing pan-Indian movement took hold after the war. Groups such as the National Congress of American Indians held meetings at which representatives from dozens of tribes met and discussed mutual problems, thus helping to reduce some intertribal differences and convincing many that they needed to cooperate with one another to survive.

By the late 1940s serious objections by whites to the New Deal program of encouraging Indians to preserve their distinct cultures had reappeared. Indeed, in 1950 the government launched a new program—termination—designed to eliminate itself from the Indian business. Despite the objections of skeptics, who claimed that private lumber and mining interests hoped to get their hands on Indian-held resources, Congress passed several termination bills that cut tribes loose from federal supervision. Only about ten thousand Indians received this treatment before a chorus of criticism forced the bureaucrats into a hasty retreat. Many of those terminated encountered disaster. The Menominee of Wisconsin saw much of their tribal land sold to outsiders and the sharp curtailment of their medical and educational benefits. The Klamath in Oregon came close to losing most of their vast timber holdings before the federal government altered its policy. Proponents of termination claimed it would put the Indian on an equal footing with the rest of society. Unfortunately, for many this meant being handed over to the tender mercies of state and local officials, traditional enemies of tribal interests. In 1958 the secretary of the interior halted termination, and by 1970 the government repudiated its policy.

Meanwhile, members of tribes unaffected by the termination controversy worked to combine traditional ways with new ideas and practices learned from the rest of American society. The Tohono O'odham, formerly the Papago tribe, which lives on a sprawling reservation in the southern Arizona desert, offers a good example of this. Many of these people live in small villages scattered widely across the reservation without a nearby store or even electricity. They support themselves by raising livestock, hunting, harvesting cactus fruit, and weaving and selling baskets to tourists. Most of those who leave get unskilled or semiskilled jobs in nearby Arizona communities.

Although life in the desert is rigorous, it is not impossible, and the O'odham have adapted items such as pickup trucks and television sets to their way of life. Their housing is a good example of cultural blending, as the tribesmen live in mud-and-stick and adobe dwellings, as well as modern, government-financed homes. Medical practices also reflect how the Indians have merged elements of their culture with those of white society. In addition to treatment from tribal healers and singers, some reservation dwellers receive care from lightly trained community health representatives or even may go to the outpatient clinics or hospitals staffed by the doctors and nurses of the Public Health Service.

Despite the continuing pressures on these people to shed their traditional ways, during the 1980s a dramatic shift in the opposite direction took place. This effort brought a sharply increased sense of cultural pride and tribal identity, even among the young, educated, and off-reservation O'odham. On the reservation the tribal schools now give bilingual instruction, so that for the first time in a generation or more Indian children are learning their own language

TABLE 9.4. Ten Largest Places in Total Population and in American Indian and Alaska Native Population, 2000

Place	Total population		American Indian and Alaska Native alone		American Indian and Alaska Native alone or in combination		Percent of total population	
							American Indian and Alaska Native alone	American Indian and Alaska Native alone or in combination
	Rank	Number	Rank	Number	Rank	Number		
New York, NY	1	8,008,278	1	41,289	1	87,241	0.5	1.1
Los Angeles, CA	2	3,694,820	2	29,412	2	53,092	0.8	1.4
Chicago, IL	3	2,896,016	9	10,290	8	20,898	0.4	0.7
Houston, TX	4	1,953,631	11	8,568	10	15,743	0.4	0.8
Philadelphia, PA	5	1,517,550	24	4,073	21	10,835	0.3	0.7
Phoenix, AZ	6	1,321,045	3	26,696	3	35,093	2.0	2.7
San Diego, CA	7	1,223,400	13	7,543	9	16,178	0.6	1.3
Dallas, TX	8	1,188,580	18	6,472	18	11,334	0.5	1.0
San Antonio, TX	9	1,144,646	10	9,584	12	15,224	0.8	1.3
Detroit, MI	10	951,270	40	3,140	25	8,907	0.3	0.9
Oklahoma City, OK	29	506,132	6	17,743	5	29,001	3.5	5.7
Tucson, AZ	30	486,699	8	11,038	11	15,358	2.3	3.2
Albuquerque, NM	35	448,607	7	17,444	7	22,047	3.9	4.9
Tulsa, OK	43	393,049	5	18,551	4	30,227	4.7	7.7
Anchorage, AK	65	260,283	4	18,941	6	26,995	7.3	10.4

(For information on confidentiality protection, nonsampling error, and definitions, see *www.census.gov/prod/cen2000/doc/sf1.pdf*)

and history. This new cultural pride has brought some disagreement, too. The young and vigorous leaders persuaded their followers to drop the Spanish name Papago and return to using their aboriginal name, the Tohono O'odham Nation. Although this caused discomfort to some tribal members, these young people seem clearly more aware of their traditional culture, beliefs, and practices than many of their predecessors during the past half-century.

Historically, groups intending to help tribesmen usually included whites, but this changed abruptly after mid-century. In 1961 a number of young, educated, and articulate Indians organized the National Indian Youth Council (NIYC), which they hoped would speak for all Indians rather than taking the more tribally oriented approach of earlier associations. Recognizing the successes of militant black civil rights demonstrations, the NIYC gained national publicity in 1964 by staging a "fish-in" in Washington state, with help from Marlon

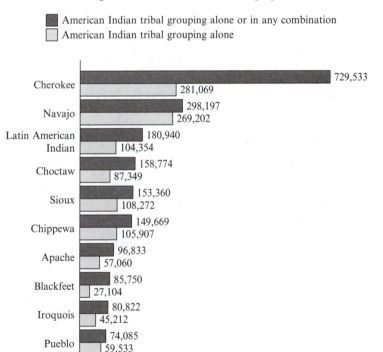

Ten Largest American Indian Tribal Groupings: 2000

■ American Indian tribal grouping alone or in any combination
☐ American Indian tribal grouping alone

Tribe	Alone or in any combination	Alone
Cherokee	729,533	281,069
Navajo	298,197	269,202
Latin American Indian	180,940	104,354
Choctaw	158,774	87,349
Sioux	153,360	108,272
Chippewa	149,669	105,907
Apache	96,833	57,060
Blackfeet	85,750	27,104
Iroquois	80,822	45,212
Pueblo	74,085	59,533

(For information on confidentiality protection, nonsampling error, and definitions, see *www.census.gov/prod/cen2000/doc/sf1.pdf*)
Source: U.S. Census Bureau, Census 2000 Summary File I.

Brando and other Hollywood notables, to remind the public of special Indian treaty rights and show that state and local actions tended to weaken or destroy them. Lapel buttons and bumper stickers calling for "Red Power" and reminding whites that "Custer Died for Your Sins" appeared to show the increasing strength of Indian commitment to this movement.

Responding to growing public support, Congress passed the 1968 Civil Rights Act, which contained a so-called Indian Bill of Rights. This was meant to protect individual tribesmen from any exercise of arbitrary power by either white or tribal officials, but it tended to disrupt and displace tribal laws and customs. Soon it brought sharp disagreements on reservations between the elected tribal governments and those who disapproved of electing officials and preferred a return to the traditional hereditary leadership. In late 1969 Indian frustration with government unresponsiveness led to the seizure of Alcatraz Island in San Francisco Bay. Claiming "the Rock" as unoccupied federal territory and thus subject to use by the Indians under the Sioux treaty of 1868, the militants hoped to turn the island into a pan-Indian cultural center. In 1971, however, the government forced them to leave.

The militants became increasingly active as other civil rights groups seemed to achieve their goals. In 1972 members of the radical American Indian Movement (AIM) occupied the offices of the BIA in Washington, D.C. After some days they departed peacefully, but only after "trashing" the offices and stealing or ruining many tribal records. In other widely scattered sit-ins, Indians demonstrated from New Mexico to Maine. Their most spectacular activity, however, was the 1973 occupation of Wounded Knee, South Dakota. A carefully staged media event that depended on both the immense popularity of Dee Brown's best-selling *Bury My Heart at Wounded Knee* and extensive television news coverage, the occupation thrust AIM leaders Dennis Banks and Russell Means into national headlines. Although the organization failed to achieve its stated goals of overthrowing the elected tribal leaders at the Pine Ridge, South Dakota, reservation or obtaining recognition for the tribes as independent nations within the general society, this movement should not obscure Indians' real discontent.

It is uncertain what AIM represented, but clearly, through its militant leaders, men and women from tribes across the country were mobilized into a semblance of cohesion. During the 1970s a generation of college-educated Indians moved into positions of leadership in both the tribes and the BIA. They used their knowledge and organizational skills to focus public attention on tribal problems and to exploit the guilt of many Americans, while at the same time defending traditional Indian culture and tribal aspirations. They encouraged the tribes to assume control of their own schools, and in many places Indian children now receive instruction in bilingual classes.

The tribes have moved aggressively to use education to help themselves improve their standard of living. Under provisions of federal legislation passed during the 1970s, tribal governments now routinely contract to operate their own schools, much as cities and school districts do. The long-term impact of these educational initiatives remains unclear, but both the tribes and the BIA have greatly increased spending for schools. For the BIA-operated schools, the results as of 2000 remain unsatisfactory. According to their own figures, the average achievement test scores for Indian children in both the second and sixth grades remain mired at only the twenty-first percentile of children nationally. That figure, however, represents only schools operated by the government, not by the tribes, and so it does not provide a complete picture.

If one looks at higher education, the picture seems a bit brighter. Between 1968 and 2000, thirty-one tribally controlled colleges have been organized. Current enrollment stands between five and six thousand Indian students. Only a few of these fledgling institutions have more than three or four hundred students, so the impact of this tribally sponsored higher education remains modest. Most Indian students who attend colleges or universities do so in publicly supported institutions, in which their enrollments have increased from seventy-eight thousand in 1978 to nearly one hundred thousand in 2000. Most of the students are women, and they usually attend public two-year institutions. Even with tribal schools and colleges and the training received at public schools, Indians still have less education per capita than any other significant minority in American society. In 2000 about 11 percent of tribal people had received a college degree, and 71 percent of the adults had graduated from high school.

Despite their educational gap, various tribes have succeeded in obtaining or retaining traditional lands and resources. In 1965 the people of Taos Pueblo, New Mexico, won a cash settlement from the Indian Claims Commission for having lost their sacred Blue Lake to the United States Forest Service. They rejected the money and continued to press for the return of the lake and surrounding forest area. In 1971 they succeeded, as the Nixon administration supported legislation for that purpose. That same year the federal government negotiated the Alaska Native Claims Settlement, which awarded forty million acres of land to the Indians, Aleuts, and Eskimo (Inuit) people of Alaska. The controversy over who got what land and how to best use the resources there continues, even though the agreement was a major step in getting a secure title to the lands in question.

In other parts of the country, when tribes regained rights to use resources they had lost over the years, bitter reactions occurred. A decision in *United States v. State of Washington* (1974) awarded the tribes of the Pacific Northwest the right to engage in salmon fishing at their traditional sites, dating back to the 1850s treaties their ancestors had signed. In addition, the court ruled that half of the current annual salmon catch belonged to the tribal people. This brought howls of rage from commercial and sport fishermen alike, and much violence occurred. Angry whites slashed the nets of Indian fishermen, dynamited their boats, and in every way possible tried to prevent tribal people from exercising their rights. In Wisconsin federal court rulings allowed the Ojibwa people to spear walleyed pike each spring before the regular fishing season opened. This also led to repeated protests by white fishermen and resort owners who claimed that Indian spearing harmed fishing and the area's tourist business. Pickup trucks sporting stickers that read "Spear an Indian, Save a Walleye" indicated the depth of anger the issue had created. Eventually state officials mediated, and physical confrontations have faded, but the deep anti-Indian antipathy remains.

Civil rights and tribal self-determination have been slow in coming for some groups. Many tribes still retain a continuing "special relationship" to the federal government because of nineteenth-century treaty rights. Others faced discrimination because of federal regulations. For example, the so-called Five Civilized Tribes of Oklahoma could not elect their own leaders between 1906 and 1970, when the government relented and stopped appointing tribal executives. Unreasonable and uneven law enforcement, particularly in urban areas and in small towns near the reservations, caused frequent trouble. Much of the early involvement of AIM resulted from police heavy-handedness in dealing with urban Indian people. The case of Raymond Yellow Thunder, who was beaten to death by a mob in Gordon, Nebraska, during the early 1970s, brought the issue to national attention. Eventually the courts convicted two men of manslaughter. Although ethnic tensions remain near a few of the large reservations, violent incidents have almost disappeared.

Because of growing awareness and ethnic pride, Indian groups long thought to have disappeared have emerged and now demand recognition as legal entities. Particularly strong in the East, their movement led the Indians to launch damage claims against both state and federal authorities over compensation for lost lands and for reinstatement as tribes with treaty rights. The first such group to draw major national attention was the Maine Passamaquoddy. In 1975 they won a judgment against the Interior Department and since then have negotiated a settlement worth $81.5 million. Perhaps as important as the cash settlement was their achievement of federal recognition as a tribe. Their suit and similar actions by other Indian groups led the BIA to establish a new office for tribal acknowledgement. In 1978 the BIA announced the first guidelines for the process of gaining tribal recognition, and since then almost two hundred groups have applied for tribal status. By 2000 more than twenty of them succeeded, and about the same number of claims were rejected. Many of the others remain somewhere in the process; how many will be recognized as legal tribes is difficult to predict.

Since the late 1940s Indian people have grown in numbers, visibility, and competence in dealing with the rest of American society. Yet despite increased education, better health care, and the shift of more than half of them off the reservation, they continue to rank at the bottom of the list of economic, social, and health indicators. Their insistence that they be allowed to retain parts of their aboriginal culture continues to trouble many other Americans, and the general public gives few indications that it is willing to accept tribal differences with any enthusiasm. This is perhaps best illustrated by President Ronald Reagan's remarks about Indians during the March 1988 summit meetings in Russia. Speaking to students at Moscow State University there, he said, "Maybe we [the U.S. government] made a mistake in trying to maintain Indian cultures. Maybe we should not have humored [Indians] in wanting to stay in that kind of primitive lifestyle." This comment brought sharp criticism from Indian rights groups, but the public paid little attention.

On the other hand, Americans have been somewhat more attentive to other developments. In 1988 Congress passed the Indian Gaming Regulation Act. This legislation allowed recognized tribal groups to offer gambling facilities on their properties after negotiating contracts with the individual states. The most spectacularly successful, Foxwoods Casino, stands in Ledyard, Connecticut, on the 318-member Mashantucket Pequot reservation. Opened in 1993, this venture grossed more than $800 million dollars during 1994, more than any other gambling establishment in the country. Its success set off a stampede of efforts by ninety-five other tribes, who operate everything from bingo halls to full-fledged casinos. Millions of white Americans patronize these reservation businesses, and the tribes are working hard to ensure that the bonanza will bring long-term benefits to their people.

Whereas few Americans are unfamiliar with Indian gaming facilities, many have never heard of the 1990 Native American Graves Protection and Repatriation Act. This legislation put the tribes on a collision course with museums, universities, and scholars who study North American prehistory by calling for the return of identifiable human remains, such as skeletons, to their descendants. At first museums and scholars objected bitterly, but now most of them work in apparent cooperation with tribal groups to decide which material will go back to the tribes and which they will retain. Indians hail this as another step in getting equal rights within American society. At the same time, many other Americans voice uncertainty about what they see as special treatment for Indians, and that idea continues to make things difficult for tribal people in contemporary society.

The White Ethnic Groups

The dramatic protests made by members of contemporary minority groups frequently antagonized the children and grandchildren of the southern and eastern

European immigrants from another era. By the end of the 1960s the descendants of Slavs, Italians, and other groups believed that society overlooked their problems and that they, too, needed social programs to aid their movement into the middle class or, conversely, that they had received no governmental largesse and that therefore no one else should.

White ethnic groups particularly objected because the liberal establishment in universities, foundations, and the federal administration had ignored them while condemning bigotry against Indians, African Americans, and Spanish-speaking Americans. These white ethnic minorities resented the racial integration being forced on their neighborhoods by government bureaucrats and courts while the "limousine liberals" lived in homogeneous middle-class communities or exclusive residences and sent their children to high-priced private or fancy suburban schools. In an impassioned defense of the white ethnic minorities who felt that their interests were being shunted aside while they themselves were being condemned, Barbara Mikulski, a Polish American woman later elected to the Senate, described the United States as a

sizzling cauldron for the ethnic American who feels that he has been politically extorted by both government and private enterprise. The ethnic American is sick of being stereotyped as a racist and dullard by phony white liberals, pseudo-black militants and patronizing bureaucrats. He pays the bill for every major government program and gets nothing or little in the way of return. Tricked by the political rhetoric of the illusionary funding for black-oriented social programs, he turns his anger to race—when he himself is the victim of class prejudice. He has worked hard all of his life to become a "good American"; he and his sons have fought on every battlefield—then he is made fun of because he likes the flag.

Banding together in groups such as the Italian American Civil Rights League, the Portuguese Congress in America, and a variety of other national and religious groups, these whites demanded more governmental sensitivity to their concerns and a larger share of the benefits. The Italian American Civil Rights League, for example, staged rallies and protested against the alleged slurs made by the FBI and television stations concerning ties between the Italian American community and organized crime. The League lost much of its vitality after its leader, Joseph Columbo, was shot in 1970, but other groups made similar demands. The Polish American Congress sued the American Broadcasting Company because the network refused to allow its representatives equal time on the air to respond to four jokes on one of its shows that the group believed constituted "personal attacks on the character, intelligence, hygiene or appearance" of Americans of Polish descent. The Congress of Italian American Organizations, formed in 1965, argued that "the government is blatantly insensitive to the needs of the Italian-American community," and its director declared, "We are going to fight for our share of the pie."

A significant minority of Jews, who had formerly been aligned with liberal causes, now feared that their hard-won gains of previous decades were endangered. Because many of them had qualified for professional and executive positions, they interpreted affirmative action as a euphemism for the quota system and, particularly in the contracting economy of the 1970s, as discrimination against them. Hence a spokesperson for this minority, Norman Podhoretz, editor of the prominent American Jewish monthly *Commentary,* spoke out vigorously against a changed American policy that seemed to be ignoring whites and favoring blacks. He wrote that Jews should start questioning public policies and asking themselves, "Is it good for the Jews? That is to say, I think that Jews must once again begin to look at proposals and policies from the point of view of the Jewish interest, and must once again begin to ask what [are] the consequences, if any, of any proposals or policy are likely to be so far as the Jewish position is concerned."

The lessons of the Jewish example were not lost on immigrants from the Middle East, particularly Arab Americans and Muslims whose numbers grew substantially after 1960. Many of these people believed that the mass media portrayed them unfairly and that American foreign policy was too closely allied to Israel. Muslims experienced violent personal attacks and complained that thugs desecrated mosques and even burned some of them to the ground. (That was especially true after the disaster at the World Trade Center on September 11, 2001.) They organized groups such as the American-Muslim Research Center and the Council on American-Islamic Relations to combat adverse views of Islam in the United States. In addition, in 1980 former United States Senator James G. Abourezk of South Dakota organized the American-Arab Anti-Discrimination Committee (ADC). The ADC was a Washington-based group that sought change in American foreign policy in the Middle East and an end to what it perceived as a proliferation of unfair images of Arab Americans spread across America's newspapers, magazines, and television screens.

ADC believes that the American public lacks clear information about the issues involving wars between Israel and her neighbors. A crisis had arisen when a United States citizen who was neither Arab nor Muslim blew up a truck filled with explosives in front of a federal office building in Oklahoma City on April 19, 1995. The driver escaped but was later captured and was executed after a trial. The Council on American-Islamic Relations reported that many members of the media had hastily blamed Muslims for the attack. But this episode was minor compared with the attacks on the Pentagon and the World Trade Center on September 11, 2001. A horrified nation watched on television as the twin towers of the trade center collapsed after being struck by two airplanes hijacked by terrorists. When it was revealed that Islamic and Arab extremists were responsible for the attacks, once again organizations such as the ADC rushed to assure other Americans that the foreigners responsible for the atrocities did not represent American Muslims or Islam generally. They insisted that true Muslims did not condone such violence and pointed to the fact that Muslim and Arab Americans were patriotic and supported the subsequent war against terrorism begun by President George W. Bush. Although incidents of violence occurred in some Arab American communities and Arab immigrants and visitors to the United States were rounded up by the Justice Department, other Americans defended the loyalty and dedication of Arab Americans in their midst. President Bush also made a big effort to show that he thought most Arab Americans were loyal. He visited a mosque in Washington, D.C., and urged that Americans judge people on an individual basis and not simply by the behavior of a few foreigners.

The heavy emphasis in American society during the 1960s and 1970s on helping members of the more noticeable minority groups "uplift" themselves and develop pride in their heritages also stimulated the descendants of European and Asian immigrants to demand equal attention to their own pasts. As a result, Congress passed the Ethnic Heritage Act of 1973, which funded programs designed to enhance the image of numerous American subgroups. In addition, a growing number of books, such as Michael Novak's *The Rise of the Unmeltable Ethnics* and Irving Howe's *World of Our Fathers,* celebrated the cultures and values of the immigrant groups of yesteryear. As usual, academic institutions responded with alacrity. A survey by the United States Office of Education found that in the 1973 academic year, 135 colleges and universities offered 315 courses concerning the ethnicity of white groups, including many in the area of Jewish, Italian, Greek, Basque, and Polish American studies. Many of these courses had been only the forerunners of ethnic studies programs and departments that now flourish in universities throughout the nation.

The renewed assertions of ethnic pride and identity are still evident, but not as strongly as they were thirty years ago. Migrants from one section of the country to another often seek out the Swedish American Club, the Greek association, or some other ethnic or religious organization as a way of meeting people and helping ease the transition to a new community; nonetheless, most second- and third-generation Americans of foreign ancestry are not so anxious to remain "ethnic" as they are to blend into the dominant society. Although they retain certain foods and festivals for culinary or nostalgic satisfaction and often associate with individuals of a similar heritage, they do not want to revert to an isolated ethnic experience. Educated people in the United States can no more go back to a ghetto culture than Eliza Doolittle, in George Bernard Shaw's *Pygmalion* (later made into the musical *My Fair Lady*), could go back to being a flower girl after Professor Henry Higgins trained her for another station in life.

The institutions of society—the schools, the media, and especially television—promote an American culture that only the most secluded can escape. The propaganda agencies of the government, the civil rights legislation of the 1960s, and the United States Supreme Court decisions demanding "equal protection of the laws" have combined to accelerate the pace of Americanization, the ending of discriminatory treatment, and the accordance of respect to all individuals regardless of heritage. Ironically, this improved treatment hastens the cultural breakdown of white ghettos rather than cementing them. Minorities stick together most closely in times of stress and during threats to group identity. With greater acceptance of variety by the dominant community, the gradual disappearance of white minority cultures seems likely for all except a few groups, such as the Amish, who voluntarily isolate themselves from the rest of society.

The assimilation of so many descendants of European immigrants should not lead one to conclude that America lacked ethnic diversity by the twenty-first century. Many of the millions of immigrants who arrived after the enactment of the 1965 Immigration Act had middle-class aspirations and wished to join the mainstream of American society. But, like so many millions of immigrants before them, they still retained much of their culture, as the Greeks, Colombians, and Brazilians of New York City and the Mexicans, Koreans, and Asians of Los Angeles have demonstrated. The civil rights movement had opened doors for many minority group members, but others remain trapped in the nation's urban ghettos with little hope. Although Spanish-speaking people had been in the United States for generations, the poorer ones and recent arrivals were often segregated from American life. The nation's oldest and least affluent group, the American Indians, also kept distinct cultures. Many moved to the cities in search of jobs, and in 2000 the largest contingents of Indian groups dwelled in New York City and Los Angeles. The people left behind on the reservations still faced continuing poverty and isolation. Thus, whatever path American society and economy followed, and whatever the role of various white ethnic groups in determining this direction, it appeared that cultural diversity would be a part of the future as it had been part of the past.

Contributing to the diversity of America was the renewed immigration of the post-World War II era that brought many Europeans to America. The most recent of these newcomers were dealing with the problems of immigration adaptation, just as others had done before them. But more important were the millions of immigrants coming from areas other than Europe. In 1970 there were 9.6 million foreign-born persons in the United States. In 2009 the foreign-born exceeded 38 million, and of this figure, 16 million came from Latin America and 8 million came from Asia. These new immigrants added to the cultural mosaic of American society and helped reshape areas of the country in directions different from those of the past.

10

A New Global Immigration

From 1945 through 2010 more than 30 million people entered the United States. This figure was comparable to the number of "new immigrants" who reached our shores between 1880 and 1940. The numbers of newcomers increased decade by decade, reaching six million during the 1980s and nearly ten million during the 1990s. The highest annual total of immigrants for any year, in fact, occurred in 1991, when the United States added another 1.8 million people, mostly from Latin America and Asia. That boost came after the enactment of a 1986 amnesty for those in the country illegally. As a result, the 1990s surpassed the years 1900–1910 as the largest decade of immigration in American history. Yet between 2000 and 2009 more than 8 million newcomers arrived in the United States. These figures do not tally undocumented entrants, whose numbers can only be estimated. The amnesty of 1986 gave three million undocumented individuals the right to become legal immigrants, but it failed to slow the continuing movement of others into the country. By the mid-1990s, unauthorized immigration increased sharply to more than 500,000 a year. In 2010 the census estimated that foreign-born people made up over 12 percent of the population, or over 38 million people. Before then, the highest percentage ever recorded had occurred in 1910, when just fewer than 15 percent of America's population came from other nations.

Beyond Europe: The Global Immigrants

As a result of the Hart-Cellar bill passed in 1965, a dramatic shift occurred in the sources of immigrants to the United States. Mexicans, Dominicans, Brazilians, Asian Indians, Iranians, Cubans, Vietnamese, Cambodians, Laotians, Koreans, Filipinos, Chinese, Haitians, and English-speaking West Indians dominated the post-1970 immigration statistics. Mexicans had a long history of large-scale immigration, and Filipinos and Koreans had established modest-sized communities here earlier. But these Asians had remained small in number. Now these older communities experienced dramatic growth, and by 2009 whole new communities of Vietnamese, Cambodians, Laotians, and Cubans hurried to became part of the American ethnic mosaic.

Immigrants to the United States by Decade:
Fiscal Years, 1821 to 2007
(Numbers millions)

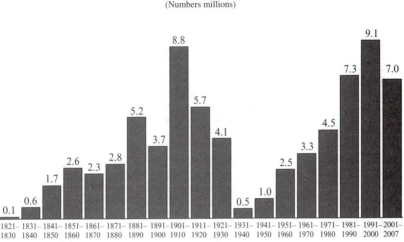

| 1821– | 1831– | 1841– | 1851– | 1861– | 1871– | 1881– | 1891– | 1901– | 1911– | 1921– | 1931– | 1941– | 1951– | 1961– | 1971– | 1981– | 1991– | 2001– |
| 1830 | 1840 | 1850 | 1860 | 1870 | 1880 | 1890 | 1900 | 1910 | 1920 | 1930 | 1940 | 1950 | 1960 | 1970 | 1980 | 1990 | 2000 | 2007 |

Source: U.S. Immigration and Naturalization Service, 2000, 2007, Table 1.

Like their predecessors, the new immigrants have settled in every part of the country, though they tended to concentrate in half a dozen states and in the major metropolitan areas. Today, Los Angeles has replaced New York City as the leading port of entry. New York is still the center for much of the immigration from the Caribbean, but because Los Angeles is closer to Mexico and Asia, that city has become the first stop for newcomers from Latin America and Asia. Central Americans and Mexicans travel north by car, Asians arrive by plane. No longer are the millions coming into New York harbor by ships, passing the Statue of Liberty, and docking at Castle Garden or Ellis Island. The population of Los Angeles County in 1992 topped nine million inhabitants, one-quarter of whom arrived within the previous decade. Broken down by ethnicity, estimates are that the city is 40 percent Anglo (those of European origin), 30 percent Hispanic, 20 percent black, and 10 percent Asian. Only twenty years earlier 72 percent of the population was Anglo.

Today Hollywood, once a place associated with moviemaking and glamour, is one of the centers of new immigrant settlement. In the fall of 1980, when the principal of Hollywood High School spoke to a parents' association meeting, translators immediately repeated his words in Spanish, Korean, and Armenian. Los Angeles's foreign-language television stations also reflect the new wave of immigrants. The city's Spanish station KMEX carries five daily newscasts and live coverage of events of interest to its Hispanic audience. Each December it

TABLE 10.1.   Legal Permanent Resident Flow by Region and
Country of Birth, Fiscal Years 2005–2007

Region/Country of Birth	2007		2006		2005	
	Number	Percent	Number	Percent	Number	Percent
Total	1,052,415	100.0	1,266,129	100.0	1,122,257	100.0
Region						
Africa	94,711	9.0	117,422	9.3	85,098	7.6
Asia	383,508	36.4	422,284	33.4	400,098	35.7
Europe	120,821	11.5	164,244	13.0	176,516	15.7
North America	339,355	32.2	414,075	32.7	345,561	30.8
Caribbean	119,123	11.3	146,768	11.6	108,591	9.7
Central America	55,926	5.3	75,016	5.9	53,463	4.8
Other North America	164,306	15.6	192,291	15.2	183,507	16.4
Oceania	6,101	0.6	7,384	0.6	6,546	0.6
South America	106,525	10.1	137,986	10.9	103,135	9.2
Unknown	1,394	0.1	2,734	0.2	5,303	0.5
Country						
Mexico	148,640	14.1	173,749	13.7	161,445	14.4
China, People's Republic	76,655	7.3	87,307	6.9	69,933	6.2
Philippines	72,596	6.9	74,606	5.9	60,746	5.4
India	65,353	6.2	61,369	4.8	84,680	7.5
Colombia	33,187	3.2	43,144	3.4	25,566	2.3
Haiti	30,405	2.9	22,226	1.8	14,524	1.3
Cuba	29,104	2.8	45,614	3.6	36,261	3.2
Vietnam	28,691	2.7	30,691	2.4	32,784	2.9
Dominican Republic	28,024	2.7	38,068	3.0	27,503	2.5
Korea	22,405	2.1	24,386	1.9	26,562	2.4
El Salvador	21,127	2.0	31,782	2.5	21,359	1.9
Jamaica	19,375	1.8	24,976	2.0	18,345	1.6
Guatemala	17,908	1.7	24,133	1.9	16,818	1.5
Peru	17,699	1.7	21,718	1.7	15,676	1.4
Canada	15,495	1.5	18,207	1.4	21,878	1.9
United Kingdom	14,545	1.4	17,207	1.4	19,800	1.8
Brazil	14,295	1.4	17,903	1.4	16,662	1.5
Pakistan	13,492	1.3	17,418	1.4	14,926	1.3
Ethiopia	12,783	1.2	16,152	1.3	10,571	0.9
Nigeria	12,448	1.2	13,459	1.1	10,597	0.9
All other countries	358,185	34.0	462,014	36.5	415,621	37.0

Source: U.S. Department of Homeland Security, Computer Linked Application Information Management System (CLAIMS), legal immigrant data, fiscal years 2005–2007.

TABLE 10.2.   Legal Permanent Resident Flow by
Metropolitan Area of Residence, Fiscal Years 2005–2007

	2007		2006		2005	
Metropolitan Areas of Residence	Number	Percent	Number	Percent	Number	Percent
Total	1,052,415	100.0	1,266,129	100.0	1,122,257	100.0
New York-Northern New Jersey-Long Island, NY-NJ-PA	175,753	16.7	224,439	17.7	172,844	15.4
Los Angeles-Long Beach-Santa Ana, CA	95,413	9.1	120,881	9.5	98,241	8.8
Miami-Fort Lauderdale-Pompano Beach, FL	78,172	7.4	98,918	7.8	79,558	7.1
Washington-Arlington-Alexandria-Rockville, DC-VA-MD-WV	40,698	3.9	54,549	4.3	37,146	3.3
Chicago-Naperville-Joliet, IL-IN-WI	39,504	3.8	49,748	3.9	49,015	4.4
San Francisco-Oakland-Fremont, CA	35,652	3.4	38,348	3.0	33,876	3.0
Houston-Sugar Land-Baytown, TX	26,850	2.6	31,557	2.5	34,788	3.1
Boston-Cambridge-Quincy, MA-NH	24,679	2.3	28,469	2.2	27,135	2.4
Dallas-Fort Worth-Arlington, TX	23,272	2.2	26,639	2.1	28,961	2.6
Atlanta-Sandy Springs-Marietta, GA	22,056	2.1	25,270	2.0	25,347	2.3
Other	490,366	46.6	567,311	44.8	535,346	47.7

Note: Metropolitan areas defined based on Core-based Statistical Areas (CBSAs).
Source: U.S. Department of Homeland Security, Computer Linked Application Information Management System (CLAIMS), legal immigrant data, fiscal years 2005–2007.

holds a telethon to raise money for Latin immigrants. Although Spanish stations claim the largest audience, the city's KSCI-TV also carries Korean news, Islamic programs, and a costume drama called *Chinese World.*

Aware of the growing Hispanic population in the Los Angeles region, Von's Grocery Company, a large grocery chain, became the first supermarket to actively court California's Hispanic market. In early 1987, Von's opened its 191st supermarket in Montebello, a city of fifty-eight thousand Hispanics in eastern Los Angeles County. The new store had a staff of three hundred persons, all of whom were bilingual, and it was stocked with goods that catered to Mexican American tastes.

Like Los Angeles, other cities have had to adjust to the recent waves of foreigners. Even though New York City fell behind the Los Angeles metropolitan area in admission of numbers of immigrants, it became instead even more diverse and truly global in its population mix. The thousands of Asians who arrived after 1970 added a distinctive flavor to New York City's more than seven million residents. Accustomed to huge colonies of Europeans, blacks, and Puerto Ricans, in the 1990s and 2000s the city acclimated itself to Koreans, Asian Indians, Thais, Filipinos, Chinese, and people from the Caribbean. The city's black population is hardly monolithic; in 2005 over five hundred thousand of its more than two million blacks were born abroad, hailing from African nations, as well as the Caribbean.

Miami is known for its large Cuban population, but in the mid-2000s it claimed a sizable Haitian community and many immigrants from Nicaragua. Toledo, Ohio, is home to immigrant communities from the Philippines, India, Korea, and China. Arabs pray five times a day in Dearborn, Michigan, and have transformed streets in their neighborhoods into a Middle Eastern phantasmagoria. Nearby, in Detroit, Chaldeans, an Aramaic-speaking Christian minority from Iraq, own many of the city's grocery stores. Moreover, 125,000 of the two million Arabs in the United States live in the Detroit area. Hoboken, New Jersey, houses small colonies from India, many of them well-educated professionals who had limited opportunities for advancement in their native land.

These amazing and diverse new immigrants bolstered declining neighborhoods by opening new shops and businesses. In addition, they provided the labor for restaurants, hotels, factories, car services, and construction. They formed new ethnic organizations, published new foreign-language newspapers, and put on plays in their neighborhood theaters. By the end of the twentieth century it became clear that they were also diversifying American religion. Although Protestants, Catholics, and Jews remained the major religious groups, the rapid growth of Muslims, Buddhists, Hindus, and Sikhs gave a dimension to American religion virtually unheard of before World War II.

Even before its admission into the union as a state in 1959, Hawaii had no majority group in its population. Persons of Japanese ancestry were the most numerous, but they fell short of being half of the people. By 2005 California, the nation's largest state, became the second in which no one ethnic group composed half of the population, and Texas seemed headed in the same direction by the end of the first decade of the twenty-first century. In fact, the U.S. Census Bureau reported that in 2007 it classed more than three hundred American counties as having a "majority minority." Clearly, a major shift in the ethnic makeup of society was under way, and the rapid growth of the Hispanic and Asian communities suggests that these dramatic changes will continue. For New York City residents, however, the minorities had been the majority for over a generation.

TABLE 10.3. Percent of Foreign Born in the
United States by Region of Birth

	Europe	Latin America	Asia
1850	92.2		
1880	86.2		
1900	86.0		
1930	83.0	5.6	
1960	75.0	9.4	5.1
1970	61.7	19.4	8.9
1980	39.0	33.1	19.3
1990	22.9	44.3	26.3
2000	15.3	51.0	25.5

Mexicans

In 2009 Latinos account for almost 15 percent of the American population and for nearly one-third of all immigrants in the United States. Sixty percent of this group hails from Mexico. That same year persons born in Mexico numbered over10 million, and that figure was likely an undercount. Mexicans made up more than one-half of the three million persons granted amnesty under the 1986 Immigration Reform and Control Act and made up over one-half of the eleven million undocumented immigrants in the United States today.

After the deportations of the 1930s the Mexican government frowned on its citizens going north again; many Mexicans were also reluctant to seek new lives in the United States. But World War II created labor shortages in American agriculture. As a result, the United States and Mexico signed an agreement in 1942 that allowed the temporary entry of Mexican nationals into America. The Mexican government screened the laborers, and then the American government placed them on farms, in fields, or in other enterprises in which the need seemed the greatest. The workers also received transportation to their jobs, food, shelter, and medical care. Usually they earned substandard wages,

TABLE 10.4. Growth of Hispanic Population by Region

	Hispanics 1990	Hispanics 2000	Increase	% Change
Northeast	3.754389	5,254,087	1,499,698	39.95%
Midwest	1,726,509	3,124,532	1398,023	80.97%
South	6,767,021	11,586,696	4,819,675	71.22%
West	10,106,140	15,340,503	5,234,363	51.79%
USA	22,354,059	35,305,818	12,951,759	57.94%

although even those sums were greater than the men could have made at home. The agreements, intended to be of short duration, were extended, with periodic interruptions, through 1964. Over the years almost five million *braceros,* as these temporary workers were called, came to the United States. Although many growers resented having to pay the Mexicans first 30¢, then 50¢ an hour for their labor, the *braceros* rarely earned more than $500 a year.

More important than the *braceros* in Southwestern agriculture after the 1940s, however, were unauthorized immigrants, dubbed "wetbacks," whose numbers probably exceeded five million. The *bracero* program may have inadvertently stimulated the illegals. Many of those who came illegally had wanted to be *braceros,* but their government did not include them. They knew, however, that work existed in the United States, and they were desperate for it. Many rural Mexicans lived in poverty, having little opportunity at home, so they willingly took any means necessary to get work in the United States. American agribusiness interests, on the other hand, welcomed the cheap and illegal migrants. They could pay them even less than *braceros* earned, and because the workers could not complain about conditions without fear of being deported, the growers' profits soared. At the beginning of the twentieth first

Attempt to smuggle illegal aliens in the back of a camper. The number of undocumented aliens coming to America increased after 1970. Many walked across the Mexican border, but some, like this group, were smuggled into the country in trucks and cars and even campers. (Immigration and Naturalization Service)

century it was estimated that the undocumented immigrants make up roughly one-half of the agricultural workers in the Southwest.

This growing number of undocumented migrants working on America's farms alarmed some public officials, and under growing pressure in 1954 President Dwight Eisenhower authorized "Operation Wetback." Federal agents swept through large western farms and rounded up and helped deport about one million workers who lacked proper work papers. At the same time, the government doubled the number of *braceros* to replace those sent home under this program. The next year immigration authorities insisted that they had secured the border and pointed out that in 1955 they had apprehended and deported to Mexico only 78,000 persons.

However, when the 1965 immigration act placed a ceiling on entrants from the Western Hemisphere shortly after the *bracero* program ended, the Mexican ambassador to the United States warned that undocumented migration from Mexico would increase again, and he was right. After that year a steady number of persons tried to cross the border. Federal officials said that by the early 1970s America was once again being flooded with migrants without proper immigration papers. These officials realized how porous the southern border of the United States was. So their solution was to make it a crime for business owners to hire persons who lacked documents. Twice in the early 1970s the House of Representatives passed legislation to outlaw the employment of unauthorized immigrants.

Some years later, after much debate and frequent compromise, in 1986 Congress passed the Simpson-Rodino Act. One provision of the law outlawed knowingly hiring undocumented workers, in theory removing the incentive—finding employment—for those entering without government approval. A second clause was the aforementioned amnesty for those who had arrived without proper papers before 1982 and had lived here since that time. A third provision granted legal status to those who had worked illegally in agriculture, a concession to growers who claimed that without undocumented workers they could not harvest their crops.

Beginning in May 1987, the government gave eligible undocumented immigrants one year (later extended) to apply for amnesty so that they might become legal resident aliens and eventually United States citizens. About 1.6 million did so, a figure less than that predicted by Immigration and Naturalization Service (INS) authorities. The turnout was good in Los Angeles and Houston, but poor in New York City. As expected, the largest group was Mexicans living in the Southwest and in California. The claims of the vast majority of these persons appeared to be valid, but no one knew what would happen to those who arrived illegally after 1982.

If the general amnesty produced fewer applications than expected, the program for agricultural amnesty produced considerably more—about 1.3 million—than anticipated. Some officials said that many of these agricultural worker claims were fraudulent, but the INS lacked the personnel to check them.

The sanctions against employer's hiring undocumented aliens led to a drop in the number of persons apprehended at the Mexico–United States border, from a high of 1.6 million to less than a million when the law went into effect. Apprehensions rose again in the 1990s when the number of persons apprehended increased to over one million annually. The entry of authorized Mexican immigrants also remained high from 1990 to 2010, and Mexico remained the largest source for new immigrants to America.

Although some *braceros* without proper papers remained to work on farms, more important was the fact that they were able to find jobs in American cities and towns. From the farms, the *braceros* followed the paths to the towns. Legal immigrants, who came in greater number from Mexico after 1965, labored mostly in cities.

The urbanization of Mexican immigrants grew after 1965, and it is estimated that in the first decade of the twenty-first century nearly 90 percent of Mexican immigrants lived in cities. About one-third of them lived in the metropolitan regions around San Antonio, San Diego, San Francisco, Los Angeles, El Paso, Tucson, and Phoenix. Many of the earlier migrants who came to the United States during World War II had also found employment in defense plants that had been established in the nation's Midwest cities. Other wartime opportunities had beckoned in the sugar beet fields of Michigan. When the war ended, most of these people moved on to garment factories, auto plants, and the building trades in cities such as Detroit and Chicago. They and their children also obtained civil service appointments, which proved to be another means of advancement.

Although many immigrants remained almost destitute with a bleak future ahead of them, a growing number succeeded in business. In 1986 *Money* magazine told its readers of Jose de Santiago. At age seventeen he crossed the border illegally. "I came here with nothing to lose and everything to gain," he later recalled. Beginning with a low-wage job, so common to undocumented aliens, he found better employment, became a citizen, and eventually formed his own business in Houston, Texas. By 1986 he was running a $2-million-a-year enterprise, and he had been awarded the 1985 Minority Small Business Person Award by President Ronald Reagan. Perhaps the most remarkable success story of an undocumented Mexican immigrant was that of Dr. Alberto Quinones-Hinojosa, who crossed by hopping over a fence. He worked as a common laborer while attending night school. He eventually graduated from

Harvard University Medical School and then became a prominent neurosurgeon at Johns Hopkins's prestigious medical school.

Not all of the undocumented have been so skilled or so lucky. By 2009 the undocumented and their children had become a majority of the new Mexicans in the United States. A few of them found jobs in garment factories, and many more in meat and chicken processing plants, but many others became employed by Americans to care for their children and do housework. As nannies, they often had long hours, with only one day a week off. As a result most sought housework jobs that gave them time to rush home to care for their own families. Supporting their families proved difficult, and they lived in fear of being deported. For those women who left their families behind, their decision to go to America to earn money was not easy. One said, "But I had to give them [her children] a better life. I told them I would go and work, and we could buy a small plot of land and a little house and have a dog."

Her reference to using her earnings at home points to a major goal for going north: to send money home to one's family. Many migrants had little chance for a better life in Mexico, so they trekked north, where they could get work, save, and send cash home. In fact, undocumented workers often had no intention of staying in America. One study estimated that between 1965 and 1986 27.9 million undocumented people crossed into the United States, and of these 84 percent returned to Mexico after working here for short periods. After the 2001 terrorist attack in New York, however, it became increasingly more difficult to enter the country illegally, and many unauthorized immigrants remained permanently or for longer periods of time than had been the case earlier.

In the past two decades Mexicans, like many of the other post-1970 immigrants, formed communities in places where few others of their background had gone before. New York City, for example, recorded only twenty thousand Mexicans in 1980. One Mexican woman in that city stated, "There were no Mexicans in New York in 1979—none that I could find. It took me a month of deep-cover detective work to find out where I could buy tortillas." But by 2009 New York City's Mexican population exceeded two hundred thousand, with another one hundred thousand estimated to be living in the surrounding suburbs. This occurred across the country. In May 2008 Mexico opened its forty-seventh consulate in the United States, this one in Little Rock, Arkansas, to look out for the interests of workers in the chicken processing industry there. Mexican officials also announced that they would continue to issue *matricula consular* (cards stating that the workers were Mexican citizens) so that the newcomers could open bank accounts and thus reduce the cost of sending money home. Western Union had charged much more for that service.

The greatest percentage growth, however, occurred in North Carolina (394 percent), Arkansas (337 percent), Georgia (300 percent), Tennessee (278 percent), and South Carolina (211 percent). One now finds new Mexican settlements in places such as Noel, Missouri, and Strom Lake, Iowa. In many of the small towns of the Midwest and South, newcomers often work in garment shops or along "the chicken trail," virtual factories that produce chickens or meat for American tables. These jobs scarcely pay over the minimum wage, and working conditions are terrible. The labor turnover is high, but employers know that the workers who stay also send word back home for others to come north, where wages are better than at home, even though working conditions are dreadful.

However, not all recent Mexican immigrants have been unskilled laborers willing to take whatever jobs were available in the United States. A recent Pew Hispanic Center report characterized the immigrants from Mexico between 1995 and 2005 as likely to be older, to have higher levels of education, and to have jobs in the construction industry rather than in the lower-wage factory and agricultural sector that beckoned to earlier migrants. The Center also found that the number of Hispanic immigrants in the lowest fifth of wage distribution had decreased from 42 to 36 percent. Other studies showed that the children and grandchildren of previous generations of foreign laborers are better educated and earn more money than their elders. At the same time, one cannot deny that many Hispanics still live in poverty and that large groups of them are behind both blacks and other whites in income and education.

Cubans

Unlike Mexicans, who simply came north across the land, Cubans arrived by boat and air into Florida, where they formed an important community. Some Cubans settled in New York, New Jersey, and other states, but the vast bulk remained in Florida, especially the Miami area. They arrived in several waves. First came the elite from 1959 to 1962, and then after their migration was interrupted for three years, middle-class Cubans again headed for Miami from 1965 to 1973. These two waves numbered about six hundred thousand, and they mostly traveled by air to Miami.

After 1973, the exodus slowed, but another wave entered in the spring of 1980. This group, called the *Marielitos,* who numbered roughly 130,000, were picked up by Cuban Americans piloting boats at the port of Mariel and brought to Florida. President Jimmy Carter and his administration finally realized that the exodus was uncontrolled, especially when it was learned that Fidel Castro was also loading criminals and mentally ill persons on the ships. As a result, American officials finally halted boats from picking up additional Cubans. Some of the *Marielitos* found themselves in prison because they could not satisfy United States immigration requirements or were convicted of crimes in this country. Cuba did not want to take these few thousand people back. Because the individuals did not want to return to Cuba, the prisoners staged riots in the Atlanta, Georgia, federal prison and at an INS facility at Oakland, Louisiana. After negotiating with the prisoners and the Cuban government, the United States heard pleas for asylum, but officials rejected most of those and returned to Cuba those ineligible for immigration status.

In 1994 another Cuban group sailed to Florida on rafts, and once again it appeared that a disorderly exodus was under way. Then the Clinton administration moved quickly and concluded an agreement with the Cuban government, which, in turn, carefully screened potential emigrants. In this way Cuban officials stopped the raft exodus.

At one time, in the 1960s, the United States put its welcome mat out for Cubans and attempted to embarrass the communist regime of Fidel Castro by this action. Cubans were also provided with refugee benefits when Congress passed the Cuban Adjustment Act in 1966. The funds provided special training programs for refugee professionals, medical aid, and English-language training. The benefits no doubt aided these immigrants, but it must also be noted that the groups for whom these funds were allocated were mostly a population of the literate, educated, and well-to-do Cubans. The *Marielitos,* on the other hand, tended to come from the lower classes of society and had difficulty adapting to American society.

Because of their high economic status and marketable skills, Cubans generally adjusted to life in the United States fairly quickly. In 2000 they constituted the majority of Miami's population and were well represented in business and professional positions. They even became bank presidents and began the Trade Fair of the Americas, which became a showcase of Latin American international trade. Cubans have also followed the path of inclusion by electing one of their own, Xavier Suarez, as mayor of Miami in 1965.

The Cuban refugees did not limit their political activities to local issues at home. Perhaps no other immigrant group had such strong attachments to their homeland as they did. Many considered themselves exiles waiting to return to Cuba. They elected two of their members to the United States House of Representatives. Mostly Republicans, they pressured the federal government to support a trade embargo against their homeland and participated in anti-Castro measures, including a badly defeated 1961 attempt to overthrow the Castro regime. In 2008, over forty years after they arrived, their prayers seemed to be answered as Fidel Castro, in failing health, gave up his power. Although most of Florida's Cubans cheered, the future of their beloved homeland remains unclear. Castro's brother Raul has taken the leadership position. Whether he will be more moderate than Fidel is uncertain. Yet another factor, the growing age of the 1960s exiles, is important. As many of the first-generation leaders retired or died, a new generation has become important in Cuban American communities. They do not remember the Havana of old, and many of them realize that their future is in the United States, not in a return to a Castro-free Cuba.

Other Latinos

The Dominicans are another Hispanic group that has made an impact in American society since 1965. Because some of them have entered this country illegally and many return home, the precise number of Dominicans living here is not known, but in the 1990s immigration officials annually recorded more than twenty thousand newcomers, many of whom planned to settle here. Mostly they went to New York City, especially the Washington Heights and Inwood sections in Manhattan, making those areas the second largest "Dominican" city in the world outside of Santo Domingo. In 2010 Dominicans were the largest foreign-born group in the city. Though not prosperous by American criteria, these immigrants are well off by Dominican standards, and many have achieved a lower-middle-class status. Yet these emigrants have

TABLE 10.5.   Hispanics at Mid-Decade:
Population by Race and Ethnicity, 2000 and 2005

	2005 Population	2000 Population	Percent of Population 2005	Percent Change 2000–2005	Share of Total Change (%)
Hispanic	41,926,302	34,494,801	14.5	21.5	50.3
Native Born	25,085,528	20,488,299	8.7	22.4	31.1
Foreign Born	16,840,774	14,006,502	5.8	20.2	19.2
White alone, not Hispanic	192,526,952	189,520,003	66.8	1.6	20.4
Black alone, not Hispanic	34,410,656	32,036,110	11.9	7.4	16.1
Asian alone, not Hispanic	12,331,128	9,893,205	4.3	24.6	16.5
Other, not Hispanic	7,203,781	7,693,277	2.5	−6.4	−3.3
Total	288,398,819	273,637,396	100.0	5.4	100.0

Universe: 2000 and 2005 Household Population.

Note: "Other, not Hispanic" includes persons reporting single races not listed separately and those reporting more than one race.

Source: Pew Hispanic Center tabulations of 2000 Census and 2005 American Community Survey.

experienced a high unemployment rate. The lack of opportunities in their own land, however, stimulated emigration to America, where they joined friends and families.

Many Dominicans hope to make money and return home, like some of turn-of-the-twentieth century immigrants, and some have done so. However, it has not always been easy to get a high-paying job in America. Many found employment in New York's reviving garment industry, working in small shops at low pay, though by the 1990s these opportunities faded. Others worked in the city's service industries. As New York's Hispanic population grew, many stores originally run by Puerto Ricans became increasingly managed by Dominicans. These stores, described by some observers as combination mom-and-pop groceries, drugstores, and neighborhood social clubs, carried a variety of products desired by Hispanics. One Puerto Rican owner of a chain of *bodegas* (grocery stores) explained their appeal: "The supermarkets, with all their advanced sales, will never wipe out the *bodegas* because they are part of the community."

For many Dominican women, the United States contained new opportunities for work and personal independence. Historian Jesse Hoffnung-Garskof reported that one woman told her that "On a visit to Juan Pablo [in the Dominican Republic], my cousin saw the way my husband made me wait on him hand and foot, and the way he'd yell if everything was not perfect. But she told me that one did not see that kind of behavior in New York, concluding, 'Wait till you get there. You'll have your own paycheck, and I tell you, he won't be pushing you around there the way he is here.'"

The downside of such freedom was that women headed nearly half of the Dominican households. Usually their only employment came in low-wage manufacturing, or else they had to remain at home. In either case, their incomes remained low, and many of them lived below the poverty line. Their low levels of education and lack of English kept many from finding better jobs, but they also faced discrimination. Many arrived in the country with only visitors' visas, so when their permits expired, they remained as undocumented aliens. As if those issues weren't enough, the Washington Heights section of Manhattan was overcrowded, had poor schools, and was rumored to be the center of the drug trade.

Poor education is a major handicap for Dominicans, who have higher than average drop out rates and lower than average rates of college attendance. They earned college degrees at only half the national rate. Some of their handicap is due to the fact that the educational system of the Dominican Republic is poor. A special school for immigrant teenagers in New York found many Dominicans in attendance who lacked schooling in the Dominican Republic. In 2009 it was reported that students from the rural areas of the Dominican Republic did not attend school because "it was too far away or because they working to support their families."

Another group from south of our border that became noticeable in New York City and environs hailed from Brazil. Whereas 22,310 people from the largest nation in South America came to the United States between 1966 and 1979, another forty thousand have arrived since that time. Together with their children they now constitute perhaps 150,000 in New York, New England, and New Jersey. Brazilians as a group do not usually stand out, because most are educated and middle class, refugees from a roller-coaster economy back home. Within New York City the less affluent, like so many other contemporary immigrants, live in the borough of Queens, especially Astoria, whereas those better off have found homes in the city's northern and northeastern suburbs. The least affluent Brazilians are likely to reside in Newark, New Jersey. One in-group joke refers to a woman assaulted in Newark who kept calling for "help" to no avail. Had she used the Portuguese term for assistance and screamed *"socorro, soccoro,"* she no doubt would have received assistance from passersby.

Central and South Americans usually settled in places where Cubans, Puerto Ricans, and Mexicans had gone, in cities such as New York, Miami, Los Angeles, San Antonio, Chicago, San Diego, New Orleans, and Houston. In New Orleans, for example, a settlement of Hondurans had originally begun when they entered on the banana boats, found jobs, opened shops, and sent for their compatriots.

The nation's capital, Washington, D.C., also became one center for this migration. Small numbers had lived there before, and by 1980 the census found ninety-three thousand Hispanics in the Washington, D.C., area, about nineteen thousand in the city proper. Their numbers increased rapidly in the 1980s, when many people fled from violence in Nicaragua, El Salvador, and Guatemala. A Hispanic marketing firm estimated that in 1980 and 1981 twenty thousand Central Americans arrived in the Washington, D.C., area. Emigration pressure eased somewhat in the 1990s, when peace returned to Central American countries. However, peace did not bring a halt to migration from Central Americans. In the 2000s Central Americans actually came in larger numbers (at least legally) than before the end of hostilities.

Many newcomers took jobs in the city's restaurants as dishwashers, busboys, and eventually waiters. A Hispanic leader told the *Washington Post,* "There's a top-notch French restaurant in Washington where the maitre d' speaks with a French accent and the waiter who comes up and takes your order is from El Salvador. He's one of the top waiters there. I asked him, 'How do you get a job like this?' He said, 'You come in at the lowest possible rung and demonstrate you are a hard worker and you go up.' " Symbolic of the growing

Hispanic presence in the area was the construction of a new mall called Plaza International. Although many Central Americans fleeing violence headed for Washington, D.C., by no means did all of these refugees. For Nicaraguans Miami became the main area of settlement. There they joined Cubans, other Hispanics, and Haitians to make that city a major point of entry for America's new immigrants.

In the Miami area Nicaraguans could hear Spanish spoken because of the Cuban domination of the city. Some Cubans saw Nicaraguans as fellow exiles from communism and assisted them in their settlement. When the left-wing government of Nicaragua was voted out of power in the 1990s that tie disappeared.

San Francisco also attracted a growing number of Central Americans. The 1980 census reported eighty-three thousand persons, or more than 12 percent of the city's population, to be Hispanics. The largest groups were Nicaraguans, then Salvadorans, and then Mexicans. The newcomers gave the Mission District of that city a distinct Latin flavor. Spanish movie houses provided an alternative to television in English, and one could hear Spanish spoken in churches and on the streets.

The scattering of Central Americans was not limited to Miami, San Francisco, or Washington, D.C. Some immigrants followed "the chicken trail," working in chicken processing plants alongside Mexicans in states such as North Carolina, which had few Hispanic immigrants before 1990. In the 2000s others settled in suburban communities, where young men stood on street corners in the mornings waiting and bargaining for daily employment. The fortunate ones landed jobs in construction that kept them busy for weeks and months, but most found short-term work in landscaping or as day laborers. The few women took jobs as domestics. Most of these immigrants were young men, however, willing to accept low wages. Central Americans worked for low wages because opportunities in their countries were limited, and by living frugally they could send money home. Remittances were important to the villages they left behind and provided the main source of income in the towns the migrants had come from. Remittances also proved important for many Mexican communities, as well, and it was not uncommon to find villages in Mexico and Central America where most of the young men worked in the United States. However, with the beginning of the severe downturn in the American economy, remittances dropped. Remittances to Mexico fell 3.6 percent in 2008 and were expected to decrease further in 2009.

The exact size of the Central American population was unknown because so many were without proper immigration documents. Congress did pass a law in 1997 that placed Nicaraguans on a footing similar to that of Cubans. But supporters of an amnesty for other Central Americans were unable to convince the legislators that all Central Americans and Cubans should be treated alike. The INS did grant Central Americans the right to remain until conditions quieted at home and while their pleas for asylum or immigrant status were being heard. For most, however, prospects for becoming legal were dim.

Not all Central Americans, or Mexicans for that matter, could be considered Hispanic. A number were Indians who spoke their own dialect and little Spanish. Mayans from Guatemala lived in Indiantown, Florida, where they harvested crops during the growing season. Other Mayans lived in Houston, Texas, and in southern California in the late 2000s.

Puerto Ricans, who mainly settled on the East Coast, were not immigrants. The United States acquired Puerto Rico from Spain as a result of the Spanish-American War in 1898, and in 1917 Puerto Ricans became American citizens. That gave them the right to come to the mainland, and ever since they have done so. Their exact numbers on the continent are not known, but by 1930 they numbered fifty thousand. Not many came during the Great Depression and World War II, but beginning in 1945 the flow swelled to a torrent. Relatively cheap air transportation and an abundance of skilled and unskilled jobs in New York City served as the magnets. Today there are over two million Puerto Ricans on the mainland, with roughly eight hundred thousand in the New York City area. Other major centers for them are Chicago and Philadelphia, but there are also Puerto Rican communities in Bridgeport, Connecticut; Rochester, New York; Dayton, Ohio; Boston, Massachusetts; Milwaukee, Wisconsin; and numerous cities in New Jersey.

As American citizens, they do not share the same legal status with immigrants, but they do resemble European immigrants who landed on the East Coast and settled in urban areas. Arriving with little education and lacking English, many replaced the European immigrants in lower-level factory jobs—especially the Jews and Italians in the garment district—and in the city's worst slums. Like most Europeans who arrived in the United States, they spoke a foreign language, but, unlike the Europeans, they encountered a color problem. Many Puerto Ricans are the descendants of centuries of racial mixing between the island's white and black populations. Although higher status is afforded those of lighter complexions, darker skin does not have quite the impact in Puerto Rico that it has in the United States. Those with darker skins have greater difficulty in gaining acceptance and being able to adjust to the dominant culture on the mainland. As a result of racism in the United States and the disappearance of low-skilled jobs from New York City after 1970, Puerto Ricans found themselves at the bottom of the economy. In the 1990s women headed nearly half of their families, and most of these families lived below the poverty line; they made up half of the poorest group in New York City in the

1990s, having roughly half the income of other New Yorkers. Whereas a Puerto Rican middle class has emerged in the New York City area, high dropout rates from high school seem to trap many in poverty. Outside of New York, they fared better. Indeed, by 2009 many Puerto Ricans concluded that conditions were better elsewhere, including Puerto Rico. Then an exodus began, with more Puerto Ricans returning to their roots than seeking new opportunities in New York City.

New Asian Immigrants

Like Latinos, the new Asian immigrants represented a variety of people and cultures. The largest groups came from China, Korea, the Philippines, Vietnam, and India. From 1951 to 1960 only 24,201 persons entered the United States from mainland China, Taiwan, and Hong Kong; however, during the following forty years more than one million arrived. At first they hailed from Hong Kong and Taiwan, but after 1981, when the United States gave mainland China a separate quota, many came from there, as well. The impact of such immigration is potentially staggering when one realizes that the Chinese American population in 1960 was less than 250,000. Moreover, these people were generally concentrated in the Chinatowns of a few American cities, such as San Francisco, New York, and Honolulu. The new immigrants headed for these cities, substantially swelling the population already there. San Francisco's Chinatown more than doubled its population from 1952 to 1972, and New York City's Chinese population grew from thirty-three thousand in 1960 to nearly four hundred thousand by 2000, thus becoming the nation's largest. The rapid influx of immigrants strained housing. In the mid-1980s some experts estimated that nearly two thousand new immigrants were searching monthly for apartments in New York City's Chinatowns. In addition, restaurants and garment shops also sought Chinatown locations. The old Chinatown spread north into "Little Italy" and east into the famed Lower East Side, home for tens of thousands of Europeans decades before. These crowded conditions prompted many to find housing in Queens, another New York City borough.

A disaster shattered New York City's main concentration of Chinese people and businesses when two planes deliberately flew into the World Trade Center on September 11, 2001, and destroyed the complex. Because Chinatown was so close to the World Trade Center, the tourist trade spiraled downward. Restaurants, fruit and vegetable stands, and other shops lost customers; manufacturing plants also had to shut down. Some garment shops could locate to other neighborhoods in the city, but for many entrepreneurs the lost revenue was too large, and they were forced out of business.

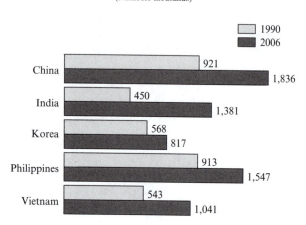

Top Countries of Birth of the Foreign-Born
Population From Asia: 1990 and 2006
(Numbers thousands)

Note: China includes Hong Kong and Taiwan.

Like earlier immigrants without language and labor skills, Chinese immigrants could be exploited. Even when they had mastered English, they had trouble finding high-paying work. One Chinese man described his parents' situation in a garment factory. "There [are] no vacations, no pensions; they just work and work all their lives. We're willing to work, but can't find [good] jobs." In 1992 an estimated twenty-two thousand Chinese, most of them immigrants and many of them women, worked in 250 garment factories—virtual sweatshops in New York City's Chinatown—for wages as low as $2.50 per hour. A Labor Department administrator said these "employees in Chinatown are one of the worst exploited groups in the metropolitan area."

As new migrants poured into San Francisco and New York, the garment industry expanded. Wages improved somewhat as the number of shops grew and were unionized. New York's 250 garment shops in 1972 numbered 550 by 1987 and employed twenty-two thousand, mostly unionized, workers. The city's old garment district gave way to the new center in Chinatown, though by the 1990s many shops experienced difficulty because of competition from abroad.

Chinese immigrants also included a number of highly educated professionals. From 1965 to 1985, 150,000 students from Taiwan studied in the United States, and many were able to change their visa status to documented immigrants by finding jobs in colleges, universities, businesses, and research centers in which they could utilize their education. They did not have to live in

Chinatowns, and often, as did so many highly educated immigrants, settled in the nation's suburbs.

Whereas the number of Taiwanese students and immigrants fell in the 1990s, the number from the People's Republic of China (PRC) rose. Few entrants had come from there until 1977 when China ended the Cultural Revolution and began to admit students to its universities. Thousands of young Chinese took the entrance examinations when they were given for the first time in twelve years. In 1981 the United States gave China a separate immigration quota, and many of the students came to American colleges and universities. Many remained in the country and took jobs in California's Silicon Valley, where they helped pioneer the computer industry.

At the other end of the spectrum, poor and desperate immigrants from Fujian Province paid thousands of dollars to get to America with the aid of smugglers, who were called "snakeheads." Once in the United States, they had to work long hours at low-paying jobs to settle their debts with the "snakeheads." If fortunate, they managed to do so within a few years and then were in a position to help others to emigrate or to send remittances to China. Not all were fortunate. Some were caught en route and sent back to China, and not a few lived as virtual indentured servants trying to pay their debts.

The first post-1943 entrants from China, the Philippines, Japan, and Korea owed their opportunities to World War II and the Cold War that followed. During World War II, the United States permitted Filipinos who had served in the American army or navy to become citizens, which meant that they could sponsor their immediate families as immigrants. China received its small quota of 105 persons in 1943 in recognition for being a wartime ally. Chinese soldiers, who came under the War Brides acts, sponsored six thousand women shortly after the war ended. In the immediate years after the end of World War II, few Japanese, other than women who married American servicemen, arrived. When the United States entered the Korean War in 1950, it opened its doors to Korean women married to American soldiers serving there. The existence of American naval and air bases in the Philippines until the early 1990s led to frequent American-Filipino marriages there.

Almost all of these women had a difficult time adjusting to their new status. Many Japanese and Korean families opposed their daughters' marriages because of the bad reputation of the "Camptowns" surrounding military bases. They considered these as little more than strings of bars and houses of prostitution, and the Asian families feared that their daughters would come to be seen as nothing more than prostitutes.

Yet Asian immigration had other bases besides the cold war. American penetration of Filipino culture had been going on for decades. Many Filipinos spoke English and knew much about American culture while living in poverty and, until 1972, under a political dictatorship. Their schools had been modeled on those in the United States, and, when faced with poor economic conditions at home, many emigrated eagerly. From 1970 to 2009 Filipino immigration to the United States averaged over 40,000 annually. Indeed, the two million Filipinos in 2005 ranked second only to the Chinese among Asian immigrants.

Desire to migrate was one issue; another was the structure of immigration law. The Philippine quota of only 100 people a year in 1946 had to change for immigration to reach such numbers less than two decades later. Often Filipino doctors and nurses led the way, and after the enactment of the 1965 immigration law that encouraged people with vital skills to enter, over 9,000 physicians came to America. This flow slowed after the legislation of the 1970s made it more difficult to enter the United States.

Nurses remained in high demand, and Filipino women had been educated in American methods, so hospitals across the country recruited them actively. Those who had difficulty getting green cards entered as temporary workers and later changed their status. Some Americans complained that no shortage of nurses existed but that, because wages remained low, few citizens would accept the jobs. Yet the salaries were far higher here than at home for the Filipino nurses, and they continued to arrive. Overall, one-half of the foreign-born nurses in the country came from the Philippines. Once in the United States with green cards and later citizenship, Filipino nurses could sponsor their relatives to become immigrants, or they could send remittances home.

A large contingent settled on the West Coast, especially in California, the state that attracted many Asians. Many of the better-educated Filipinos were drawn to urban areas such as New York City and Chicago. There is hardly a hospital in San Francisco, Los Angeles, or Chicago without Filipino nurses. Medical and nursing schools in the Philippines train their students in American methods, and until the early 1990s they found a ready market for their skills in the United States. Then, as wages rose and more Americans turned to nursing, it became more difficult to find positions in most American hospitals. Even so, hospitals still experienced shortages of nurses after 2000 and continued to recruit foreign born nurses, either as immigrants or as temporary workers.The lure of America to Filipino men and women is indicative of the U.S. impact on Philippine culture and the attractiveness of the United States to many people there.

As striking as the Filipinos are the Koreans. The number of Koreans in America before 1950 was not large. Then came a few students, a few businessmen, and—after the Korean War ended in 1953—wives of American

TABLE 10.6. Education of Immigrants:
Persons by Educational Attainment and Region of Birth, 2006

	Less than 9th grade	9th to 12th grade	High school graduate	Some college	College graduate	Advanced degree	Total
Total native born	6,457,486	14,875,477	51,808,235	47,336,609	28,594,722	16,050,016	165,122,545
Total foreign born	6,287,167	3,581,449	7,353,835	5,391,300	4,888,413	3,356,157	30,858,321
Mexico	3,639,072	1,692,834	2,171,646	908,014	319,403	120,041	8,851,010
South and East Asia	708,732	492,716	1,334,440	1,337,744	2,208,441	1,518,241	7,600,314
Caribbean	420,324	364,612	893,719	654,221	367,381	191,785	2,892,042
Central America	706,843	337,872	559,473	333,915	163,851	63,478	2,165,432
South America	79,472	172,925	620,846	496,622	389,551	202,373	2,061,789
Middle East	99,692	66,176	235,451	202,125	264,320	212,625	1,080,389
All other	533,032	454,314	1,538,260	1,458,659	1,175,466	1,047,614	6,207,345
Percent Distribution							
Total native born	3.9	9.0	31.4	28.7	17.3	9.7	100.0
Total foreign born	20.4	11.6	23.8	17.5	15.8	10.9	100.0
Mexico	41.1	19.1	24.5	10.3	3.6	1.4	100.0
South and East Asia	9.3	6.5	17.6	17.6	29.1	20.0	100.0
Caribbean	14.5	12.6	30.9	22.6	12.7	6.6	100.0
Central America	32.6	15.6	25.8	15.4	7.6	2.9	100.0
South America	8.7	8.4	30.1	24.1	18.9	9.8	100.0
Middle East	9.2	6.1	21.8	18.7	24.5	19.7	100.0
All other	8.6	7.3	24.8	23.5	18.9	16.9	100.0

Universe: 2006 resident population ages 25 and older.

Notes: "Some college" includes persons who have attained an associate's degree; "college graduate" consists of persons who have attained a bachelor's degree. Middle East consists of Afghanistan, Iran, Iraq, Israel/Palestine, Jordan, Kuwait, Lebanon, Saudi Arabia, Syria, Turkey, Yemen, Algeria, Egypt, Morocco and Sudan.

Source: Pew Hispanic Center tabulations of 2006 American Community Survey (1% IPUMS).

servicemen. The Korean War also had an impact on Korean society, for Koreans learned about opportunities in the United States. The penetration of American culture triggered immigration, especially after passage of the 1965 Immigration Act. In the nineteenth century, Europeans had learned about America from letters, newspapers, guidebooks, and the stories of those who had already emigrated. This word of mouth was also true for Koreans, who learned of our country from the wives of American servicemen and from students, many of whom stayed after their period of study ended. Korean newspapers also told of life here; in 1976 one series of articles was published as a book, *Day and Night of Komericans,* which became a best-seller. Knowledge was one thing, the law was another; not until the 1965 reforms was it possible for many Koreans to emigrate. First came the doctors and nurses, and once they were settled they sent for their relatives.

The INS recorded that more than one million Korean immigrants had arrived between 1950 and 2000. Included among them were thousands of orphans adopted by Americans. During the period 1960–90 the largest source for the adoption of foreign children was Korea, whose numbers peaked at 6,150 in 1986. After that the numbers dropped, and American parents turned to China as the leading source for adopted children.

New Asian immigration: Self-employed Korean immigrant with small street-side business, New York City. (Photo by Elliott Barkan)

Immigration from Korea numbered about thirty-three thousand annually in the 1980s, but it dropped to about half that amount in the next decade. Moreover, the immigrants of the post-1990 era were more apt to be working-class Koreans. Los Angeles, with more than 150,000, houses the largest contingent, but there are sizable numbers in New York City and Chicago. In Los Angeles these Asians mixed with other immigrants, including Samoans, Mexicans, and Chinese, but maintained their own community life and neighborhoods. For Koreans the church was an important institution. Because so many were Protestants, they affiliated with Presbyterian and Methodist congregations and began to hold separate services in their own language. In some cases this meant that Koreans gave new life to declining Protestant churches. In 1985 the First United Methodist Church of Flushing, in Queens, New York City, had only thirty members in its English-speaking congregation but more than four hundred fifty in its Korean congregation.

These new Koreans are particularly successful in running small businesses; they control about six thousand enterprises in Los Angeles. In New York City the most prosperous Koreans were the health professionals, but in traditional immigrant fashion, they have also taken over businesses that had been run by those who came before them. They have just about replaced Italians and Jews in the fruit and vegetable stores in the nation's largest city. In 1987 Koreans ran about 80 percent of the greengroceries in New York City. However, by 2008 Koreans were giving up these stores. Competition from super markets and other new immigrants made many head for the suburbs where they became noted for running dry cleaning shops Despite the move the focus on education for their children did not change.

Their urban entrepreneurial activities were not confined to Los Angeles, New York City, or Chicago. They also moved into declining neighborhoods in cities such as Newark, New Jersey. In El Paso, Texas, only one Korean store existed in 1982, but thirty were reported there three years later. Many of the newcomers at first had lived and worked in California before moving to El Paso. In that Texas city, as elsewhere, they quickly earned a reputation for successful merchandising. As one El Paso merchant put it, "They're moving in like crazy—it seems every space that's available, they take it. They're very hard-working and industrious."

These small businesses offered chances for success, but they posed serious risks, too. The market for greengroceries was saturated in New York City by the 1990s, and in 1992 a major racial and ethnic riot in Los Angeles destroyed many Korean-run shops and their owners' hopes to fulfill the American dream. As a result some Koreans returned home, but more important, the number immigrating to American dropped although about 20,000 arrived annuually after 2000.

As remarkable as the growth of the Korean community was that of people from India. Unlike Koreans, the number of immigrants from India increased from 1990 to 2002, and India had become one of the leading sources for immigrants to the United States. There were nearly two million Indians in the United States by 2009. The figures of INS or the Department of Homeland Security (DHS), which replaced the INS in 2004, are less than those of the census, because many Indians had come from West Indian nations such as Guyana and from Africa. Those from the West Indies came for better opportunities, but many Africans left their homelands because of persecution.

The first waves of them to arrive from Asia in the United States, early in the twentieth century, were uneducated Sikh agricultural workers. Sikhs still arrived after passage of the Immigration Act of 1965, but most Indian immigrants were Hindus, and they were highly educated. Many engineers, doctors, and scientists came to the United States to take advantage of opportunities in the nation's businesses, hospitals, and universities. Along with the Chinese, they made up the largest number of foreign computer experts in California's Silicon Valley. Twenty percent of American physicians are foreign born, and the largest number by far were Indians, who amounted to 35,000 of the total in the 2000s.

Of the nation's newcomers, these immigrants had the highest incomes and even earned more than the national average. The educated elite did well economically in professional positions, as did others who went into business, especially those running newsstands and motels. Perhaps the largest successful business was founded by two brothers, Suesch and Bawnesh Kapor, who arrived in the 1970s. In 1983 they won the contract to operate 143 of New York City's Transit Authority newsstands, and they also ran others along the railroad lines to the suburbs. Their personal success collapsed when they were convicted of failure to pay income taxes, but this did not detract from the overall accomplishments of Asian Indians.

In California, another center of Indian settlement, these new immigrants bought and ran many inexpensive motels. The first Indian immigrant to purchase one was Nanlal Patel, who bought a motel in Sacramento in the 1940s. Many others followed him, and by 1985 Indians operated an estimated 80 percent of the state's independent motels. Branching out from the West Coast, they began to buy motels across the country. One owner observed, "You can travel from San Francisco to New York, and there's not a town where an Indian, a Patel, is not there." In the 1990s they began to run many Days Inn motels, a national chain; by 2005 they managed about 30 percent of these hostelries.

The numbers of people emigrating from Pakistan, Thailand, and Bangladesh were not large, but they grew after 1990, with the potential for future increases. Some of the first Thais to emigrate were women who married American soldiers stationed there during the Vietnam War. Others were professionals who satisfied the occupational preferences of the 1965 Immigration Act, some of whom remained in the United States after studying here. The largest settlement of Thais, who were Buddhists, was in California.

Larger than the Thai migration was that from Pakistan. Yet Pakistan's numbers were only one-tenth of India's. Professionals often studied in the United States and stayed by finding employment. The overwhelming majority were Muslims, who joined with others in the nation's fast-growing Islamic population. The Pakistani community was large enough to support a variety of ethnic organizations and to publish newspapers. The networks formed in the 1980s and 1990s served as a base for future immigration by using family preferences.

Few Bangladeshi lived in the United States prior to that nation's independence from Pakistan. Bangladesh, a nation of 120 million people, was a poor country that experienced many natural disasters, thus creating powerful incentives for those with the necessary funds to leave. The immigration laws were a problem, but a few professionals did manage to obtain visas. The 1990 immigration law's provision for "diversity visas," given to people from those nations that had low immigration totals after 1965, aided several thousand Bangladeshi who won these visas in a lottery and managed to immigrate to the United States.

The experiences of Vietnamese, Cambodians, and Laotians were different from those of most other Asians. These people, who numbered more than one million by 2000, came as refugees. A few entered before 1973, but the vast bulk arrived after the fall of the American-backed government in South Vietnam in that year. The first group of approximately 140,000 left in 1975; several thousand more emigrated in the next few years. Then, in 1978, a new crisis developed in Vietnam and soon enveloped neighboring Kampuchea and Laos. Hundreds of thousands of refugees fled across the border to Thailand or escaped by boat to neighboring Southeast Asian nations. Many were victimized by sea pirates; others found themselves living in squalid refugee camps. In response, the United States began to take in large numbers of "boat people" and other stranded emigrants after 1978. The number admitted after the mid-1980s declined, but by 2008 well over one million had settled in the United States.

The federal government first placed the 1975 refugees, many of whom were Roman Catholic and well educated, at military enclaves such as Camp Chafee, Arkansas, and Camp Pendleton, California, and a variety of private organizations helped the government find jobs and homes for the newcomers. Federal surveys indicated that the heads of household of the first Vietnamese refugees were well educated, with a significant proportion having attended college and possessing skills that could be put to productive use in the American economy.

Many Southeast Asian refugees who arrived after 1978 had horrible experiences in escaping Indochina and were less well educated than the original Vietnamese. They had many difficulties adjusting in their new land, and in the 1990s a number of these families still relied on government welfare programs for support. Indochinese women seemed to have a particularly hard time. They came from a culture so different from that in the United States that they found the immigrant experience profoundly depressing. A refugee official working among the Hmong (Laotian) people noted that these newcomers had never encountered checkbooks, birth control pills, or modern freeways filled with autos. He concluded, "This is like Disneyland to them. It's like going to Mars and starting all over again."

Near Easterners

From another part of Asia, the Near or Middle East, a growing number of immigrants came to America. The changes in immigration policy and the end of European colonialism meant that nations in the Near East had the same quotas as all other countries. One of the largest groups came from Iran. Many of those arriving between 1950 and 1980 first studied in the United States and gained a foothold by using the occupational or family preferences of the 1965 Immigration Act. Many of these immigrants were highly educated professionals. Then came the Iranian revolution of 1979 that displaced the pro-American government and for over four hundred days held hostage fifty-three Americans who were part of the diplomatic mission. The revolution prompted many Iranians to seek a better and safer life elsewhere. As the new regime was hostile to the United States and to many upper- and middle-class Iranians, the American government granted refugee status to those seeking to immigrate to the United States. However, after 1980 most still received no help from the United States government, but many continued to arrive under the regular immigration preferences. By 2008 300,000 had come to the United States.

The Iranians who arrived were generally well educated and had no difficulty finding white-collar positions. Some established their own businesses. California claimed the largest number of Iranians, but they were also found in metropolitan New York and Chicago. A good number spoke English, but many preferred to speak their own languages at home, and they organized groups to maintain their ethnic culture. They represented a variety of religions, such as Baha'i, but followers of Baha'i were outnumbered by Muslims who were much more secular than the Islamic character of post-1979 Iran. Some of the Iranians were Jews whose children began to associate with other Jews in the United States.

Arabs came in several waves after World War II. From 1948 to 1966, the conflict between Israel and her Arab neighbors uprooted many Arabs, some of whom eventually immigrated to the United States. Government figures recorded only a few Palestinians, but thousands of others came by way of Arab nations such as Jordan and Syria. Unlike the pre-World War I wave of Arabs, who were Christians, these exiles were mostly Muslims.

A second wave from the Middle East entered from 1967 to 1985, in response to new Arab-Israeli battles, a bitter civil war in Lebanon, and the Iran-Iraq conflict. Many were Palestinians, though their countries of origin were listed as Jordan, Syria, Lebanon, and the Persian Gulf nations. Some experts believe that since 1945 as many as two hundred thousand Palestinians have come to the United States. Like other Third World immigrants, many are well-educated professionals. A prominent Middle East journal reported that in 1983 as many as half of all Arab science and engineering Ph.D.s had left the Arab world, many to immigrate to the United States.

Although Muslims made up a majority of the Middle Eastern émigrés, Christians also constituted a considerable number. These included Egyptian Copts, who settled in California and New Jersey, and Chaldean immigrants from Iraq. The center of Chaldean settlement is Detroit, with other communities in Washington, D.C., and Jacksonville, Florida. Chaldeans are unique among immigrants to America. About 70 percent are bilingual and speak English, and many are professionals. In Detroit they are associated frequently with groceries and milk and ice cream distributorships. Ironically, many of the Christian Chaldeans who left Iraq because they were afraid they would lose their identity among Muslims have settled in or near Detroit, the center for Arabic-speaking people in America.

In Detroit the Chaldeans encountered, among other Arabs, Yemenis. Yemeni immigrants are mostly men who sought jobs in the automobile industry as temporary workers, intending to return home later. When the motor industry experienced unemployment after 1970, many of these Yemeni workers found unskilled jobs in restaurants or as seafarers on the Great Lakes. They also opened shops to serve their fellow workers.

Just as the Chaldeans ran grocery stores in Detroit, Christian Palestinians purchased and operated similar shops in California. One Palestinian estimated that in the mid-1980s Palestinians ran nearly half of San Francisco's small grocery stores. Mostly these were family businesses. Said one owner, "The wife, the little kid can work behind the cash register. You use your family. How else are you going to make it?"

Israel, a nation of immigrants, began to watch more people leaving than entering in the early 1980s. That movement prompted officials to encourage the immigration of Russian Jews to offset the losses. The lure, or the "magic of

America," was strong. As one migrant put it, "I don't think there is so much 'push' pushing people out of Israel as there is a 'pull' or magnet drawing them to the West—mostly to America." Israelis, like other Middle Eastern people, were thoroughly familiar with the United States, through American goods, television programs, and magazines and from letters sent by those already settled there describing the wonders of America. And with modern air travel it was easy to get to the United States.

Another factor motivating Israeli emigration is the political instability in the Middle East. Conflict between Arabs and Jews has been continual and has been punctuated by two wars, in 1967 and 1973. President Jimmy Carter used his offices to get Egypt and Israel to sign a peace treaty in 1978, but conflicts between other Arabs and Jews in the region have not yet subsided. New violence erupted in the 1990s, and then escalated again in 2001, in Israel and the Palestinian territories on the west bank of the Jordan River, as well as in the Gaza Strip in southern Israel. This almost ceaseless conflict in the Middle East has prompted even more Israelis and Arabs to immigrate to America. About 10 percent of those with visas from Israel are Muslims and Christians.

The Israeli-Arab conflict was not the only violence that wracked the Middle East after 1990. American-led forces pushed Iraqi soldiers out of Kuwait in 1991, and this led to an exodus of some Kuwaiti and Iraqi refugees, as well as Kurds living in the northern part of Iraq who were persecuted by the established Iraqi government.

Although the numbers of refugees from these conflicts was not large, they added to the ethnic mix of the American people. So did a new flow of refugees from Afghanistan. When the Soviet Union invaded that nation in 1979 to support a new and more radical regime, thousands of Afghans fled. The Soviets withdrew ten years later, but fighting among various Afghan factions destroyed still more homes. Then came the American war on terrorism after the September 11, 2001, bombing of the World Trade Center, and another exodus began. Untold numbers fled to neighboring Pakistan and Iran; others found a haven in Europe and the United States. Several thousand Afghans entered this country after 1989, but they used regular immigrant channels to get here. In 1994, for example, only twenty-one Afghans were recorded as refugees; ten times that number came under the regular immigration laws.

The vast majority of these Afghans were Muslims who did not share the beliefs of the Taliban, who came to power in 1995. Most were middle- and upper-class individuals who wanted to escape the pervasive violence in their nation. Life was not always satisfying in the United States, however, because they arrived with few resources, financial or social. In contrast to many other refugees from the developing world, only a few had been students in the United

Number of Mosques in the United States
Founded in Each Decade

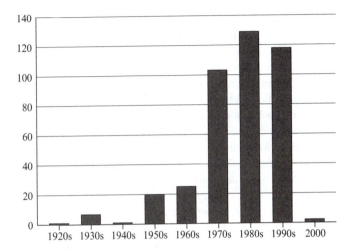

States and knew English. The center of America's Afghan community was in Fremont, California. If lucky, the men learned English quickly and found jobs with the help of American friends or other Afghans. For the women, American culture posed difficulties. They usually had not been in the paid labor market in Afghanistan, but working in the United States became a must if their families

TABLE 10.7.   Ethnic Breakdown of Regular Mosque Participants

	Percentage of Mosques with at Least Some	Estimated Participants* Nationally
South Asian (Pakistani, Indian, Bangladeshi, Afghani)	87	159,588
African American	87	135,408
Arab	90	68,913
African (Sub-Saharan)	40	15,717
European (Bosnian, Tartar, Kosovar, etc.)	25	7,979
White American	41	5,561
Southeast Asian (Malaysian, Indonesian, Filipino)	29	4,715
Caribbean	15	4,715
Turkish	22	3,869
Iranian	18	1,934
Hispanic/Latino	18	1,572

*Calculated by multiplying the average number by the total mosques in the country (1,209).

were to survive. Needless to say the attack on the World Trade Center and the American military role in toppling the Taliban in 1991 was keenly watched by Afghans. Some hoped to return to Afghanistan and help rebuild the nation, but in 2009 the future was hard to predict. The Taliban appeared to be gaining in 2007 and 2008, which prompted calls for more American troops. How the conflict would end was not certain in 2009 but outside nations had a poor record of trying to control Afganistan.

The immigration of so many Muslims from the Middle East, Asia, and even Africa diversified the American religious mosaic. Islamic leaders claimed that Muslims had overtaken Jews as the third largest religious group behind Protestants and Catholics. Scholars disputed this claim, and because the United States census does not count religious identification, it was left to sociologists of American religion to find the exact numbers. But they were also unable to come up with precise figures. The number of Muslims and mosques in America grew rapidly. A survey conducted by the Council on American-Islamic Relations reported that from 1994 to 2001 the number of mosques increased by 25 percent. By 2009 there were more than 1,200 mosques in the United States, and that 20 percent of them supported full-time religious schools. Muslims had become more visible in the American workplace, and several had even been appointed chaplains in the United States military.

Yet American Islam itself reflected many ethnic and theological differences, from fundamentalist to secular. African Americans accounted for about one-third of Muslims, followed by large numbers from south Asia and the Arab nations of the Near East. The numbers included, for example, Bosnian Muslims from Europe. The war on terrorism in 2001 elicited strong support for the American position from American Muslim leaders, although a few imams supported the Taliban. The theological and cultural differences meant that American Muslims practiced their faith in diverse ways. Whatever the future of Islam in America, it was certain to grow, given the number of people from the Islamic world who wished to migrate to America.

West Indians

Although people whose native language was Spanish made the largest presence among American immigrants from the Western Hemisphere after 1970, significant numbers of English-speaking and Haitian Creole-speaking newcomers joined the migration north. The new law made possible substantial increases from several English-speaking island nations. The exodus of people from Jamaica to the United States was probably the largest from the islands. It was not unusual for women from Jamaica to begin the migration process, arriving to work here as nurses or maids. New York City housed the largest contingent of West Indians, Jamaicans, and other English-speaking immigrants. Although Jamaicans participated in existing activities, they also had their own cultural institutions. Cricket, a popular game at home, was now played in Brooklyn, Philadelphia, and other cities by these newcomers.

From Haiti, French- and Creole-speaking migrants fled the dictatorial regime of François Duvalier and a severely depressed economy. At first a number of relatively well-educated Haitians emigrated, followed by those with fewer skills. Once in the United States, they took whatever jobs they could get, often being paid poorly. They suffered because they were black, as well as immigrants. Like other newcomers before them, they congregated together; by the 1980s one Haitian colony in the Crown Heights section of Brooklyn already had about seventy-five thousand people. In the late 1970s some Haitians, who could not qualify as immigrants under American laws, were so desperate to leave that they sailed in boats for hundreds of miles to the Florida coast. Once in the United States, they were seized by immigration authorities who insisted that they were illegal immigrants and not entitled to remain here.

Those who arrived before 1982 eventually won immigrant status, but many continued to arrive later. This exodus slowed when the Duvalier regime was overthrown in 1986, only to pick up again when a military unit seized power. The Reagan and Bush administrations pursued an interdiction policy, stopping Haitian boats and returning the passengers to Haiti. In the 1992 election Democratic candidate Bill Clinton criticized the Republican policy, but he continued it when he took office. The American government allowed some Haitians onto its naval base in Cuba and then admitted them to the United States as refugees. In the fall of 1994 the United States occupied Haiti and restored democracy, thus lessening the Haitian desire for immigration.

New African Immigrants

Many of the African immigrants who came after 1960 were white or Asian, but a growing number were black. By far the largest numbers of black immigrants were from the Caribbean, but the increases from Africa became noticeable after 1980. The first black Africans to arrive were men who studied at American colleges and universities. Like other immigrants, the students found jobs and sent for their families in Africa or sent money home or both. When a Marxist revolution seized power in Ethiopia in the 1970s, many of the well educated fled, and some were admitted as refugees. In the 1990s they were joined by Muslim refugees from Somaliland. Africa experienced a great deal of violent conflict in the 1980s and 1990s, and by 2000 the largest number of the world's refugees was found in that continent. The refugee quota for African nations was only a few thousand, but under the administration of Bill Clinton, it was increased. In 1999 the president set the allotment of refugees at twenty thousand, which was one-quarter of the world's total and higher than any previous year. Others, such as Liberians, were admitted temporarily in the hope that they could return to their homes when conditions improved. Under President George W. Bush the refugee quota for Africa was raised again to 25,000.

In addition, the 1990 law that provided for diversity visas favored Africa, which received twenty thousand of the world's total of fifty-five thousand annually. The establishment of small African communities laid the groundwork for using the family unification system to bring more migrants to America. By the mid-1990s African immigrants, mostly from the sub-Sahara, were entering at the rate of more than thirty thousand annually, and they were usually family members of those who had gone before. The numbers continued to grow after 2000, and in 2006 they constituted ten percent of all immigrants. Not all were refugees, students turned professionals, family members, or persons with diversity visas. Some who could not get visas arrived as tourists and stayed when their visas expired to work illegally. Many were from Senegal and hawked goods on the streets of major cities such as New York.

Although New York City attracted the largest number of African immigrants, other important communities developed in Minneapolis and Washington, D.C. Ethiopians and Eritreans were especially to be found in Washington, D.C., driving cabs and running restaurants and small businesses. Somalis ended up in the cold climate of Minnesota or in San Diego. Like so many other newcomers, they formed their own organizations, published newspapers, and frequented the same religious institutions. They generally stayed aloof from native African Americans, but some did join churches and mosques in their neighborhoods.

The growing presence of Haitians and of English speakers from Jamaica and other West Indian nations and from Africa, as well as small countries such as the Cape Verde Islands, brought increasing diversity to the American black population. African Americans had never been monolithic; historically, issues such as social class, education, and religion and the question of whether they were urban or rural had divided them. Now, with so many new black immigrants arriving, this population became increasingly disparate, just as the Hispanic and Asian populations had.

Renewed Anxiety over Immigration

The presence of so many new immigrants has caused apprehension among those Americans who arrived before World War II. Although overt bigotry declined after 1945 and Congress and the president lifted some of the more restrictive features of our laws, uneasiness about immigration continued. After 1970 the Civil Rights Commission and the media recorded numerous incidents of violence and interethnic friction. In Michigan, Dearborn's Fordson High School, of which 40 percent of the 1,755 students were Arab Americans, conflicts continually arose. Bathroom graffiti included ugly slogans such as "Kill the Arabs" and "Death to America." A minor fight in the cafeteria in 1984 brought both the police and negative publicity for the school. A young Arab man was thrown off a Jet Blue aircraft because he wore a t-shirt with both English and Arabic saying "We shall Not Be Silent." He sued the airline and two years later, in 2009, won a $240,000 settlement.

The most violent racial/ethnic incident occurred in Los Angeles in 1992. African Americans, angry over the failure of a jury to convict four white policemen who were seen on video beating a black man, took to the streets to vent their frustrations. The situation quickly degenerated into a full-scale riot. Mobs roamed the streets and vandalized stores and buildings, burning whatever they chose and injuring and killing many people before police finally brought the riots under control. The violence hit Korean immigrants particularly hard because many of their stores in predominantly African American and Hispanic neighborhoods were destroyed and burned to the ground. In several cities blacks had boycotted Korean-owned stores in their neighborhoods for alleged insults, but these were minor episodes compared with the Los Angeles multiethnic riot.

The Mariel Cubans received much attention because of the criminals within the group, but bigots singled out other immigrants as undesirable as well. Some Americans even attributed the nation's serious drug problems to foreigners in our midst. Police and public officials noted that the nation's Chinatowns experienced gang wars for control of businesses, and they also noted that Chinese, Colombians, Dominicans, and other immigrants were involved in the drug trade, so they urged a crackdown on immigrant criminals. For a brief period in the mid-1980s, INS officials saw Haitians as likely carriers of AIDS and hence undesirables to be kept out of the United States.

In the past, restrictionist groups had claimed that certain people were inassimilable. This charge reappeared in the 1980s and seemed especially directed at Hispanics. In 1981 Senator Alan Simpson of Wyoming insisted that a "substantial proportion of these new persons and their descendants do not assimilate into our society.... If language and cultural separation rise above a certain level, the unity and political stability of our nation will—in time—be seriously eroded."

Some went beyond Simpson's statements and insisted that bilingual programs had failed. They opposed electoral ballots in a foreign language, as mandated by federal law, and they held that educational programs in other than the English language fostered segregation. Yet in most states not enough bilingual teachers could be found to help those immigrants who wanted to learn English. In the 1980s, however, an organization called U.S. English emerged with the purpose of making English the official language of the United States, which seems superfluous as English has always been this country's language. By 1996 twenty-two states had passed propositions stating the obvious, but some prohibited the use of any other language by government employees who were working in authorized activities. Nowhere was the controversy over the official use of English so heated as in California, with its large number of Mexicans and Asian Americans. Hispanic leaders called the proposition "racist in character," but in 1986 California voters approved it by a two-to-one margin. These laws were not enforced, and when they were the courts declared them to be unconstitutional. Nor did all Americans accept them. In January, 2009, the voters of Nashville rejected a proposal to make English the city's official language and prevent government workers from communicating in other languages.

The meaning of officially sanctioning the English language remained unclear. The Los Angeles School Board approved a master plan for an expansion of bilingual programs and specifically provided for the teaching of most courses in the students' own language until they mastered English. The school board had its eye on perhaps the nations' most diverse student body, in which more than eighty languages were spoken in the city's schools. Of the 600,000 pupils in the schools, 163,000 could speak little or no English. About 90 percent of these students were Spanish-speaking, with Koreans, Cantonese, Vietnamese, Kampucheans, and Armenians constituting the other minorities. Critics attacked the proposal as retarding assimilation, but its defenders responded, "It's clear now that academic progress must continue while students learn English. It's not enough to become English proficient but to fall behind in content."

The debates over assimilation and bilingualism will no doubt continue. Yet assimilation and bilingualism were not the only aspects of immigration that troubled Americans. Another controversy involved the refugee issue. A growing influx of undocumented immigrants fleeing both poverty and bloody civil wars came from such Central American countries as El Salvador, Guatemala, and Nicaragua. As political refugees they sought sanctuary on the basis of international law and the 1980 Refugee Act. That law granted political asylum to those who had fled from lands in which their freedom might be threatened or in which, based on race, religion, nationality, social association, or political opinions, their lives might be in jeopardy. The Reagan administration considered most of these individuals to be fleeing from economic rather than politically life-threatening causes and hence would not approve their presence in the United States. Some Nicaraguans, claiming to be refugees from communism, were accepted.

As conditions deteriorated and violence remained common in the late 1980s, a growing number of Central Americans sought refuge in the United States. They traveled mainly from Nicaragua, but also from Guatemala and El Salvador, through Mexico and across the southern border of the United States. Once on American territory, they applied for asylum as political refugees. With visions of thousands of asylum seekers coming to the United States, the immigration authorities insisted that they must stay at their entry point in Texas and refused them work permits while their cases were pending. In early 1989 a federal judge nullified these rulings and granted the refugees permission to leave. Many did so, heading for the Miami area, home to so many Cuban, Haitian, and Nicaraguan refugees.

Florida politicians did not want this latest immigrant influx. Bob Graham, a U.S. senator from Florida, declared: "Florida has suffered enough. We've been strained to the breaking point of crisis immigration. The current system is out of control and unfair to Florida." Miami officials did not have adequate housing for these latest newcomers, so some Central Americans found themselves living in tents in the city's baseball and football stadiums.

Friendly groups seeking to assist the refugees used the courts to delay their departures. Church leaders, especially in the Southwest, were among those who founded a movement to give sanctuary in churches to Central Americans. Members of the sanctuary movement interpreted the law to favor those whose lives were in danger, but their position conflicted with the positions taken by the State Department and the INS. Two celebrated cases developed in Arizona and New Mexico with apparently different results; the nuances of the law differed in each state. In 1985 in Tucson, federal government officials successfully challenged church leaders who had illegally smuggled refugees into this country. The defendants received suspended sentences as the courts upheld the official position of the Reagan administration. However, circumstances in New Mexico in 1988 were different, and those prosecuted for providing sanctuary escaped conviction on the grounds that the former governor of the state, Toney Anaya, had proclaimed New Mexico a sanctuary state in 1986 and that the defendants acted on the belief that the governor's edict in effect legalized their decision to provide assistance to political refugees. The sanctuary movement became quiet after 1990, when Congress granted Salvadorans the right to remain in the United States temporarily, and especially when the civil war ended in that country and Nicaragua.

Central Americans were not the only ones having difficulty winning asylum. Practically all refugees brought into America, or those persons who obtained asylum once in the United States, were fleeing communism. Before 1980 American law indicated that only persons escaping communism could qualify for political sanctuary. The Refugee Act of 1980 changed the definition to be in accord with the United Nations protocol on refugees, which stipulated that if you had a well-founded fear of persecution based on religion, race, or membership in a political organization, you could be considered a political refugee. Thus persons fleeing totalitarian regimes other than communist ones might qualify for admission. But most persons, such as Afghans who won asylum, continued to be admitted to this country because they were fleeing communism. There were exceptions: during the 1980s Iranians escaping the fundamentalist Islamic state got asylum. On the other hand, it generally proved difficult to apply this stipulation, especially for Salvadorans and Haitians, who were not escaping communism yet were trying to get into the United States as political refugees. INS officials were not particularly sympathetic to them, but they tried anyway.

The fact that so many of these persons then entered our country without proper immigration papers highlighted another major issue troubling Americans—undocumented aliens. During the 1950s the numbers of these immigrants increased until "Operation Wetback," a 1954 INS sweep of farms in the Southwest to catch illegal agricultural workers, seemed to eliminate the problem. But when the United States ended the *bracero* temporary-workers program and enacted a new immigration law in 1965, the number of undocumented or illegal entrants, which had been relatively low at that point, started increasing. By the mid-1980s undocumented immigration had become a national issue.

Because immigration was a federal issue, the debate shifted to Washington, D.C. In 1996, after discussing a variety of proposals, Congress enacted new regulations about the admission of immigrants and their eligibility for economic benefits. The legislators also provided more funds for increased border control to keep out undocumented aliens. However, Congress did not decrease the number of immigrants to be admitted each year.

In fact, the economy was doing very well in 1996 and continued to grow from that date until 2001. After a recession in 2001, the economy picked up again. Undocumented and regular immigrants were needed for the job market, and Congress was well aware of that fact. Within a few years, the federal government restored some of the cuts, and states picked up the slack. President George W. Bush suggested in 2001 that a new amnesty of some type be adopted for unauthorized Mexicans. Immigrant rights supporters wanted the amnesty proposal extended to other immigrants. Then came September 11, 2001. When the nineteen men who turned their planes into bombs were revealed to be from Arab countries (fifteen from Saudi Arabia alone), the legislators were in no mood to ease controls. Actually most of the men were not immigrants but possessed another status to permit them to enter the United States. Several had stayed beyond the terms of their visas.

The Justice Department and Congress moved quickly to tighten immigration. First, President Bush's proposal for an amnesty for Mexicans became a dead letter. The attorney general rounded up more than one thousand men from the Middle East, and men from Arab-speaking lands had more difficulty getting visas to the United States. The USA Patriot Act of 2001 gave the executive greater powers to force cooperation between the INS and FBI. The act also permitted the Justice Department to detain persons suspected of having connections to terrorist organizations and gave American officials the right to share more intelligence about terrorism with other nations.

In an attempt to assure Arab Americans that the government only wanted to find those involved with terrorists, the legislators expressed their concern about discrimination against Arabs and Muslims. Just how sensitive federal authorities would be was left undecided, but many Arab Americans and Muslims did point to harassment in the wake of September 11. These measures indicated how clearly the United States maintained its historical ambivalence about immigration.

By 2006, with the numbers of undocumented immigrants growing and regular immigrants averaging roughly one million annually, Congress once again turned its attention to immigration. The House of Representatives passed a bill providing for increasing border security, making undocumented immigration a crime and penalizing those aiding immigrants. The Senate passed a different bill providing for a partial legalization for undocumented immigrants and a temporary workers program. In 2007 the Senate tried again to fashion a bill that might be acceptable to the house, but it also included a provision to change the immigration laws to emphasize skills.

The Senators could not agree, even with President Bush's support. Both the President and Congress then turned to enforcement of the laws against hiring undocumented aliens and border enforcement. Funds were provided for hiring more men and women for the border patrol and building nearly 700 miles of additional fences along with border separating the Untied States and Mexico. In addition, government agents raided several plants suspected of employing unauthorized workers. Agents arrested and jailed many workers and then deported them. In 1986 the border patrol numbered 3,000, but in early 2009 18,000 agents were on duty. Yet the task of controlling the border was large, and rounding up and deporting eleven million illegal immigrants was huge. Thus just how government would be able to control immigration was left unclear especially in view of economic factors. Scholars suggest that the number of undocumented immigrants trying to enter in 2008 fell, simply because employment was hard to find in the depressed American economy. Economic conditions, rather than harsh tactics along the border might have a bigger impact in controlling undocumented immigration.

Afterword

In the twenty-first century Americans are keenly aware of how the various minorities in their midst combine to make the United States a unique nation. The growth of the country began with the English colonization of Jamestown, Virginia, and Plymouth, Massachusetts, more than 150 years before the colonies declared their independence in 1776. At the time America was still a relatively weak, agrarian society, with fewer than three million Europeans and Africans settled along the Eastern seaboard and a smaller number of Indians scattered throughout the country. Although the colonists laid the foundations of American society in that era, the years of great growth and the transformation of the nation into an urban and industrial one came much later.

In this process Americans experienced developments similar to those of Western European societies. They accumulated capital and invested it, constructed a transportation network, cleared and tilled the land, built cities, suburbs, and factories, invented and improved machinery and gadgets, organized large corporations, and reached out for foreign markets. Yet in many ways the American experience differed from that of Europe. In the seventeenth century, America needed to import labor. The English colonies and later the new nation sought workers overseas. From Africa, Americans brought back men and women in chains, and from all over Europe, they enticed strong laborers. In the nineteenth century they also welcomed, temporarily, immigrants from Asia; and in the twentieth century they looked to Mexico, South America, and Canada, as well as Europe and Asia again.

The labor of these millions helped transform the nation. But the mingling of so many peoples also had enormous consequences for the social history of the United States. Whereas society enslaved Africans and prized voluntary immigrants for their strong backs and skillful hands, it scorned Indians because the white people believed that the tribes stood in the way of progress and economic growth. Because the Indians held the land, they bore the brunt of the white Americans' greed as they moved across the continent.

Although the nation welcomed slaves and immigrants for their economic contributions, it did not mean that these people experienced an easy time. These newcomers differed from the early Englishmen, who set the tone for

285

American society and culture. Anglo Americans expected them to conform to the then-dominant culture and frequently abused them when they did not. But many did change, and the gradual loss of an Old World heritage has been an integral part of American ethnic history. When people did not assimilate fast enough for some Americans, or were considered unassimilable by others, they encountered the wrath of nativism. Black men and women, slaves at first, suffered more than immigrants. No matter what they did, they were held to be different and inferior, a race apart.

Thus conflicts occurred in spite of the indispensable contributions the newcomers made to the building and shaping of modern society. Sometimes they were fierce and violent; at other times these conflicts exposed minorities to more subtle forms of discrimination and exclusion. It seems as if some ethnic struggles marked every period of American history. In recent years, the nation apparently has come to a public acceptance of ethnic differences and a growing toleration for all peoples. Certainly anti-Catholicism and anti-Semitism have abated, and even white racism has lessened. Perhaps the best example of this is the acceptance of a black man as President of the United States.

Nevertheless, personal feelings and prejudices have not kept pace with contemporary public and constitutional realities. Places of purely social recreation, such as country clubs, still show signs of "ethnic purity," and private comments to close friends and family often contain the most brutal kinds of racial and religious bigotry. In the past decade, some of the comments made by extremist groups and individuals, as well as those expressed on some radio talk shows, suggest that ethnic animosity still sparks outrageous outbursts.

After the World Trade Center was destroyed on September 11, 2001, Muslims became the favorite scapegoats for American bigots. Many Middle Easterners were subsequently attacked in the streets all over the United States.

Finally, individual perceptions of reality are significant. Children who attend integrated schools and people who live and work in integrated communities base their attitudes on whom and what they see about them. Although living and working with others often bring understanding, they do not always encourage greater acceptance and tolerance of different cultural values.

That the nation would eventually lay aside ethnic antagonism and seek a pluralistic society in which all groups were accepted and treated with respect, even if they remained different, seemed more likely in the twenty-first century than it did in previous periods of American history.

In 2009, more than forty years after the enactment of the Voting Rights Act of 1965, African Americans were participating in the political process in growing numbers. They were also recognized for their achievements to a greater degree than they ever had been before. In 2002, for example, Denzel Washington and Halle Berry, both African Americans, won the coveted Oscars as the best actor and actress, respectively. It was the first time in American history that a black woman had won the award and only the second time that a black male received it. After Berry's name was announced, talk show host Oprah Winfrey exclaimed, "I can't believe I'm still walking on earth! I am over the moon! Ecstatic!" Such an achievement warranted celebration as it proved that accomplishment, rather than race, dictated the direction motion picture academy voters took. Winfrey herself was widely known and was the richest single woman in America, reportedly worth over one billion dollars.

Blacks in popular culture, and not simply the movies, were becoming familiar to audiences after the 1980s. The Bill Cosby TV program was extraordinarily popular during its run, and high achieving athletes, especially in basketball and football, were permanent fixtures in American sports. In the first decade of the twenty-first century the Williams sisters, Venus and Serena, impressed the world with their prowess in In the realm of scholarship John Hope Franklin won the presidency of the Southern Historical Association, the Organization of American Historians, and the American Historical Association—the three most prestigious organizations for professionals who write about American history. The presidency of the Southern Historical Association was especially noteworthy in view of the segregation and racism that Franklin faced when using southern libraries while researching his doctoral dissertation in North Carolina in the late 1930s. As notable as these high-achieving blacks have been, few would have predicted the election of Barack Obama in 2008 as president of the United States.

Shortly after Barack Obama assumed the office of the President in January, 2009, the Republican Party chose Michael W. Steel as head of its national committee. Steele was the first person of African American heritage to assume leadership of the party of Abraham Lincoln. Moreover, the Republican Party is made up mostly of WASPs and members of white ethnic groups. Steele's appointment, as well as Obama's election, of course, shows how far Americans have come over the past fifty years when even the appointment of an African America to a President's Cabinet would have raised eyebrows.

Clearly, American tolerance and broad-mindedness have expanded during the past half century. As the United States has become much more involved in world affairs, and as the nation has become the cultural leader in so many different areas, it behooves us to act as if we believed in the rhetoric of the nation and the philosophy taught to American school children: we favor democracy and equal opportunity for all persons. Now one's innate talents and work ethic are far more important for individual accomplishment than it had been in an earlier era when one's gender, creed, and color created artificial barriers.

Newcomers to America often start out at the bottom of the socioeconomic pecking order and endure problems that a more humane society might handle differently. Nevertheless, most Americans believe that good people, given opportunities, will pick themselves up by their bootstraps, and move on. It is impossible, therefore, to predict who will or who will not "make it" in the United States. All that we can be certain of is that ethnicity by itself is no longer an impediment. People from all over the world still want to come here and take advantage of whatever opportunities they might find. And even if they have to struggle to survive, many nurture the belief that their children will have better lives in this country than they would have had elsewhere. In the United States, neither social class nor governmental edicts preclude the most talented individuals from working to achieve their goals.

In the twenty-first century, the United States is committed to nurturing cultural pluralism, even if not all Americans are equally enthusiastic about the idea. We know from past history, however, that when educational and entrepreneurial opportunities are available, most people will achieve a modicum of success. Although there may never be full comprehension of the richness of ethnic contributions to the nation's cultural and economic development, it is important to recognize that significant changes in attitudes have occurred over time. "The country has, of course, made considerable progress since the days of Know-Nothings and the Klan," *The New York Times* editorialized on February 1, 2009. "But racism has a nasty habit of never going away, no matter how much we may want it to, and thus the perpetual need for vigilance."

SELECTED BIBLIOGRAPHY

Two sweeping and comprehensive works are Elliott Robert Barkan, ed., *A Nation of Peoples: A Sourcebook on America's Multicultural Heritage* (Westport, CT: Greenwood Press, 1999) and David Levinson, ed., *Encyclopedia of American Immigrant Culture* (New York: Macmillan, 1997). For African Americans, one might use James Oliver Horton and Lois E. Horton, *Hard Road to Freedom: The Story of African America* (New Brunswick: Rutgers University Press, 2001) and John Hope Franklin's *From Slavery to Freedom* (8th ed.; New York: Alfred A. Knopf, 2000). Roger L. Nichols, *American Indians in U. S. History* (Norman: University of Oklahoma Press, 2003); Nichols, *The American Indian* (6th ed.; Norman: University of Oklahoma Press, 2008); and Philip J. Deloria and Neal Salisbury, eds., *A Companion to American Indian History* (Malden, MA: Blackwell, 2002) provide good introductions to the topic. On Asians, we would start with Gary Y. Okihiro, *The Columbia Guide to Asian American History* (New York: Columbia University Press, 2001) and Ronald Takaki, *Strangers from a Different Shore* (Boston: Little, Brown, 1989). An overview of Mexican history from 1521 through 1998 is Manuel G. Gonzales, *Mexicanos: A History of Mexicans in the United States* (Bloomington: Indiana University Press, 2000).

A controversial account about immigrants and ethnicity is Paul Spicard, *Almost All Aliens: Immigration, Race, and Colonialism in American History and Identity* (New York: Routledge, 2007). Other works one might look through include include Frank Bean and Gillian Stevens, *America's Newcomers and the Dynamics of Diversity* (New York: Russell Sage Foundation, 2003); Mary C. Waters and Reed Ueda, eds., *The New Americans: A Guide to Immigration since 1965* (Cambridge, MA: Harvard University Press, 2006); and Richard Alba and Victor Nee, *Remaking the American Mainstream: Assimilation and Contemporary Immigration* (Cambridge, MA: Harvard University Press, 2003).

Especially good on women is Donna Gabaccia, *From the Other Side: Women, Gender, and Immigrant Life in the U. S., 1820–1990* (Bloomington: Indiana University Press, 1994) and Maxine S. Seller, ed., *Immigrant Women* (2nd ed.; Albany: State University of New York, 1994). More specialized are Martha Gardner, *The Qualities of a Citizen: Women, Immigration, and Citizenship, 1870–1965* (Princeton, NJ: Princeton University Press, 2005) and Hasia R. Diner and Beryl Lief Benderly, *Her Works Praise Her: A History of Jewish Women in America from Colonial Times to the Present* (New York: Basic Books, 2002).

Chapter 1

For an overview of European migration to the New World in the seventeenth and eighteenth centuries, one might look through Alison Games, *Migration and the Origins of the English Atlantic World* (Cambridge, MA: Harvard University Press, 1999) and Marianne Sophia Wokeck, *Trade in Strangers: The Beginning of Mass Migration to North America* (University Park: Pennsylvania State University Press, 1999).

For relationships among blacks, whites, and Indians, consult Gary B. Nash, *Red, White and Black: The Peoples of Early America* (3rd ed.; Englewood Cliffs, NJ: Prentice-Hall, 1992). The development of slavery is treated in Edmund S. Morgan, *American Slavery, American Freedom: The Ordeal of Colonial Virginia* (New York: Norton, 1975); Peter Wood, *Black Majority: Negroes in Colonial South Carolina from 1670 through the Stono Rebellion* (New York: Knopf, 1974); Gerald W. Mullin, *Flight and Rebellion: Slave Resistance in Eighteenth-Century Virginia* (New York: Oxford University Press, 1975); Ira Berlin, *Many Thousands Gone: The First Two Centuries of Slavery in North Carolina* (Cambridge, MA: Harvard University Press, 1998); David Brion Davis, *Inhuman Bondage: The Rise and Fall of Slavery in the New World* (New York: Oxford University Press, 2006); and Simon Schama, *Rough Crossings: Britain, the Slaves and the American Revolution* (New York: HarperCollins, 2006). A study of New York City's fears about slave rebellion is Jill Lepore, *New York Burning: Liberty, Slavery, and Conspiracy in Eighteenth-Century Manhattan* (New York: Knopf, 2005).

On the major white groups in colonial America, one might begin with Bernard Bailyn, *Voyagers to the West* (New York: Knopf, 1986), and follow up with David H. Fischer, *Albion's Seed: Four British Folkways in America* (New York: Oxford University Press, 1989). For two other important groups, see Aaron Spencer Fogleman, *Hopeful Journeys: German Immigration, Settlement, and Political Culture in Colonial America, 1717–1775* (Philadelphia: University of Pennsylvania Press, 1996) and Patrick Griffin, *The People with No Name: Ireland's Ulster Scots, America's Scots Irish, and the Creation of a British Atlantic World, 1689–1764* (Princeton, NJ: Princeton University Press, 2001).

For a brief treatment of Indians before the European arrival, see Alice Beck Kahoe, *America before the European Invasions* (New York: Longman, 2002). Another worthwhile work on the Indians in early America is James Axtell, *Natives and Newcomers: The Cultural Origins of North America* (New York: Oxford University Press, 2001). Two books on the conflict between whites and Indians in the eighteenth century are Patrick Griffin, *American Leviathan: Empire, Nation and the Revolutionary Frontier* (New York: Hill & Wang, 2007) and Peter Silver, *Our Savage Neighbors: How Indian Wars Transformed Early America* (New York: Norton, 2008).

Chapters 2 and 3

For American development in the early national and Jackson eras, worthwhile books include Robert L. Heilbroner and Aaron Singer, *The Economic Transformation of America* (New York: Harcourt Brace Jovanovich, 1977); David R. Meyer, *The Roots of American Industrialization* (Baltimore: Johns Hopkins University Press, 2003); and Daniel Walker Howe's Pulitzer Prize-winning *What Hath God Wrought: The Transformation of America, 1815–1846* (New York: Oxford University Press, 2007).

Peter Way presents Irish laborers' perspectives in *Common Labour: Workers and the Digging of North American Canals, 1780–1860* (Cambridge, England: Cambridge University Press, 1993). For general views of the South, see Bertram Wyatt-Brown, *The Shaping of Southern Culture: Honor, Grace, and War, 1760s–1890s* (Chapel Hill: University of North Carolina Press, 2001) and Robert F. Durden, *The Self-Inflicted Wound: Southern Politics in the Nineteenth Century* (Lexington: University Press of Kentucky, 1985).

For slavery, the following would be good places to start: Peter Kolchin, *American Slavery* (New York: Hill & Wang, 1993) and Walter Johnson, *Soul by Soul: Life inside the Antebellum Slave Market* (Cambridge, MA: Harvard University Press, 1999). Insightful older works include Ira Berlin, *Slaves without Masters: The Free Negro in the Antebellum South* (New York: Pantheon, 1974); Eugene Genovese, *Roll Jordan Roll: The World the Slaves Made* (New York: Pantheon, 1974); John Blassingame, *The Slave Community: Plantation Life in the Antebellum South* (New York: Oxford University Press, 1972); and Lawrence W. Levine, *Black Culture and Black Consciousness: Afro-American Folk Thought from Slavery to Freedom* (New York: Oxford University Press, 1977). James Oliver Horton and Lois E. Norton, *In Hope of Freedom: Culture, Community, and Protest among Northern Free Blacks, 1700–1860* (New York: Oxford University Press, 1997), gives a different regional perspective.

Revealing accounts on African American girls and women are Linda Brent, *Incidents in the Life of a Slave Girl: Written by Herself*, edited by Lydia Marie Child (1861; reprint, Cambridge, MA: Harvard University Press, 1987); Deborah Gray White, *Ar'n't I a Woman?: Female Slaves in the Plantation South* (New York: Norton, 1985); and Elizabeth Fox-Genovese, *Within the Plantation Household: Black and White Women in the Old South* (Chapel Hill: University of North Carolina Press, 1988).

Among the best books on southern Indian tribes are Dale Van Every, *Disinherited: The Lost Birthright of the American Indian* (New York: Morrow, 1966); Joel W. Martin, *Sacred Revolt: The Muskogees' Struggle for a New World* (Boston: Beacon Press, 1991); William G. McLoughlin, *Cherokee Renascence in the New Republic* (Princeton, NJ: Princeton University Press, 1986); and Theda Perdue, *Cherokee Women: Gender and Culture Change, 1700–1835* (Lincoln: University of Nebraska Press, 1998). More recent scholarship on Indians includes Alfred A. Cave, *Prophets of the Great Spirit: Native American Revitalization Movements in Eastern North America* (Lincoln: University of Nebraska Press, 2006) and Douglas R. Hurt, *The Indian Frontier, 1763–1846* (Albuquerque: University of New Mexico Press, 2002).

Chapters 4–6

For a good summary of the experiences of each of the ethnic groups mentioned, see Stephan Thernstrom, ed., *Harvard Encyclopedia of American Ethnic Groups* (Cambridge, MA: Belknap Press, 1980). For ethnic groups in the West, the best place to start is Elliott Robert Barkan, *From All Points: America's Immigrant West, 1870–1952* (Bloomington: Indiana University Press, 2007).

There are a number of individual monographs on various groups. Among the best on the Irish are Kerby A. Miller, *Emigrants and Exiles: Ireland and the Exodus to North America* (NewYork: Oxford University Press, 1985); J. J. Lee and Marion R. Casey, eds., *Making the Irish American: History and Heritage of the Irish in the United States* (New York: New York University Press, 2006); Timothy J. Meagher, *Inventing Irish America: Generation, Class, and Ethnic Identity in a New England City, 1880–1928* (Notre Dame, IN: Notre Dame University Press, 2001); Jay P. Dolan, *The Immigrant Church: New York's Irish and German Catholics, 1815–1865* (Baltimore: Johns Hopkins University Press, 1975); and David M. Emmons, *The Butte Irish: Class and Ethnicity in an American Mining Town, 1875–1925* (Urbana: University of Illinois Press, 1989). The classic work on the Boston Irish is Oscar Handlin's *Boston's Immigrants* (revised ed.; Cambridge, MA: Belknap Press, 1959).

For the Germans, there are also a large number of works worth reading. One might begin with Russell A. Kazal, *Becoming Old Stock: The Paradox of German-American Identity* (Princeton, NJ: Princeton University Press, 2004); Stanley Nadell, *Little Germany: Ethnicity, Religion, and Class in New York City, 1845–1880* (Urbana: University of Illinois Press, 1990); and Kathleen Neils Conzen, *Immigrant Milwaukee, 1836–1860: Accommodation and Community in a Frontier City* (Cambridge, MA: Harvard University Press, 1976).

Italian immigrants in the United States are covered by Christopher Sterba, *Good Americans: Italian and Jewish Immigrants during the First World War* (New York: Oxford University Press, 2003); Thomas A. Guglielmo, *White on Arrival: Italians, Race, Color, and Power in Chicago, 1890–1945* (New York: Oxford University Press, 2003); Humbert S. Nelli, *From Immigrants to Ethnics: The Italian American* (New York: Oxford University Press, 1983); Gary Ross Mormino and George E. Pozetta, *The Immigrant World of Ybor City: Italians and Their Latin American Neighbors in Tampa, 1885–1985* (Urbana: University of Illinois Press, 1987); and Mormino, *Immigrants on the Hill: Italian Americans in St. Louis, 1882–1985* (Urbana: University of Illinois Press, 1985).

Other good books on European ethnic groups include Jon Gjerde, *From Peasants to Farmers: The Migration from Balestrand, Norway, to the Upper Middle West* (Cambridge, England: Cambridge University Press, 1985); Theodore Saloutos, *The Greeks in the United States* (Cambridge, MA: Harvard University Press, 1964); and Eva Morawska, *For Bread with Butter: Life-Worlds of East Central Europeans in Johnstown, Pennsylvania* (Cambridge, England: Cambridge University Press, 1985). Morawska has also written about Jews in the same community: *Insecure Prosperity: Small-Town Jews in Industrial America, 1890–1940* (Princeton, NJ: Princeton University Press, 1996). A good read on East European Jews in New York City at the end of the nineteenth and beginning of the twentieth centuries is Irving Howe, *World of Our Fathers* (New York: Harcourt Brace Jovanovich, 1976).

The literature on ethnic women is far better than it was when the first edition of this book came out. All of the following are quite enlightening: Karen Anderson, *Changing Women: A History of Racial and Ethnic Women in Modern America* (New York: Oxford University Press, 1996), which focuses on American Indian, African American, and Mexican women in the twentieth century. See also Hasia R. Diner, *Erin's Daughters in*

America: Irish Immigrant Women in the Nineteenth Century (Baltimore: Johns Hopkins University Press, 1983); Elizabeth Ewen, *Immigrant Women in the Land of Dollars: Life and Culture of the Lower East Side, 1890–1925* (New York: Monthly Review Press, 1985); Linda S. Pickle, *Contented among Strangers: Rural German-Speaking Women and Their Families in the Nineteenth-Century Midwest* (Urbana: University of Illinois Press, 1996); Sydney S. Weinberg, *World of Our Mothers* (Chapel Hill: University of North Carolina Press, 1988); Susan Glenn, *Daughters of the Shtetl: Life and Labor in the Immigrant Generation* (Ithaca, NY: Cornell University Press, 1990); Miriam Cohen, *Workshop to Office: Two Generations of Italian Women in New York City, 1900–1950* (Ithaca, NY: Cornell University Press, 1993); and Sarah Deutsch, *No Separate Refuge: Culture, Class, and Gender on an Anglo-Hispanic Frontier in the American Southwest, 1880–1940* (New York: Oxford University Press, 1987). Two works on African American women are Jacqueline Jones, *Labor of Love, Labor of Sorrow: Black Women, Work, and the Family from Slavery to the Present* (New York: Basic Books, 1985) and Dorothy Sterling, ed., *We Are Your Sisters: Black Women in the Nineteenth Century* (New York: Norton, 1984). Two works that cover a number of different minority women are Joan M. Jensen, *With These Hands: Women Working on the Land* (New York: Feminist Press, 1981) and Cathy Luchetti and Carol Olwell, *Women of the West* (St. George, UT: Antelope Press, 1984). Lillian Schlissel, Byrd Gibbens, and Elizabeth Hampsten explore what life was like in the West in *Far from Home: Families of the Westward Journey* (New York: Shocken Books, 1989). Gretchen M. Batille and Kathleen Mullen Sands focus on *American Indian Women: Telling their Lives* (Lincoln: University of Nebraska Press, 1984).

An extraordinary work dealing with African Americans during the Reconstruction era is Eric Foner, *Reconstruction: America's Unfinished Revolution, 1863–1877* (New York: Harper and Row, 1988). For the South after Reconstruction see Edward Ayers, *The Promise of the New South: Life after Reconstruction* (New York: Oxford University Press, 1992). Two newer works that follow black experiences from the nineteenth and first half of the twentieth centuries are Douglas A. Blackmon, *Slavery By Another Name: The Re-Enslavement of Black Americans from the Civil War to World War II* (New York: Doubleday, 2008) and Steven Hahn, *A Nation under Our Feet: Black Struggles in the Rural South from Slavery to the Great Migration* (Cambridge, MA: Harvard University Press, 2003). Two older classics about African American urban experiences are Gilbert Osofsky, *Harlem: The Making of a Ghetto, Negro New York, 1890–1920* (New York: Harper & Row, 1966) and Allan H. Spear, *Black Chicago: The Making of a Negro Ghetto, 1890–1920* (Chicago: University of Chicago Press, 1967).

The literature dealing with Indians in the West is both varied and voluminous. The two works by Roger L. Nichols, mentioned at the beginning of this bibliography, are the latest, but one might also look at Francis P. Prucha, *The Great Father: The United States Government and the American Indians* (2 volumes; Lincoln: University of Nebraska Press, 1984); Robert M. Utley, *The Indian Frontier of the American West, 1846–1890* (Albuquerque: University of New Mexico Press, 1984); and David Wallace Adams, *Education for Extinction: American Indians and the Boarding School Experience, 1825–1928* (Lawrence: University Press of Kansas, 1995).

Works on other groups associated with the West are Nels Anderson, *Desert Saints: The Mormon Frontier in Utah* (Chicago: University of Chicago Press, 1942); William A. Douglass and Jon Bilboa, *Americanuak: Basques in the New World* (Reno: University of Nevada Press, 1975); William H. Leckie, *The Buffalo Soldiers: A Narrative of the Negro Cavalry* (Norman: University of Oklahoma Press, 1967); and Philip Durham and Everett L. Jones, *The Negro Cowboy* (New York: Dodd, Mead, 1965).

Chapter 7

The classic book on nativism is John Higham, *Strangers in the Land: Patterns of American Nativism, 1860–1925* (2nd ed.; New York: Atheneum, 1970). Ethnic tensions are also dealt with in most of the previously mentioned works about African Americans, American Indians, and European immigrants. Other books worth going through on this topic include two by David R. Roedinger, *Black on White: Black Writers on What It Means to Be White* (New York: Shocken Books, 1998) and *The Wages of Whiteness: Race and the Making of the American Working Class* (New York: Verso, 1999). Joel Williamson explored prejudice in *The Crucible of Race* (New York: Oxford University Press, 1984). A more recent study is Kevin Boyle, *Arc of Justice: A Saga of Race, Civil Rights and Murder in the Jazz Age* (New York: Henry Holt, 2004). C. Vann Woodward's classic, *The Strange Career of Jim Crow* (3rd ed.; New York: Oxford University Press, 1974), has three outstanding virtues: it is short, readable, and extremely telling.

In much of the country, other victimized groups include American Indians, the Chinese, the Japanese, and the Mexicans. Some of the better works on these groups include Robert F. Berkhofer Jr., *The White Man's Indian: Images of the American Indian from Columbus to the Present* (New York: Knopf, 1978); Brian W. Dippie, *The Vanishing American: White Attitudes and U. S. Indian Policy* (Middletown, CT: Wesleyan University Press, 1982); Charles Wilkinson, *Blood Struggle: The Rise of Modern Indian Nations* (New York: Norton, 2005); and Joanne Nagle, *American Indian Ethnic Renewal* (New York: Oxford University Press, 1996).

Next to the Indians, the Chinese were the most hated group in the western states. Consult Stuart Creighton Miller, *The Unwelcome Immigrant: The American Image of the Chinese, 1785–1882* (Berkeley: University of California Press, 1969); Judy Yung, *Unbound Feet: A Social History of Chinese Women in San Francisco* (Berkeley: University of California Press, 1995); and George Anthony Peffer, *If They Don't Bring Their Women Here: Chinese Female Immigration before Exclusion* (Urbana: University of Illinois Press, 1999). They all detail the venomous feelings experienced. For the struggle against discrimination, see Charles J. McClain, *In Search of Equality: The Chinese Struggle against Discrimination in Nineteenth-Century America* (Berkeley: University of California Press, 1994). A comprehensive account of Asians is presented in Roger Daniels, *Asian America: Chinese and Japanese in the United States since 1850* (Seattle: University of Washington Press, 1988). For the Chinese after 1882, see Erika Lee, *At America's Gates: Chinese Immigrants during the Exclusion Era: 1882–1943* (Chapel Hill: University of North Carolina Press, 2003).

Almost any work by Roger Daniels exposes American hostility toward Japanese and Japanese Americans. One might start with *Concentration Camps USA: Japanese Americans and World War II* (New York: Holt, Rinehart & Winston, 1972), but his first book, *The Politics of Prejudice: The Anti-Japanese Movement in California, and the Struggle for Japanese Exclusion* (Gloucester, MA: Peter Smith, 1966), has much greater breadth. Other insightful works on Japanese American experiences during World War II are Jeanne Wakotsuki Houston and James D. Houston, *Farewell to Manzanar* (Boston: Houghton Mifflin, 1973) and Yoshika Uchida, *Desert Exile: The Uprooting of a Japanese American Family* (Seattle: University of Washington Press, 1982).

There are a number of excellent works on Mexican American history. They include David Montejano, *Anglos and Mexicans in the Making of Texas, 1836–1936* (Austin: University of Texas Press, 1987); Oscar J. Martinez, *Border People: Life and Society in the U.S.* (Tucson: University of Arizona Press, 1994); and George J. Sanchez, *Becoming Mexican American: Ethnicity, Culture, and Identity in Chicano Los Angeles, 1900–1945* (New York: Oxford University Press, 1993). An older, but insightful, work is Carey McWilliams, *North from Mexico* (reprint; New York: Greenwood Press, 1968).

Works on immigration restriction include Matthew Frye Jacobson, *Whiteness of a Different Color: European Immigrants and the Alchemy of Race* (Cambridge, MA: Harvard University Press, 1998); Desmond King, *Making Americans: Immigration, Race, and the Origins of Diverse Democracy* (Cambridge, MA: Harvard University Press, 2000); and Mae Nagi, *Impossible Subjects: Illegal Aliens and the Making of Modern America* (Princeton, NJ: Princeton University Press, 2004). A fine and insightful monograph is Robert Zeidel, *The Dillingham Commission* (De Kalb: Northern Illinois University Press, 2004). Gary Gerstle's *American Crucible: Race and Nation in the Twentieth Century* (Princeton, NJ: Princeton University Press, 2001) won the Immigration History Society's prize for best book on the subject published that year.

Chapters 8–10

There are several issues that have dominated the discussion about immigration and minorities since the end of World War II. Among them are: Whom should we welcome, what should our immigration policies be, and how should we deal with undocumented immigrants? Moreover, the civil rights movement took the front burner. Should all Americans have equal rights and opportunities, regardless of heritage or gender? Who is white, and what difference does it make? Is affirmative action necessary or appropriate? The list that follows includes some of the works on these topics. Practically all of the books listed have points of view that should contribute to enlightening discussions about how to deal with contemporary problems.

There is no adequate history of immigration and immigration policy since 1945. Nonetheless, there are a variety of monographs on aspects of these topics. Among them are David M. Reimers, *Still the Golden Door: The Third World Comes to America* (2nd ed.; New York: Columbia University Press, 1992); Reimers, *Other Immigrants: The Global Origins of the American People* (New York: New York University Press, 2005);

Roger Daniels, *Guarding the Golden Door: American Immigration Policy and Immigrants since 1982* (New York: Hill & Wang, 2004); Daniel J. Tichenor, *Dividing Lines: The Politics of Immigration Control in America* (Princeton, NJ: Princeton University Press, 2002); Aristide R. Zolberg, *A Nation by Design: Immigration Policy Making in the Fashioning of America* (Cambridge, MA: Harvard University Press, 2007); Bill Hing, *Defining America through Immigration Policy* (Philadelphia: Temple University Press, 2004) and *Deporting Our Souls: Values, Morality, and Immigration Policy* (New York: Cambridge University Press, 2006). For cold war refugees, consult Carl J. Bon Tempo, *Americans at the Gate: The United States and Refugees during the Cold War* (Princeton, NJ: Princeton University Press, 2008).

Books with both broad and deep analyses of civil rights concerns, whiteness, and affirmative action include Taylor Branch's trilogy on the impact of Martin Luther King Jr., *Parting the Waters, 1954–1963; Pillars of Fire*; and *At Canaan's Edge, 1965–1968* (New York: Simon & Schuster, 1988, 1998, and 2006, respectively). For whites, see Eric Goldstein, *The Price of Whiteness: Jews, Race and American Identity* (Princeton, NJ: Princeton University Press, 2006); David R. Roediger, *Toward Whiteness: How America's Immigrants Became White* (New York: Basic Books, 2006); Ira Katznelson, *When Affirmative Action Was White: An Untold History of Racial Inequality in Twentieth-Century America* (New York: Norton, 2005); Matthew Frye Jacobson, *Roots Too: White Ethnic Revival in Post Civil Rights America* (Cambridge, MA: Harvard University Press, 2006); Terry H. Anderson, *The Pursuit of Fairness: A History of Affirmative Action* (New York: Oxford University Press, 2004); William G. Bowen and Derek Bok, *The Shape of the Long-Term Consequences of Considering Race in College and University Admissions* (Princeton, NY: Princeton University Press, 1998); Barbara A. Perry, *The Michigan Affirmative Action Cases* (Lawrence: University of Kansas Press, 2007); and Hugh David Graham, *Collision Course: The Strange Convergence of Affirmative Action and Immigration Policy* (New York: Oxford University Press, 2002). An outstanding book on civil rights in the North is Thomas J. Sugrue, *Sweet Land of Liberty: The Forgotten Struggle for Civil Rights in the North* (New York: Random House, 2008).

On individual groups, see Linda Dowling Almeida, *Irish Immigrants in New York City, 1945–1995* (Bloomington: Indiana University Press, 2001); Annelise Orleck, *The Soviet Jewish Americans* (Westport, CT: Greenwood, 1999); Peter Kwong and Dusanke Miscevic, *Chinese Americans: A History in the Making* (New York: The New Press, 2005); Xiaolon Bao, *Holding Up More Than Half the Sky: Chinese Women Garment Workers in New York City, 1948–1992* (Urbana: University of Illinois Press, 2001); Bernard Wong, *The New Chinese Immigrants in the San Francisco Bay Area* (Boston: Allyn & Bacon, 1998); Mitra S. Kalia, *Suburban Sahibs: Three Immigrant Families and the Passage to America* (New Brunswick, NJ: Rutgers University Press, 2003); Barbara Posada, *Filipino Americans* (Westport, CT: Greenwood Press, 1999); Yen Le Espiritu, *Home Bound: Filipino Americans Living across Cultures, Communities and Countries* (Berkeley: University of California Press, 2003); and Wayne Patterson, *Ilse: First Generation Korean Immigrants in Hawaii, 1902–1973* (Honolulu: University of Hawaii Press, 2000). For Koreans, see Illsoo Kim, *New Urban Immigrants: The Korean Community in New York City* (Princeton, NJ: Princeton University Press, 1981); Nancy

Abelmann and John Lie, *Blue Dreams: Korean Americans and the Los Angeles Riots* (Cambridge, MA: Harvard University Press, 1995); and Pyong Gap Min, *Ethnic Solidarity for Economic Survival: Korean Greengrocers in New York City* (New York: Russell Sage Foundation, 2008). On Brazilian immigrants see Maxine Margolis, *Little Brazil: An Ethnography of Brazilian Immigrants in New York City* (Princeton, NJ: Princeton University Press, 1994). For Puerto Ricans, consult Joseph P. Fitzpatrick, *Puerto Rican Americans* (2nd ed.; Englewood Cliffs, NJ: Prentice Hall, 1987). The best book on Cubans is Maria Cristina Garcia, *Havana USA: Cuban Exiles and Cuban Americans in South Florida, 1959–1994* (Berkeley: University of California Press, 1996). Arabs and Muslims are covered in Gregory Orfalea, *The Arab Americans: A History* (Northampton, MA: Olive Branch Press, 2005) and Yvonne Yazbeck, Jan I. Smith, and Kathleen Moore, *Muslim Women in America: The Challenge of Islamic Identity Today* (New York: Oxford University Press, 2006).

Perceptions of Indians remained mixed at best. See Fergus M. Bordewich, *Killing the White Man's Indian: Reinventing Native Americans at the End of the Twentieth Century* (New York: Doubleday, 1996); Robert Sullivan, *A Whale Hunt: Two Years on the Olympic Peninsula with the Makah and Their Canoe* (New York: Scribner's, 2000); Brett Fromson, *Hitting the Jackpot: The Inside Story of the Richest Indian Tribe in History* (New York: Atlantic Monthly Press, 2003); and David E. Wilkins, *American Indian Politics and the American Political System* (Lanham, MD: Rowman & Littlefield, 2002). For Indian initiatives and responses, see K. Tsianina Lomawaima, *They Called It Prairie Light: The Story of the Chiloco Indian School* (Lincoln: University of Nebraska Press, 1994).

Works on Latinos generally and Mexicans in particular have been mentioned previously. The following include some additional books on more recent experiences: Roberto Suro, *Strangers among Us: How Latino Immigration Is Transforming America* (New York: Knopf, 1998); Juan Gonzales, *Harvest of Empire: A History of Latinos in America* (New York: Viking, 2000); and Laura Gomez, *Manifest Destinies: The Making of the Mexican American Race* (New York: New York University Press, 2007). A work on Hispanics trying to enter the United States through the southwestern border is Jorge Ramos, *Dying to Cross: The Worst Immigrant Tragedy in American History* (New York: HarperCollins, 2005). For a view of a new group on the East Coast, see Robert Courtney Smith, *Mexican New York: Lives of New Immigrants* (Berkeley: University of California Press, 2006).

INDEX